Logic and Declarative Language

Logic and Declarative Language

MICHAEL DOWNWARD
Thames Cancer Registry, London

First Published 1998
by Taylor & Francis,
2 Park Square, Milton Park, Abingdon, Oxon, OX14 4RN

Transferred to Digital Printing 2004

British Library Cataloguing-in-Publication Data

A catalogue record for this book is available from the British Library.

ISBN 0–7484–0803–7 (HB)
ISBN 0–7484–0802–9 (PB)

Library of Congress Cataloging-in-Publication Data are available

Cover design by Youngs Design in Production

Typeset in Times 10/12pt by Graphicraft Typesetters Ltd, Hong Kong

Contents

Preface

In order to understand something of the problems facing the computer software industry we have also to understand something of its history. A great deal of computer programming is still carried out in the style of the third-generation programming languages introduced by John Backus in 1954. The basic problem of these languages is that they are derived from an earlier generation of assembler languages in which the programmer is directly responsible for allocating and manipulating memory locations in the underlying computer hardware. Languages such as Ada have added a great many details to the original formula translator produced by Backus, but the sad fact is that these changes might well have made the problem worse rather than better. In his 1977 Turing lecture the creator of FORTRAN commented, "Conventional programming languages have become fat and flabby," and noted ruefully that he bore some of the responsibility for this situation. These languages had been so successful in their early years that it became difficult to conceive any other way of implementing computer systems.

A computer program has to model a real-world situation and is best constructed by first specifying the nature of the system in some abstract form, then implementing the specification in a programming language. The problem with low-level languages such as Ada is that the gap between specification and implementation is uncomfortably large. Mistakes often arise as a result of an incorrect translation from specification to implementation. Just as important, programs written in machine-oriented languages inevitably require a great many lines of code because of their limited expressiveness. As a result, the probability of making mistakes while writing the code is greatly increased, even if the specification has been correctly understood. Programs written in these languages require comprehensive testing regimes, but even the best test routines will not catch every mistake.

It is particularly difficult to understand the meaning of machine-oriented computer programs because much of the program is concerned with movements between computer storage locations. Complete methodologies called formal methods such as the Vienna Definition Methodology (VDM) and the Z specification method were provided to define the translation from specification to machine-level code. Unfortunately these methodologies did little more than extend the problems of conventional programming languages to a higher specification level. The process of writing specifications at a high level then redrafting them at several lower levels resulted in very lengthy proofs. Some studies even suggested that formal methods of this kind might actually increase the number of mistakes as the complexity of development increased.

In fact programs written in conventional languages turned out to be more reliable than early observers expected. Traditional testing methods together with strict development regimes produce programs sufficiently reliable to control airliners and nuclear power stations. The real argument against conventional languages is not the mistakes that have to be removed from them, but the very low levels of productivity they allow. This is just one reason that explains the recent shift of interest away from procedural, machine-oriented languages to declarative languages. Conventional languages are procedural because they are used to instruct machines how to solve a problem by performing a certain sequence of actions. Declarative languages specify the problem in some form of logic, but leave the solution of the problem to a series of deductions in an underlying logic system. Programs written in declarative languages are sometimes described as "animated specifications", emphasising their similarity to specifications.

A large number of semantic modelling techniques have been invented with the intention of modelling real-world problems in some abstract form; they have much in common with declarative languages. Objects such as functions and relations found in declarative languages are much more likely to be of use in describing computer systems than statements involving machine storage locations. Specifications are statements in a form of logic and, in order to rationalise the vast number of different specification systems that have evolved, we need to understand their relationship with known logic systems. Progress has been greater than is generally realised and it seems certain that the intense effort in this direction will continue. As early as 1967 McCarthy wrote, "It is reasonable to hope that the relationship between computation and logic in the next century will be as fruitful as that between calculus and physics in the last." This vision of the future is all the more amazing in that it was written before the first papers describing relational databases, efficient logic programs, object-oriented programming, lazy functional languages, polymorphism, constructive logic and many other developments in logic and declarative language.

The task facing us in the twenty-first century is to explain all of the ad hoc developments of the past years in terms of a single coherent structure based in logic. It is already clear that classical logic alone will be inadequate and that other logics are required to act as specifications for computational structures. The interrelationship between intuitionistic logic and functional language that has been developed in recent years perhaps indicates the path we must follow. Other logics have corresponding relationships with declarative languages.

Logic has acquired a reputation for difficulty, perhaps because many of the approaches adopted have been more suitable for mathematicians than computer scientists. This book shows that the subject is not inherently difficult and that the connections between logic and declarative language are straightforward. Many exercises have been included in the hope they will lead to a much greater confidence in manual proofs, leading to a greater confidence in automated proofs.

ACKNOWLEDGEMENTS

A great debt of gratitude is owed to many friends and colleagues in and around the University of London, particularly to the academic staff at University College, Birkbeck College and King's College. My thanks also to an anonymous referee who patiently worked through the original typescript to produce valuable improvements. I am further indebted to the production staff at Taylor & Francis who guided the text through its late stages to final publication. Finally, at a very personal level, I would like to thank Margaret Dawson for her support during the long period it took to write this text.

Introduction

At the heart of the description of logic in this book there is a division between syntactic or proof theoretic reasoning and semantic or model theoretic reasoning. Syntactic reasoning proceeds through arguments based on the syntactic form of formulas and is based on the nature and order of symbols used in the formulas, whereas semantic reasoning depends on a meaning given to the formulas in some interpretation. Two forms of equality accompany this division: a syntactic equality compares strings of symbols and a semantic equality compares the values of terms. For example, the expression 6×7 is semantically equal to the number 42 because both terms denote the same value. This denotational form of equality is associated with meaning, representation or interpretation, as opposed to the syntactic form of equality, which is associated with the form or sense of an expression. Two expressions are syntactically equal when they contain the same symbols in the same order. Most people think that 6×7 is equal to 42 and are therefore implicitly using the semantic or denotational version of equality. As a result, it is usual to describe logic without the denotational form of equality simply as "logic without equality"; inclusion of denotational equality leads to "logic with equality".

Classical logic as described in Chapters 1 and 2 has evolved from the work of Frege during nineteenth century and, in common with other logics, uses predicates and terms as its major components. A predicate is either *true* or *false* in respect to some interpretation that is often expressed in the form of a relation. Such relations express information from which the truth of a predicate may be judged and are therefore concerned with semantics and meaning. A relation might consist of a collection of facts showing possible routes and distances between cities:

Route(athens,rome,distance(athens,rome))

Here a relation called *Route* has three arguments, the names of two cities and a function expressing the distance between them. Each of the three arguments is a term; the first two terms are simple constants and the third is a function that itself has two simple constant arguments. Since we know the distance in kilometres between these two cities, we know the value denoted by the application

distance(athens,rome) = 1055

and we might substitute this value in the *Route* fact above to give

*Route(athens,rome,*1055)

Term substitutions of this kind are only permitted in logic with equality because there is no concept of denotational equivalence in logic without equality.

Chapters 3 and 4 show that logic without equality can be animated to provide very expressive declarative languages that should properly be called relational languages, but are usually called logic languages. These languages are declarative in the sense that a programmer declares a collection of known and unknown terms within relations. An underlying reasoning system such as the SLD mechanism described in Chapter 3 then deduces possible values for the unknown terms. The important point is that a declarative language should arrive at its result without the need for explicit procedural directions for computing that result. Declarative languages are animated forms of specification in which computation is seen as automated deduction in an appropriate form of logic. Programming in logic first became a practical proposition when the Prolog language was introduced by Colmerauer and his group at the University of Marseilles in 1973. This fundamental work was rapidly developed by Kowalski, Van Emden and Warren at the University of Edinburgh, and efficient implementations of a language that became known as Edinburgh Prolog were widely available by 1980. One of the reasons for the success of logic languages such as Prolog is that they deliberately avoid equality because it leads to problems in logic language mechanisms.

Abstract types and object-oriented programming

Object-oriented programming has its philosophical basis in Birkhoff's work on universal algebras published during the 1930s, but the importance of this work in computer science was not recognised until the early 1970s. Separate groups led by Zilles at IBM, Guttag at the University of Southern California and Goguen at UCLA recognised the relevance of Birkhoff's work at almost the same time. The importance of this work grew from the simple observation that the concept of a type as it is used in computation is greater than that of a set. We tend, for example, to think of the set of integers $\{ \ldots, -1, 0, 1, \ldots \}$ as a type, but these elements are of little use without a defined collection of operators that can be applied to the numbers. An abstract type encapsulates the operations and constants of a type into a single self-contained package called an abstract type or abstract data type (ADT). Different representations of the constants and operations in an abstract type are possible but each representation must behave in exactly the same way as the defining abstract type. Birkhoff's original work was restricted to homogeneous algebras, describing the behaviour of objects that contain elements of only one type. This work was later extended to heterogeneous systems with objects containing elements of different types. Goguen invented a much neater notation for what he called many-sorted abstract data types, making descriptions of heterogeneous objects almost as easy as that for homogeneous objects. An abstract type is a syntactic form in logic with equality and its objects act as representations or interpretations, providing a semantics for the type.

Abstract types define equalities between terms that allow fragments of large expressions to be substituted with equivalent values until the simplest possible form of an expression is obtained. This process of reduction to a simplest, so-called normal value is called term rewriting and is described in detail in Chapters 5 and 6. In addition to providing a method of specifying objects, Goguen and his colleagues also invented an object-oriented declarative language called OBJ that automated the process of term rewriting. Complex expressions presented to OBJ are rewritten according to a set of equations in a user-specified abstract type until the simplest possible canonical form is obtained. In this way OBJ acts as a rapid prototyping system because the specification is animated directly to reveal any flaws before any translation into a low-level conventional language takes place. OBJ is especially interesting because it is a programming language with a very clear and direct rela-tionship to the first-order logic described in the early part of the text. Although it has a great deal in common with the functional languages described later in the text, it is important to note that functional languages are derived from a different starting-point. Fortunately, Goguen was able to show that the domain basis of functional languages can be seen as an extension of the object domains in a language such as OBJ. Many functional languages have an abstract type facility that allows opera-tions to be encapsulated into a module that looks almost the same as an abstract type specification. As a result, these languages can act as animated object specifica-tions in much the same way as OBJ.

Representations of abstract types are based on sets of elements called domains that may contain a special error element in each set. For example, in addition to the true and false constants of a Boolean domain there is a requirement for a third, error element. Abstract errors of this kind mean that a defined result is obtained when inappropriate arguments are submitted for evaluation. This requirement complic-ates the specifications a little, but in practice is handled without problems in the OBJ system.

Scott domains and functional languages

Scott domains are similar to the domains described above and were invented by Dana Scott to provide a semantics for a syntactic system called the lambda calculus. Domains of this kind act as a model for lambda calculus expressions in the same way that objects act as models for abstract types. Unlike simple term-rewriting sys-tems, Scott domains give a special status to an operation that has failed to produce a defined result. Lifted domains in this theory include an additional bottom or null element that represents an undefined element in that domain. More important, functions in Scott's theory are defined in a way that sometimes enables them to produce a defined result even when applied to undefined arguments. Lifted domains of this kind are essential in simulating the behaviour of very large scale integrated (VLSI) circuits. At a very simple level we can picture a transistor in which +5 volts represents true and −5 volts represents false, but in order to get from +5 to −5 the voltage level has to pass through 0. In other words, the device has to pass though an undefined state on moving between defined states. This undefined state may be explicitly modelled by the null element of a lifted domain and as a consequence the transition become predictable.

Declarative languages based on Scott domains are usually called functional languages and have a great deal in common with term-rewriting systems based on object domains. McCarthy and Backus both realised the limitations of machine-oriented programming and both suggested functional languages as a solution to the problem. McCarthy introduced a language called Lisp that has been widely used over many years and has now become something of a cult language in certain areas. Some years later Backus introduced a language called FP that never became widely used, perhaps because so many other functional languages were by then available. Progress with functional language implementations continued, so that by 1990 Augustsson and Johnsson at Chalmers University in Sweden were able to announce a very efficient functional language called LML. Programs written in LML run almost as efficiently as those written in machine-oriented languages and have the additional advantage that they are more rapidly written and tested. The wide variety of functional languages available led a group of leading researcher workers in the field to define a "standard" functional language called Haskell. Although this language is now widely used in the research community and in some universities, it has not yet displaced the more familar functional languages. Chapter 8 of this book provides an outline of the Miranda functional language, probably the most popular system available at the moment.

Constructive logic

One of the most exciting developments in recent years has been the extension of type theory through constructive logic. Roughly stated, the early work of Curry and Howard establishes a one-to-one relationship between intuitionistic logic statements and type declarations. According to the Curry–Howard isomorphism, these apparently unconnected features of specifications and programming languages are two aspects of a single property. Constructive or intuitionistic logic differs from classical logic in that statements are always accompanied by their proof objects and these objects are in fact functional programs. As a result, a direct connection between logic and computation is established in a way never before possible. Using these techniques, the structures of computer programs are derived directly from logic statements. Existential quantifiers in constructive logic are identified with abstract types whereas universal quantifiers are identified with polymorphic programs. Consequently, two of the most important areas of modern computing are seen to arise naturally from constructive logic and new possibilities arise for the translation of specifications into programs.

Relational databases

Relational databases (RDBs) emerged from a paper published by Codd in 1970 and have since grown to become one of the most important software products in the computing industry. The success of relational databases has occurred in spite of, or perhaps because of, the remarkable simplicity of the relational model. A relational database consists of sets of records such as

```
{(123, 'Smith', 45.78),
(456, 'Gupta', 67.28),
(789, 'Patel', 87.36), ... }
```

and these sets are called tables in RDBs. Individual elements (attributes) within the records have to be entered in some arbitrary order, but the position of an element in the record is of no importance. Every column in the table is named and access to an element is through the column name, not through its position. A small number of relational database operations are then defined to operate on the tables of various databases, producing new sets of records as a result. Three of these operations are the familiar set union, set intersection and set difference operations; a further three or four are simple extensions of basic set theory operations. Relational database theory is little more than an extension of basic set theory, yet it is a sufficient basis for a huge industry.

One interesting feature of the relational model is that it is really a special case of a term-rewriting declarative language such as those described in the second half of this book. It is special in the sense that only set operations are applicable and only sets of records such as those described above are taken as arguments or operands. An interactive declarative language called Sequel (SQL) evolved as a user-friendly method of writing logic statements to describe relationships between known and unknown information in the database. The advantage of the relational model over earlier file-oriented processing languages such as COBOL follows the general advantage of declarative languages over procedural languages. A query is presented and satisfied by underlying software in an RDB without the explicit procedural instructions required in conventional languages.

Deductive databases

Logic languages such as Prolog are more expressive and capable of answering some queries that cannot be answered in the relational database model. On the other hand, the set-oriented processing approach adopted in RDBs is much more efficient than the exhaustive searches used in logic languages. A new set-oriented logic language called Datalog has been defined, combining many of the desirable features of both relational databases and logic languages. Developments of Datalog languages continued throughout the 1980s and eventually the Microelectronics and Computer Technology Corporation (MCC) produced a powerful extended Datalog system called LDL. This system has been implemented both on a parallel-processing machine and in a standard Unix environment. The increased use of parallel-processing machines should improve the speed of "data dredging", which these systems seem to do so well.

Functional databases

Databases are distinguished from file-oriented declarative languages by their ability to incorporate data changes in secondary storage incrementally as such changes are made. Persistent storage of this kind can be added to the basic features of a functional language to give functional databases that have some advantages over the longer-established relational databases. The advantages of functional databases over their relational counterparts flow from the ease with which specifications can be converted to implementations. The basic structures used in functional databases have much more in common with the semantic modelling techniques that can be used to describe real-world situations. Functional databases face the same efficiency problems that faced early relational databases, but because of the inherent advantages of the functional model, efforts to resolve these problems will continue.

Unified languages and parallel processing

Relations and functions are defined in logic and are used in conjunction with each other in describing theories in logic. Declarative languages, on the other hand, tend to be either exclusively relational or exclusively functional, and separate traditions have grown up in line with this division. This is unfortunate because many of the skills required to develop declarative language programs are derived from a declarative way of thinking rather than from a particular approach. Programmers have to learn to express what is required in an approriate form rather than provide explicit instructions for a machine. Much thought has been given to the idea of merging the two styles of declarative language into a single language that would then use relations or functions as appropriate. Chapter 10 includes a brief outline of the progress already made in this area.

Another major challenge facing computer scientists in the new century will be the production of software for computers with many processors. Parallel-processing machines are in fact already available, but our ability to write programs for them is sadly lacking. Hidden dependencies within conventional language programs prevent the easy migration of such programs to parallel-processing machines. Declarative language programs should not contain these dependencies, hence fragments of such programs may be distributed between processors in the computer. Research into the implementation of declarative languages on parallel processors continues at many centres around the world.

PART ONE

Logic without equality

CHAPTER ONE

Propositional logic

1.1 SYNTAX OF PROPOSITIONAL LOGIC

A formal system consists of a set of symbols called an alphabet and a set of rules describing the way in which these symbols may be joined together to form strings of symbols. Our initial formal system is built from the following alphabet:

$p, q, r, s, \ldots,$

$\perp,$

$\neg,$

$\wedge, \vee, \rightarrow, \leftrightarrow,$

$(,)\,,\,,\,,$

Symbols $p, q, r, s, \ldots$ represent an infinite number of atomic statements in the alphabet and may be seen as the building blocks of propositions. Three rows of symbols then show logical connectives that bind these atomic elements together according to the following rules:

a. Symbols $\perp, p, q, r, s, \ldots$ are themselves propositions.

b. If A is a proposition then $\neg A$ is also a proposition.

c. If A and B are both propositions then $A \wedge B$, $A \vee B$, $A \rightarrow B$, and $A \leftrightarrow B$ are also propositions.

d. Strings of symbols not built up according to these rules are not propositions.

Unlike the atomic statement symbols $p, q, r, \ldots$, symbols A and B represent any proposition and are not themselves part of the formal system being described. Symbols of this kind are often called metasymbols. The rules above define the number of arguments that each logical connective requires to produce a correctly formed proposition, producing a form of valency called the *arity*. Statement symbols

$p, q, r, \ldots$ and the connective $\bot$ are themselves propositions and thus have an arity of zero. A zero-arity connective might at this point seem a little fraudulent, but later we shall see that it does have properties in common with the other connectives. Only one connective symbol is defined with an arity of one, limiting the form of propositions that might be constructed from this symbol and atomic statement symbols. Increasingly large propositions may be constructed by the repeated attachment of this connective to a simple atomic statement as follows:

$$\neg(\neg p) \qquad \neg(\neg(\neg p)) \qquad \neg(\neg(\neg(\neg p)))$$

or to the special connective $\bot$, e.g. $\neg\bot$, $\neg(\neg(\bot))$. All remaining connectives are defined to be of arity two, giving propositions of the form

$$p \wedge q \qquad r \vee (\neg p) \qquad \neg(\neg(\neg q)) \to \neg q \qquad \bot \leftrightarrow (\neg p)$$

with simple or negated atomic statements. Such connectives may take arguments that are themselves formed from arity-two connectives, creating propositions such as

$$(\neg(\neg q)) \to (r \vee (\neg p)) \qquad (\neg q) \wedge (r \vee (\neg p))$$

Parentheses are defined as part of the formal system to record the order in which a proposition is constructed from its atomic symbols. A proposition might be built from atomic statements p and q as follows:

$$p \qquad \neg q \qquad \neg p \qquad q$$
$$(p \wedge (\neg q)) \qquad ((\neg p) \wedge q)$$
$$(p \wedge (\neg q)) \vee ((\neg p) \wedge q)$$

but if the same starting propositions are combined in a different order, a different proposition is obtained:

$$p \qquad \neg q \qquad \neg p \qquad q$$
$$p \qquad ((\neg q) \vee (\neg p)) \qquad q$$
$$p \wedge ((\neg q) \vee (\neg p)) \wedge q$$

In order to reduce the number of brackets used in formulas a precedence order for arity one and two connectives is defined as follows:

> low precedence $\leftrightarrow \to \vee \wedge \neg$ high precedence

Connectives with the highest precedence bind most tightly to the objects that they connect. Thus $\neg p \wedge q$ is understood to mean $(\neg p) \wedge q$ because a $\neg$ symbol has greater precedence than a $\wedge$ symbol. Explicit bracketing would have to be included if the alternative proposition, $\neg(p \wedge q)$, were intended. Similarly, proposition $p \wedge \neg q \vee \neg p \wedge q$ represents the first of the two examples constructed above and brackets would have to be retained to represent the second possibility. Symbol $\wedge$ has a higher precedence than $\to$, so the formula $p \wedge q \to r$ is assumed to represent $(p \wedge q) \to r$, a formula in which connective $\wedge$ is first applied to statements p and q then this proposition itself becomes an argument. The alternative proposition, $p \wedge (q \to r)$ requires brackets to overide the precedence rule.

Sometimes the legal or allowed propositions are called well-formed propositions or well-formed formulas, but we shall simply call them propositions or formulas because we have no interest in constructions that are not well formed. An ill-formed formula such as $p \land \lor q$ looks odd, even to the inexperienced eye, so no great analysis is required to remove such problems. In fact, an algorithm that decides whether or not a given proposition is well formed may be written, and the proposition property is said to be decidable. All it requires is a procedure that breaks propositions into symbols and arguments according to the formation rules until only statement symbols or the constant $\bot$ remain.

At this point we should be careful not to attribute a meaning to any of the symbols or propositions: all that is defined is an alphabet of symbols and some rules that specify the ways in which these symbols can be grouped together. In addition to the rules of construction, we might also have rules of deduction that allow further propositions to be derived from an existing set. The simplest and best-known rule may be written as

$$A, A \to B \vdash B$$

and is known as *modus ponens*. Here a syntactic turnstile symbol ($\vdash$) shows that proposition B follows from propositions with the forms A and $A \to B$ in which A and B are metasymbols representing any proposition. Thus, from p and $p \to q$ we may deduce q and from $(r \land s)$ and $(r \land s) \to (p \land q)$ we may deduce $p \land q$ by making appropriate substitutions in *modus ponens*. Multiple applications of *modus ponens* have a chaining effect as in the following derivation:

$$p, p \to q, q \to r \vdash r$$

in which q is deduced from the first two propositions then used with the third to produce the final proof. Derivations of this kind may be shown as follows:

1. p assumption
2. $p \to q$ assumption
3. q 1, 2 *modus ponens*
4. $q \to r$ assumption
5. r 3, 4 *modus ponens*

Propositions on the left of the syntactic turnstile are assumed, then the proposition on the right is proven from these assumptions. Each line of the derivation follows from earlier proven or assumed propositions in the proof and is in itself a proof. Reasoning of this kind is described as proof theoretic because it depends only on the application of a rule, making no appeal to any meaning that might be given to the symbols. Later in this chapter the Hilbert proof system using *modus ponens* and three axioms is described. In contrast a Gentzen proof system that has eight rules of deduction but only one axiom schema is also described. Chapter 3 includes a proof system called resolution that also has just one deduction rule, but this might be considered a special case of the Gentzen system.

1.2   SEMANTICS OF PROPOSITIONAL LOGIC

A formal system with the alphabet and proposition building rules described in the previous section may be used to construct propositions or to decide if a given string of symbols is a proposition. However, even when correctly formed, a proposition is no more than a string of symbols because it is defined by its syntactic form, the arrangement of its symbols. None of the symbols represents anything more than itself and we should avoid reading any meaning into the symbols themselves at this stage. One possible meaning for the symbols is provided by the semantic functions below, and this particular interpretation of the symbols has such widespread use that the symbols and this particular interpretation are easily confused. A meaning (a semantics) is provided for each of the symbols by defining semantic functions with arities corresponding to the syntactic forms as follows:

Syntactic form	Semantic function	Name
$\perp$	*false*	false
$\neg$	*not*	negation
$\wedge$	*and*	conjunction
$\vee$	*or*	disjunction
$\rightarrow$	*implies*	implication
$\leftrightarrow$	*iff*	mutual implication

First of all, a constant interpretation *false* is provided for the arity-zero symbol $\perp$ then an interpretation *not* is provided for the arity-one symbol $\neg$ in the form of a table as follows:

A	*not(A)*
false	*not(false)*
not(false)	*false*

Thus proposition $\neg\perp$ has the interpretation *not(false)* whereas proposition $\neg(\neg\perp)$ has the interpretation *not(not(false))* defined in the table as equivalent to the constant *false*. This interpretation represents the principle of the excluded middle because it forces a proposition to be either *false* or *not(false)*, excluding any other possibility. Later we outline an alternative semantics that is not so restrictive and proves to have useful properties, but for the moment we remain with two-valued logic. Our interpretation of *false* is the familiar one: something is *false* if it does not accord with our reasoning, if we would consider it wrong. In two-valued logic a statement is true if it is not *false*, so a new symbol *true* may be introduced into the semantic domain as an abbreviation for *not(false)*. This allows a more compact semantic function definition:

A	not(A)
false	true
true	false

It would have been possible to include a symbol in the alphabet of the formal system which would then have been interpreted as the constant *true*. An interpretation of the $\neg$ symbol could then operate directly on the interpretations *true* and *false*. Instead we use the word *true* simply as an abbreviation for *not(false)*. This might seem an unecessary distinction, but later we shall see that there are sometimes advantages in using a minimum number of symbols in an alphabet. More important, it will become clear that the alphabet described above already contains many more connective symbols than are strictly necessary.

Each of the statement symbols p, q, r, s, ... is mapped to a truth value in a valuation which may be shown as a number of valuation functions such as $val(p) = true$. Statements like "grass is red" or "the earth is spherical" are mapped to truth values in valuations, but the choice of truth value involves extralogical considerations connected to colour perception and physics. In electronics these statement symbols might simply represent transistor switches that may be either on or off and an allocation of truth is straightforward. At this point we are not concerned with the philosophical problems of assigning truth values to statements. Instead we just describe the consequences of different assignments to statement symbols p, q, r, ... A set of n statement symbols permits 2^n combinations of possible truth values that are conveniently displayed in the form of a truth table.

Interpretations for the symbols $\wedge$ and $\vee$ are provided by the conjunction and disjunction semantic functions defined as follows:

A	B	A and B	A or B
true	true	true	true
true	false	false	true
false	true	false	true
false	false	false	false

A conjunction of two argument propositions is *true* only when both arguments evaluate to *true*, whereas a disjunction is *false* only when both arguments are *false*.

A valuation provided for each individual atomic statement in a proposition decides the value of the proposition itself because the interpretation of the connectives is fixed by the semantic function definitions. For example, valuations $val(p) = true$ and $val(q) = false$ decide the value of proposition $\neg(\neg p \vee \neg q)$ as follows:

1. $val(\neg(\neg p \vee \neg q))$
2. $not(val(\neg p \vee \neg q))$
3. $not(val(\neg p) \text{ or } val(\neg q))$

4. *not(not val(p) or not val(q))*
5. *not(not true or not false)*
6. *not(false or true)*
7. *not(true)*
8. *false*

Valuation *val(¬proposition)* is replaced by the equivalent expression *not(val proposi-tion)* when the outer ¬ symbol is replaced by its meaning. Gradually the valuation moves inwards until all the connective symbols are replaced by their meanings. In practice this is simply a matter of replacing syntactic symbols with their inter-pretations to give a result like that in line 4. Once this result is obtained, the state-ment valuations are inserted and the expression evaluated according to the truth table definitions. All of this work produces a result for just one valuation, the valu-ation for which *val(p)* is *true* and *val(q)* is *false*. In order to economise on effort, all four possible valuations could be deduced in a single truth table with an intermediate valuation:

p	*q*	*¬p ∨ ¬q*	*¬(¬p ∨ ¬q)*
true	*true*	*false*	*true*
true	*false*	*true*	*false*
false	*true*	*true*	*false*
false	*false*	*true*	*false*

When a particular set of atomic valuations makes a proposition *true* that valuation is said to "satisfy" the formula or the valuation is said to be a "model" for the for-mula. But if a valuation makes the proposition *false*, it is said to falsify the formula and is not a model.

The final column in the truth table for proposition $¬(¬p ∨ ¬q)$ is exactly the same as that shown in the table defining the interpretation of the ∧ symbol, i.e. corresponding atomic valuations produce the same truth values. These two proposi-tions are said to be logically equivalent and this property is shown by the logical equivalence symbol (≅)

$$A ∧ B ≅ ¬(¬A ∨ ¬B)$$

Logical equivalences allow one proposition to be substituted for another without changing the meaning of an overall expression. This allows propositions to be simplified while retaining their meaning, or perhaps manipulated into special forms that have useful properties. The equivalence noted above is one form of De Morgan's relation, the other form being

$$A ∨ B ≅ ¬(¬A ∧ ¬B)$$

Logical equivalence means that two syntactically different formulas evaluate to the same truth value for all valuations. The equivalence symbol used is another metasymbol because it is not part of the formal system under discussion. Like the natural language used for writing this text, it provides a method of describing the formal system without being part of it.

1.2.1 Tautology and contradiction

Propositions that evaluate to *true* in all valuations are called tautologies whereas those that evaluate to *false* in every valuation are said to be contradictory or unsatisfiable. Propositions that evaluate to *true* in some valuations and *false* in others are said to be satisfiable or contingent. A simple example of a tautology is provided by the disjunction of a proposition and its negation in an expression $A \lor \neg A$ that evaluates as follows:

$val(A \lor \neg A)$
$val(A)$ *or* $val(\neg A)$
$val(A)$ *or* $val(not\ A)$

When proposition A evaluates to *true* the first part of this disjunct is *true* and when A evaluates to *false* the second part evaluates to *true*. Since A has to evaluate to either *true* or *false*, the expression above always evaluates to *true*, regardless of the nature of proposition A. In a similar way, the conjunction of a proposition and its negation, $A \land \neg A$, always leads to a contradiction because it is unsatisfiable in this interpretation:

$val(A \land \neg A)$
$val(A)$ *and* $val(\neg A)$
$val(A)$ *and* $not\ val(A)$

Clearly this valuation must always produce a false result. Both $val(A)$ and *not* $val(A)$ must be *true* for the conjunction to be *true*, but this can never occur. Tautology and contradiction statements of this kind may be placed in an equivalence relation with the constants *true* and *false* as follows:

$A \lor \neg A \cong true$
$A \land \neg A \cong false$

Since a propositional tautology is equivalent to the constant *true*, a negated tautology such as $\neg(A \lor \neg A)$ is equivalent to the constant *false* and vice versa. This is in fact a very important relationship because we shall later see that a standard approach to proving tautology is to prove the negated formula to be a contradiction.

Equivalence relations might permit a reduction in the number of brackets required for a proposition. For example, the propositions

$(A \land B) \land C \cong A \land (B \land C)$
$(A \lor B) \lor C \cong A \lor (B \lor C)$

make it clear that the order of evaluation is unimportant when two conjunctions or two disjunctions are applied within a single proposition. The semantic functions defining these connectives are said to be associative, allowing these expressions to be written without brackets as $A \wedge B \wedge C$ and $A \vee B \vee C$.

Two logical equivalences called the distribution rules have the following form:

$$A \vee (B \wedge C) \cong (A \vee B) \wedge (A \vee C)$$
$$A \wedge (B \vee C) \cong (A \wedge B) \vee (A \wedge C)$$

The first case distributes a disjunction over a conjunction; the second case distributes a conjunction over a disjunction. These rules are used to manipulate propositions into the normal forms described later and to simplify propositions by extracting common propositional fragments. For example, proposition p is common to both parts of the following disjunction and may be withdrawn to simplify the formula as follows:

$$(p \wedge r) \vee (p \wedge \neg r) \cong p \wedge (r \vee \neg r)$$
$$\cong p \wedge true$$
$$\cong p$$

One part of the resulting proposition is a tautology and may be replaced by the constant *true*, but in conjunction with this constant, the proposition simply reproduces itself.

A generalised form of De Morgan's relation proves to be very useful in later sections and is justified as an extension of the above equivalence definitions. Conjunctions of three propositions may be substituted by equivalences as follows:

$$(A \wedge B) \wedge C \cong \neg(\neg(A \wedge B) \vee \neg C) \quad \text{De Morgan}$$
$$\cong \neg((\neg A \vee \neg B) \vee \neg C) \quad \text{De Morgan}$$
$$\cong \neg(\neg A \vee \neg B \vee \neg C) \quad \text{distribution}$$

and it is clear that this equivalence holds for repeated conjunctions with any number of arguments. Thus

$$A \wedge B \wedge C \wedge D \wedge \ldots \cong \neg(\neg A \vee \neg B \vee \neg C \vee \neg D \vee \ldots)$$

and a similar equivalence holds for repeated disjunctions:

$$A \vee B \vee C \vee D \vee \ldots \cong \neg(\neg A \wedge \neg B \wedge \neg C \wedge \neg D \wedge \ldots)$$

Interpretations for the symbols $\rightarrow$ and $\leftrightarrow$ are provided by the arity-two semantic functions *imp* and *iff*, standing for implies and "if and only if":

A	B	A imp B	A iff B
true	true	true	true
true	false	false	false
false	true	true	false
false	false	true	true

An implication $A \rightarrow B$ has left- and right-hand subformulas, A and B, called the antecedent and the consequent. A *false* antecedent makes the implication *true* because anything can be implied from a *false* premiss. On the other hand, a *true* antecedent must lead to a *true* consequent: it would not be correct to deduce a wrong conclusion from the *true* facts. As a result, an implication is only *false* when it is claimed that a *true* antecedent implies a *false* consequent. Truth tables may be used to justify the following equivalences involving implication:

$$A \rightarrow B \cong \neg A \vee B$$
$$\cong \neg(A \wedge \neg B) \quad \text{De Morgan}$$

Mutual implication is logically equivalent to the conjunction of two implications:

$$A \leftrightarrow B \cong (A \rightarrow B) \wedge (B \rightarrow A)$$

and, since the implications have to be true in both directions, this only occurs when both arguments are *true* or both are *false*. The following alternative logical equivalence follows from this simple observation:

$$A \leftrightarrow B \cong (A \wedge B) \vee (\neg A \wedge \neg B)$$

A mutual implication between two logically equivalent propositions always produces a tautology. For example, a tautology based on De Morgan's relation simply joins two equivalent formulas by a mutual implication:

$$\neg(\neg A \vee \neg B) \leftrightarrow A \wedge B$$

In noting this relationship, we should also note that symbol $\leftrightarrow$ is part of the formal system being described whereas $\cong$ is a metasymbol used to describe the formal system.

An arity-two function requires a truth table of four rows to describe its semantics. Since the outcome of each row may be either *true* or *false*, there are two possible outcomes for each row and a total of $2 \times 2 \times 2 \times 2 = 16$ possible functions that might be defined. These functions may be divided into two groups of eight, the first of which includes the four connectives already described (*and,or,imp,iff*) together with a further group of four defined as follows:

A	B	A rimp B	fst(A,B)	snd(A,B)	tconst(A,B)
true	*true*	*true*	*true*	*true*	*true*
true	*false*	*true*	*true*	*false*	*true*
false	*true*	*false*	*false*	*true*	*true*
false	*false*	*true*	*false*	*false*	*true*

The first of these functions is a reverse implication that might have been given the symbol $\leftarrow$ in the formal system. But since this is just an ordinary implication written in reverse, it is not usually included. Nevertheless, this form of implication is particularly useful in logic programming because program statements are more naturally written in the reversed form. Functions *fst* and *snd* are projection operators that project their first or second arguments out as the value of the function.

Notice that these functions are written in prefix notation as opposed to the infix notation used for all other expressions. This notation is standard in functional programming, an area in which the two functions are of fundamental importance. The remaining function maps every argument combination onto the constant *true* and is of little interest in practice.

A second set of eight semantic functions is obtained by negating the results of the first eight described above. Negations of the original four (*and,or,imp*, *iff*) produce the following functions:

A	B	A nand B	A nor B	A nimp B	A niff B
true	true	false	false	false	false
true	false	true	false	true	true
false	true	true	false	false	true
false	false	true	true	false	false

This table may be seen as an interpretation of the propositions $\neg(A \land B)$, $\neg(A \lor B)$, $\neg(A \rightarrow B)$ and $\neg(A \leftrightarrow B)$ using the semantic functions already provided for the connectives within these expressions. In fact, it has to be seen in these terms because the formal system defined above contains no symbols that these semantic functions might interpret. It would be possible to add more symbols to the original alphabet and then interpret these symbols with the semantic functions. Three of the functions have accepted syntactic forms: the semantic functions *nand*, *nor* and *niff* are often given syntactic forms |, ↓ and ⊕ and these symbols could be included in a formal system. The vertical bar of the *nand* syntax is called a Sheffer stroke and the *niff* function symbol is more often described as the exclusive-or (exor) symbol.

We have shown that interpretations for the symbols $\{\rightarrow, \leftarrow, \leftrightarrow, \land\}$ may all be expressed in terms of negation and disjunction interpretations. Semantic functions for the remaining three cases of the first group of eight may be written without any other connectives as

$$fst(A,B) = A$$
$$snd(A,B) = B$$
$$tconst(A,B) = true$$

Since the second group of eight semantic functions is formed by prefixing negations to the earlier eight, we conclude that all sixteen may be expressed in terms of negation and disjunction alone. Thus the set of symbols $\{\neg, \lor\}$ interpreted as above is adequate to generate all sixteen possible semantic functions. There are other adequate sets of symbols containing the connective $\neg$ with an arity-two connective, notably the sets $\{\neg, \land\}$ and $\{\neg, \rightarrow\}$. Perhaps more surprising, the *nand* and *nor* semantic functions interpreting symbols | and ↓ are individually adequate sets, so that either one alone could represent all sixteen semantic functions. Integrated circuit devices that implement either *nand* or *nor* logic are relatively easy to produce because these functions reflect the physical behaviour of transistors. Since any circuit can be implemented from collections of these elements, they are widely used as building blocks in electronics.

EXERCISES 1.2

1. Produce truth tables representing each of the following propositions and state whether each proposition is a tautology, a contradiction or a contingent proposition.

   a. $(p \wedge \neg q) \vee (\neg p \wedge q)$

   b. $(p \vee \neg q) \wedge (\neg p \vee q)$

   c. $(p \wedge q) \rightarrow (p \vee q)$

   d. $(p \vee q) \rightarrow (p \wedge q)$

   e. $(p \wedge q) \rightarrow r$

   f. $(p \vee (q \wedge r)) \rightarrow ((p \vee q) \wedge (p \vee r))$

   g. $((p \rightarrow q) \wedge (q \rightarrow r)) \wedge \neg(p \rightarrow r))$

2. Consider the following propositions:

$$(p \rightarrow q) \rightarrow ((q \rightarrow r) \wedge (p \rightarrow r))$$
$$(p \rightarrow (q \rightarrow r)) \rightarrow ((p \rightarrow q) \rightarrow (p \rightarrow r))$$

   a. Express them in terms of negations and disjunctions alone.

   b. Express them in terms of negations and conjunctions alone.

3. Produce truth tables to evaluate the following propositions for all possible interpretations of their atomic symbols:

$$p \oplus q \rightarrow p \vee q$$
$$p \mid q \downarrow p \mid q$$

1.3 SEMANTIC TABLEAUX

A semantic tableau is a graphical method of showing the conditions under which a proposition evaluates to *true*. For example, according to the interpretations given earlier, the formula

$$p \wedge \neg q \vee \neg p \wedge q \cdot$$

evaluates to *true* when either subformula $p \wedge \neg q$ or subformula $\neg p \wedge q$ evaluates to *true*. The fact that there are two ways of making the formula *true* is shown in the semantic tableau of Figure 1.1 as a splitting between lines 1 and 2. Next we need to know when subformula $p \wedge \neg q$ evaluates to *true* and from the interpretation given earlier it is clear that this occurs only when both p and $\neg q$ both evaluate to *true*. Thus p and $\neg q$ appear along a single path below the subformula in the tableau. A

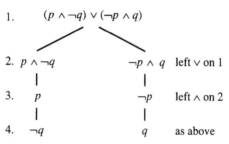

Figure 1.1   Tableau for $(p \wedge \neg q) \vee (\neg p \wedge q)$

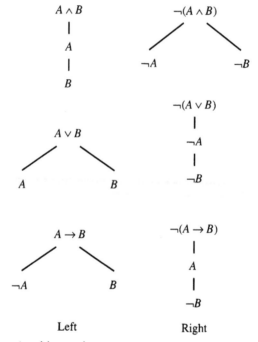

Figure 1.2   Semantic tableau rules

similar argument applies to the subformula on the right-hand side of the tableau. Once a rule has been applied, the formula to which it is applied is of no further interest and might be marked with a tick as having been discharged. Only the subformulas it produces are of further interest. Eventually a situation is reached where no further rule can be applied, and at this point the tableau is complete.

The arguments used here can be generalised into two of the rules shown in Figure 1.2. Formulas with $\vee$ symbols as a principal connective are decomposed by the "left $\vee$" rule whereas an $\wedge$ symbol is decomposed by the "left $\wedge$" rule. At this point, left and right rules are simply those on the left and right of Figure 1.2, but later the left and right tags acquire greater significance. Earlier it was shown that formula $A \rightarrow B$ is logically equivalent to formula $\neg A \vee B$ and is *true* when either $\neg A$ *or* B is *true*. As a result, the "left $\rightarrow$" rule looks like the "left $\vee$" rule except that one of its subformulas is negated.

Each rule on the right-hand side of Figure 1.2 relates to the same connective as the left, but the whole proposition lies within the scope of a $\neg$ symbol. A justification for the "right $\wedge$" rule is provided by one of the De Morgan equivalences given earlier:

$$\neg(A \wedge B) \cong \neg A \vee \neg B$$

A proposition of form $\neg(A \wedge B)$ is *true* when either $\neg A$ *or* $\neg B$ is *true* (or both are *true*) and therefore causes branching in the tableau. Justification for the "right $\vee$" rule is also provided by a De Morgan rule, this time in the form

$$\neg(A \vee B) \cong \neg A \wedge \neg B$$

A proposition subject to a "right $\vee$" rule is *true* only if both $\neg A$ and $\neg B$ are *true*, so its structure resembles the "left $\wedge$" rule but with negated subformulas. Finally the truth of a negated implication proposition follows from the "right $\rightarrow$" rule because of the following equivalences:

$$\neg(A \rightarrow B)$$
$$\neg(\neg A \vee B)$$
$$A \wedge \neg B$$

A negated formula with an implication principal connective is only *true* when both A and $\neg B$ are *true*, so its structure is that of a "left $\wedge$" with one negated subformula. These inference rules are sometimes divided into two classes: a class of non-branching rules called the alpha or conjunctive set and a class of branching rules called the beta or disjunctive set.

A Hintikka set S is a set of propositions with the following properties:

a. If P is a conjunctive (alpha type) formula in S then both of its subformulas are also in set S.

b. If P is a disjunctive (beta type) formula then one of its subformulas is in set S.

c. An atom and its negation must not both occur in set S.

Looking back at the tableau in Figure 1.1, we see that a Hintikka set may be obtained by collecting propositions along a path from the root to a leaf of a semantic tableau. Since the tree in this figure has two branches, there are two Hintikka sets:

$$S1 = \{p \wedge \neg q \vee \neg p \wedge q, p \wedge \neg q, p, \neg q\}$$
$$S2 = \{p \wedge \neg q \vee \neg p \wedge q, \neg p \wedge q, \neg p, q\}$$

Every formula in a Hintikka set must evaluate to *true* in order to make the root proposition *true*. Consequently, the subset of atoms and negated atoms in a Hintikka set provides a valuation that is a model for the proposition. Every proposition in Hintikka set S1 evaluates to *true* for valuations $val(p) = true$ and $val(q) = false$, and

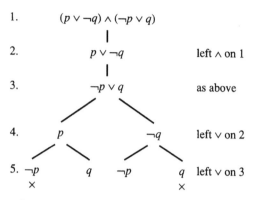

Figure 1.3   Tableau for $(p \vee \neg q) \wedge (\neg p \vee q)$

this set of valuations is a model for the proposition. Similarly, every proposition in set S2 is *true* for the pair of valuations $val(p) = false$ and $val(q) = true$, providing a further model for the proposition. In this simple example the tableau did not tell us anything that could not have been seen in the original formula, but as formulas become larger and more complex the tableau becomes more useful.

The same two rules can be applied to formula $(p \vee \neg q) \wedge (\neg p \vee q)$, giving the tableau of Figure 1.3, but here the result is less obvious than before. A single application of the "left $\wedge$" rule is followed by two applications of the "left $\vee$" rule, producing four paths down through the resulting tableau. Two of these paths are incapable of producing a Hintikka set because they contain both an atom and its negation: one contains both p and $\neg p$, the other q and $\neg q$. Every formula in a Hintikka set has to evaluate to *true* for a valuation indicated by its atomic components, but there can be no valuation of (say) p that makes both p and $\neg p$ *true*. A branch may be closed and marked with a cross as soon as a clashing pair of atoms appears because it could not lead to a satisfying valuation. Hintikka sets may be read from the remaining two open paths of the tableau as follows:

$$S1 = \{(p \vee \neg q) \wedge (\neg p \vee q), p \vee \neg q, \neg p \vee q, p, q\}$$
$$S2 = \{(p \vee \neg q) \wedge (\neg p \vee q), p \vee \neg q, \neg p \vee q, \neg q, \neg p\}$$

Set S1 indicates that valuations $val(p) = true$ and $val(q) = true$ provide a model for the proposition and S2 indicates a further model $val(p) = false$ and $val(q) = false$. Thus, the proposition is satisfied in valuations where both p and q are interpreted as *true* or when both p and q are interpreted as *false*, suggesting an alternative equivalent proposition:

$$(p \wedge q) \vee (\neg p \wedge \neg q)$$

Semantic tableaux are very useful for producing certain equivalent forms of propositions called normal forms; this feature is explored in more detail in Section 1.6.

Inference rules are applied to propositions containing implication symbols in much the same way as in the examples above. A tableau constructed by applying rules to the proposition $(p \rightarrow q) \rightarrow (\neg q \rightarrow \neg p)$ is shown in Figure 1.4. Three open

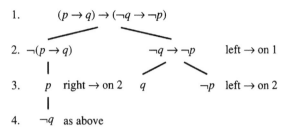

Figure 1.4   Implications in a semantic tableau

paths are visible and three corresponding Hintikka sets suggest that this formula is satisfied by the following three sets of valuations:

	val(p)	*val(q)*
model1	*true*	*false*
model2	*	*true*
model3	*false*	*

Asterisks in the table represent "don't care" situations in which atomic valuations of *true* or *false* do not affect the truth of the formula. This table clearly shows that the formula is *true* when $val(p) = true$ and $val(q) = false$ OR when $val(q) = true$ OR when $val(p) = false$, yielding an equivalent formula $(p \wedge \neg q) \vee q \vee \neg p$. Again a special form of the proposition has been obtained from the tableau, but this is not our immediate concern. If the table above is expanded by including explicit *true* and *false* values for each "don't care" value, it produces a larger table of five lines, but one of these lines is repeated. There are only four possible pairs of valuations for a two-symbol proposition, and from the table we deduce that all four are models for the formula. In other words, the formula is *true* in any valuation and is therefore a tautology, but this is not immediately obvious from the tableau of the proposition itself.

Tautologies are important in the applications of logic to computer science, and methods of deciding if a proposition is a tautology are of great interest. The example above suggests that the direct use of semantic tableaux does not provide an easy procedure for deciding if a given proposition is a tautology, but an alternative approach is possible. If a proposition is a tautology, it is satisfied by every set of valuations and its negation is a contradiction that cannot be satisfied by any valuation. As a result, the semantic tableau produced from a negated tautology has only closed branches containing clashing pairs. This property provides a convenient decision procedure for deciding tautologies. A tableau constructed from the negated formula is shown in Figure 1.5 and confirms the original (unnegated) proposition to be a tautology. Notice that the proposition in line 3 is first broken down by a "right →" inference rule to give lines 4 and 5, then the proposition in line 2 is decomposed by a "left →" rule to give line 7. It was not essential to apply the rules in this

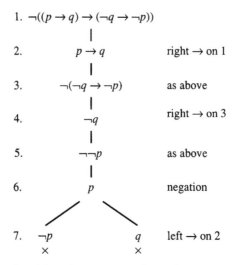

Figure 1.5 A semantic tableau from a negated tautology

order, so the proposition in line 2 could have been discharged before the proposition in line 3. The order in which inferences are applied does not affect the outcome of a deduction, but it does affect the shape of the tableau produced and the efficiency with which a result is obtained. Whenever a choice between a branching and non-branching step is possible, the non-branching inference should be applied first because it delays tableau spanning until it is unavoidable. Directives of this sort are often called *heuristics*.

1.3.1   Extended tableau rules

Disjunction and conjunction are associative operations and the equivalent representations

$$(A \lor B) \lor C \cong A \lor (B \lor C)$$
$$(A \land B) \land C \cong A \land (B \land C)$$

may be represented by the unbracketed propositions $A \lor B \lor C$ and $A \land B \land C$. Since it is unimportant which pair of arguments is evaluated first, it is equally unimportant which connective is first removed in the semantic tableau. As a result, it is possible to define rules that remove two connectives at a time for these operations, leading to the extended tableau rules in Figure 1.6. These new rules are equivalent to two applications of the previous two-symbol rules and are only possible because of the associative nature of the connectives. Extensions of the "right" rules follow from the generalised form of De Morgan's relation:

$$\neg(A \land B \land C) \cong \neg A \lor \neg B \lor \neg C$$
$$\neg(A \lor B \lor C) \cong \neg A \land \neg B \land \neg C$$

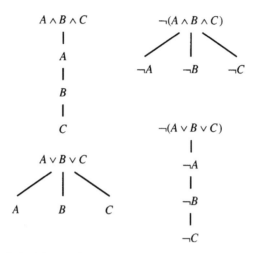

Figure 1.6 Extended tableau rules

A "right ∧" is *true* when any one of its subformulas is *false* whereas a "right ∨" is *true* only when all of its subformulas are *false*. In effect, the negated formulas are also associative.

Extended tableau rules are not permitted for the → symbol because the interpretation provided for this connective is not associative. As a result, the two formulas $A → (B → C)$ and $(A → B) → C$ have different meanings and cannot be reduced with a single extended "left →" rule. It would of course be possible to assume left association or right association and build extended tableaux on this basis, but this would not be very helpful. In practice the extended tableaux are required for propositions containing only ∧ and ∨ symbols, so a generalised implication is not required.

1.3.2 Soundness and completeness

Proof systems are said to be sound if any theorem proven by the system is indeed valid, i.e. in the case of propositions every theorem is a tautology. A propositional theorem is proven by a semantic tableau when it is shown that the negated theorem produces a closed semantic tableau. A negated tautology is certainly a contradiction, so it is sufficient to be sure that a contradiction always produces a closed tableau. This is easily done because the semantic tableau rules implement a systematic search for a satisfying valuation. If one existed it would be found as an open path with a corresponding Hintikka set; the absence of such a path must indicate a contradiction.

Conversely, a proof system is said to be complete if every valid proposition may be proven within the system. In this case we have to show that a closed semantic tableau may be constructed for every contradictory proposition. First of all, we note that a finite tableau may be constructed for any finite proposition. The argument here is simple: each time a rule is applied, the number of connectives is reduced and eventually there are no more connectives to which rules may be applied. Thus any finite root proposition yields a tableau of some sort. A contradictory root proposition is unsatisfiable and is connected through the rules to closed paths. This may be proven by showing that a satisfiable proposition has a tableau with at least one open path that defines a satisfying valuation. In fact, we have already shown that the Hintikka set defines a model for a satisfiable root proposition and the absence of a Hintikka set implies an unsatisfiable root proposition.

EXERCISES 1.3

1. Produce a semantic tableau for each of the following propositions. From each tableau produce Hintikka sets to show the conditions under which the proposition is true:

   a. $q \rightarrow (p \rightarrow q)$

   b. $(p \vee q) \rightarrow (p \wedge q)$

   c. $(p \wedge q) \rightarrow r$

2. Use semantic tableaux to show that each of the following propositions represents a tautology:

   a. $(p \wedge q) \rightarrow (q \wedge p)$

   b. $(p \wedge q) \rightarrow (p \vee q)$

   c. $(p \rightarrow q) \rightarrow ((q \rightarrow r) \wedge (p \rightarrow r))$

   d. $(p \vee q) \leftrightarrow (q \vee p)$

   e. $((p \rightarrow r) \wedge (q \rightarrow r)) \rightarrow ((p \wedge q) \rightarrow r)$

   f. $(\neg p \vee \neg r) \leftrightarrow \neg(p \wedge r)$

1.4   SEMANTIC ENTAILMENT

Formula A is said to entail formula B if every valuation that makes A *true* also makes B *true*. In other words, any set of atomic valuations that is a model for A is also a model for B. A semantic entailment, sometimes called a logical consequence, is shown with the aid of the semantic turnstile symbol:

$$A \vDash B$$

Although formula B must evaluate to *true* in any valuation where A evaluates to *true*, it might also be *true* in valuations where A is *false*. Consider as an example the following entailment:

$$(p \wedge \neg q) \vee (\neg p \wedge q) \vDash p \vee q$$

Truth tables for the propositions on each side of the turnstile are easily constructed:

p	q	$(p \wedge \neg q) \vee (\neg p \wedge q)$	$p \vee q$
true	true	false	true
true	false	true	true
false	true	true	true
false	false	false	false

The formula on the left of the turnstile is in fact the exclusive-or function and evaluates to *true* when just one but not both of its arguments is *true*. An ordinary or function, on the other hand, is *true* when either or both of its arguments are *true*. Clearly the ordinary or function is *true* whenever exclusive-or is *true*, but it is also *true* in one valuation where the exclusive-or is *false*. An entailment such as the one above is equivalent to a valid implication, i.e. the proposition $(p \wedge \neg q) \vee (\neg p \wedge q) \rightarrow p \vee q$ is a tautology because its consequent must be *true* whenever its antecedent is *true*. A tautology can always be written from a semantic entailment in this way, and the semantic tableau of the negated proposition in Figure 1.7 confirms this particular example. Notice, however, that the semantic entailment symbol is a metasymbol and is outside propositional logic, whereas the implication symbol is part of the formal system being examined.

More generally, a proposition B is entailed by (or is a logical consequence of) a set of propositions M, represented as $M \vDash B$. A specific example is provided by the entailment

$$\{p \rightarrow q, q \rightarrow r\} \vDash p \rightarrow r$$

1. $\neg((p \wedge \neg q \vee \neg p \wedge q) \rightarrow p \vee q)$

2. $p \wedge \neg q \vee \neg p \wedge q$ right $\rightarrow$ on 1

3. $\neg(p \vee q)$ as above

4. $\neg p$ right $\rightarrow$ on 3

5. $\neg q$ as above

6. $\cdot p \wedge \neg q$ $\neg p \wedge q$ left $\vee$ on 2

7. p $\neg p$ left $\wedge$ on 6

8. $\neg q$ q as above
    ×   ×

Figure 1.7 Tableau for an entailment

and a first attempt to check this entailment could involve writing a truth table for each of the formulas:

p	q	r	$p \rightarrow q$	$q \rightarrow r$	$p \rightarrow r$
true	true	true	true	true	true
true	true	false	true	false	false
true	false	true	false	true	true
true	false	false	false	true	false
false	true	true	true	true	true
false	true	false	true	false	true
false	false	true	true	true	true
false	false	false	true	true	true

It is clear that no valuation simultaneously makes both $p \rightarrow q$ and $q \rightarrow r$ *true* but $p \rightarrow r$ *false*, so the entailment is proven. In fact, there was no need to write out the full truth table because it is only necessary to check that no valuation makes every formula on the left *true* while making the one on the right *false*. Only the rows in which the entailed formula ($p \rightarrow r$) is *false* need to be checked and, since this only occurs when p is *true* and r is *false*, just rows 2 and 4 have to be checked. This semantic entailment confirms the tautology

$$(p \rightarrow q) \wedge (q \rightarrow r) \rightarrow (p \rightarrow r)$$

and this is further confirmed by the semantic tableau of Figure 1.8.

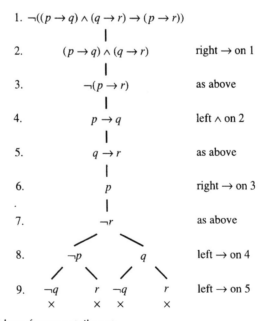

Figure 1.8 Tableau for an entailment

A larger example with more proposition symbols illustrates the advantage of not considering every possible valuation:

$$p, p \rightarrow (q \vee r), q \rightarrow s, r \rightarrow s \vDash s$$

We have to check there is no valuation that satisfies every proposition on the left while falsifying the proposition on the right of the turnstile. Since the formula on the right is a single symbol s, only a valuation of *false* for this symbol has to be considered. Equally, since all propositions on the left have to be *true*, only valuations that set p to *true* have to be considered and the truth table is reduced to four lines:

q	r	$p \rightarrow (q \vee r)$	$q \rightarrow s$	$r \rightarrow s$
true	true	true	false	false
true	false	true	false	true
false	true	true	true	false
false	false	false	true	false

No valuation makes all of these propositions *true*, so there is no valuation that makes every formula on the left *true* at the same time as making the entailed formula *false*. As a result, the entailment is proven and the following formula must be a tautology:

$$p \wedge (p \rightarrow (q \vee r)) \wedge (q \rightarrow s) \wedge (r \rightarrow s) \rightarrow s$$

In each of the examples above, an implication was derived from an entailment, and for the general case this may be shown as

$$A_1 \wedge A_2 \wedge A_3 \wedge \ldots \wedge A_n \rightarrow B$$

If any of the subformulas joined by conjunctions in the antecedent evaluates to *false*, the whole antecedent is *false* and formula B may be either *true* or *false*. If every subformula is *true* the antecedent as a whole is *true* and formula B has to be *true* in order to make the implication *true*. Thus an entailment has the properties indicated by an implication.

It is worth reviewing the procedure used to establish semantic entailment because it has much in common with the Gentzen G system described in the next section. This procedure takes a proposed entailment of the form

$$\{A_1, A_2, A_3, \ldots, A_n\} \vDash B$$

and systematically attempts to satisfy every formula on the left while falsifying formula B on the right. It is a systematic search for a counterexample that will disprove the entailment, i.e. an attempt to find one set of valuations where each formula on the left evaluates to true when B evaluates to *false*. Failure to find such a valuation set establishes the entailment.

A set of n formulas

$$M = \{A_1, A_2, A_3, \ldots, A_n\}$$

is said to be consistent if there is at least one valuation that makes every formula in the set *true*, i.e. there exists at least one model for the set of formulas. An inconsistent set of formulas has no model and therefore entails any other formula: if there is no valuation that makes every formula on the left *true*, the result of a valuation on the right-hand formula is irrelevant. But if the set M is consistent, an entailment imposes the requirements described above on formula B, then

   $M \vDash B$

and B has to be *true* when all of M are *true*. It follows that, if B is entailed by set M, the set of formulas

   $\{A_1, A_2, A_3, \ldots, A_n, \neg B\}$

is inconsistent because $\neg B$ evaluates to *false* whenever the other formulas in the set all evaluate to *true*. Consistency and inconsistency are the proof theoretic equivalents of satisfiability and contradiction in interpretations. Just as it is easier to prove tautology by showing that the negated formula is a contradiction, it is easier to prove entailment by showing the set $\{A_1, A_2, A_3, \ldots, A_n, \neg B\}$ to be inconsistent. Indirect proofs of this kind are usually described as refutation techniques because they work by refuting negated forms rather than demonstrating the feature directly.

   Truth tables may be used to evaluate formulas and to establish entailments, tautologies and contradictions in the way shown above, but the procedure becomes more difficult as the number of statements to be interpreteted increases. A formula with n symbols has 2^n possible valuations, so the size of a truth table increases exponentially with the number of symbols involved. Relatively small examples with four or five symbols require truth tables of 16 or 32 lines, so the approach is already becoming impractical. Modern integrated circuits often have more than a million transistors that have to be represented by distinct symbols and a truth table of greater than $2^{1\,000\,000}$ lines. Clearly we have to develop methods of establishing the truth of a formula without the use of truth tables, and it is this purpose we now address.

EXERCISES 1.4

1. Prove the following entailments by deriving truth tables for propositions on each side of the entailment symbol:

   a. $p \wedge q \vDash p \vee q$
   b. $\neg p \rightarrow p \vDash p$
   c. $q \vDash p \vee q$
   d. $(p \rightarrow r) \wedge (q \rightarrow r) \vDash (p \vee q) \rightarrow r$
   e. $(p \rightarrow (q \wedge r)) \vDash (p \rightarrow q) \wedge (p \rightarrow r)$

   Each entailment $A \vDash B$ indicates that the corresponding proposition $A \rightarrow B$ is a tautology. Draw semantic tableaux to confirm each entailment above.

2. Prove the following entailments from sets of propositions:

   a. $\{p \rightarrow q, r \rightarrow s\} \vDash (p \wedge r) \rightarrow (q \wedge s)$

   b. $\{p \rightarrow q, r \rightarrow s\} \vDash (p \vee r) \rightarrow (q \vee s)$

   c. $\{p \leftrightarrow \neg q, q \leftrightarrow \neg r\} \vDash p \leftrightarrow r$

3. Show that the following entailments do not hold:

   a. $p \vee q \vDash p \wedge q$

   b. $p \rightarrow q \vDash p \wedge q$

1.5   A GENTZEN PROOF SYSTEM FOR PROPOSITIONS

In 1935 Gerhard Gentzen laid down deduction rules for two formal proof systems which he called the LK and LJ calculi. The first of these is equivalent to a simpler approach called the G system of deduction later developed by Lyndon. Any LK proof may be translated into an equivalent G proof and, since this latter approach is easier, it makes a better starting-point than the LK form. We shall see that the inference rules of such a Gentzen-style proof system are compatible with the interpretation described in Section 1.2. This particular interpretation of propositional logic symbols has the advantage that it is very easily related to the rules of proof systems. Gentzen himself recognised a close relationship between what he called sequent systems and the concept of an entailment or logical consequence described in the preceding section. An LJ proof system may also be expressed in the style of Lyndon and rules for this variation are presented in Chapter 7. Although there are only small differences between the rules given here and those provided later, the effect of these changes is to define a completely different formal system called intuitionistic logic.

A G proof system may be seen as a proof theoretic form of the reasoning that establishes the extended semantic entailment

$$\{A_1, A_2, \ldots, A_m\} \vDash \{B_1, B_2, \ldots, B_n\}$$

This entailment is *true* if valuations that make every formula on the left *true* also make at least one of the formulas on the right *true*. In other words, there is no valuation that makes all of the formulas on the left *true* at the same time as making all formulas on the right *false*. As before, the entailment is proved by systematically searching for valuations that make formulas on the left *true* while making the right-hand side *false*. A proof of the entailment is provided by the failure of a systematic and exhaustive search for a counterexample. A Gentzen-style proof system applies rules to sequents of the form

$$[A_1, A_2, \ldots, A_m] \Rightarrow [B_1, B_2, \ldots, B_n]$$

in which the left- and right-hand lists, called respectively the antecedent and succedent, are separated by the sequent symbol ($\Rightarrow$). In the original (LK) formulation

1. $\quad (p \lor \neg q) \land (\neg p \lor q) \Rightarrow$

2. $\quad \overline{(p \lor \neg q), (\neg p \lor q) \Rightarrow} \qquad\qquad$ left $\land$ on 1

3. $\overline{(p \lor \neg q), \neg p \Rightarrow} \qquad \overline{(p \lor \neg q), q \Rightarrow} \qquad$ left $\lor$ on 2

4. $\overline{p, \neg p \Rightarrow} \quad \overline{\neg q, \neg p \Rightarrow} \quad \overline{p, q \Rightarrow} \quad \overline{\neg q, q \Rightarrow} \qquad$ left $\lor$ on 3

5. $\quad p \Rightarrow p \qquad \Rightarrow p, q \qquad p, q \Rightarrow \qquad q \Rightarrow q \qquad$ negations

$\qquad \times \qquad\qquad\qquad\qquad\qquad\qquad\qquad\qquad \times$

Figure 1.9 A deduction tree

the order of formulas in the lists is important and rules are provided to change the order in which objects appear. This order is unimportant in the G proof system described here, allowing the antecedent and succedent to be treated as sets rather than lists. Nevertheless, the square brackets are sometimes retained to keep the notation compatible with LK usage and in practice we show neither set nor list brackets. Just as in the entailment, a sequent is valid if there is no valuation that makes all of its antecedent formulas *true* without making at least one of the succedent formulas *true*.

As a first example, we demonstrate the conditions under which the proposition $(p \lor \neg q) \land (\neg p \lor q)$ is *true* by making it the antecedent of a sequent

$$(p \lor \neg q) \land (\neg p \lor q) \Rightarrow$$

A semantic tableau has already been provided for this formula in Figure 1.3 and the G system deduction tree is shown in Figure 1.9. The reasoning now is similar to that used in building the semantic tableau, but the notation in which it is expressed is rather different. In order to make the antecedent *true*, subformulas $(p \lor \neg q)$ and $(\neg p \lor q)$ have separately to be made *true*, so these subformulas are placed in the revised lower antecedent. If one of the subformulas had to be made *false* in order to make the initial antecedent *true*, it would then be moved to the new succedent. Subformula $(p \lor \neg q)$ is in turn *true* when either one of propositions p or $\neg q$ is *true*, generating two subsequents with p in one antecedent and $\neg q$ in the other. Finally in the leftmost branch we see that the sequent is *true* if p and $\neg p$ are both *true* or, equivalently, that p occurs in the antecedent where it has to be satisfied and in the succedent where it has to be falsified. A sequent containing the same atom in both its antecedent and its succedent is called an axiom. A branch may be terminated and marked with a cross whenever an axiom occurs. Similar reasoning is used to build the right-hand side of the deduction tree.

In addition to two axiom sequents labelled with crosses, the deduction tree in Figure 1.9 contains two non-axiom leaf sequents, indicating there are valuations capable of making the proposition true. From the non-axiom sequents $\Rightarrow p, q$ and $p, q \Rightarrow$ we deduce that the original formula is satisfied (is *true*) when both propositions are *false* or when both are *true*. The informal arguments used above may be formalised into a set of inference rules similar to those given earlier for semantic tableaux. Figure 1.10 shows eight G system inference rules as opposed to the six rules required for semantic tableau construction. Two extra rules arise because

$$\frac{X, A \wedge B \Rightarrow Y}{X, A, B \Rightarrow Y} \qquad \frac{X \Rightarrow Y, A \wedge B}{X \Rightarrow Y, A \qquad X \Rightarrow Y, B}$$

$$\frac{X, A \vee B \Rightarrow Y}{X, A \Rightarrow Y \qquad X, B \Rightarrow Y} \qquad \frac{X \Rightarrow Y, A \vee B}{X \Rightarrow Y, A, B}$$

$$\frac{X, A \rightarrow B \Rightarrow Y}{X \Rightarrow Y, A \qquad X, B \Rightarrow Y} \qquad \frac{X \Rightarrow Y, A \rightarrow B}{X, A \Rightarrow Y, B}$$

$$\frac{X, \neg A \Rightarrow Y}{X \Rightarrow Y, A} \qquad \frac{X \Rightarrow Y, \neg A}{X, A \Rightarrow Y}$$

Left   Right

Figure 1.10   G system rules

formulas in the antecedent are distinguished from those in the succedent and "not" rules are required to transfer between the two. If a formula occurs on one side of a sequent symbol, it may be moved to the other side, provided an appropriate correcting negation is made. This seems quite reasonable: if we seek to satisfy antecedent formulas and falsify succedent formulas, a move from one to the other has to be accompanied by negation. Apart from the addition of a "left ¬" rule, the left G rules correspond almost exactly to the semantic tableau rules. At first, the obvious correspondence between right tableau and G system rules might seem surprising, but it has a simple explanation. The right tableau rules derive conditions under which a negated proposition is *true* whereas G rules derive conditions under which the formula itself is *false*. This amounts to the same thing, hence the similar rule structure. Like the semantic tableau in Figure 1.3, the deduction tree in Figure 1.9 required the application of "left ∧", "left ∨" and "left ¬" rules before it reached a point where no further rules could be applied. Unlike the semantic tableau, it required final negation rules to produce axioms.

The whole purpose of G system rules is to demonstrate the subformula conditions under which antecedent formulas are *true* and succedent formulas are *false*. These requirements are entered into subsequents that become the subjects of further applications of the rules. Eventually it becomes impossible to apply any more rules because all the connectives have been exhausted. If the initial antecedent proposition is a contradiction such as $p \wedge \neg p$, the following steps are observed:

$$p \wedge \neg p \Rightarrow$$
$$p, \neg p \Rightarrow$$
$$p \Rightarrow p$$

Antecedent $p \wedge \neg p$ is *true* if both p and $\neg p$ are separately *true*, so the single proposition is replaced by two separate propositions on the left. Proposition $\neg p$ is in turn *true* only if p is *false*, so $\neg p$ on the left may be replaced by p on the right-hand side. In terms of the G system rules, this deduction consists of a "left $\wedge$" followed by a "left $\neg$" and results in a single-axiom sequent.

If the initial sequent contains an empy antecedent together with the tautology $p \vee \neg p$ in the succedent position, a similar sequence of steps is observed:

$$\Rightarrow p \vee \neg p$$
$$\Rightarrow p, \neg p$$
$$p \Rightarrow p$$

Proposition $p \vee \neg p$ is shown *false* if both p and $\neg p$ are separately shown *false*, and a single proposition on the right of the sequent symbol is replaced by two separate propositions. Proposition $\neg p$ in turn is *false* only if p is shown *true*, so $\neg p$ on the right, false side can be replaced by p on the left, true side. In terms of the rules, we see a "right $\wedge$" followed by a "right $\neg$", leading to an axiom.

Both of these small examples lead to an axiom that does not contain any other propositions, but in the more general case an axiom takes the form

$$X, P, Y \Rightarrow W, P, Z$$

in which symbol P represents the common proposition and X, Y, W, Z represent any other propositions. If P is *false* the sequent is *true* because an antecedent formula is *false*. If P is *true* the sequent is *true* because the succedent has at least one *true* element. In this case other elements of the antecedent may be *true* or *false*, but the sequent can never be falsified. An axiom in the G system proof derived from an antecedent contradiction has much in common with a clashing pair along a path in a semantic tableau.

In the more general case a deduction tree beginning with a sequent of the form

contradiction $\Rightarrow$

must lead to a tree in which every branch terminates in an axiom. A deduction tree with this property is called a proof tree. The object of the systematic search is to find valuations that make the antecedent true, but no valuation can make a contradiction true. In the same way, an initial sequent of the form

$\Rightarrow$ tautology

leads to a proof tree because the search for a valuation that makes a tautology false inevitably ends in failure. This line of thought suggests a method of proving propositions to be tautologies: make the proposition a succedent in a sequent and apply the G system rules until the tree is complete. If every branch of the tree terminates with an axiom, the initial proposition is indeed a tautology because an exhaustive search has failed to find any valuation to falsify it. If every possible rule has been applied to a branch and no axiom has resulted, the branch remains open, producing a counterexample to the proof.

As an example of a proof tree produced from a tautology, we now consider a proposition called the contrapositive:

1. $\Rightarrow (\neg p \to \neg q) \to (q \to p)$

---

2. $(\neg p \to \neg q) \Rightarrow (q \to p)$ right $\to$ on 1

---

3. $(\neg p \to \neg q), q \Rightarrow p$ right $\to$ on 2

---

4. $q \Rightarrow p, \neg p$ $\neg q, q \Rightarrow p$ left $\to$ on 3

---

5. $p, q \Rightarrow p$ $q \Rightarrow p, q$ negations
        $\times$ $\times$

Figure 1.11   A proof tree for a tautology

$(\neg p \to \neg q) \to (q \to p)$

In order to prove this, we could prefix the formula with a negation symbol and systematically attempt to satisfy the negated formula. This was the procedure adopted to demonstrate a tautology with a semantic tableau. A failure to find any valuation at all in which the negated formula is *true* then indicates that the original unnegated formula is a tautology. This approach is equivalent to proving the sequent

$\neg((\neg p \to \neg q) \to (q \to p)) \Rightarrow$

but the first inference rule to be applied to such a sequent would be the "left $\neg$" rule and would result in the sequent

$\Rightarrow (\neg p \to \neg q) \to (q \to p)$

Now the objective is to falsify the succedent, to decompose the sequent into subformulas with the objective of showing this succedent to be *false*. Successive decompositions generate subsequents with antecedents to be shown *true* and succedents to be shown *false*. Figure 1.11 shows that two applications of the "right $\to$" rule followed by a single "left $\to$" rule result in subsequents that are easily converted to axioms by the "left $\neg$" and "right $\neg$" rules. The succedent proposition produces a proof tree containing only leaf axioms and is therefore a tautology. It is interesting to note that a semantic tableau proof beginning with the negated formula uses equivalent inference rules in the same order. A sequent is deemed valid if it produces a proof tree, so a valid sequent containing only a succedent formula implies the validity of that formula.

No rule has been offered for mutual equivalence, but this connective can be implemented by substituting one of the following equivalent propositions:

$(A \leftrightarrow B) \cong (A \to B) \land (B \to A)$
$(A \leftrightarrow B) \cong (A \land B) \lor (\neg B \land \neg A)$

after which the existing rules may be applied. Consider as an example the following mutual implication:

$((p \to q) \to r) \leftrightarrow (p \to (q \to r))$

Using the first logical equivalence, this problem may be divided into two separate sequents with implications as principal connectives. The first of them is

$$\frac{\Rightarrow (p \rightarrow (q \rightarrow r)) \rightarrow ((p \rightarrow q) \rightarrow r)}{}$$

$$\frac{(p \rightarrow (q \rightarrow r)) \Rightarrow ((p \rightarrow q) \rightarrow r)}{} \qquad \text{right} \rightarrow \text{on 1}$$

$$\frac{(p \rightarrow (q \rightarrow r)), (p \rightarrow q) \Rightarrow r}{} \qquad \text{right} \rightarrow \text{on 2}$$

$$\frac{q \rightarrow r, p \rightarrow q \Rightarrow r \qquad\qquad\qquad p \rightarrow q \Rightarrow r, p}{} \qquad \text{left} \rightarrow \text{on 3}$$

$$\frac{p \rightarrow q \Rightarrow r, q \qquad r, p \rightarrow q \Rightarrow r \qquad\qquad \Rightarrow r, p, p \quad q \Rightarrow r, p \quad \text{left} \rightarrow \text{on 4}}{\times}$$

$$q \Rightarrow r, q \qquad \Rightarrow r, q, p$$
$$\times$$

Figure 1.12 A counterexample tree

$$\Rightarrow ((p \rightarrow q) \rightarrow r) \rightarrow (p \rightarrow (q \rightarrow r))$$

It produces a proof tree and is therefore a tautology. Figure 1.12 shows a deduction tree for the reverse implication

$$\Rightarrow (p \rightarrow (q \rightarrow r)) \rightarrow ((p \rightarrow q) \rightarrow r)$$

It is clear this tree contains a number of leaf sequents that are not axioms. Consequently, the original mutual implication is not valid because counterexample valuations may be deduced from the tree.

A sequent is valid if at least one succedent formula is *true* in every valuation that makes all of its antecedent formulas *true*. A single *false* antecedent formula is sufficient to make the whole antecedent *false* and the sequent valid. Conversely, a single *true* succedent formula is sufficient to make the whole succedent *true* and the sequent valid. This suggests that the formulas might be written in the following form:

$$A_1 \wedge A_2 \wedge \ldots \wedge A_m \Rightarrow B_1 \vee B_2 \vee \ldots \vee B_n$$

in which antecedent formulas are explicitly joined by conjunctions and succedent formulas are explicitly disjuncted. Explicit connectives may also be shown in the entailment

$$A_1 \wedge A_2 \wedge \ldots \wedge A_m \vDash B_1 \vee B_2 \vee \ldots \vee B_n$$

so the meaning of the sequent is expressed in the following entailment:

$$\vDash A_1 \wedge A_2 \wedge \ldots \wedge A_m \rightarrow B_1 \vee B_2 \vee \ldots \vee B_n$$

A sequent may be interpreted as a general implication from a conjunction of its antecedent formulas to a disjunction of its succedent formulas.

1.5.1   Proof systems, soundness and completeness

Although G rules have been explained in terms of making propositions *true* and *false*, the whole procedure should be seen purely as a proof system without regard to the interpretation. A sequent is proven if it is constructed in a proof tree, i.e. a deduction tree in which every leaf sequent is an axiom. Previously we thought of decomposing sequents in a way that makes antecedents *true* and succedents *false*, but in proof theory we think of building large sequents from collections of axioms. Instead of seeing leaf sequents as the final step of a decomposition, a proof system sees them as a collection of premisses from which the sequent at the root of the tree is concluded. This means the reasoning steps are upwards in the deduction trees, as shown in this chapter, and the G system rules take the form

conclusion   or   conclusion

premiss   premiss1   premiss2

It would of course be possible to draw the diagrams the other way up so that initial premisses occur at the top and are joined together on moving down the page to reach a conclusion at the bottom. This approach might have some merit in a final presentation, but nobody actually attempts to prove a sequent by joining together a collection of axioms. It is far better to arrive at the necessary axioms by using G system rules to decompose sequents. One attractive feature of the G proof system is that its rules preserve validity in both directions, so there is no real distinction between premiss and conclusion. An LK system on the other hand only preserves validity in one direction, that of moving from axioms towards the final sequent. As a result, LK sequent deduction trees have traditionally been written with the root sequent at the bottom of the page.

A deduction that begins with the formula to be proven is sometimes said to be *goal oriented* and the reasoning procedure is said to be *top-down* or *backward chained*. A deduction that begins with a set of axioms that are then joined together through inference rules is described as a *bottom-up* or *forward-chained* procedure. Top-down and bottom-up may be interpreted literally in the G system deduction trees as they have been presented here.

A theorem is proven in the G proof system by showing that a sequent with the theorem as succedent can be constructed from axioms alone. However, we need to be sure that the G proof system is both sound and complete, meaning that every proven theorem is actually valid and that every valid theorem is provable. Soundness is easily demonstrated. Axioms are valid sequents and validity is preserved when sequent rules are applied, therefore a final concluding sequent must be valid.

To show completeness, we have to show that a proof tree may be constructed for any valid sequent, but first we need to be sure that a proof tree is always constructed with a finite number of inference rules. To do this, we note that the premiss or premisses of every rule contain fewer logical connectives than the conclusion. It follows that the total number of connectives in subsequents must reduce as we work backwards from the conclusion to more distant premisses. Since the sequent is of finite size, a point must be reached at which all the connectives are used and leaf sequents are visible. Thus the deduction tree obtained from a finite proposition is of finite size and must be either a proof tree or a counterexample tree. A root sequent is valid if and only if every leaf sequent in the tree is an axiom and falsifiable if and only if at least one leaf sequent is not an axiom. We can be sure that every falsifiable sequent yields a counterexample because this requirement motivated the construction of the rules. Conversely, we are sure that every valid sequent is provable from some proof tree.

EXERCISES 1.5

1. Show that each of the following propositions is valid by adopting each proposition as a root succedent in a G system proof tree:

   a. $q \rightarrow (p \rightarrow q)$
   b. $(p \rightarrow q) \rightarrow (\neg q \rightarrow \neg p)$
   c. $((p \rightarrow r) \wedge (q \rightarrow r) \wedge (p \vee q)) \rightarrow r$
   d. $(p \wedge q) \rightarrow (p \vee q)$
   e. $(\neg p \vee q) \leftrightarrow (p \rightarrow q)$
   f. $(p \vee (q \wedge r)) \rightarrow ((p \vee q) \wedge (p \vee r))$
   g. $\neg (((p \rightarrow q) \wedge (q \rightarrow r)) \wedge \neg (p \rightarrow r))$
   h. $((p \rightarrow q) \rightarrow r) \rightarrow (p \rightarrow (q \rightarrow r))$
   i. $((p \vee r) \wedge (q \vee \neg r)) \rightarrow (p \vee q)$

2. Show that the following propositions are not valid by producing counterexamples:

   a. $(p \vee q) \rightarrow (p \wedge q)$
   b. $(p \rightarrow q) \rightarrow \neg (q \rightarrow p)$
   c. $(p \rightarrow q) \wedge (\neg q \rightarrow \neg p)$

1.6   NORMAL FORMS

The dual proposition of an atomic statement p is the proposition $\neg p$ whereas the dual of $\neg p$ is proposition p, i.e. a statement is converted to its dual by adding or detaching a negation symbol. Atomic propositions and their negations are usually described as literals, and the dual proposition above is sometimes also called the complement of a literal. Propositions are called cubes if they contain just literals and conjunctions or clauses if they contain just literals and disjunctions. These two forms are illustrated by the following examples:

$p \wedge \neg q \wedge r \wedge \neg s$ cube
$p \vee \neg q \vee r \vee \neg s$ clause

Either a cube or a clause may be negated as a whole then simplified by the generalised De Morgan rule. Taking the clause above as an example, we obtain

$\neg (p \vee \neg q \vee r \vee \neg s)$ negated clause
$\neg p \wedge \neg \neg q \wedge \neg r \wedge \neg \neg s$ generalised De Morgan
$\neg p \wedge q \wedge \neg r \wedge s$ simplify

producing the complementary form as a result. A moment's reflection reveals that the dual of a clause is always a cube that may be written directly from an inspection of the clause. Disjunctions are changed to conjunctions and literals are replaced by their duals. Conversely, the dual of a cube always simplifies to a clause.

A proposition is said to be in negation normal form (NNF) if it contains only the connectives $\wedge$ and $\vee$ together with literals and any necessary bracketing. Any proposition not already in NNF may be converted to this form by the application of logical equivalences followed by the movement of negations into literals. Formulas containing implications are converted by the following procedure:

a. Eliminate all occurrences of implication and mutual implication using the following logical equivalences:

$$(A \leftrightarrow B) \equiv (A \rightarrow B) \wedge (B \rightarrow A)$$
$$\equiv (\neg A \vee B) \wedge (\neg B \vee A)$$
$$(A \leftrightarrow B) \equiv (A \wedge B) \vee (\neg B \wedge \neg A)$$
$$(A \rightarrow B) \equiv \neg A \vee B$$

b. Move negation symbols inwards using De Morgan's rules until each one stands directly in front of an atomic statement, i.e. until it is contained in a literal.

Thus, formula $p \rightarrow q$ is not in negation normal form because it contains an implication, but it may be converted to the formula $\neg p \vee q$, which is in NNF. Equally, $\neg(p \wedge \neg q)$ fails to satisfy the requirement because a leading negation sign applies to the whole subformula inside the brackets, but it can be converted as follows:

$$\neg(p \wedge \neg q)$$
$\neg p \vee \neg\neg q$ De Morgan
$\neg p \vee q$ double negation

Any proposition may be expressed in an equivalent negation normal form, but the form obtained is not unique: every proposition has many equivalent NNF propositions.

Two special cases of NNF are defined: disjunctive normal form (DNF) consists of cubes joined together by disjunctions; conjunctive normal form (CNF) consists of clauses joined together by conjunctions. These two forms have the general appearance

$(p \wedge \neg q \wedge r) \vee (s \wedge \neg t) \vee u$ DNF
$(p \vee \neg q \vee r) \wedge (s \vee \neg t) \wedge u$ CNF

CNF has a dual form that is easily found by negation and simplification as follows:

$\neg((p \vee \neg q \vee r) \wedge (s \vee \neg t) \wedge u)$ negated CNF
$\neg(p \vee \neg q \vee r) \vee \neg(s \vee \neg t) \vee \neg u$ De Morgan
$(\neg p \wedge q \wedge \neg r) \vee (\neg s \wedge t) \vee \neg u$ De Morgan

Clearly the dual of a CNF proposition simplifies easily to a DNF proposition and vice versa, but some caution needs to be exercised here. The dual of a given formula is actually a different formula from the original, equivalent in fact to a negation of the original formula, and in later sections this conversion has the required properties. On other occasions it is necessary to find a CNF for the proposition itself, rather than its negation, and the techniques described below are then used. Any proposition can be expressed in either DNF or CNF, so we immediately have two possible equivalent NNFs. Later we shall see how a conversion to normal form can be a useful first step in deciding the truth of a proposition, so methods of converting formulas to normal forms are required.

1.6.1   Finding disjunctive normal forms

There exists a simple but tedious method of converting a proposition to its equivalent DNF: simply write out the truth table for the formula and read off the valuations that are a model of the formula. The proposition $(p \rightarrow q) \rightarrow r$ evaluates as follows:

p	q	r	$(p \rightarrow q) \rightarrow r$
true	true	true	true
true	true	false	false
true	false	true	true
true	false	false	true
false	true	true	true
false	true	false	false
false	false	true	true
false	false	false	false

A DNF of the proposition is obtained by extracting the five valuations for which the proposition is true:

$$(p \wedge q \wedge r) \vee (p \wedge \neg q \wedge r) \vee (p \wedge \neg q \wedge \neg r) \vee (\neg p \wedge q \wedge r) \vee (\neg p \wedge \neg q \wedge r)$$

Although this approach provides an equivalent proposition in DNF, the resulting formula is not as simple as it might be. However, the size of this proposition may be reduced by pairing off cubes and joining such pairs through the distributive rule. For example, cubes 2 and 3 above are joined and simplified as follows:

$(p \wedge \neg q \wedge r) \vee (p \wedge \neg q \wedge \neg r)$
$(p \wedge \neg q) \wedge (r \vee \neg r)$ distributive rule
$(p \wedge \neg q)$ tautology: $(r \vee \neg r) \equiv true$

because proposition $r \vee \neg r$ is equivalent to *true* and has no effect in conjunction with the other subproposition. If this procedure is repeated for other pairs of cubes, the large DNF is reduced to a much simpler form then to the minimal form

$(p \wedge r) \vee (p \wedge \neg q) \vee (\neg p \wedge r)$
$(p \wedge \neg q) \vee (p \wedge r) \vee (\neg p \wedge r)$ rearrangement
$(p \wedge \neg q) \vee r$ distributive rule

1. $(p \to q) \to r \Rightarrow$
2. $\Rightarrow (p \to q) \quad r \Rightarrow$ left $\to$ on 1
3. $p \Rightarrow q$ right $\to$ on 2

Figure 1.13   Finding the DNF of $(p \to q) \to r$

In fact, this much simpler result could have been found directly by using formula equivalences:

$(p \to q) \to r$
$\neg(\neg p \lor q) \lor r$ logical equivalence
$(p \land \neg q) \lor r$ De Morgan

Semantic tableaux and G system proofs incorporate the meaning of truth tables in a display and should be capable of producing normal forms for a formula. Figure 1.13 shows the deduction tree that arises when this proposition is made the antecedent of a sequent and G system rules are applied until termination. Leaf sequents $p \Rightarrow q$ and $r \Rightarrow$ arise, indicating that the formula is *true* if p is *true* when q is *false* or, reading from the second leaf sequent, if r is *true*. This requirement is expressed in DNF as $(p \land \neg q) \lor r$, the same result as above.

1.6.2   Finding conjunctive normal forms

Those valuations that falsify the proposition $(p \to q) \to r$ are read from the truth table above to produce a disjunctive normal form

$(p \land q \land \neg r) \lor (\neg p \land q \land \neg r) \lor (\neg p \land \neg q \land \neg r)$

and this proposition is therefore equivalent to the negated proposition $\neg((p \to q) \to r)$. It follows that the formula $(p \to q) \to r$ itself is equivalent to the proposition

$\neg((p \land q \land \neg r) \lor (\neg p \land q \land \neg r) \lor (\neg p \land \neg q \land \neg r))$

and this expression might be simplified to negation normal form by the application of De Morgan's rules. However, as explained earlier, the result of simplifying a negated DNF expression is the dual CNF

$(\neg p \lor \neg q \lor r) \land (p \lor \neg q \lor r) \land (p \lor q \lor r)$

This formula may be simplified with the distributive rules to give a simpler but equivalent CNF

$(p \lor r) \land (\neg q \lor r)$

In summary, a truth table approach to finding equivalent CNFs proceeds as follows:

a. Write a DNF proposition from those valuations that falsify the truth table proposition.

b. Write the dual CNF of this proposition (a step equivalent to negation and simplification).

c. Use the distributive rule to remove clashing literals from the result of step b.

Although the truth table approach provides considerable insight into the relationships between truth tables, valuations and normal forms, it is not a very practical approach. A truth table has to be constructed before the DNF can be extracted and, as the number of statement variables increases, this method becomes increasingly intractable. The procedure has an obvious exponential complexity because the number of truth table lines to be considered doubles with each extra variable.

A CNF proposition may be found by the direct application of a distributive rule to a DNF expression. Thus the DNF of proposition $(p \rightarrow q) \rightarrow r$ is converted to a CNF in one step:

$(p \wedge \neg q) \vee r$ DNF
$(p \vee r) \wedge (\neg q \vee r)$ distributive rule

Although this algebraic approach appears attractively simple, it too hides an underlying exponential complexity that creates problems when the examples become larger.

The above example showed that a truth table approach to finding CNFs proceeds by forming a DNF from those valuations that falsify a proposition then taking the dual of the resulting proposition. Apart from having to create the table, the process of simplifying the resulting proposition makes this method unattractive in practice. However, a simplified propositional DNF that falsifies a given proposition may be obtained by constructing a deduction tree with the proposition as its succedent. A CNF may then be written directly as the dual of this formula. Figure 1.14 shows that if the earlier example is made a succedent and inference rules are applied, it generates leaf sequents $\Rightarrow r, p$ and $q \Rightarrow r$, producing the DNF formula

$(\neg p \wedge \neg r) \vee (q \wedge \neg r)$

but the dual form of this proposition is easily written as

$(p \vee r) \wedge (\neg q \vee r)$

A little practice allows the CNF of a proposition to be read directly from the deduction tree by making the appropriate corrections for the dual form.

As a slightly larger example, we now convert

$(p \rightarrow (q \rightarrow r)) \rightarrow ((p \wedge s) \rightarrow r)$

$$
\begin{array}{ll}
1. \Rightarrow (p \rightarrow q) \rightarrow r & \\
\hline
2. \quad (p \rightarrow q) \Rightarrow r & \text{right} \rightarrow \text{on 1} \\
\hline
3. \Rightarrow r, p \quad q \Rightarrow r & \text{left} \rightarrow \text{on 2}
\end{array}
$$

Figure 1.14   Finding a CNF of $(p \rightarrow q) \rightarrow r$

to normal form. A truth table approach is possible, but this proposition has four distinct statement symbols and would require a table of 16 rows. The substitution of equivalent propositions followed by an algebraic manipulation of the substituted symbols provides the following conversion:

$(p \to (q \to r)) \to ((p \wedge s) \to r)$
$\neg(\neg p \vee (\neg q \vee r)) \vee (\neg(p \wedge s) \vee r)$ equivalences
$(\neg\neg p \wedge \neg(\neg q \vee r)) \vee ((\neg p \vee \neg s) \vee r)$ De Morgan
$(p \wedge (q \wedge \neg r)) \vee ((\neg p \vee \neg s) \vee r)$ De Morgan
$(p \wedge q \wedge \neg r) \vee (\neg p \vee \neg s \vee r)$ brackets

In fact, the resulting formula is not only in negation normal form but also in disjunctive normal form. Applications of the distributive rule allow a further conversion to CNF:

$(p \vee (\neg p \vee \neg s \vee r)) \wedge (q \vee (\neg p \vee \neg s \vee r)) \wedge (\neg r \vee (\neg p \vee \neg s \vee r))$
$true \wedge (q \vee (\neg p \vee \neg s \vee r)) \wedge true$
$q \vee \neg p \vee \neg s \vee r$

Clearly the direct use of equivalences followed by an algebraic simplification has become rather more complex than was the case in the earlier example. Although the algebraic method looked attractive with a small proposition, the size of that example disguised the exponential complexity of this procedure. Like the truth table approach, it quickly becomes intractable as the size of the problem increases.

Negation normal forms for this proposition are obtained when a counterexample tree is constructed using the proposition as either the antecedent or succedent. Figure 1.15 shows the tree obtained when this formula is taken as the antecedent, leading to four leaf sequents of the form

$p, q \Rightarrow r \quad\quad \Rightarrow p \quad\quad \Rightarrow s \quad\quad r \Rightarrow$

from which a DNF is read as

$(p \wedge q \wedge \neg r) \vee \neg p \vee \neg s \vee r$

A counterexample tree constructed with the proposition as succedent is shown in Figure 1.16, producing the leaf sequents

$p, s \Rightarrow r, p \quad\quad r, p, s \Rightarrow r \quad\quad p, s \Rightarrow r, q$

but the first two of these sequents are axioms and the remaining sequent produces a single clause of CNF

$$\dfrac{(p \to (q \to r)) \to ((p \wedge s) \to r) \Rightarrow}{\dfrac{\Rightarrow p \to (q \to r) \quad\quad\quad (p \wedge s) \to r \Rightarrow}{\dfrac{p \Rightarrow (q \to r)}{p, q \Rightarrow r} \quad\quad \dfrac{\Rightarrow p \wedge s \quad\quad r \Rightarrow}{\Rightarrow p \quad\quad \Rightarrow s}}}$$

Figure 1.15   A deduction tree to obtain DNF

$$\cfrac{\cfrac{\cfrac{\cfrac{\cfrac{p, s \Rightarrow r, p \quad \times \qquad\qquad \cfrac{q \to r, p, s \Rightarrow r}{p, s \Rightarrow r, q \quad r, p, s \Rightarrow r \quad \times}}{(p \to (q \to r)), p, s \Rightarrow r}}{(p \to (q \to r)), p \wedge s \Rightarrow r}}{(p \to (q \to r)) \Rightarrow ((p \wedge s) \to r)}}{\Rightarrow (p \to (q \to r)) \to ((p \wedge s) \to r)}}$$

Figure 1.16   A deduction tree to obtain CNF

$\neg p \vee \neg s \vee r \vee q$

A small increase in the size of the problem and in the number of statement symbols has made the deduction tree approach much more attractive compared to the alternatives. Perhaps more important, the rules of the G system are easily implemented in computer programs, so the process is easily mechanised.

1.6.3   Normal forms in proofs

Propositional normal forms have characteristic features that make them more suitable for certain purposes than propositions in general form. However, the concept of a normal form may be extended to proofs arising from the propositions: specific normal forms of proof are defined by characteristic deduction trees. To illustrate such normal forms, we first find an equivalent normal form for the proposition

$$(p \to (q \to r)) \to ((p \to q) \to (p \to r))$$

This proposition is an instance of Hilbert's second axiom and is therefore valid, i.e. it is a propositional tautology, *true* in all valuations. A deduction tree developed with this formula as its initial succedent has only leaf axioms, confirming that the formula cannot be falsified. A tree developed from a sequent taking this proposition as antecedent is shown in Figure 1.17 and it generates the leaf sequents

$$p, q \Rightarrow r \quad\quad p \Rightarrow q \quad\quad \Rightarrow p \quad\quad r \Rightarrow$$

This information allows an equivalent DNF proposition to be written as

$$(p \wedge q \wedge \neg r) \vee (p \wedge \neg q) \vee \neg p \vee r$$

The resulting proposition is in both NNF and DNF, and since it is equivalent to the formula from which it was derived, it should behave equivalently. In particular, a sequent of the form

$$\Rightarrow (p \wedge q \wedge \neg r) \vee (p \wedge \neg q) \vee \neg p \vee r$$

should produce a proof tree when subjected to G system inference rules, and Figure 1.18 shows this is indeed the case. The proof in Figure 1.18 uses a generalised

$$(p \rightarrow (q \rightarrow r)) \rightarrow ((p \rightarrow q) \rightarrow (p \rightarrow r)) \Rightarrow$$

$\Rightarrow (p \rightarrow (q \rightarrow r))$	$(p \rightarrow q) \rightarrow (p \rightarrow r) \Rightarrow$	left $\rightarrow$ on 1
$p \Rightarrow (q \rightarrow r)$	$\Rightarrow p \rightarrow q \qquad p \rightarrow r \Rightarrow$	left $\rightarrow$ on 2
$p, q \Rightarrow r$	$p \Rightarrow q \qquad \Rightarrow p \quad r \Rightarrow$	

Figure 1.17 A deduction from Hilbert's second axiom

$$\Rightarrow (p \wedge q \wedge \neg r) \vee (p \wedge \neg q) \vee \neg p \vee r$$

$$\Rightarrow (p \wedge q \wedge \neg r), (p \wedge \neg q), \neg p, r$$

$\Rightarrow (p \wedge q \wedge \neg r), \neg p, r, p \qquad\qquad \Rightarrow (p \wedge q \wedge \neg r), \neg p, r, \neg q$

$p \Rightarrow (p \wedge q \wedge \neg r), r, p \qquad\qquad \Rightarrow p \wedge q, \neg p, r, \neg q \qquad \Rightarrow \neg r, \neg p, r, \neg q$

$\qquad \times$

$\Rightarrow p, \neg p, r, \neg q \quad \Rightarrow q, \neg p, r, \neg q \qquad r \Rightarrow \neg p, r, \neg q$

$\qquad\qquad\qquad\qquad\qquad\qquad\qquad\qquad\qquad\qquad \times$

$p \Rightarrow p, r, \neg q \quad q \Rightarrow q, \neg p, r$

$\qquad \times \qquad\qquad \times$

Figure 1.18 A normal form of proof

"right $\vee$" inference rule that removes all disjunction symbols in one step. This might appear simply as a form of shorthand, since the individual steps could have been written, but they would have produced exactly the same sequent. After this step, the only rules that can be applied are the "right $\wedge$" inference rule and negation inference on the literals.

Suppose more generally that a formula is the succedent in a sequent:

$\Rightarrow$ formula

and the application of inference rules generates a proof tree. Suppose further that the formula is converted to disjunctive normal form and again taken as the succedent of a sequent:

$\Rightarrow$ formula$_{dnf}$

It too must lead to a proof tree, though different inference rules are required to produce axioms. If a particular formula is valid, any other formula claiming to be its equivalent must also be valid. Reasoning from the G system "not" rule, it is clear that the sequent

$\neg$(formula$_{dnf}$) $\Rightarrow$

must also lead to a proof tree because the first rule to be applied would be the "left $\neg$" rule and the sequent would be returned to its previous form. However, the negation of a DNF formula is an easily derived CNF formula, so a sequent of the form

formula$_{cnf}$ $\Rightarrow$

must also lead to a proof tree (provided the original formula is valid).

$$(\neg p \vee \neg q \vee r) \wedge (\neg p \vee q) \wedge p \wedge \neg r \Rightarrow$$

$$\overline{(\neg p \vee \neg q \vee r), (\neg p \vee q),\ p, \neg r \Rightarrow}$$

$(\neg p \vee \neg q \vee r), \neg p, p, \neg r \Rightarrow$	$(\neg p \vee \neg q \vee r), q, p, \neg r \Rightarrow$

$(\neg p \vee \neg q \vee r), p, \neg r \Rightarrow p$ $\qquad\qquad \neg p \vee \neg q, q,\ p, \neg r \Rightarrow \qquad\qquad r, q, p, \neg r \Rightarrow$

$\qquad\qquad \times$

$\neg p, q,\ p, \neg r \Rightarrow \qquad \neg q, q, p, \neg r \Rightarrow \qquad\qquad r, p, q \Rightarrow r$

$\qquad\qquad\qquad\qquad\qquad\qquad\qquad\qquad\qquad\qquad\qquad \times$

$q, p, \neg r \Rightarrow p \qquad\qquad q, p, \neg r \Rightarrow q$

$\qquad\qquad \times \qquad\qquad\qquad\qquad\qquad \times$

Figure 1.19 A deduction tree from a CNF antecedent

Returning to the example above, we negate and simplify the DNF to obtain an equivalent CNF formula:

$$\neg((p \wedge q \wedge \neg r) \vee (p \wedge \neg q) \vee \neg p \vee r)$$
$$\neg(p \wedge q \wedge \neg r) \wedge \neg(p \wedge \neg q) \wedge \neg\neg p \wedge \neg r \qquad \text{De Morgan}$$
$$(\neg p \vee \neg q \vee r) \wedge (\neg p \vee q) \wedge p \wedge \neg r \qquad\qquad \text{De Morgan}$$

Note how this is the CNF of the negated formula and could have been obtained from the DNF by inspection, since one is the dual of the other. Having converted the formula to the CNF style of NNF, it might now be made the antecedent of a sequent

$$(\neg p \vee \neg q \vee r) \wedge (\neg p \vee q) \wedge p \wedge \neg r \Rightarrow$$

and inference rules applied to this sequent should produce a proof tree. The resulting tree is shown in Figure 1.19 and from this we see an interesting property: the whole proof appears to be the dual of that given in Figure 1.18. First of all, a generalised "left ∧" rule is used to remove all conjunctions then a number of "left ∨" rules are applied until axioms are obtained through negation inferences. The important point here is that proofs have dual forms related to the dual forms obtainable in NNF.

The familiar style of proof, producing axioms from formulas taken as the succedent of a sequent, is called proof normal form. This procedure systematically attempts to falsify the formula until every branch of the deduction tree produces axioms or counterexamples. If every branch produces an axiom, the falsification attempt has failed and the formula must be valid. The alternative style introduced above, taking the negation normal form of the negated proposition as antecedent, is called refutation normal form. Here the objective is to satisfy the negated form, i.e. to show that the formula has a satisfying valuation. A systematic attempt is made to find such satisfactions, but if every branch of the tree is an axiom, the negated formula represents a contradiction and the original unnegated formula is valid. This technique of demonstrating the validity of a formula by refuting its negation is more characteristic of semantic tableaux and is developed in the resolution method of Chapter 3.

EXERCISES 1.6

1. Use truth tables, equivalences and G system proofs to deduce DNF and CNF equivalents from the following contingent propositions:

   a. $p \rightarrow (q \rightarrow r)$
   b. $(p \rightarrow q) \wedge (q \rightarrow r)$
   c. $(p \rightarrow q) \rightarrow (r \rightarrow \perp)$

2. Use equivalences and G system proofs to produce DNF and CNF equivalents of the following contingent propositions:

   a. $((p \rightarrow q) \rightarrow r) \rightarrow s$
   b. $p \rightarrow (q \rightarrow (r \wedge s))$
   c. $(\neg p \vee q) \rightarrow (\neg r \rightarrow s)$

3. Find disjunctive normal forms for the following tautologies by making each one in turn the antecedent of a G system deduction tree:

   a. $(p \rightarrow q) \wedge (p \rightarrow r) \rightarrow (p \rightarrow (q \wedge r))$
   b. $(p \rightarrow (q \rightarrow r)) \rightarrow (q \rightarrow (p \rightarrow r))$
   c. $((p \rightarrow r) \wedge (q \rightarrow r)) \rightarrow ((p \vee q) \rightarrow r))$

   Check that the equivalent DNFs obtained are still tautologies by making each one the succedent in a proof tree. Show that the dual CNF propositions produce refutation trees.

4. Find negation normal forms for each of the propositions in the previous exercise by substituting equivalences and simplification.

1.7   A HILBERT PROOF SYSTEM FOR PROPOSITIONS

The Gentzen proof system contained just one axiom scheme and eight rules of deduction. It is easily related to the semantic tableau method because its inference rules are chosen to reflect the intended semantics of the formal system. A Hilbert proof system does not relate to the semantics in such an obvious way but we shall see that the theorems it proves are exactly those proved by the G system. First of all, an alphabet and a set of rules for combining elements of this alphabet are provided as in Section 1.1 then a proof system is defined by giving three axioms and a single deduction rule. Whereas the Gentzen system described earlier has one axiom and eight inference or deduction rules, the Hilbert system defined here has three axioms and just one deduction rule. The structural rules, axioms and deduction rule are as follows:

a. An alphabet of symbols:

$$\neg, \rightarrow, (,) , , , , p, q, r, s, \ldots$$

b. Rules for building up propositions from the alphabet:

   1. Atoms such as p, q, r are propositions.

   2. If A and B are both propositions then $\neg A$ and $A \to B$ are propositions.

   3. Nothing else is a proposition.

c. The following axiom schemata:

   1. $(A \to (B \to A))$

   2. $((A \to (B \to C)) \to ((A \to B) \to (A \to C)))$

   3. $((\neg A \to \neg B) \to (B \to A))$

d. A rule of deduction called *modus ponens* (MP):

   $A, (A \to B) \vdash_H B$

This alphabet obviously contains fewer symbols than the alphabet in Section 1.1, but it was clear from Section 1.2 that the original alphabet contained several connectives that are redundant in the usual interpretation of these symbols. In fact, distinguishable but equivalent Hilbert proof systems may be constructed from any adequate set of connectives. If interpretations are provided by truth tables, there is no great disadvantage in using a more than adequate set of connectives. On the other hand, a Hilbert system is a pure proof system that encapsulates the traditional meaning of logical connectives in a number of axioms, so a larger alphabet requires a greater number of axioms. Although a reduced number of connectives makes the formal system less expressive, it is easier to prove properties for those that are defined. Connectives not contained in this alphabet may then be defined as abbreviations for propositional fragments using elements within the alphabet.

   The fact that A can be proven from $\neg\neg A$ within the Hilbert system is indicated by a syntactic turnstile with an H subscript

   $\neg\neg A \vdash_H A$

A proof of the above statement runs as follows:

1.	$\neg\neg A$	assumption
2.	$\neg\neg A \to (\neg\neg\neg\neg A \to \neg\neg A)$	axiom 1
3.	$\neg\neg\neg\neg A \to \neg\neg A$	1,2 MP
4.	$(\neg\neg\neg\neg A \to \neg\neg A) \to (\neg A \to \neg\neg\neg A)$	axiom 3
5.	$\neg A \to \neg\neg\neg A$	3,4 MP
6.	$(\neg A \to \neg\neg\neg A) \to (\neg\neg A \to A)$	axiom 3
7.	$\neg\neg A \to A$	5,6 MP
8.	A	1,7 MP

A propositional statement to the left of the turnstile is seen as a hypothesis, a basic point from which reasoning begins. The proposition in line 2 is obtained by substituting $\neg\neg A$ for A and $\neg\neg\neg\neg A$ for B in axiom 1 and is therefore an instance of the axiom. *Modus ponens* is then applied to the formulas in lines 1 and 2 to obtain the result in line 3. Every line in a proof of this sort contains a formula proven on the basis of some assumptions, the axioms and *modus ponens*. Further substitutions using axiom 3 are both followed by applications of *modus ponens*, leading eventually to the desired result. It is clear that Hilbert-style proofs are much more difficult and far less intuitively reasonable than corresponding G system proofs. Worse still, apparently trivial relationships sometimes require inordinately many lines to prove them. To counter this problem, it is usual to work from a stock of proven relations, substituting them in later proofs as required. This procedure is justified by a law usually described as the deduction rule.

1.7.1 The deduction rule

The deduction rule states that if a proposition B is deduced from proposition A and a set of propositions M (possibly empty), the proposition $A \rightarrow B$ may be deduced directly from the set M. Symbolically

If $M \cup \{A\} \vdash B$ then $M \vdash A \rightarrow B$

In practice this means that propositions may be taken from the left of the syntactic turnstile and made the antecedent of a new propositional implication on the right. Already we have shown a deduction of the formula A from the formula $\neg\neg A$ and this is represented as follows:

$\neg\neg A \vdash_H A$

According to the deduction rule, this result might equally well be shown as

$\vdash_H \neg\neg A \rightarrow A$

and we have a proposition that may be assumed without any hypotheses. A proposition with this property is called a theorem, and one of the purposes of the deduction rule is to build up a stock of theorems that may be used in deductions in much the same way that axioms are used. This particular example is called the double-negation theorem and its existence permits an occurence of $\neg\neg A$ in a proof to be replaced by A through *modus ponens*. Notice that the implication is only proved in one direction and a further proof is required before it can be used in the other direction:

1. $\neg\neg\neg A \rightarrow \neg A$ dubneg of $\neg A$
2. $(\neg\neg\neg A \rightarrow \neg A) \rightarrow (A \rightarrow \neg\neg A)$ axiom 3
3. $A \rightarrow \neg\neg A$ 1, 2 MP

As a result of this deduction, we are able to state another theorem:

$\vdash_H A \rightarrow \neg\neg A$

Another useful theorem can be derived from the following deduction:

$A, A \rightarrow B, B \rightarrow C \vdash_H C$

This deduction is easily proved without any axioms:

1. A assumption
2. $A \rightarrow B$ assumption
3. $B \rightarrow C$ assumption
4. B 1, 2 MP
5. C 4, 3 MP

Having proven this result, the deduction theorem can now be applied to give a very useful theorem called the chain rule:

$A \rightarrow B, B \rightarrow C \vdash_H A \rightarrow C$

As the name implies, this rule allows implications to be chained along a series. A glance at the proof should be enough to show that the method could be applied to chains longer than three symbols and is really just an extended version of *modus ponens*.

In order to derive another rule, we prove the following deduction:

$(B \rightarrow A) \vdash_H (\neg A \rightarrow \neg B)$

Taking the single proposition from the left as an assumption, the derivation is as follows:

1. $B \rightarrow A$ assumption
2. $\neg\neg B \rightarrow B$ dubneg
3. $\neg\neg B \rightarrow A$ 2, 1 + chain
4. $A \rightarrow \neg\neg A$ dubneg
5. $\neg\neg B \rightarrow \neg\neg A$ 5, 6 MP
6. $((\neg\neg B) \rightarrow (\neg\neg A)) \rightarrow (\neg A \rightarrow \neg B)$ axiom 3
7. $\neg A \rightarrow \neg B$ 5, 6 MP

This is modified through the deduction rule to give

$\vdash_H (B \rightarrow A) \rightarrow (\neg A \rightarrow \neg B)$

and is usually called the contrapositive rule.

One more useful rule is obtained after we prove the deduction

$A \rightarrow (B \rightarrow C) \vdash_H B \rightarrow (A \rightarrow C)$

1. $A \rightarrow (B \rightarrow C)$ assumption
2. $(A \rightarrow (B \rightarrow C)) \rightarrow (A \rightarrow B) \rightarrow (A \rightarrow C)$ axiom 2
3. $(A \rightarrow B) \rightarrow (A \rightarrow C)$ 1, 2 MP
4. $B \rightarrow (A \rightarrow B)$ axiom 1
5. $B \rightarrow (A \rightarrow C)$ 4, 3 + chain

After an application of the deduction theorem, the "exchange of antecedent rule" is obtained:

$\vdash_H (A \rightarrow (B \rightarrow C)) \rightarrow (B \rightarrow (A \rightarrow C))$

Finally we show that $A \rightarrow A$ is a theorem in the Hilbert proof system with the following deduction:

1. $A \rightarrow ((A \rightarrow A) \rightarrow A) \rightarrow ((A \rightarrow (A \rightarrow A)) \rightarrow (A \rightarrow A))$ axiom 2
2. $A \rightarrow ((A \rightarrow A) \rightarrow A)$ axiom 1
3. $(A \rightarrow (A \rightarrow A)) \rightarrow (A \rightarrow A)$ 1, 2 MP
4. $(A \rightarrow (A \rightarrow A))$ axiom 1
5. $(A \rightarrow A)$ 3, 4 MP

No assumptions have been made in the above deduction and we can state the final result in the form

$\vdash_H A \rightarrow A$

This theorem is equivalent to the law of the excluded middle in classical logic, i.e. the proposition $\neg A \vee A$ is also a theorem.

1.7.2 Soundness and completeness

A deductive system is sound if every theorem proven in the system is in fact valid. For the propositional Hilbert deduction system this means that a proven theorem is a tautology, true in all valuations, and this requirement may be expressed as

$\vdash_H$ proposition implies $\vDash$ proposition

As a first step, we note that every theorem is derived from assumptions, axioms and the rule *modus ponens*. Assumptions are discharged at the point where the deduction rule is applied and are in a sense built into the resulting theorem. However, we do have to be sure that the steps leading from assumptions to conclusion preserve the meanings of the assumptions. This will be the case if we can show that the axioms are universally valid, i.e. they are tautologies, and that this validity is preserved by the deduction rule. It is relatively easy to show in a semantic tableau that each of the Hilbert axioms is a tautology and an example for one of the axioms was given earlier. Next we note that the *modus ponens* rule is equivalent to an assumption that implication is a tautology, i.e. in this usage we assume the truth of implication. Now, if A is always true and $A \rightarrow B$ is always true, it follows that B is always true, i.e. it too is a tautology. Thus a Hilbert deduction system is sound.

A formal system is complete if every valid proposition is derivable within the system, essentially the converse of soundness, i.e.

$\vDash$ proposition implies $\vdash_H$ proposition

If a proposition is a tautology it must be derivable within the deduction system. Luckily, we have already shown that the G proof system is complete, so all we need to show is that a proof in this system can be converted to a Hilbert proof. A deduction above showed that $\neg A \lor A$ is a theorem in the Hilbert system and we know that it is also equivalent to an axiom in the G system, so any proof in G may be converted to an equivalent proof in H. Thus the Hilbert system is complete.

EXERCISES 1.7

1. Use the Hilbert calculus to prove the following propositions:

   a. $\neg p \rightarrow (q \rightarrow \neg p)$

   b. $\neg(p \rightarrow q) \rightarrow p$

   c. $(p \rightarrow \neg p) \rightarrow \neg p$

   d. $(p \rightarrow q) \rightarrow ((\neg p \rightarrow \neg q) \rightarrow (q \rightarrow p))$

2. Using metasymbols A, B, C, ... to represent any proposition, show that the following formulas represent theorems:

   a. $\neg(A \rightarrow A) \rightarrow B$

   b. $\neg(A \rightarrow B) \rightarrow \neg B$

   c. $\neg B \rightarrow (B \rightarrow A)$

   d. $A \rightarrow (\neg B \rightarrow \neg(A \rightarrow B))$

   e. $\neg(A \rightarrow B) \rightarrow (B \rightarrow A)$

CHAPTER TWO

First-order logic

Atomic propositions are non-decomposable statements that have to be interpreted as a single entity by either a *true* or *false* valuation. Symbols such as p, q and r might represent the following statements:

p john is taller than mary
q mary is taller than tim
r john is taller than tim

and appropriate valuations for the statements are decided by a little extralogical activity such as applying a tape-measure to the people concerned. A brief examination of the statements reveals that the truth of statements p and q implies the truth of statement r, and this observation might be expressed as an implication

$p \wedge q \rightarrow r$

This statement encodes something we know about the property of tallness: if it is *true* that john is taller than mary and that mary is taller than tim, it follows that john is taller than tim. There is nothing wrong with descriptions of this sort, but a problem becomes apparent when the same reasoning is applied to greater numbers of people. Separate atomic statements have to be written for another comparison, say s, t and u, and another formula is required to bind these statements together in an implication relationship like the one above.

Propositional logic by itself has limited expressiveness because each statement has to be accepted as a whole, even though the statement has an obvious internal structure. The property or predicate "is taller than" relates two objects in a sentence and, although the objects being compared might differ in each sentence, the predicate has a common interpretation that might be applied to many pairs of people. Obviously, a human reader decides the truth of a statement such as $p \wedge q \rightarrow r$ by examining the names of the individuals in the atomic statements while interpreting the predicate "is taller than" in the accepted way. Predicate logic extends propositional reasoning by defining a new form of statement that allows a property or predicate to be separated from the objects to which it is applied. The statements above may be written in this more flexible notation as

Is_taller_than(john, mary)
Is_taller_than(mary, tim)
Is_taller_than(john, tim)

When the person named in the first argument is indeed taller than the person in the second argument, the atomic formula is interpreted as *true* in much the same way as for the propositions above. Furthermore, the transitive nature of tallness is equally well expressed in the predicate form

Is_taller_than(john, mary) ∧ *Is_taller_than(mary, tim)* →
Is_taller_than(john, tim)

conveying the same information as before. However, there is a major difference in that the predicated statements are now connected to each other through their arguments. Each of the argument objects, *john*, *mary* and *tim*, appears twice in the formula above, connecting atomic predicates in a way not possible with propositions. The real advantage of this separation into predicates and objects is that statements may be generalised by introducing variables that represent arbitrary individuals:

Is_taller_than(x,y) ∧ *Is_taller_than(y,z)* → *Is_taller_than(x,z)*

This is far more satisfactory because it expresses the relationship in a general form.

None of the propositional work described in Chapter 1 is wasted because that form of logic occurs as a subset of the more extensive logic now described. Predicated statements of the kind described above might contain variables such as *x* and *y*, but these variables have to be instantiated with values such as mary and tim, returning us to statements that are essentially propositional in nature. All that is required now is the addition of extra symbols, interpretations and rules that describe the more complex structures outlined above.

2.1 SYNTAX FOR FIRST-ORDER LOGIC

First-order logic introduces strings of symbols called terms and predicates that do not occur in propositional logic, and these new strings have to be correctly formed in just the same way that propositions have to be well formed. Correctly formed terms may be embedded as arguments within predicates that are then joined together by the propositional connectives described earlier.

2.1.1 Terms

A term is defined to be one of the following:

a. Zero-arity symbols called constants, often represented by lower case letters from the beginning of the alphabet, i.e. a, b, c, ... or any one of these letters with numeric subscripts. An infinite number of such constants is available, but the examples that follow use only a small number of constants.

b. Symbols called variables that may be substituted by any other term, usually represented by lower case letters from the end of the alphabet, typically w, x, y and z.

c. Constant symbols that have arity greater than zero and so require other terms as arguments before they themselves are terms. Symbols of this kind, called functions, are given lower case letters in the range f, g, h, ...

Terms are easily constructed from constants and variables because these symbols are themselves terms and any more complex term has to be constructed with the aid of function symbols. If function symbols f and g have arities of one and two, each of the following strings of symbols represents a term:

$$f(a) \qquad f(f(c)) \qquad g(b,c) \qquad g(f(c), f(a)) \qquad g(g(b,a), f(b))$$

so the procedure for constructing a term is very similar to the procedure for constructing a proposition in the previous chapter. Terms constructed with just constants and function symbols are called ground terms because they represent unchangeable forms. Each one of the examples above is a ground term.

Variables in terms may be substituted with ground terms or even with a different variable. The substitution of term t for variable x is generally shown as $\{t/x\}$, so the substitution of constant c for variable x in a term may be shown as

$$g(f(x), h(b,y))\{c/x\} = g(f(c), h(b,y))$$

Only variable x is replaced by term c; other constants and variables remain unchanged. This pattern of substitutions is summarised in the following rules:

$$b\{a/x\} = b$$
$$y\{a/x\} = y$$
$$y\{a/y\} = a$$
$$f(t_1, t_2, \ldots, t_n) \{a/x\} = f(t_1\{a/x\}, t_2\{a/x\}, \ldots, t_n\{a/x\})$$

which tell us that the result of substituting a for x in constant b is to leave b unchanged. Variable y is similarly unchanged when another variable is substituted, but is replaced by the new term when it is the object of substitution. Substitutions in functions are achieved by making the same substitutions in each function argument.

2.1.2 Predicates

First-order logic extends the simple notion of statement symbols to the concept of predicate symbols, usually represented by the upper case letters P, Q, R, ... Each predicate symbol has an associated arity or rank indicating a number of terms required as arguments to make it into a well-formed formula. A predicate might have an arity of zero and is then equivalent to the simple proposition described in Chapter 1, but upper case symbols are used in full first-order logic. Predicate symbols P and R with arities of two and three have correctly formed strings $P(a,f(b))$ and $R(g(a),b,c)$ and, since the arguments used here are all ground terms, these strings may be described as ground predicates or ground formulas. Variable terms that occur within predicate arguments may be substituted as in the following example:

$$R(g(x), h(f(y,b),c))\{a/y\} = R(g(x), h(f(a,b),c))$$

In general, the substitution of term t_s for variable x in a predicate R results in the substitution being made in each argument term:

$$R(t_1,t_2, \ldots ,t_n)\{t_s/x\} = R(t_1\{t_s/x\}, t_2\{t_s/x\}, \ldots , t_n\{t_s/x\})$$

Terms and relations might differ in each first-order language, depending on the intended interpretation of the language. In addition to this differing base of symbols, there exists a fixed set of logical symbols consisting largely of the propositional symbols described earlier. As we might expect, a small number of additional symbols are required to extend logical reasoning to term symbols.

2.1.3 Logical symbols

In addition to the term and predicate symbols defined above, first-order logic has the following alphabet of logical symbols:

$\perp$

$\neg$

$\wedge, \vee, \rightarrow, \leftrightarrow$

$(,),$

$\forall, \exists$

and it is clear that all of these symbols except the last two are inherited from propositional logic. At the moment, we are only concerned with the syntax of first-order logic, but it might be helpful to note that the interpretations (semantics) we shall give to the symbols $\forall$ and $\exists$ are respectively "for all" and "there exists". The symbols are usually read as such, but are also described as the universal and existential quantifiers.

Given correctly formed terms and predicates, a formula is defined from the logical symbols by the following rules:

a. Predicates are formulas and the constant $\perp$ is a formula.

b. If A is a formula then $\neg A$ is also a formula.

c. If A and B are formulas then $A \wedge B$, $A \vee B$, $A \rightarrow B$, $A \leftrightarrow B$ are also formulas.

d. Given a variable x and a formula A then $\forall xA$ and $\exists xA$ are also formulas.

e. A string of symbols not constructed in accordance with these rules is not a formula.

Thus the simplest formula consists of either the constant $\perp$ or a single predicate symbol with an appropriate number of terms as arguments, e.g. $P(b)$, $Q(a,b)$ and $R(a,b,c)$ are formulas. Predicates such as these may be joined together by the logical symbols from propositional logic in much the same way as simple statements were constructed from proposition statements. Thus formulas $\neg Q(a,b)$ and $P(b) \wedge Q(b,c)$ are well formed because they comply with the above rules and are ground formulas bécause they contain only ground terms.

A formula with unquantified variable terms such as $P(x,y)$ is said to contain free variable arguments that could be substituted with other terms, whereas a formula of the type

$$\forall x \forall y P(x,y)$$

has two variables bound by universal quantifiers. A variable in a formula is bound by a quantifier if it lies within the scope of an appropriate quantification, otherwise it is free. For example, the formula

$$\forall x P(x,y) \vee Q(x)$$

contains one occurrence of x bound by a universal quantifier and a second occurrrence of x that lies outside the scope of the quantifer and is therefore free. The single occurence of y is also free. Increasingly large formulas are constructed from smaller ones according to the four rules for creating formulas. Looking in the other direction, we see that a large formula contains correctly formed subformulas and the behaviour of the whole depends on the behaviour of these subformulas.

2.1.4 Substitutions in formulas

Substitutions in formulas are really substitutions in the arguments of predicates within formulas and they follow the pattern of term substitutions described earlier. An attempt to substitute a variable in the constant $\perp$ or in ground formulas has no effect:

$$\perp \{a/x\} = \perp$$
$$Q(b,c)\{a/x\} = Q(b,c)$$

but a substitution applied to a formula with unbound variables reduces to substitutions in the appropriate arguments of each predicate, thus

$$P(x) \wedge Q(x,y)\{a/x\} = P(a) \wedge Q(a,y)$$

Substitutions in a quantified formula are similar, except that only free occurrences of the variable are substituted.

Sets of substitutions are usually labelled with lower case letters from the Greek alphabet, giving the general form

$$\tau = \{t_1/x_1, t_2/x_2, \ldots, t_n/x_n\}$$

For example, the substitution

$$\sigma = \{y/x, d/y\}$$

is applied to formula $P(f(x,a), h(y,z))$ as follows:

$$P(f(x,a), h(y,z))\ \sigma = P(f(y,a), h(d,z))$$

the important point being that constant d is only substituted for the existing y variable, not for the first substituted item, i.e. the substitutions do not "chain" along.

Any term, including another variable, can be substituted in the place of a variable; it amounts to renaming the variable. However, a substituted variable should not become captured on substitution, i.e. it should not be substituted within the scope of a quantification for that symbol. This possibility is illustrated in the substitution

$$\forall x P(x,y)\{x/y\} = \forall x P(x,x)$$

in which free variable argument y is replaced by variable x within the scope of the $\forall x$ quantification, binding the variable and preventing any further substitution. A substituted variable should not change the properties of the formula in which it is substituted and should not become bound on substitution. A substituted term should be free for the variable it replaces, but in this example the variable x is not free for y in the initial formula.

2.1.5   Compositions of substitutions

Multiple substitutions carried out separately might produce a different result from that obtained when the same individual replacements are contained in a single substitution. For example, two substitutions defined as

$$\pi = \{y/x\}$$
$$\rho = \{d/y\}$$

might by applied to a formula one after the other. The composition of substitutions $\pi \circ \rho$, read as "π followed by ρ" indicates that substitution π is followed by ρ, giving the result

$$P(f(x,a), h(y,z))\ \pi \circ \rho = P(f(y,a), h(y,z))\ \rho$$
$$= P(f(d,a), h(d,z))$$

In this case the second substitution is able to use the previously substituted variable to obtain a result different from that obtained in a single substitution σ.

EXERCISES 2.1

The following substitution sets are used in the examples below:

$\pi = \{a/x, y/z\}$ $\theta = \{b/y\}$ $\rho = \{a/x, y/z, b/y\}$ $\sigma = \{c/x, d/y, d/z\}$

1. Carry out the following term substitutions:

   a. $g(x, f(y,x), h(z))\ \pi$
   b. $g(x, f(y,x), h(z))\ \pi \circ \theta$
   c. $g(x, f(y,x), h(z))\ \rho$
   d. $P(h(x,y,z), f(x))\ \rho$

2. Carry out the following substitutions in formulas:

   a. $(P(x,a) \wedge \neg Q(y,z))\ \pi$
   b. $(P(y) \rightarrow \exists y Q(x,y))\ \theta$
   c. $\forall y(P(y) \rightarrow Q(x,z))\ \pi$
   d. $(\forall y P(f(x,y)) \rightarrow Q(g(y), h(z)))\ \rho$
   e. $\forall x(\exists y P(f(x,z),y) \vee \exists z R(z,h(x,y)))\ \sigma$
   f. $Q(x,y,z,f(x,y))\ \theta \circ \rho$
   g. $Q(x,y,z,f(x,y))\ \rho \circ \theta$

2.2 SEMANTICS FOR FIRST-ORDER LOGIC

An interpretation of a set of propositional logic symbols amounts to no more than a valuation that assigns one of the truth values *true* or *false* to each symbol. Interpretations in first-order logic extend the simple valuations of propositional logic to cover predicates that include argument terms. Just as we assigned a truth value to a single proposition P, we have to assign one to the predicate $P(a)$, but such an assigned value may be different from that of formula $P(b)$. The truth value of a predicate clearly depends on the argument to which it is applied; we need to know all of the truth values for all possible arguments. If the number of arguments is small, it might be possible to list truth values of the predicate applied to each possible argument. More often it is necessary to depend on some understanding of the interpretation of the predicate P. Once a truth value has been found for each predicate in a formula, the truth tables given earlier are used to derive a truth value for the formula as a whole.

A first-order logic interpretation must provide a non-empty universe or domain of discourse D with elements representing constants of the syntax. It must also provide

a. A mapping from constants $\{a, b, c, \ldots\}$ in the formal system to elements of the domain D in the interpretation.

b. A mapping from function symbols $\{f, g, h, \ldots\}$ in the formal system to operations of the same arity in the interpretation.

c. A mapping from predicate symbols $\{P, Q, R, \ldots\}$ in the formal system to relations of the same arity using arguments from the domain D.

A set of constants $\{a, b, c, d\}$ in a formal language might be interpreted by a domain of pet animals $\{rover, pixie, tiddles, fido\}$ as follows:

$$I(a) = rover \quad\quad I(b) = pixie \quad\quad I(c) = tiddles \quad\quad I(d) = fido$$

whereas a set of arity-one predicates $\{P, Q, R\}$ might be interpreted by the relations

$$I(P) = \{(rover), (fido)\} \quad\quad I(Q) = \{(tiddles)\} \quad\quad I(R) = \{(pixie)\}$$

An interpretation of the predicates such as this is simply a list of the arguments for which the predicate is *true*, and we conclude that formulas $P(a)$, $P(d)$, $Q(c)$ and $R(b)$ are all *true* in this interpretation. These are the only predicates that are *true* in this interpretation, ensuring that any other combination of predicate and domain element is *false*. As a result, $P(b)$ is *false* because b is interpreted as *pixie* and this domain element does not appear in the set of elements interpreting P.

An alternative approach might map each predicate symbol to another symbol of known meaning, thus the interpretation of the predicate symbols is now

$$I(P) = Dog \quad\quad I(Q) = Cat \quad\quad I(R) = Parrot$$

whereas the interpretation of the domain element set $\{a, b, c, d\}$ remains as above. Given an interpretation in terms of a meaningful name and the domain element assignment above, we would like to deduce that formulas $P(a)$, $P(d)$, $Q(c)$ and $R(b)$ are *true* in this interpretation, but here the method does not work very well. Although the predicate names clearly define a distinguishable set, it is not obvious which of the named animals belong in each set. Nevertheless, such an approach works well in applications where the predicate property may be deduced from the domain object, e.g. the prime number predicate applied to a number, $Prime(5)$. Similarly, formulas $Odd(x)$ and $Even(x)$ are predicates applied to natural numbers and their meaning is understood without an explicit listing of all satisfying constants. In this and in many other examples drawn from arithmetic, such an explicit listing is impossible.

Logical connectives are interpreted in exactly the same way as described in Chapter 1 and are necesssary to decide the truth of formulas constructed according to the syntax rules. Consider the interpretation given above applied to the formula

$$P(a) \rightarrow \neg Q(a)$$

observing that constant a is interpreted by *rover* and this domain element appears in the relation interpreting P but not in the one interpreting Q. Thus $P(a)$ is *true* in this interpretation whereas $Q(a)$ is *false*, and the atomic formulas may be replaced by truth values to give a proposition

$$true \rightarrow \neg false$$

An intepretaton of this formula reduces to the following valuation of the proposition:

val(true → ¬false)
true implies not false
true implies true

which is obviously *true*. As a result, we conclude that the formula is *true* in this interpretation. Distinguishing between the syntactic and semantic forms in this way is a heavy burden, so it makes sense to use just the syntactic form and decide how it is to be used from the context.

Formulas may be manipulated with propositional equivalences in just the same way as simple propositions. Thus the formula above might be expressed in either of the following forms:

$\neg P(a) \vee \neg Q(a)$
$\neg(P(a) \wedge Q(a))$

using a logical equivalence and the De Morgan relation. The last formula might be interpreted as a more recognisable statement that a pet may not be both a dog and a cat.

Variables allow formulas such as the one above to be expressed in a more general way, allowing any constant to replace symbol x in the formula

$P(x) \rightarrow \neg Q(x)$

Each different mapping of variables to constants is called an assignment, but in this particular case only the assignment of x influences the value of the formula. When x is assigned to constant b it produces an instantiated formula

$P(b) \rightarrow \neg Q(b)$

and in the interpretation given above this formula evaluates to true. In fact, this formula evaluates to *true* "for all" assignments of the variable, making the quantified expression $\forall x(P(x) \rightarrow \neg Q(x))$ *true* in this interpretation.

An arity-one function f in the formal language might be interpreted by the operation *father*, producing as its result the single domain object that is the father of the argument domain object. Such an interpretation may be written as

$I(f) = \{(rover \mapsto fido)\}$

showing that *fido* is the (only) father of *rover*. A formula may be defined with interpretations in the domain of pets in mind, thus

$\forall x(P(x) \rightarrow P(f(x)))$

and is interpreted as a requirement that the father of any dog is also a dog. This interesting biological fact applies to all animals, not just dogs, and the formula

$\forall x(Q(x) \rightarrow Q(f(x)))$

is interpreted to restrict fathers of cats to be cats. Since the same property applies to all predicates, we might be tempted to write a general formula as follows:

$\forall Animal\forall x(Animal(x) \rightarrow Animal(f(x)))$

intending to range over both types of animals and instances of animals of one type. Quantifications over instances of the predicate belong to first-order logic. Quantifications over the predicates themselves would require the use of second-order logic and this introduces many unwanted complications. In practice the first-order form is sufficient to express anything of interest and the second-order form is not required.

Two quantifier symbols have been defined, but one of them is redundant in the same sense that many of the propositional connectives in Chapter 1 are redundant. Symbol $\forall$ is usually taken as the more fundamental quantifier and is interpreted as a requirement that a predicate is *true* for all domain elements. Symbol $\exists$ requires that "there exists one" domain element satisfying the predicate, though there might be more, and is defined in terms of the universal quantifier as

$$\exists xP(x) \cong \neg\forall x\neg P(x)$$

There exists one domain element that satisfies the predicate if it is not the case that all domain objects falsify the predicate. If both sides of this equivalence are negated and the right-hand side simplified with the double-negation rule, the following dual equivalence is obtained:

$$\neg\exists xP(x) \cong \forall x\neg P(x)$$

Alternatively, if the predicate in the first formula above is replaced by a negated predicate, the following equivalence arises after an application of the double-negation rule:

$$\exists x\neg P(x) \cong \neg\forall xP(x)$$

It is clear from this equivalence that negations may be "passed over" quantifiers provided the quantifer is changed to its dual form, converting existential quantifiers to universal forms and vice versa.

2.2.1 Some formulas involving natural numbers

Consider the formula

$$\forall x\exists yP(x,y)$$

with an interpretation in which the arguments are natural numbers and predicate P is the relation "greater than". Since this relation is usually represented by the more meaningful symbol $>$, the formula might be written in the more familiar form

$$\forall x\exists y(y > x)$$

indicating that for all x there exists a number y that is greater than x. Clearly this is *true* because there is no largest number, so a bigger one can always be found. But if the intended interpretation of predicate P is the relation "less than", the following modified version of the formula might be used:

$\forall x \exists y (x > y)$

This formula is *false* in such an interpretation: there does not exist a smaller number for every other natural number, so this interpretation is not a model of the formula. In moving directly from variables to domain elements, we have cheated a little by not describing the syntactic constants associated with natural numbers. Although a more detailed treatment of this relationship is postponed until Chapter 5, we note here that the familiar Arabic representation of natural numbers is an interpretation of the abstract series *zero*, *succ(zero)*, *succ(succ(zero))*, . . . described later. Every number is either *zero* or the successor of some other number.

Suppose that we have a language with predicates P and Q of arity one and two together with constants *zero*, *succ(zero)*, *succ(succ(zero))* and as many variables as required. An interpretation of this language is provided as follows:

$I(zero) = 0$,
$I(succ(zero)) = 1$,
$I(succ(succ(zero))) = 2$

$I(P) = \{(0), (1)\}$,
$I(Q) = \{(0,1), (0,2), (1,2)\}$

Thus *P(zero)*, *P(succ(zero))*, *Q(zero, succ(zero))*, *Q(zero, succ(succ(zero)))*, and *Q(succ(zero), succ(succ(zero)))* are *true* whereas all other constants make these predicates *false*. In the light of this interpretation, we now decide the truth of formula

$\forall x \exists y (P(x) \rightarrow Q(x,y))$

by checking every possible assignment of x. In order to be *true* "for all" values of x, this formula has to be *true* for the three constants defined in the formal system. In other words, we have to show that each of the formulas

$\exists y (P(zero) \rightarrow Q(zero,y))$
$\exists y (P(succ(zero)) \rightarrow Q(succ(zero),y))$
$\exists y (P(succ(succ(zero))) \rightarrow Q(succ(succ(zero)),y))$

is *true* in the interpretation. Taking the first of these, we note that *P(zero)* is *true* in the interpretation because 0 occurs in $I(P)$. As a result, the formula is only *true* if there exists a y such that *Q(zero,y)* is *true* in this interpretation. Looking at the interpretation $I(Q)$ supplied for Q, we see there are in fact two possible pairs of arguments that satisfy the requirements: (0,1) and (0,2). The second formula is satisfied in a very similar manner when the y variable is assigned to the constant *succ(succ(zero))* because *Q(zero, succ(succ(zero)))* is *true* in this interpretation. Finally the third formula is *true* because its antecedent *P(succ(succ(zero)))* is *false* and this is sufficient to satisfy the implication, regardless of the consequent. There are only three domain elements and the formula is *true* "for all" of them, making the universally quantified formula itself *true* in this interpretation.

2.2.2   Formulas with function symbols

An interpretation of a language with functions must provide an interpretation for each function, providing either an explicit listing or a known meaning. Consider a language with an arity-one predicate P, a function symbol f and with constants *zero*, *succ(zero)*, *succ(succ(zero))* and *succ(succ(succ(zero)))*. The constants are given the usual interpretation 0, 1, 2, 3, ... and function f is given the interpretation

$$I(f) = \{(0 \mapsto 1) \ (1 \mapsto 2) \ (2 \mapsto 3) \ (3 \mapsto 0)\}$$

which is just a modulo 3 increment operation. Predicate P has the interpretation

$$I(P) = \{(0), (2)\}$$

indicating that $P(zero)$ and $P(succ(succ(zero)))$ are *true* in the interpretation whereas $P(succ(zero))$ and $P(succ(succ(succ(zero))))$ are *false*. A truth value for the formula

$$\forall x(P(f(f(x))) \rightarrow \neg P(f(x)))$$

is then deduced by evaluating the formula for all domain elements. For example, substituting the first domain element, we obtain

$$P(f(f(zero))) \rightarrow \neg P(f(zero))$$

and this is evaluated only when the functions themselves have been evaluated. Element *zero* is interpreted as 0 and a single application of function f converts this to element 1. A further application of the function to element 1 results in element 2, so the interpretations are as follows:

$$I(f(zero)) = 1$$
$$I(f(f(zero))) = 2$$

Relation P given above contains element 2 but not 1, so $P(f(f(zero)))$ is *true* in this interpretation whereas $P(f(zero))$ is *false* and the formula above evaluates as follows:

$$true \rightarrow \neg false$$
$$true \rightarrow true$$
$$true$$

If this procedure is repeated for the other three domain elements, the universally quantified formula is also found to be *true*.

A formula is said to be satisfiable in an interpretation if there is some assignment that makes it *true* in that interpretation. A formula is *true* in an interpretation if every assignment makes it *true* in that interpretation. In this case the interpretation is said to be a model of the formula. It is *false* in an interpretation if there is no assignment that makes it *true*. Finally a formula is valid if it is *true* in every assignment in every interpretation; it is a contradiction if *false* in every assignment of every interpretation.

EXERCISES 2.2

1. A formal system has constants a, b, c and d with predicates P, Q, R and S with the following interpretation:

$I(a) = huey$ $I(b) = duey$ $I(c) = luey$ $I(d) = donald$

$I(P) = \{(huey), (duey)\}$
$I(Q) = \{(duey), (luey)\}$
$I(R) = \{(donald), (mickey)\}$
$I(S) = \{(donald,huey), (mickey,duey), (mickey,luey)\}$

Decide whether this interpretation is a model for the following formulas:

a. $\exists x(P(x) \wedge Q(x))$
b. $\exists x(P(x) \wedge \neg Q(x))$
c. $\forall x \forall y(R(x) \wedge (P(y) \vee Q(y)) \rightarrow S(x,y))$

2.3   SEMANTIC TABLEAUX

The move from propositional to predicate logic introduced existentially and universally quantified formulas that may be either *true* or *false* in a particular interpretation. Remember that the objective of the semantic tableau approach is to break down formulas into fragments that would have to be *true* in order to make the root formula *true*. For this reason, we need to know the conditions under which quantified formulas will be *true*. Taking first the existentially quantified formula $\exists x P(x)$, we claim it is *true* if there exists an instantiated predicate $P\{a/x\}$ that is *true*, i.e. if there is a ground formula $P(a)$ that is *true*. This is quite reasonable: the statement that there exists a domain element x which makes predicate $P(x)$ *true* is replaced by a formula containing an element that actually does so. As a result, we have the "left $\exists$" rule shown as one of the semantic tableau rules in Figure 2.1 and the fact that the truth of $P(a)$ establishes the truth of $\exists x P(x)$ is shown by placing it directly along a tableau line below the earlier formula.

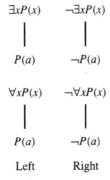

Figure 2.1   Tableau rules for quantifiers

If the left existential rule is used more than once in a given tableau, a fresh constant must be introduced with each use, otherwise a constant is endowed with properties that it might not possess. If the fragment $\exists xP(x)$ is instantiated to give $P(b)$ then $\exists yQ(y)$ is instantiated to give $Q(b)$ in the same tableau, a claim that object b has both properties P and Q is made. Such a claim is unjustified and is only avoided if a fresh constant is introduced with every use of the rule.

A similar line of reasoning leads to the establishment of a left universal rule, but there is a crucial difference in the way this rule is used in comparison with the left existential rule. An existential formula is of no further interest after a left existential inference rule has been applied and is therefore discharged in the same way that propositional formulas are discharged. The fact there exists one object that satisfies a predicate is demonstrated by instantiating just one constant. In contrast, a universally quantified formula is not discharged by the use of the left universal rule, because the quantified formula is *true* if and only if the predicate is *true* "for all" domain elements. As a result, a tableau with fragment $\forall xP(x)$ should have descendents $P(a)$, $P(b)$, etc., exhausting all the domain elements a, b, c, ... , but the rule instantiates them one at a time. Hopefully, the instantiated formulas allow every branch of the tableau to close, removing the need for any further instantiations. Since a universally quantified formula must be true for all domain elements, a left universal inference may use a constant previously introduced by other left universal or existential inference rules.

As in the propositional case, "right" rules show the conditions under which negated formulas are *true*, but two logical equivalences given earlier show a diagonal relation between left and right rules:

$$\neg\forall xP(x) \cong \exists x\neg P(x)$$

$$\neg\exists xP(x) \cong \forall x\neg P(x)$$

A "right $\forall$" inference is equivalent to a "left $\exists$" acting on a negated formula, so this rule has the properties of an existential rule. In particular, a formula is discharged when the rule has been used once, and fresh variables must be introduced with each usage. Similarly, the right existential rule has all the properties of the left universal rule.

As a first example, we demonstrate the validity of the formula

$$\exists xP(x) \rightarrow \exists yP(y)$$

by constructing a semantic tableau with the negated formula at its root. Figure 2.2 shows how a propositional "right $\rightarrow$" rule is first applied to decompose the formula into two separate quantified subformulas. Then, in line 4, the constant a is introduced through an application of the left existential rule. When an instance of an existential formula has been introduced, the original formula can be ticked as having been used. An application of the right existential rule to the formula in line 3 then produces the result on line 5 and it is clear that the single tableau path is now closed. The negated existential formula in line 3 is not discharged by the application of the rule, but the occurrence of $P(a)$ and $\neg P(a)$ on a single path ensures the

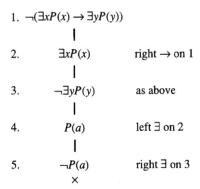

1. $\neg(\exists x P(x) \to \exists y P(y))$

2. $\exists x P(x)$ right $\to$ on 1

3. $\neg \exists y P(y)$ as above

4. $P(a)$ left $\exists$ on 2

5. $\neg P(a)$ right $\exists$ on 3
        $\times$

Figure 2.2 A proof tableau

closure of that path. Additions of $\neg P(b)$, $\neg P(c)$ and others by further applications of the rule would not change the result.

In a slightly more ambitious example, we use the same approach to prove the formula

$$\forall x(P(x) \to Q(x)) \to (\forall x P(x) \to \forall x Q(x))$$

An application of the "right $\to$" rule discharges the formula at the root of the tableau in Figure 2.3, producing a choice of two formulas that could be subjected to further inference rules. A left universal inference could be applied to line 2 or

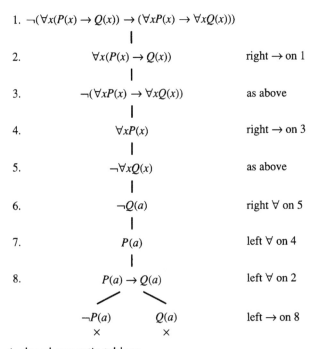

1. $\neg(\forall x(P(x) \to Q(x)) \to (\forall x P(x) \to \forall x Q(x)))$

2. $\forall x(P(x) \to Q(x))$ right $\to$ on 1

3. $\neg(\forall x P(x) \to \forall x Q(x))$ as above

4. $\forall x P(x)$ right $\to$ on 3

5. $\neg \forall x Q(x)$ as above

6. $\neg Q(a)$ right $\forall$ on 5

7. $P(a)$ left $\forall$ on 4

8. $P(a) \to Q(a)$ left $\forall$ on 2

        $\neg P(a)$ $Q(a)$ left $\to$ on 8
        $\times$ $\times$

Figure 2.3 A closed semantic tableau

a right implication to line 3, the latter option being taken in this demonstration. A "right ∀" rule is then used to discharge the formula in line 5, introducing constant *a* into line 6. Once introduced, this constant is reused when the "left ∀" rule is applied to the formula in line 4, but the formula itself is not discharged. The same constant is used yet again when the "left ∀" rule is applied to line 2, producing the formula in line 8. A single propositional "left →" inference then closes the tableau. Two universally quantified formulas in lines 2 and 4 remain undischarged and could be used to introduce further constants into the tableau, but both paths are closed and further ground formulas would not change anything. Just as it is wise to apply non-splitting rules first, in the propositional case it is equally wise to apply existential rules (either "left ∃" or "right ∀") first to quantified formulas.

In propositional examples, a tableau might close before all of its formulas have been discharged; but if this does not occur, the tableau terminates when it runs out of connectives to decompose. The introduction of universally quantified formulas generates an endless "self-generated universe" of constants that might continue indefinitely. Closure might now be the only way of obtaining a certain result. A termination problem arises in the following non-valid formula:

$$\exists x P(x) \wedge \exists x Q(x) \rightarrow \exists x (P(x) \wedge Q(x))$$

According to this formula, the existence of objects that separately satisfy predicates *P* and *Q* implies the existence of a single object that satisfies both *P* and *Q*. This is in fact the misconception avoided by instantiating existential formulas in a given tableau with different constants. Since the formula is not universally *true*, we would not expect its negation to produce a closed tableau, and as shown in Figure 2.4, this

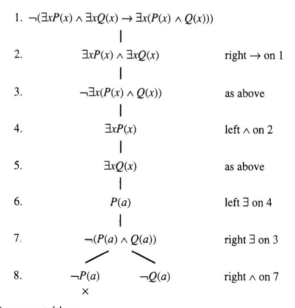

1.	¬(∃xP(x) ∧ ∃xQ(x) → ∃x(P(x) ∧ Q(x)))	
2.	∃xP(x) ∧ ∃xQ(x)	right → on 1
3.	¬∃x(P(x) ∧ Q(x))	as above
4.	∃xP(x)	left ∧ on 2
5.	∃xQ(x)	as above
6.	P(a)	left ∃ on 4
7.	¬(P(a) ∧ Q(a))	right ∃ on 3
8.	¬P(a) ¬Q(a)	right ∧ on 7
	×	

Figure 2.4   An open tableau

is indeed the case. The first part of the tableau proceeds in much the same way as the previous example, but fails to generate ground atoms capable of closing every path. The two existential subformulas in lines 4 and 5 are discharged to give ground formulas $P(a)$ and $Q(a)$, then the right existential rule is applied to the formula in line 3 to give the result in line 8. A propositional rule then produces one closed path and one open path. Since the formula in line 3 is not discharged by one use, it may be used to generate further ground formulas such as $\neg(P(b) \wedge Q(b))$ but this causes further branching. Note that further instantiations using constants c, d, e will not solve the problem, though this is less obvious than in the propositional case.

EXERCISES 2.3

1. Use semantic tableaux to demonstrate the following tautologies:

   a. $\forall x P(x) \rightarrow P(a)$

   b. $\exists x (P(x) \vee Q(x)) \rightarrow (\exists x P(x) \vee \exists x Q(x))$

   c. $(P \rightarrow \forall x Q(x)) \leftrightarrow \forall x (P \rightarrow Q(x))$

   d. $\forall x (P(x) \rightarrow Q(x)) \rightarrow \neg \exists x (P(x) \wedge \neg Q(x))$

   e. $\forall x Q(x) \rightarrow \neg \exists x \neg Q(x)$

   f. $\forall x (P(x) \wedge Q(x)) \leftrightarrow (\forall x P(x) \wedge \forall x Q(x))$

   g. $\forall x (P(x) \rightarrow Q(x)) \wedge \exists x (R(x) \wedge \neg Q(x)) \rightarrow \exists x (R(x) \wedge \neg P(x))$

2. Brackets are not absolutely necessary when writing a formula because predicates such as $P(x)$, $Q(x)$ and $R(x)$ may be written more simply as Px, Qx and Rx. Use this abbreviated notation in a semantic tableau to show that the following formula is valid:

   $$\exists x Px \wedge \forall x (Px \rightarrow Qx) \wedge \forall x (Qx \rightarrow Rx) \rightarrow \exists x (Px \wedge Rx)$$

   Predicates of greater arity, such as $Q(x,y)$ and $R(x,y,z)$ may be shown in a similar style as Qxy and $Rxyz$.

3. Show that the following formula is a contradiction by attempting (and failing) to establish its truth in semantic tableaux:

   $$\forall x \forall y \forall z (Pxy \wedge Pyz \rightarrow Pxz) \wedge \forall x \neg Pxx \wedge \exists x \exists y (Pxy \wedge Pyx)$$

2.4 SEMANTIC ENTAILMENT

Semantic entailment or logical consequence is applied to predicated formulas in exactly the same way as the propositional case. An entailment

$$A_1, A_2, \ldots, A_m \vDash B$$

is *true* if there is no interpretation that makes the formula on the right *false* when every formula on the left is *true*. Consider a potential entailment using just one predicate symbol P:

$$\neg P(x) \vDash \forall x \neg P(x)$$

in all possible interpretations with the two-element domain $\{1, 2\}$. Each domain element leads to two possible interpretations of the predicate $P(1)$ and $P(2)$, both of which might be *true* or *false*, producing the four possible interpretations in the table:

	*I*1	*I*2	*I*3	*I*4
$P(1)$	true	true	false	false
$P(2)$	true	false	true	false
$\neg P(1)$	false	false	true	true
$\neg P(2)$	false	true	false	true
$\forall x \neg P(x)$	false	false	false	true

A negation symbol in front of a predicate inverts the truth value obtained for the whole formula, just as for a propositional formula. Since there are only two domain elements in this case, the formula is *true* "for all" elements if it is *true* for both elements 1 and 2. In order to confirm the entailment, we have to show that the truth of $\forall x \neg P(x)$ follows from the truth of $\neg P(x)$. In other words, we have to show that if $\neg P(x)$ evaluates to *true* for any one domain element, the formula must evaluate to *true* for all elements. A glance at the table shows this is not the case: interpretations *I*2 and *I*3 have entries where $\neg P(x)$ evaluates to *true* but in which $\forall x \neg P(x)$ evaluates to *false*.

Turning our attention to a second possible entailment

$$\neg P(x) \vDash \neg \forall x P(x)$$

we have to show that formula $\neg \forall x P(x)$ is *true* whenever the formula $\neg P(x)$ is *true*. To do this, we first extend the table above to include two more lines:

	*I*1	*I*2	*I*3	*I*4
$\forall x P(x)$	true	false	false	false
$\neg \forall x P(x)$	false	true	true	true

This time, a glance at the formula shows the entailment does follow: the right-hand formula is *true* in the three interpretations that make the left-hand side true.

The truth values of formulas $\neg \forall x P(x)$ and $\forall x \neg P(x)$ are clearly different in each interpretation, confirming that these formulas are not equivalent. Remembering the earlier identity relating universal and existential quantifiers, this second entailment could be written as

$$\neg P(x) \models \exists x \neg P(x)$$

and the entailment seems much more obvious. When a particular instantiation makes $\neg P(x)$ *true*, there must exist a domain element that makes the formula $\exists x \neg P(x)$ *true*.

The number of cases that has to be considered increases with the number of domain elements, so this method of demonstrating entailments is very limited. An alternative approach depends on generating just those constants necessary to demonstrate the entailment, the so-called self-generated universe of the entailment. As an example, we take an entailment with quantified formulas but with a similar structure to one of the propositional entailments examined in Section 1.4:

$$\forall x(P(x) \rightarrow Q(x)), \forall x(Q(x) \rightarrow R(x)) \models \forall x(P(x) \rightarrow R(x))$$

As in the propositional examples, we have to show there is no interpretation that makes all the formulas on the left *true* while making the entailed formula on the right *false*. As a result, the entailment is only made invalid when the entailed formula $\forall x(P(x) \rightarrow R(x))$ is *false*, and this only occurs when there is some constant c that makes formula $P(c) \rightarrow R(c)$ *false*. There might be more, but one example is enough to falsify the entailment. Having generated the constant c in this way, we now note that both formulas on the left are universally quantified and should therefore be *true* for all domain elements. This being the case, they must be *true* for c, since it is one of the domain elements, and the quantified entailment above reduces to the following ground formula entailment:

$$P(c) \rightarrow Q(c), Q(c) \rightarrow R(c) \models P(c) \rightarrow R(c)$$

One constant might not seem enough to demonstrate the entailment, but constant c might be taken as any one constant that makes the entailed formula *false*. Both formulas on the left are universally quantified and therefore *true* for such an arbitrary constant, since they are *true* for all such constants.

An entailment containing only ground formulas is equivalent to a propositional form and is treated in exactly the same way. Formula $P(c) \rightarrow R(c)$ is *false* only when $P(c)$ is *true* and $R(c)$ is *false*, so these are the only valuations that need to be considered. This leaves only $Q(c)$ undecided, but a small truth table shows the consequences of assigning each truth value to this formula:

$Q(c)$	$P(c) \rightarrow Q(c)$	$Q(c) \rightarrow R(c)$	$P(c) \rightarrow R(c)$
false	false	true	false
true	true	false	false

It appears that no valuation of $Q(c)$ makes both of the formulas on the left of the entailment *true* while making the formula on the right *false*; the entailment is proven. As in the propositional case, the failure of a systematic attempt to falsify the right-hand side of the entailment while satisfying the left-hand side proves validity.

A slightly different strategy is required to demonstrate the following entailment:

$$\exists x P(x), \forall x(P(x) \rightarrow Q(x)) \vDash \exists x Q(x)$$

Again we aim to prove the entailment by failing to find a counterexample in a systematic search for interpretations that satisfy every formula on the left while falsifying the formula on the right. In this particular example, the right-hand formula is *false* if none of the domain elements makes $Q(x)$ *true*. This means that "for all" domain elements the predicate $Q(x)$ is *false*, giving the formula a universally quantified nature. An existentially quantified formula on the right-hand side of an entailment clearly behaves like a universally quantified formula on the left and is not a suitable starting-point.

However, the left-hand formula $\exists x P(x)$ is *true* if there exists a single constant c making $P(c)$ *true*, and this makes a better starting-point in the search for a counterexample. Given such a constant, we then reason that the right-hand formula $\exists x Q(x)$ is *false* if and only if formula $Q(x)$ is *false* for all domain elements. This being the case, the formula must be *false* for the element c that satisfies formula $P(x)$, since this is just an arbitrarily generated argument. The universally quantified formula on the left must also be *true* for the element c, since it has to be *true* for all domain elements. As a result, the search for a counterexample reduces to a check of the following propositional entailment:

$$P(c), P(c) \rightarrow Q(c) \vDash Q(c)$$

There is no valuation that makes both formulas on the left *true* while making the one on the right *false*, because the implication must be *false* when $P(c)$ is *true* and $Q(c)$ is *false*. The search for a counterexample fails and the entailment is proven.

EXERCISES 2.4

1. Use the truth value reasoning techniques of the preceding section to demonstrate the following entailments:

   a. $\forall x(P(x) \rightarrow Q(x)), \forall x P(x) \vDash \forall x Q(x)$

   b. $\forall x(P(x) \rightarrow Q(x)), \forall x(Q(x) \rightarrow \neg R(x)) \vDash \forall x(P(x) \rightarrow \neg R(x))$

   c. $\forall x(P(x) \vee Q(x) \rightarrow R(x)), \forall x \neg R(x) \vDash \forall x \neg P(x)$

   d. $\forall x(P(x) \rightarrow Q(x)) \vDash \forall x P(x) \rightarrow \forall x Q(x)$

2. Use truth value reasoning to demonstrate the following entailments containing existential quantifiers:

   a. $\exists x(P(x) \rightarrow Q(x)), \exists x P(x) \vDash \exists x Q(x)$

   b. $\forall x(P(x) \vee Q(x) \rightarrow R(x)), \exists x \neg R(x) \vDash \exists x \neg P(x)$

   c. $\forall x(P(x) \rightarrow Q(x)), \exists x(R(x) \wedge P(x)) \vDash \exists x(R(x) \wedge Q(x))$

2.5 A GENTZEN PROOF SYSTEM FOR FORMULAS

G system inference rules operate on two sets of formulas in a sequent with the form

antecedent $\Rightarrow$ succedent

and aim to show antecedent formulas to be *true* while showing succedent formulas to be *false*. G system rules demonstrate validity by failing to falsify the sequent itself, leading to a collection of subsequents called axioms.

The Gentzen G proof system described in Chapter 1 is extended to first-order logic by introducing the four new rules shown in Figure 2.5. These rules have a similar form to the semantic tableau rules, including the diagonal relationship between the rules. Both the "left $\exists$" and "right $\forall$" rules are considered to be existential inferences that cause formulas to be discharged after one application, leaving only the instantiated formula. The fact that the "left $\forall$" and "right $\exists$" rules do not discharge their formulas is shown by reproducing the formula below the line in the deduction tree. These four rules have to be used in conjunction with those already given for propositions in Figure 1.10.

As a first example, we consider the formula

$$\exists x(P(x) \wedge Q(x)) \rightarrow \exists x P(x) \wedge \exists x Q(x)$$

The existence of a single object making both predicates P and Q *true* implies the existence of an element making P *true* and the existence of one making Q *true*. This formula is certainly valid, unlike the reverse implication, for which the semantic tableau is given in Figure 2.4. In order to demonstrate its validity, the formula is made the succedent in a sequent and G inference rules are applied as appropriate. Figure 2.6 shows how a right implication rule first generates a sequent to which either a "left $\exists$" or "right $\wedge$" might be applied. Since the second option causes the proof tree to divide, it is delayed and the left existential formula instantiated. A dividing inference has to be applied at line 4, at which point the "right $\wedge$" rule is the only rule that can be applied. Once this is done, the right existential formulas may be instantiated with the previously introduced constant to produce axioms. Notice that the right existential formulas remain in the final sequents, but this is not a problem because these sequents are axioms, and the original formula is proven.

$$\frac{X, \exists x P(x) \Rightarrow Y}{X, P(a) \Rightarrow Y} \qquad \frac{X \Rightarrow \exists x P(x), Y}{X \Rightarrow \exists x P(x), P(a), Y}$$

$$\frac{X, \forall x P(x) \Rightarrow Y}{X, \forall x P(x), P(a) \Rightarrow Y} \qquad \frac{X \Rightarrow \forall x P(x), Y}{X \Rightarrow P(a), Y}$$

Left Right

Figure 2.5 G system quantifier rules

$$\Rightarrow \exists x(P(x) \land Q(x)) \rightarrow \exists x P(x) \land \exists x Q(x)$$

$\exists x(P(x) \land Q(x)) \Rightarrow \exists x P(x) \land \exists x Q(x)$	right $\rightarrow$ on 1
$P(a) \land Q(a) \Rightarrow \exists x P(x) \land \exists x Q(x)$	left $\exists$ on 2
$P(a), Q(a) \Rightarrow \exists x P(x) \land \exists x Q(x)$	left $\land$ on 3

$P(a), Q(a) \Rightarrow \exists x P(x)$	$P(a), Q(a) \Rightarrow \exists x Q(x)$	right $\land$ on 4
$P(a), Q(a) \Rightarrow P(a), \exists x P(x)$	$P(a), Q(a) \Rightarrow Q(a), \exists x Q(x)$	right $\exists$ on 4
$\times$	$\times$	

Figure 2.6   A G system proof tree

$$\Rightarrow \forall x(P(x) \lor Q(x)) \rightarrow \forall x P(x) \lor \forall x Q(x)$$

$\forall x(P(x) \lor Q(x)) \Rightarrow \forall x P(x) \lor \forall x Q(x)$	right $\rightarrow$ on 1
$\forall x(P(x) \lor Q(x)) \Rightarrow \forall x P(x), \forall x Q(x)$	right $\lor$ on 2
$\forall x(P(x) \lor Q(x)) \Rightarrow P(a), \forall x Q(x)$	right $\forall$ on 3
$\forall x(P(x) \lor Q(x)) \Rightarrow P(a), Q(b)$	right $\forall$ on 4
$\forall x(P(x) \lor Q(x)), P(a) \lor Q(a) \Rightarrow P(a), Q(b)$	left $\forall$ on 5
$\forall x(P(x) \lor Q(x)), P(a) \Rightarrow P(a), Q(b)$ $\times$	left $\lor$ on 6

$$\forall x(P(x) \lor Q(x)), Q(a) \Rightarrow P(a), Q(b)$$

Figure 2.7   A non-terminating tree

As a second example, we try to prove the validity of the formula

$$\forall x(P(x) \lor Q(x)) \rightarrow (\forall x P(x) \lor \forall x Q(x))$$

Figure 2.7 shows how two right propositional inference rules are followed by two applications of the right universal rule, generating two differently labelled constants. Fresh constants are required for each application of either the left existential or right universal rules, leaving two different predicates instantiated with two different constants, $P(a)$ and $Q(b)$. Finally the left universal rule is applied, generating ground atoms that close one branch of the tree. The remaining branch of the tree is the non-axiom sequent

$$\forall x(P(x) \lor Q(x)), Q(a) \Rightarrow P(a), Q(b)$$

and further instantiations of the universally quantified formula do not lead to a proof tree. The situation is similar to Figure 2.4, because a deduction has not terminated and the whole matter is left unresolved.

EXERCISES 2.5

1. Show that the following formulas are valid by constructing a proof tree, taking each formula as the initial succedent:

   a. $\forall x P(x) \rightarrow \exists x P(x)$

   b. $\forall x(P(x) \rightarrow Q) \rightarrow (\exists x P(x) \rightarrow Q)$

   c. $\neg \exists x(P(x) \wedge \neg Q(x)) \rightarrow \forall x(P(x) \rightarrow Q(x))$

   d. $\forall x P(x) \vee \exists x Q(x) \rightarrow \exists x(P(x) \vee Q(x))$

2. By constructing a proof tree, demonstrate the validity of the following formulas:

   a. $\forall x \forall y R(x,y) \leftrightarrow \forall y \forall x R(x,y)$

   b. $\exists x \exists y R(x,y) \leftrightarrow \exists y \exists x R(x,y)$

   c. $\exists x \forall y R(x,y) \rightarrow \forall y \exists x R(x,y)$

   Two of these formulas are mutual implications and one is a simple conditional. Explore the result when the conditional of the last example is reversed.

3. Prove that the following formulas are valid:

   a. $\forall x(P(x) \rightarrow \neg Q(x)) \wedge \exists x(R(x) \wedge P(x)) \rightarrow \exists x(R(x) \wedge \neg Q(x))$

   b. $\exists x(P(x) \rightarrow \neg Q(x)) \rightarrow (\forall x(R(x) \wedge P(x)) \rightarrow \exists x(R(x) \wedge \neg Q(x)))$

2.6   NORMAL FORMS

Normal forms are standard methods of writing formulas or proofs that reveal properties not obvious in the unnormalised form. A number of such forms were defined for the propositional subset of first-order logic and further definitions connected to quantified formulas are now given.

2.6.1   Prenex normal form

A formula in prenex normal form has all its quantifier symbols to the left of a collection of predicate and logical connective symbols called the matrix. If symbol Q represents either an existential or universal quantifier with its variable and M represents the matrix, a prenex normal formula has the following general form:

$$Q_1 Q_2 Q_3 \ldots M$$

Consider first a formula that is not in prenex form because two quantifiers appear within a propositional subformula

$$\forall x(P(x) \wedge \forall y \exists x(Q(x,y) \vee R(x,y)))$$

Notice further that symbol x is used for two distinct variables: the inner disjunction has variable x bound by an existential quantifier and the variable in $P(x)$ is bound by the outer universal quantifier. Since the precise symbol given to a variable in a quantified formula is unimportant, one of the occurrences of x may be relabelled with symbol z to give

$$\forall x(P(x) \land \forall y \exists z(Q(z,y) \lor R(z,y)))$$

Quantifiers can then be moved to the left, producing a formula in prenex form:

$$\forall x \forall y \exists z(P(x) \land (Q(z,y) \lor R(z,y)))$$

Notice that, in moving the quantifiers to the left, we have assumed the two quantifiers can be "carried over" a predicate such as $P(x)$. This repositioning is justified by the following logical equivalences:

$$Qx(A \land B) \equiv A \land QxB$$
$$Qx(A \lor B) \equiv A \lor QxB$$
$$Qx(A \rightarrow B) \equiv A \rightarrow QxB$$

Provided x does not occur free in A, the quantifier can be carried over this formula to the left, increasing its scope. Similar logical equivalences occur when the quantifier occurs to the left of a conjunction or disjunction symbol:

$$Qx(A \land B) \equiv QxA \land B$$
$$Qx(A \lor B) \equiv QxA \lor B$$

Again the scope of a quantifier is extended to the whole formula, so variable x should not occur free in B. Provided the movement of a quantifier is not allowed to capture a free variable on moving to the left, the change to prenex form is straightforward for conjunctions and disjunctions.

Slightly more care is necessary when a quantification on the antecedent of an implication is to be applied to the whole formula rather than just the antecedent. In this case the quantifier changes from existential to universal, or vice versa, as its scope changes:

$$\forall x(A \rightarrow B) \equiv \exists xA \rightarrow B$$
$$\exists x(A \rightarrow B) \equiv \forall xA \rightarrow B$$

Confirmation of these identities is easily obtained by replacing implications with disjunctions before increasing the scope of the quantifier:

$$\exists xA \rightarrow B \equiv \neg \exists xA \lor B$$
$$\equiv \forall x(\neg A \lor B)$$
$$\equiv \forall x(A \rightarrow B)$$

Nevertheless, formulas with implications require greater care than those with only conjunctions and disjunctions. Consider the following conversion of formula $\forall x P(x,y) \rightarrow \neg \exists y Q(y)$ to prenex form:

$\forall x P(x,y) \rightarrow \neg \exists y Q(y)$
$\forall x P(x,y) \rightarrow \neg \exists z Q(z)$ rename variable
$\forall x P(x,y) \rightarrow \forall z \neg Q(z)$ move negation inwards
$\forall z(\forall x P(x,y) \rightarrow \neg Q(z))$ extract consequent quantifier
$\forall z \exists x(P(x,y) \rightarrow \neg Q(z))$ extract antecedent quantifier

2.6.2   Normal forms of writing proofs

A formula expressed in prenex normal form is equivalent to the formula from which it was derived, but has some useful features for a task in which it is to be used. Similarly, a sequent proof has normal forms equivalent to an unnormalised proof, but the application of inferences in the normal form illustrates features not obvious in the initial proof. In earlier examples, quantifier inferences or propositional inferences were used in a sequent proof in the order that each one appeared in the decomposition of the formulas. A Gentzen normal form of proof requires that all quantifier inferences are applied before any propositional inferences are used, dividing the proof into two separate parts above and below a line called the midsequent. Working down from the root formula, the midsequent is the first sequent that does not contain any quantifier symbols. Such a normal form of proof has the general appearance shown in Figure 2.8: a formula to be proven occurs at the top of a deduction tree followed by a number of quantifier inferences, leading at some point to the midsequent. Below this, only propositional inference rules are applied until axioms are obtained.

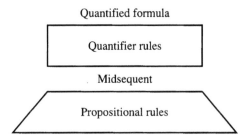

Figure 2.8 Midsequent proof pattern

Propositional and quantifier inferences have so far been applied in the order in which they arise. Applications of the two sorts of rules have been interleaved and the first inference rule to be applied has often been a propositional one. If we wish to apply every quantifier inference before any propositional rule, some modification of the procedures described in previous sections is required. One possible solution is to express all formulas in prenex normal form so that quantifier inferences are naturally the first to arise.

The following formula has already been validated by the Gentzen proof of Figure 2.6:

$$\exists x(P(x) \wedge Q(x)) \rightarrow (\exists x P(x) \wedge \exists x Q(x))$$

Using the identities given earlier, the formula is converted to prenex normal form:

$$\exists x(P(x) \wedge Q(x)) \rightarrow (\exists x P(x) \wedge \exists x Q(x))$$
$$\forall x(P(x) \wedge Q(x)) \rightarrow (\exists y P(y) \wedge \exists z Q(z)) \qquad \text{rename variables}$$
$$\forall x((P(x) \wedge Q(x)) \rightarrow (\exists x P(x) \wedge \exists x Q(x))) \qquad \text{extract quantifier}$$
$$\forall x \exists y \exists z((P(x) \wedge Q(x)) \rightarrow (P(y) \wedge Q(z))) \qquad \text{extract quantifier}$$

and a proof tree for the modified formula is shown in Figure 2.9. Since the prenex formula is equivalent to the original one, the fact that it is proven valid should not be a great surprise. The real point to be observed is that quantifier inferences are now applied first, leading to the midsequent line, then propositional rules are used to produce axioms. Only "right" quantifier rules are required in the proof and this will be the case in all proofs arising from a prenex form succedent. There can be no "right" negation or propositional rule that could move quantifiers over to the left because these connectives have been moved into the matrix. If the matrix had additionally been converted to negation normal form only, "right" propositional rules would be required.

As a larger example, we take the two formulas already in prenex form:

$$\forall x \forall y \forall z(P(x,y) \wedge P(y,z) \rightarrow P(x,z)) \qquad \forall x(\neg P(x,x))$$

and show that the prenex formula

$$\forall x \forall y(P(x,y) \rightarrow \neg P(y,x))$$

is a consequence. This might be achieved by using the semantic entailment arguments from the previous section or by building a semantic tableau from the first two formulas and a negation of the third. Equivalently, we might show that a Gentzen proof taking the first two formulas in its antecedent and the entailed formula as succedent leads to a proof tree. Figure 2.10 shows that the entailment does in fact hold and that a midsequent again divides quantifier inferences from propositional inferences.

$$\Rightarrow \forall x \exists y \exists z(P(x) \wedge Q(x) \rightarrow P(y) \wedge Q(z))$$

$$\Rightarrow \exists y \exists z(P(a) \wedge Q(a) \rightarrow P(x) \wedge Q(z)) \qquad \text{right } \forall \text{ on 1}$$

$$\Rightarrow \exists z(P(a) \wedge Q(a) \rightarrow P(a) \wedge Q(z)) \qquad \text{right } \exists \text{ on 2}$$

midsequent $\qquad \Rightarrow P(a) \wedge Q(a) \rightarrow P(a) \wedge Q(a) \qquad \text{right } \exists \text{ on 3}$

$$P(a) \wedge Q(a) \Rightarrow P(a) \wedge Q(a) \qquad \text{right } \rightarrow \text{ on 4}$$

$$P(a), Q(a) \Rightarrow P(a) \wedge Q(a) \qquad \text{left } \wedge \text{ on 5}$$

$$P(a), Q(a) \Rightarrow P(a) \qquad\qquad P(a), Q(a) \Rightarrow Q(a) \quad \text{right } \wedge \text{ on 6}$$
$$\times \qquad\qquad\qquad\qquad \times$$

Figure 2.9 Proof of a prenex formula

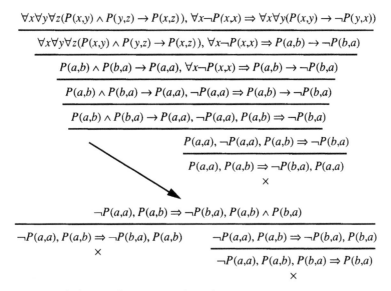

$\forall x \forall y \forall z (P(x,y) \wedge P(y,z) \rightarrow P(x,z)), \forall x \neg P(x,x) \Rightarrow \forall x \forall y (P(x,y) \rightarrow \neg P(y,x))$

$\forall x \forall y \forall z (P(x,y) \wedge P(y,z) \rightarrow P(x,z)), \forall x \neg P(x,x) \Rightarrow P(a,b) \rightarrow \neg P(b,a)$

$P(a,b) \wedge P(b,a) \rightarrow P(a,a), \forall x \neg P(x,x) \Rightarrow P(a,b) \rightarrow \neg P(b,a)$

$P(a,b) \wedge P(b,a) \rightarrow P(a,a), \neg P(a,a) \Rightarrow P(a,b) \rightarrow \neg P(b,a)$

$P(a,b) \wedge P(b,a) \rightarrow P(a,a), \neg P(a,a), P(a,b) \Rightarrow \neg P(b,a)$

$P(a,a), \neg P(a,a), P(a,b) \Rightarrow \neg P(b,a)$

$P(a,a), P(a,b) \Rightarrow \neg P(b,a), P(a,a)$
$\times$

$\neg P(a,a), P(a,b) \Rightarrow \neg P(b,a), P(a,b) \wedge P(b,a)$

$\neg P(a,a), P(a,b) \Rightarrow \neg P(b,a), P(a,b)$
$\times$

$\neg P(a,a), P(a,b) \Rightarrow \neg P(b,a), P(b,a)$

$\neg P(a,a), P(a,b), P(b,a) \Rightarrow P(b,a)$
$\times$

Figure 2.10 A deduction from prenex formulas

2.6.3 Negation normal form

A formula is said to be in negation normal form (NNF) if its logical symbols are restricted to the set $\{\exists, \forall, \wedge, \vee, \neg, \bot, (,)\}$ and every occurrence of the symbol $\neg$ stands directly before an atomic formula. Thus, the formula $\neg \forall x P(x,y)$ is not in NNF, but the equivalent form $\exists x \neg P(x,y)$ has the desired property. In fact, every first-order formula can be expressed in an equivalent negation normal form and the procedure for achieving this is an extension of that described in Chapter 1.

a. Use equivalences to replace unacceptable symbols by those in the above set. In practice this usually means the replacement of implication and mutual implication symbols.

b. Use further equivalences to drive inwards all $\neg$ symbols that do not stand directly before atomic formulas.

As a first example, we convert the formula

$\exists x (P(x) \wedge Q(x)) \rightarrow (\exists x P(x) \wedge \exists x Q(x))$

to negation normal form as follows:

$\exists x (P(x) \wedge Q(x)) \rightarrow (\exists x P(x) \wedge \exists x Q(x))$

$\neg (\exists x (P(x) \wedge Q(x))) \vee (\exists x P(x) \wedge \exists x Q(x))$ propositional identity

$\forall x \neg (P(x) \wedge Q(x)) \vee (\exists x P(x) \wedge \exists x Q(x))$ quantifier identity

$\forall x (\neg P(x) \vee \neg Q(x)) \vee (\exists x P(x) \wedge \exists x Q(x))$ De Morgan

A formula F in NNF has a dual form that is no more than the negated formula $\neg F$ adjusted so that it too is in NNF. The simplest negation normal forms are atomic formulas with or without preceding negation symbols such as $P(x)$, $\neg Q(x,y)$ and $\neg R(x,y,z)$. Such formulas are usually called literals and have dual forms that are obtained by adding or removing negation symbols, producing the dual forms $\neg P(x)$, $Q(x,y)$ and $R(x,y,z)$ from the examples above. Quantified formulas have dual forms that are obtained by the equivalences given earlier:

Formula	Dual
$\forall x P(x,y)$	$\exists x \neg P(x,y)$
$\exists x P(x,y)$	$\forall x \neg P(x,y)$
$\neg \forall x P(x,y)$	$\forall x P(x,y)$
$\neg \exists x P(x,y)$	$\exists x P(x,y)$

Dual forms are equivalent to the negated formulas and each one of the tabulated duals could have been obtained by simplification of the negated formula. The dual of formula $\forall x P(x,y)$ is obtained as follows:

$$\neg \forall x P(x,y) \equiv \exists x \neg P(x,y)$$

using the earlier identity.

The dual form of the NNF formula

$$\forall x(\neg P(x) \vee \neg Q(x)) \vee (\exists x P(x) \wedge \exists x Q(x))$$

is obtained by negation and simplification as follows:

$$\neg(\forall x(\neg P(x) \vee \neg Q(x)) \vee (\exists x P(x) \wedge \exists x Q(x)))$$
$$\neg \forall x(\neg P(x) \vee \neg Q(x)) \wedge \neg(\exists x P(x) \wedge \exists x Q(x))$$
$$\exists x(P(x) \wedge Q(x)) \wedge (\forall x \neg P(x) \vee \forall x \neg Q(x))$$

but this result might have been written by inspection of the previous formula: universal and existential symbols are exchanged, atomic formulas are replaced by their dual forms and disjunctions and conjunctions are exchanged.

A formula might be in prenex form without also being in NNF; this is certainly the case when a prenex formula contains implication connectives or if negation symbols have scope over more than one predicate. Conversely, a formula might be in NNF but not in prenex form. Given a formula in either of these forms, it should not be difficult to adjust the formula so that it is in both forms; the following prenex formula is modified to ensure it is also in NNF:

$$\forall x \exists y \exists z((P(x) \wedge Q(x)) \rightarrow (P(y) \wedge Q(z)))$$
$$\forall x \exists y \exists z(\neg(P(x) \wedge Q(x)) \vee (P(y) \wedge Q(z))) \quad \text{identity}$$
$$\forall x \exists y \exists z(\neg P(x) \vee \neg Q(x) \vee (P(y) \wedge Q(z))) \quad \text{De Morgan}$$

A formula in NNF is very easily adjusted to put it in prenex form. An NNF formula might have several quantified subformulas within a propositional statement and each subformula might use the same variable symbol. This layout appears in the following formula:

$$\exists x(P(x) \lor Q(x)) \lor (\forall x \neg P(x) \lor \forall x \neg Q(x))$$

but the variables could be renamed and the quantifiers then moved to the left to give a prenex form

$$\exists x \forall y \forall z((P(x) \lor Q(x)) \lor (\neg P(y) \lor \neg Q(z)))$$

Later we shall see that there are sometimes advantages in retaining an NNF formula in non-prenex form.

2.6.4 Refutation normal form

A formula, or set of formulas, is proven valid by making it the succedent of a sequent and applying inference rules until a proof tree is obtained. Thus the starting-point of the proof is the sequent

$\Rightarrow$ formula

but the left negation rule allows this sequent to be identified with another sequent

$\neg$formula $\Rightarrow$

A given formula may be proven from either starting-point, but in the second case the first rule to be applied is the left negation inference and the sequent is returned to the succedent form. However, if the negated antecedent formula is converted to negation normal form, the sequent becomes

$(\neg \text{formula})_{\text{nnf}} \Rightarrow$

and applications of negation rules are delayed until the very last steps of the proof.

Earlier we saw how prenex formulas lead to special normal forms of proof in which all the applications of quantifier inference rules are discharged before any of the propositional inferences. As a result, a special sequent without any quantifier symbols called the midsequent appears to divide the two different kinds of inference rules. This is possible because the quantifier inferences are naturally the first to be used in a sequent containing only prenex formulas. A second method allows all quantifier inferences to be discharged before any propositional ones are used. Especially useful in refutation form, this second method allows quantifier inference rules to be applied to quantified subformulas within sequent formulas, provided the sequent formulas are expressed in negation normal form. The need to have formulas in NNF is clear if we consider the apparent need to apply a "left $\forall$" inference rule to the subformula $\forall x P(x)$ in the following sequent:

$$Q(a,b) \lor \neg(P(b) \land \forall x P(x)) \Rightarrow$$

but when this formula is converted to NNF it becomes

$$Q(a,b) \lor \neg P(b) \lor \exists x \neg P(x) \Rightarrow$$

$$\exists x(P(x) \land Q(x)) \land (\forall x \neg P(x) \lor \forall x \neg Q(x)) \Rightarrow$$

$$(P(a) \land Q(a)) \land (\forall x \neg P(x) \lor \forall x \neg Q(x)) \Rightarrow$$

$$(P(a) \land Q(a)) \land (\neg P(a) \lor \forall x \neg Q(x)) \Rightarrow$$

midsequent $$(P(a) \land Q(a)) \land (\neg P(a) \lor \neg Q(a)) \Rightarrow$$

$$P(a) \land Q(a), \neg P(a) \lor \neg Q(a) \Rightarrow$$

$$P(a), Q(a), \neg P(a) \lor \neg Q(a) \Rightarrow$$

$$P(a), Q(a), \neg P(a) \Rightarrow \qquad\qquad P(a), Q(a), \neg Q(a) \Rightarrow$$

$$P(a), Q(a) \Rightarrow P(a) \qquad\qquad P(a), Q(a) \Rightarrow Q(a)$$
$$\times \qquad\qquad\qquad\qquad\qquad \times$$

Figure 2.11 A refutation tree

and it is clear that what is really required is an application of the "left ∃" rule to give the subsequent

$$Q(a,b) \lor \neg P(b) \lor \neg P(c) \Rightarrow$$

Formulas in NNF only contain negation symbols within literals and we can be certain that in this case the subformula quantifiers really are what they appear to be.

Earlier it was shown that the formula

$$\exists x(P(x) \land Q(x)) \rightarrow (\exists x P(x) \land \exists x Q(x))$$

is valid by making it the succedent in the proof tree of Figure 2.6. This formula was converted to NNF as an example and its dual form was derived as

$$\exists x(P(x) \land Q(x)) \land (\forall x \neg P(x) \lor \forall x \neg Q(x))$$

If this formula is taken as the antecedent in a root sequent and quantifier rules are applied to quantified subformulas, the deduction tree in Figure 2.11 is obtained. All of the quantifier inferences can be applied before any of the propositional inferences; this is because subformulas can be instantiated when the formula is in NNF. The tree is divided by a line called the midsequent, above which there are only quantifier inferences and below which there are only propositional inferences. Every branch of this tree terminates with an axiom, indicating that an attempt to demonstrate the truth of the negated formula has failed. This in turn indicates that the negated formula is a contradiction and the original unnegated formula must be a tautology, i.e. it is a valid formula. Proofs of this kind are called refutations because they achieve their objective by refuting a dual, negated formula.

2.6.5 Skolem functions

Skolem functions may be used to replace existentially quantified variables in a formula such as

$\exists x(Woman(x) \land Loves(mike,x))$

simply by replacing the quantified variable by a specific though unknown object

$(Woman(a) \land Loves(mike,a))$

The claim that "there exists" such an object is replaced by a label for the object itself in a process resembling an application of the "left $\exists$" inference rule. Suppose, however, that we try to extend this reasoning to the following formal expression of "every man loves a woman":

$\forall x(Man(x) \rightarrow \exists y(Woman(y) \land Loves(x,y)))$

by instantiating a specific object in the place of the existentially quantified variable

$\forall x(Man(x) \rightarrow (Woman(a) \land Loves(x,a)))$

Unfortunately, constant a represents a specific though unknown woman, so the formula suggests that every man loves the same woman. The problem arises because the variable of the existential quantifier occurs within the scope of a universal quantifier and the simple constant a above does not take this into account. Every man loves a woman, but the woman may be different for each man and any substitution for the existentially quantified variable must reflect this. Skolem solved the problem by introducing a function $f(x)$ to represent an existentially quantified object within the scope of a universal quantifier. Function $f(x)$ is substituted in place of the simple constant a to give the formula

$\forall x(Man(x) \rightarrow (Woman(f(x)) \land Loves(x, f(x))))$

In this Skolemised form, $Man(a)$ loves $Woman(f(a))$, $Man(b)$ loves $Woman(f(b))$ and so forth, allowing the individual instances of men a, b, c, ... to be mapped to distinct women $f(a)$, $f(b)$, $f(c)$, ...

Going still further, we formalise the well-known claim that every sailor loves a woman in every port he visits:

$\forall x(Sailor(x) \rightarrow \forall y(Port(x,y) \rightarrow (\exists z Woman(z) \land Loves(x,z))))$

Now the woman who is loved depends not only on the sailor but also on the port, i.e. it is a function of two variables and the Skolem function $f(x,y)$ used to replace the existentially quantified variable takes this into account:

$\forall x(Sailor(x) \rightarrow (\forall y Port(x,y) \rightarrow (Woman(f(x,y)) \land Loves(x, f(x,y)))))$

A simple rule emerges from these examples: the arity of a Skolem function used to replace an existentially quantified variable depends on the number of universally quantified variables within whose scope the existential variable is placed. An existentially quantified variable that is not within the scope of any universally quantified variable is replaced by a simple constant, an arity-zero function. Each additional universally quantified variable increases the arity of the Skolem function by one.

There is an implicit assumption that the formula being Skolemised appears in the antecedent of a sequent. Thus the sequent

$\forall x \exists y P(x,y) \Rightarrow$

is Skolemised to give

$\forall x P(x, f(x)) \Rightarrow$

However, the initial sequent might equally well be written in the following succedent form:

$\Rightarrow \exists x \forall y \neg P(x,y)$

and the Skolemised form could also be transformed to the succedent form

$\Rightarrow \exists x \neg P(x, f(x))$

The replacement of existential quantified variables in an antecedent is clearly equivalent to the replacement of universally quantified variables in a succedent. The procedure for antecedent formulas outlined above is now inverted: universally quantified variables are now replaced by functions of arity equal to the number of existential quantifiers within whose scope they are positioned. There is a dual system of Skolem functions corresponding to the dual forms of formulas described earlier. Skolem functions applied to succedent formulas are sometimes called Herbrand functions because they were used by Herbrand in the theorem described below.

The following example shows the care necessary in inserting Herbrand or Skolem functions in a formula:

$\Rightarrow \forall x (\exists y P(x,y) \rightarrow \forall z Q(x,z))$

Here the inner universally quantified variable might appear to be within the scope of an existential quantifier, but the scope of the y variable is limited to the first sub-formula. As a result, both universally quantified variables are replaced by constants

$\Rightarrow (\exists y P(a,y) \rightarrow Q(a,b))$

The following sequent formula requires the use of arity-one and arity-two Skolem functions:

$\Rightarrow \exists w \forall x \exists y \forall z ((\neg P(w,x) \vee Q(w)) \rightarrow R(y,z))$

because variable x is in the scope of $\exists w$ and variable z is within the scope of both $\exists w$ and $\exists y$. This gives the formula

$\Rightarrow \exists w \exists y ((\neg P(w, f(w)) \vee Q(w)) \rightarrow R(y, g(w,y)))$

2.6.6   Herbrand's theorem

A sequent containing only prenex formulas can be rearranged to place all such formulas in the succedent of a sequent:

$\Rightarrow$ formulas

and the first inferences to be applied will then be the right existential and universal rules. Herbrand's theorem states that a quantified formula is provable if and only if the quantifier-free formula obtained by the application of quantifier inference rules is provable. In terms of normal form proofs, the initial sequent is provable if and only if its midsequent is provable. New constants are introduced into succedent formulas by each application of the right universal rule, then existential inferences are free to reuse any such constants. As a proof proceeds towards its midsequent, the order in which these introductions occurred is lost, so the form of the original formula is lost. Herbrand compensated for this loss of information by instantiating Skolem functions rather than simple constants, thus recording the order in which introductions are made. In the simplest case, represented by the sequent

$$\Rightarrow \forall x \exists y \exists z ((P(x) \wedge Q(x)) \rightarrow (P(y) \wedge Q(z)))$$

the replacement of an existentially quantified variable with a constant produces a result identical to that obtained from the right universal rule:

$$\Rightarrow \exists y \exists z ((P(a) \wedge Q(a)) \rightarrow (P(y) \wedge Q(z)))$$

Only functions with an arity of one or more have a significant effect in the Herbrand proof procedure and the following sequent is therefore of more interest:

$$\Rightarrow \exists t \forall u \neg P(t,u), \exists v \forall w \neg Q(v,w), \forall x \exists y \exists z (P(x,y) \wedge Q(y,z))$$

A deduction tree for this formula is constructed as far as the midsequent in Figure 2.12a, then propositional inferences may be used to produce a proof tree. This sequent may be Skolemised to give

$$\Rightarrow \exists t \neg P(t,f(t)), \exists v \neg Q(v,g(v)), \exists y \exists z (P(a,y) \wedge Q(y,z))$$

and a proof tree tree derived from the Skolemised form is shown in Figure 2.12b.

Axioms can be produced from the midsequent of Figure 2.12b using the same two propositional steps required to produce axioms from the midsequent in Figure 2.12a. The important difference between the two approaches is that the original root formula can be reconstructed from the Skolemised midsequent, allowing the direct connection between a formula and its midsequent required for Herbrand's theorem.

2.6.7 Skolem–Herbrand–Gödel theory

Herbrand's theorem asserts a claim that the provability of a formula rests on the provability of a quantifier-free formula derived from the quantified form. An alternative approach called the Skolem–Herbrand–Gödel (SHG) theory makes a similar claim for the semantic concept of unsatisfiablity. According to this theory, a formula is unsatisfiable if and only if a quantifier-free formula derived by the application of quantifier rules is itself unsatisfiable. A formula may be shown to be valid through the refutation of its negation, i.e. by the failure of a systematic attempt to

$\Rightarrow \exists t \forall u \neg P(t,u), \exists v \forall w \neg Q(v,w), \forall x \exists y \exists z (P(x,y) \wedge Q(y,z))$

$\Rightarrow \exists t \forall u \neg P(t,u), \exists v \forall w \neg Q(v,w), \exists y \exists z (P(a,y) \wedge Q(y,z))$

$\Rightarrow \forall u \neg P(a,u), \exists v \forall w \neg Q(v,w), \exists y \exists z (P(a,y) \wedge Q(y,z))$

$\Rightarrow \neg P(a,b), \exists v \forall w \neg Q(v,w), \exists y \exists z (P(a,y) \wedge Q(y,z))$

$\Rightarrow \neg P(a,b), \forall w \neg Q(b,w), \exists y \exists z (P(a,y) \wedge Q(y,z))$

$\Rightarrow \neg P(a,b), \neg Q(b,c), \exists y \exists z (P(a,y) \wedge Q(y,z))$

(a) $\Rightarrow \neg P(a,b), \neg Q(b,c), (P(a,b) \wedge Q(b,c))$

$\Rightarrow \exists t \neg P(t,f(t)), \exists v \neg Q(v,g(v)), \exists y \exists z (P(a,y) \wedge Q(y,z))$

$\Rightarrow \neg P(a,f(a)), \exists v \neg Q(v,g(v)), \exists y \exists z (P(a,y) \wedge Q(y,z))$

$\Rightarrow \neg P(a,f(a)), \neg Q(f(a),g(f(a))), \exists y \exists z (P(a,y) \wedge Q(y,z))$

$\Rightarrow \neg P(a,f(a)), \neg Q(f(a),g(f(a))), \exists z (P(a,f(a)) \wedge Q(f(a),z))$

(b) $\Rightarrow \neg P(a,f(a)), \neg Q(f(a),g(f(a))), P(a,f(a)) \wedge Q(f(a),g(f(a)))$

Figure 2.12 Midsequents: (a) with simple constants and (b) with Skolem functions

satisfy that formula. However, as explained in Chapter 1, an attempt to produce a deduction tree from the succedent

$\neg(\text{formula}) \Rightarrow$

would quickly reproduce the proof form. But if the antecedent is converted to NNF, the left subformula quantifier rules can be directly applied to the formula. Like Herbrand's original theorm, the SHG theorem depends on the separation of quantifier and propositional rules in the deduction tree; but if the antecedent is in NNF, only left rules are required. The SHG theorem uses Skolem functions to replace existential quantifiers in a dual approach to that taken in the Herbrand theorem. It is only of real interest when existentially quantified variables lie in the scope of universal quantifiers, generating Skolem functions of arity one or more. Consider as an example the formula

$\exists x((P(x) \vee \exists y Q(x,y)) \rightarrow (\exists z Q(x,z) \vee P(a)))$

from which an equivalent NNF is derived as follows:

$\exists x((P(x) \vee \exists y Q(x,y)) \rightarrow (\exists z Q(x,z) \vee P(a)))$
$\exists x(\neg(P(x) \vee \exists y Q(x,y)) \vee (\exists z Q(x,z) \vee P(a)))$ remove $\rightarrow$
$\exists x(\neg P(x) \wedge \forall y \neg Q(x,y)) \vee (\exists z Q(x,z) \vee P(a))$ De Morgan

Since we wish to work in refutation form, we derive the dual of the above NNF by inspection:

$\forall x(P(x) \vee \exists y Q(x,y)) \wedge (\forall z \neg Q(x,z) \wedge \neg P(a))$

$$\frac{\forall x(P(x) \vee \exists y Q(x,y)) \wedge (\forall z \neg Q(x,z) \wedge \neg P(a)) \Rightarrow}{\dfrac{(P(a) \vee \exists y Q(a,y)) \wedge (\forall z \neg Q(a,z) \wedge \neg P(a)) \Rightarrow}{\dfrac{(P(a) \vee Q(a,b)) \wedge (\forall z \neg Q(a,z) \wedge \neg P(a)) \Rightarrow}{(P(a) \vee Q(a,b)) \wedge (\neg Q(a,b) \wedge \neg P(a)) \Rightarrow}}}$$

(a)

$$\frac{\forall x(P(x) \vee Q(x,f(x))) \wedge (\forall z \neg Q(x,z) \wedge \neg P(a)) \Rightarrow}{\dfrac{(P(a) \vee Q(a,f(a))) \wedge (\forall z \neg Q(a,z) \wedge \neg P(a)) \Rightarrow}{(P(a) \vee Q(a,f(a))) \wedge (\neg Q(a,f(a)) \wedge \neg P(a)) \Rightarrow}}$$

(b)

Figure 2.13   Midsequents: (a) with simple constants and (b) with Skolem functions

and the deduction of a midsequent from this formula as an antecedent is shown in Figure 2.13a. When the formula above is Skolemised, we obtain

$$\forall x(P(x) \vee Q(x,f(x))) \wedge (\forall z \neg Q(x,z) \wedge \neg P(a))$$

and a deduction tree produced when this formula is taken as the initial antecedent is shown in Figure 2.13b. Both of these deduction trees terminate in refutations, but the Skolemised version allows the original formula to be reconstructed.

EXERCISES 2.6

1. Convert the following formulas to prenex normal form:

    a. $\exists x(P(x) \vee \forall y(Q(x,y) \wedge \forall x R(x)))$

    b. $\forall x(\forall y R(x,y) \wedge \exists y(S(x,y) \vee \forall x T(x)))$

2. Express the following valid formulas in equivalent prenex normal form:

    a. $\forall x(P(x) \wedge Q(x)) \rightarrow \forall x P(x) \vee \forall x Q(x)$

    b. $\forall x P(x) \wedge \forall x Q(x) \rightarrow \forall x(P(x) \vee Q(x))$

    c. $\forall x(P(x) \wedge Q(x)) \wedge \forall x P(x) \rightarrow \forall x Q(x)$

    d. $\forall x(P(x) \rightarrow \neg Q(x)) \rightarrow (\exists x(R(x) \wedge Q(x)) \rightarrow \exists x(R(x) \wedge \neg P(x)))$

3. Show normal form proof trees for each of the formulas derived in the previous exercise, indicating the midsequent in each tree.

4. Convert each of the formulas of Exercise 2 into equivalent negation normal forms.

5. Take the dual forms of each of the formulas resulting from Exercise 4 and produce a refutation tree for each one.

6. Prove the following sequent is valid:

    $$\forall x \exists y \forall z R(x,y,z) \Rightarrow \forall x \forall z \exists y R(x,y,z)$$

Skolemise both sides of the sequent and repeat the proof.

7. Convert each of the following formulas to NNF then Skolemise out any existentially quantified variables:

a. $\forall x \exists x P(x,y)$

b. $\forall x \forall y \exists z R(x,y,z) \wedge \forall x \exists y \forall z R(x,y,z)$

c. $\forall x \exists y (P(x,y) \rightarrow \exists z Q(x,y,z))$

d. $\exists x (\forall y P(x,y) \rightarrow \exists z Q(x,z))$

e. $\forall x \exists y \forall z \exists w ((\neg P(x,y) \vee Q(x)) \rightarrow R(x,z))$

2.7 A HILBERT PROOF SYSTEM FOR FORMULAS

The Hilbert proof system described in Chapter 1 is expanded to first-order logic in each of the four components described earlier:

a. An alphabet consisting of the following logical symbols:

$\neg, \rightarrow, \forall, (,),$

and the following non-logical symbols:

$a, b, c, \ldots$	constants
$x, y, z \ldots$	variables
$f, g, h,$	function symbols
$P, Q, R, \ldots$	atomic formulas

b. Rules for building formulas from the alphabet:

1. Every atomic formula is a formula.
2. If A and B are formulas then so are $\neg A$, $A \rightarrow B$ and $\forall x A$ where x is any variable.
3. Nothing else is a formula.

c. Five axioms, three of which are inherited from the propositional subset.

1. $(A \rightarrow (B \rightarrow A))$
2. $((A \rightarrow (B \rightarrow C)) \rightarrow ((A \rightarrow B) \rightarrow (A \rightarrow C)))$
3. $((\neg A) \rightarrow (\neg B)) \rightarrow (B \rightarrow A)$
4. $\forall x A(x) \rightarrow A(a)$
5. $\forall x(A \rightarrow B(x)) \rightarrow (A \rightarrow \forall x B(x))$

d. Two rules of deduction:

1. *Modus ponens* (MP): from A and $(A \rightarrow B)$ deduce B.
2. Generalisation: if A is a formula and x is any variable from A, deduce $\forall x A$.

It is possible to recognise a subset of symbols, rules and axioms identical to those defined for the propositional Hilbert proof system within the proof system described above. The previous alphabet is extended with terms, formulas and quantifier symbols to allow the construction of full first-order logic formulas. Notice, however, that the logical symbols available in the alphabet are restricted to a minimal set and that only a universal quantifier is defined. A Hilbert proof system may be defined with a larger alphabet, but more axioms are then required to encode the required properties into the system. In practice a limited set of symbols is not a major problem because the missing symbols can be introduced as abbreviations for formulas expressed within the above system. For example

$A \vee B$ abbreviates $\neg A \to B$
$A \wedge B$ abbreviates $\neg(A \to \neg B)$

Similarly, the existential expression $\exists x A x$ may be seen as an abbreviated method of writing a formula $\neg \forall x \neg A x$, using only symbols from the alphabet above. This is justified by the equivalences described earlier. The two additional axioms are, like the previous three, really axiom schemata in which metasymbols A and B represent any formula.

A Hilbert proof begins with a number of assumptions to which axioms and rules of deduction are applied until a formula of some interest is obtained. The fact that the resulting formula is derived from those assumptions using the Hilbert axioms and rules of deduction is then expressed by the syntactic turnstile:

assumptions $\vdash_H$ formula

2.7.1   The deduction rule

The rule of generalisation may be expressed in a Hilbert deduction as

$A \vdash_H \forall x A(x)$

but it does not generally follow that

$\vdash_H A \to \forall x A(x)$

so the deduction theorem cannot be applied as simply as in the formal system of propositions. The use of the deduction theorem as above is only possible if there is no application of generalisation to a variable that occurs free in A. Certainly, if A is a closed formula, this problem does not arise.

A small proof using quantifier rules shows how formula $\forall x(A \to B(x))$ is proven from the assumption $A \to \forall x B(x)$:

1. $A \to \forall x B(x)$ assumption
2. $\forall x B(x) \to B(a)$ axiom 4
3. $A \to B(a)$ 1, 2 chain
4. $\forall x(A \to B(x))$ generalisation of 3

This deduction is then expressed through the turnstile:

$$A \rightarrow \forall x B(x) \vdash_H \forall x(A \rightarrow B(x))$$

and since x does not occur free in A, the deduction theorem can be applied to give

$$\vdash_H (A \rightarrow \forall x B(x)) \rightarrow \forall x(A \rightarrow B(x))$$

A second example seeks to prove the formula

$$\forall x(P(x) \rightarrow Q(x)) \rightarrow (\forall x P(x) \rightarrow \forall x Q(x))$$

by noting that two applications of the deduction rule might produce such a form. For this reason, the two antecedents make suitable assumptions from which the right-hand subformula might be derived as follows:

1.	$\forall x(P(x) \rightarrow Q(x))$	assumption
2.	$\forall x P(x)$	assumption
3.	$\forall x P(x) \rightarrow P(a)$	axiom 4
4.	$P(a)$	2, 3 *modus ponens*
5.	$\forall x(P(x) \rightarrow Q(x)) \rightarrow (P(a) \rightarrow Q(a))$	axiom 4
6.	$P(a) \rightarrow Q(a)$	1, 5 *modus ponens*
7.	$Q(a)$	4, 6 *modus ponens*
8.	$\forall x Q(x)$	generalisation of 7

The deduction is then expressed in turnstile form:

$$(\forall x(P(x) \rightarrow Q(x))), \forall x P(x) \vdash_H \forall x Q(x)$$

then two applications of the deduction theorem give the desired result:

$$(\forall x(P(x) \rightarrow Q(x))) \vdash_H \forall x P(x) \rightarrow \forall x Q(x)$$
$$\vdash_H (\forall x(P(x) \rightarrow Q(x))) \rightarrow (\forall x P(x) \rightarrow \forall x Q(x))$$

Existential quantifiers are so useful in practice that it is useful to have an existential equivalent of the generalisation property. Such a formula would appear as the theorem

$$\vdash_H P(a) \rightarrow \exists x P(x)$$

and this is easily proven:

1.	$\forall x \neg P(x) \rightarrow \neg P(a)$	axiom 4
2.	$(\forall x \neg P(x) \rightarrow \neg P(a)) \rightarrow (P(a) \rightarrow \neg \forall x \neg P(x))$	contrapositive
3.	$P(a) \rightarrow \neg \forall x \neg P(x)$	1, 2 *modus ponens*
4.	$P(a) \rightarrow \exists x P(x)$	definition

The strategy is to prove the deduction in terms of fragments such as $\neg \forall x \neg P(x)$ then to replace such fragments with the equivalent existential form. Such a strategy has to be adopted in proving the theorem

$$\vdash_H \forall x(P(x) \rightarrow Q(x)) \rightarrow (\exists x P(x) \rightarrow \exists x Q(x))$$

The two antecedents again provide some guidance on the assumptions to be used in proving the formula, but the reason for the second assumption is only clear at the end of the proof:

1. $\forall x(P(x) \rightarrow Q(x))$ assumption
2. $\forall x\neg Q(x)$ assumption
3. $\forall x(P(x) \rightarrow Q(x)) \rightarrow (P(a) \rightarrow Q(a))$ axiom 4
4. $P(a) \rightarrow Q(a)$ 1, 3 *modus ponens*
5. $(P(a) \rightarrow Q(a)) \rightarrow (\neg Q(a) \rightarrow \neg P(a))$ contrapositive
6. $\neg Q(a) \rightarrow \neg P(a)$ 4, 5 *modus ponens*
7. $\forall x\neg Q(x) \rightarrow \neg Q(a)$ axiom 4
8. $\neg Q(a)$ 2, 7 *modus ponens*
9. $\neg P(a)$ 6, 8 *modus ponens*
10. $\forall x\neg P(x)$ generalisation of 9

confirming the following Hilbert deduction:

$$\forall x(P(x) \rightarrow Q(x)), \forall x\neg Q(x) \vdash_H \forall x\neg P(x)$$

from which a final result may be obtained after two applications of the deduction theorem:

$$\forall x(P(x) \rightarrow Q(x)) \vdash_H \forall x\neg Q(x) \rightarrow \forall x\neg P(x) \qquad \text{deduc}$$
$$\vdash_H (\forall x(P(x) \rightarrow Q(x))) \rightarrow (\forall x\neg Q(x) \rightarrow \forall x\neg P(x)) \quad \text{deduc}$$

This is not quite the formula required, but the replacement of one subformula by its contrapositive, followed by a simplification, yields the desired result:

$$\vdash_H (\forall x(P(x) \rightarrow Q(x))) \rightarrow (\neg\forall x\neg P(x) \rightarrow \neg\forall x\neg Q(x))$$
$$\vdash_H (\forall x(P(x) \rightarrow Q(x))) \rightarrow (\exists xP(x) \rightarrow \exists xQ(x))$$

The formulation of proofs in a Hilbert system requires much more experience than the development of a proof for the same formula in the Gentzen G system described earlier. A G system proof arises from the decomposition of a formula whereas a Hilbert proof requires some foresight or experiment to arrive at suitable starting assumptions.

2.7.2 Soundness and completeness

It can be shown that any formula proven in Hilbert's system is valid and the proof system is therefore sound. Thus if M is some set of formulas and F is a formula proven in the deduction system, then

$$M \vdash_H F \text{ implies } M \vDash F$$

Conversely, Gödel's completeness theorem assures us that any valid theorem is provable in the calculus, i.e.

$$M \vDash F \text{ implies } M \vdash_H F$$

Since any valid formula may be proven and anything proven is valid, it might seem that any formula at all may be either proved or disproved. However, soundness and completeness are defined only with respect to valid formulas; they say nothing about an invalid formula. The real problem is that, unlike propositional logic, first-order logic is not decidable, i.e. there is no algorithm that can decide whether or not a formula is valid.

During the early part of the twentieth century, many researchers struggled to find algorithms that would decide the validity of first-order formulas, but none succeeded. Eventually in the mid 1930s Turing and Church separately showed that no such algorithm could ever be developed. Fortunately, this negative result was accompanied by a positive one: Church defined the limit of what could be computed in terms of partial recursive functions. The Church–Turing thesis tells us that first-order logic is partially decidable and that the parts that may be decided are formulated as partial recursive functions. This group of computable functions includes some expressions that are in principle computable, but in practice have exponential complexities, so they rapidly become intractable. A subgroup of primitive recursive functions contains all those computable functions that are needed in practice, and this subgroup is exactly what is required to produce the midsequent in Herbrand's theorem. Church originally formulated his arguments in a notation called lambda calculus, but this is equivalent to the (initial) semantics of terms in first-order logic. More important, this whole area of work gave rise to the functional programming languages described later in this book.

EXERCISES 2.7

1. Use Hilbert axioms to prove the following formulas:

    a. $\forall x P(x) \rightarrow \exists x P(x)$

    b. $\forall x P(x) \rightarrow \forall y P(y)$

    c. $\neg \forall x P(x) \rightarrow \exists y \neg P(y)$

    d. $\forall x (P(x) \wedge Q(x)) \rightarrow \forall x P(x) \wedge \forall x Q(x)$

    e. $\forall x \forall y R(x,y) \rightarrow \forall x R(x,x)$

    f. $\forall x \forall y (Q(x,y) \rightarrow \neg Q(y,x)) \rightarrow \forall x \neg Q(x,x)$

CHAPTER THREE

Principles of logic programming

3.1 REFUTING PROPOSITIONS

G system proofs may be constructed in either of the two normal forms described earlier: proof normal form and refutation normal form. The first of these approaches places formulas in the succedent position then endeavours to falsify the formula and thus the sequent. A deduction tree in which each branch terminates with an axiom, a valid sequent, is sufficient to prove the original formula valid. Refutation normal form, on the other hand, places a negation normal form of the negated formula in the antecedent then systematically attempts to satisfy the formula and thus the sequent. A deduction tree in which each branch terminates with an axiom now indicates contradiction and indirectly shows the validity of the original unnegated proposition.

In order to show the relationship between the normal forms described earlier and the resolution technique described in this chapter, we consider again the proposition

$$(p \rightarrow q) \wedge (q \rightarrow r) \rightarrow (p \rightarrow r)$$

which we already know to be a tautology from its semantic tableau given in Figure 1.8. Using the method of substituting equivalences described in Chapter 1, an NNF of the above formula is derived as follows:

$(p \rightarrow q) \wedge (q \rightarrow r) \rightarrow (p \rightarrow r)$
$\neg((\neg p \vee q) \wedge (\neg q \vee r)) \vee (\neg p \vee r)$ remove implications
$\neg(\neg p \vee q) \vee \neg(\neg q \vee r) \vee (\neg p \vee r)$ De Morgan
$(p \wedge \neg q) \vee (q \wedge \neg r) \vee \neg p \vee r$ De Morgan

In fact, this result is also in DNF and, since the original formula is a tautology, a deduction tree taking either the original formula or its DNF equivalent as the initial succedent would produce only leaf axioms and is a proof tree.

$$\frac{\dfrac{(\neg p \vee q) \wedge (\neg q \vee r) \wedge p \wedge \neg r \Rightarrow}{(\neg p \vee q), (\neg q \vee r), p, \neg r \Rightarrow}}{(\neg p \vee q), \neg q, p, \neg r \Rightarrow \qquad (\neg p \vee q), r, p, \neg r \Rightarrow}$$

$$\neg p, \neg q, p, \neg r \Rightarrow \qquad q, \neg q, p, \neg r \Rightarrow$$

gen left ∧

left ∨ on 2

left ∨ on 3

Figure 3.1   A refutation deduction

Proof normal form does not in fact require the proposition itself to be in any special form, but we saw earlier that an especially interesting case arises when the succedent formula is in DNF, i.e. has the form

$\Rightarrow$ formula$_{dnf}$

In this case all disjunctions may be removed in a general "right ∨" rule, leaving only "right ∧" rules to be applied. Refutation normal form requires the negated antecedent formula to be in NNF, but again an especially interesting property was observed when the formula was also in CNF:

$(\neg$formula$)_{cnf} \Rightarrow$

Now all the conjunctions may be removed in a general "left ∧" inference, leaving only "left ∨" and "left ¬" rules to be applied. Since we are more interested here in refutation normal form, an NNF of the negated formula is required, but this is easily obtained as the dual of the previous proposition:

$(\neg p \vee q) \wedge (\neg q \vee r) \wedge p \wedge \neg r$

Remembering this formula is the negation of one that we wish to prove valid, it is made the antecedent of a sequent which then produces the refutation-style deduction shown in Figure 3.1. All the "left ∧" inferences have been carried out in the first step, leaving an antecedent containing clauses that are then subjected to the "left ∨" rule. Subsequents with dual literals in their antecedents are eventually obtained and the "left ¬" rule might be applied to convert each of them to an axiom. Alternatively, we might simply accept that an antecedent containing these clashing pairs is equivalent to an axiom and stop the tree at this point. Although the form of the deduction tree is illustrated by a particular example, it should be clear that a deduction tree whose root is a CNF antecedent always follows this form. A generalised "left ∧" inference followed by several "left ∨" produces a tree of leaf axioms if the root formula is inconsistent. Since the initial "left ∧" and final "left ¬" operations are little more than formatting procedures, the only effective operation in these deductions is the "left ∨" inference. Thus the refutation is achieved with only one rule in a way similar to the resolution procedure described later.

CNF formulas have a particularly simple structure that admits a simplified notation called clausal form in which logical connectives are not shown. For example, the CNF formula above is represented by the clausal form

$\{\neg p, q\}, \{\neg q, r\}, \{p\}, \{\neg r\}$

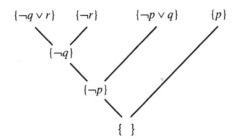

Figure 3.2   Resolution to produce an empty clause

with the understanding that literals within set brackets are joined by disjunctions whereas sets themselves are joined by conjunctions. A resolution proof shows this proposition to be inconsistent by removing clashing pairs of literals from clauses until an empty clause is obtained. Figure 3.2 shows how the dual pair of literals clashing in clauses $\{\neg q, r\}$ and $\{\neg r\}$ is removed to produce a new clause $\{\neg q\}$ that undergoes further resolution. Obtaining an empty clause through this procedure is equivalent to obtaining a tree containing only axioms in a G system refutation. In fact, the three clashing pairs based on r, q and p in Figure 3.2 are quickly related to the three axioms based on the same symbols in Figure 3.1.

In summary, the method of resolution proceeds as follows:

a. Convert the negated formula to CNF.

b. Rewrite the result in clausal form.

c. Apply the resolution step, i.e. from $\{A, X\}$ and $\{B, \neg X\}$ deduce $\{A, B\}$ until an empty clause is obtained.

The three Hilbert propositional axioms are certainly tautologies and this should be easily demonstrated with the resolution procedure. An instance of the first axiom is converted to NNF as follows:

$$p \to (q \to p)$$
$$\neg p \vee (\neg q \vee p) \quad \text{equivalences}$$
$$\neg p \vee \neg q \vee p \quad \text{remove brackets}$$

producing a DNF in which three unit cubes are joined by disjunctions. Notice that in this case the resulting proposition is also in CNF because the resulting proposition may be seen as a single clause. Negation then produces the dual of this proposition

$$p \wedge q \wedge \neg p$$

and when this is shown in clausal form as

$$\{p\}, \{q\}, \{\neg p\}$$

the production of an empty clause is obvious. Although a very small example, this refutation is interesting because it achieves its result without using all of its clauses. One form of a logic law called the compactness theorem states that a clausal form

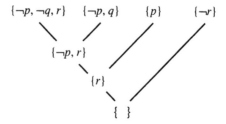

Figure 3.3   Refutation of the negated second axiom

is unsatisfiable if any subset of the clauses is unsatisfiable. Thus if any subproposition is unsatisfiable, the whole proposition is unsatisfiable.

Hilbert's second axiom has the form

$$(p \rightarrow (q \rightarrow r)) \rightarrow ((p \rightarrow q) \rightarrow (p \rightarrow r))$$

and the equivalent DNF of this proposition was derived in Section 1.6 as

$$(p \wedge q \wedge \neg r) \vee (p \wedge \neg q) \vee \neg p \vee r$$

A negated form of this proposition is easily expressed through its dual, automatically in CNF:

$$(\neg p \vee \neg q \vee r) \wedge (\neg p \vee q) \wedge p \wedge \neg r$$

which is expressed in clausal form as

$$\{\neg p, \neg q, r\}, \{\neg p, q\}\{p\}, \{\neg r\}$$

and a resolution diagram leading to an empty clause is shown in Figure 3.3.

Finally, Hilbert's third axiom $(\neg p \rightarrow \neg q) \rightarrow (q \rightarrow p)$ has the negation normal form derived below:

$$(\neg p \rightarrow \neg q) \rightarrow (q \rightarrow p)$$
$$\neg(\neg \neg p \vee \neg q) \vee (\neg q \vee p) \quad \text{equivalences}$$
$$(\neg p \wedge q) \vee \neg q \vee p \qquad \text{De Morgan}$$

producing a result conveniently in DNF. The negation of this proposition is easily expressed in CNF by the following dual form:

$$(p \vee \neg q) \wedge q \wedge \neg p$$

and the clausal form $\{p, \neg q\}, \{q\}, \{\neg p\}$ has obvious clashing literals.

As one further example, consider the semantic tableau of the following proposition, already in CNF:

$$(p \vee \neg q) \wedge (\neg s \vee q) \wedge (\neg s \vee \neg q) \wedge s$$

Figure 3.4a shows that a semantic tableau built from this proposition closes before all of its clauses have been used. Similarly, the resolution diagram of Figure 3.4b produces an empty clause from the equivalent clausal form

$$\{p, \neg q\}, \{\neg s, q\}, \{\neg s, \neg q\}, \{s\}$$

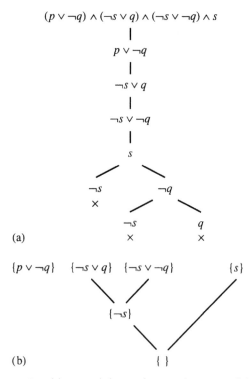

$(p \vee \neg q) \wedge (\neg s \vee q) \wedge (\neg s \vee \neg q) \wedge s$

$p \vee \neg q$

$\neg s \vee q$

$\neg s \vee \neg q$

s

$\neg s$ $\neg q$

$\times$

$\neg s$ q

$\times$ $\times$

(a)

$\{p \vee \neg q\}$ $\{\neg s \vee q\}$ $\{\neg s \vee \neg q\}$ $\{s\}$

$\{\neg s\}$

(b) $\{\ \}$

Figure 3.4   (a) Semantic tableau and (b) resolution of a negated formula

without using the clause $\{p, \neg q\}$. As noted above, any subset of clauses that produces the empty clause is sufficient to refute the whole formula, so the existence of $\{x\}$ and $\{\neg x\}$ in any clausal form is sufficient. When this occurs, the semantic tableau also closes without using all of its clauses.

A resolution step only depends on an implication from left to right:

$$((A \vee X) \wedge (B \vee \neg X)) \rightarrow (A \vee B)$$

and the validity of this formula is shown in the semantic tableau of Figure 3.5. The following proposition is, however, not valid:

$$((A \vee X) \wedge (B \vee \neg X)) \leftrightarrow (A \vee B)$$

Some valuations of the atoms in this mutual implication are a model for the formula, i.e. they make the overall formula *true*, but not all of them do so. It is a useful exercise to derive truth tables for the left- and right-hand sides of the mutual implication and to show that the two are not equivalent.

Figure 3.1 showed how a proposition in CNF is refuted when it is the antecedent of a root sequent in a deduction tree. The form of the example with its CNF antecedent is

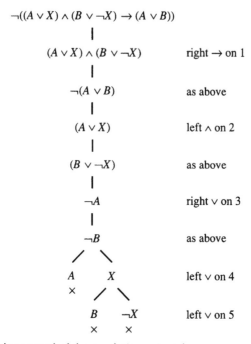

Figure 3.5 A tableau proof of the resolution principle

$$(\neg p \vee q) \wedge (\neg q \vee r) \wedge p \wedge \neg r \Rightarrow$$

but we might be curious to know how the example would have proceeded if the antecedent had been in DNF rather than CNF. In order to find out, we have to find the equivalent formula, rather than the dual form, using algebraic techniques. Since the DNF is equivalent to the previous form, another refutation tree should result, but it is the form of this tree that is of interest. To convert CNF to DNF, the clauses are "multiplied out" rather like arithmetic formulas; for example, the first two clauses multiply out to give a product proposition

$$(\neg p \vee q) \wedge (\neg q \vee r) \cong (\neg p \wedge \neg q) \vee (\neg p \wedge r) \vee (q \wedge \neg q) \vee (q \wedge r)$$

and this result is "multiplied" by proposition $p \wedge \neg r$:

$$((\neg p \wedge \neg q) \vee (\neg p \wedge r) \vee (q \wedge \neg q) \vee (q \wedge r)) \wedge (p \wedge \neg r)$$
$$\cong (\neg p \wedge \neg q \wedge p \wedge \neg r) \vee (\neg p \wedge r \wedge p \wedge \neg r) \vee (q \wedge \neg q \wedge p \wedge \neg r)$$
$$\vee (q \wedge r \wedge p \wedge \neg r)$$

A Gentzen style refutation taking the resulting proposition as antecedent immediately divides through a generalised "left ∨" into four subsequents of the form

$$\neg p \wedge \neg q \wedge p \wedge \neg r \Rightarrow$$

then a generalised "left ∧" applied to each subsequent produces sequents of the form

$$\neg p, \neg q, p, \neg r \Rightarrow$$

with a clashing pair of literals. Every cube in the DNF contains a pair of complementary literals that immediately produces an axiom, so a refutation of this kind always stops after the first step.

EXERCISES 3.1

1. Convert each of the following tautologies into disjunctive normal form then derive the dual to give a formula in conjunctive normal form:

   a. $(p \vee q) \rightarrow (q \vee p)$
   b. $((p \rightarrow q) \wedge \neg q) \rightarrow \neg p$
   c. $(p \rightarrow (q \rightarrow r)) \rightarrow (p \wedge r \rightarrow q)$
   d. $(p \rightarrow r) \wedge (\neg q \rightarrow \neg r) \rightarrow (p \rightarrow q)$
   e. $(p \rightarrow r) \wedge (q \rightarrow r) \rightarrow (p \vee q \rightarrow r)$

2. Produce refutation trees smilar to Figure 3.1 for each of the CNF propositions obtained in the previous exercise.

3. Express each of the CNF propositions from Exercise 1 in clausal form and show through resolution that the formula is unsatisfiable.

4. The converse of the resolution proposition is

   $$(A \vee B) \rightarrow (A \vee X) \wedge (B \vee \neg X)$$

   Show that this proposition is not valid, by tableau and by writing out the truth table.

5. Prove the following mutual equivalence by proving two separate implications in tableaux or G system proofs:

   $$((A \vee X) \wedge (B \vee \neg X)) \leftrightarrow (A \vee X) \wedge (B \vee \neg X) \wedge (A \vee B)$$

3.2   REFUTING FORMULAS

The previous section showed a close relationship between the refutation normal form of a G system deduction and resolution applied to the same proposition. Now we have to extend this connection to deductions involving the quantified formulas described in Chapter 2.

Figure 2.3 shows a semantic tableau for the negation of formula

$$\forall x(P(x) \rightarrow Q(x)) \rightarrow (\forall x P(x) \rightarrow \forall x Q(x))$$

and it is clear from the tableau that every path is closed, the negated formula is a contradiction and the original formula is therefore valid. This formula might equally well have been made the succedent of a sequent and the same series of inference rules applied as in the tableau construction. A proof tree in which every leaf is an axiom then shows the validity of the original formula. In the manner of the previous section, we now convert this formula to its equivalent negation normal form:

$$(\forall x(P(x) \rightarrow Q(x)) \rightarrow (\forall x P(x) \rightarrow \forall x Q(x)))$$
$$\neg \forall x(\neg P(x) \vee Q(x)) \vee (\neg \forall x P(x) \vee \forall x Q(x)) \quad \text{identity}$$
$$\exists x \neg(\neg P(x) \vee Q(x)) \vee \exists x \neg P(x) \vee \forall x Q(x) \quad \text{identity}$$
$$\exists x(P(x) \wedge \neg Q(x)) \vee \exists x \neg P(x) \vee \forall x Q(x) \quad \text{De Morgan}$$

A G system proof taking the resulting NNF formula as its succedent produces a proof tree, but obviously the series of inferences required to achieve this is different from that required for the original formula. At this point, we are more interested in a refutation normal form of the Gentzen-style deduction, so the above NNF is negated and manipulated back into NNF as follows:

$$\neg(\exists x(P(x) \wedge \neg Q(x)) \vee \exists x \neg P(x) \vee \forall x Q(x))$$
$$\neg \exists x(P(x) \wedge \neg Q(x)) \wedge \neg \exists x \neg P(x) \wedge \neg \forall x Q(x) \quad \text{De Morgan}$$
$$\forall x \neg(P(x) \wedge \neg Q(x)) \wedge \forall x \neg \neg P(x) \wedge \exists x \neg Q(x) \quad \text{identities}$$
$$\forall x(\neg P(x) \vee Q(x)) \wedge \forall x P(x) \wedge \exists x \neg Q(x) \quad \text{De Morgan}$$

noting that the result could have been written directly as the dual of the earlier NNF formula. The resulting formula may be made the antecedent of a sequent and deduction might proceed using the subformula rules introduced in Chapter 2. A refutation shown in Figure 3.6 adopts this approach, creating a midsequent after three quantifier inferences and axioms after further propositional operations. Notice that after the midsequent is obtained, the process of deduction is exactly that described in the preceding section on propositions. A single generalised "left ∧" rule may be used to convert the midsequent to a list of clauses and the "left ¬" rule might be completely avoided if we accept an antecedent with dual literals as an axiom. As a result, only the "left ∨" rule is significant in the production of the final result.

In order to develop a resolution refutation approach for quantified formulas, we first replace existentially quantified variables with Skolem functions. In this particular case, a single variable is replaced by a constant to give the formula

$$\forall x(\neg P(x) \vee Q(x)) \wedge \forall y P(y) \wedge \neg Q(a)$$

Figure 3.6   A refutation deduction

At the same time, the second use of variable x has been replaced by a distinct variable y. Since all remaining variables are represented by distinct symbols and must be universally quantified, there is no longer any need to show quantifier symbols and the formula appears as

$$(\neg P(x) \vee Q(x)) \wedge P(y) \wedge \neg Q(a)$$

or, if written in clausal form, as follows:

$$\{\neg P(x), Q(x)\}, \{P(y)\}, \{\neg Q(a)\}$$

Resolution steps can now be applied to the clausal form in a development of the procedure explained earlier. Again the object is to resolve out new clauses from pairs of existing clauses that contain clashing atoms, but the existence of terms in the atoms makes this more complicated than before. Although $\neg P(x)$ and $P(y)$ do not appear to clash, if x is substituted for y or vice versa, the atoms become identical and $Q(x)$ or $Q(y)$ may be resolved from the pair. Similarly $Q(x)$ and $\neg Q(a)$ do not immediately clash, but the constant a may be substituted for variable x and a clash obtained. Notice that the substitution may be carried out either way round when both are variables, but in only one direction if one is a constant. When a choice exists, it is better to take the option that leaves the greatest number of variables in the resolvant, allowing further resolutions to take place. Figure 3.7 shows how these interleaved substitutions and resolutions lead to an empty clause, proving that the formula being resolved is unsatisfiable. Since this formula is the negation of the one in which we are really interested, the original unnegated formula must be valid.

Gentzen-style proofs become increasingly difficult as the size and complexity of the sequent to be proven or refuted increases. Left universal quantifications present particular problems because they might have to be used several times to obtain different ground-state formulas that might then be subjected to propositional rules. It is difficult in such deductions to know which instantiations are required to close the final deduction tree, so much experimentation is required. The problem is one of needing to see ahead in order to instantiate universally quantified formulas with appropriate constants. Repeated resolution of Skolemised formulas, on the other hand, leads to a systematic method of attempting every possible instantiation until a refutation is achieved. Furthermore, resolution is mechanised in a fairly direct way to produce the logic languages described in the following sections.

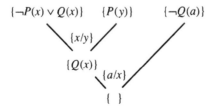

Figure 3.7 A resolution diagram with predicates

$$\forall y P(a,y) \wedge \forall x \neg P(x,b) \Rightarrow$$

	$P(a,b) \wedge \forall x \neg P(x,b) \Rightarrow$	left $\forall$ on 1
midseq	$P(a,b) \wedge \neg P(a,b) \Rightarrow$	left $\forall$ on 2
	$P(a,b), \neg P(a,b) \Rightarrow$	left $\wedge$ on 3
	$P(a,b) \Rightarrow P(a,b)$	left $\neg$ on 4

Figure 3.8 A refutation deduction

A hint of the problems that might be encountered in a G system proof appears in a deduction from the following small formula:

$$\exists x \forall y P(x,y) \rightarrow \forall y \exists x P(x,y)$$

This example is quickly translated into negation normal form

$$\forall x \exists y \neg P(x,y) \vee \forall y \exists x P(x,y)$$

Refutation requires that we take the dual of this formula which, by inspection, we are able to write as

$$\exists x \forall y P(x,y) \wedge \exists y \forall x \neg P(x,y)$$

Existentially quantified variables may then be replaced by Skolem constants to give the simpler form

$$\forall y P(a,y) \vee \forall x \neg P(x,b)$$

We can then show this to be unsatisfiable in the deduction tree of Figure 3.8. The deduction tree clearly demonstrates unsatisfiability, but the way in which this result is obtained indicates problems ahead. Notice that formula $\forall y P(a,y)$ is instantiated to $P(a,b)$, but it could have been instantiated with domain element a to $P(a,a)$ or with any other available domain element. Equally, $\forall x \neg P(x,b)$ might have been instantiated to $\neg P(b,b)$ but this was not done because it was obvious that $\neg P(a,b)$ was required to terminate the deduction. In this case there are just two formulas in the initial antecedent and the necessary instantiations are obvious; but as the examples get larger, the required instantiations become less obvious. If the above formula is drafted in clausal form as $\{P(a,y)\}\ \{\neg P(x,b)\}$, it is clear that substitution $\{a/x,\ b/y\}$ produces a clash of atoms and no other substitutions need be considered. In larger examples the guidance provided by the need to produce clashing pairs makes problems tractable.

3.2.1 Substitution and resolution

Clauses derived from full first-order logic formulas are resolved when a clashing pair occurs in two different clauses in much the same way as clauses of propositions. A general scheme for resolving formula literals might be written as

$$\{A(x), P(z)\} \wedge \{B(y), \neg P(z)\} \rightarrow \{A(x), B(y)\}$$

However, unlike the propositional case, it is possible to have pairs of literals that clash only after appropriate substitutions of terms have been made in the atomic arguments. One approach is to instantiate all terms to ground states, i.e. to replace all variables by constants, and then attempt to resolve the resulting ground clauses. The problem here is that a great many different ground clauses are possible and it is not always easy to see which ones are required to produce a refutation. This is in fact much the same problem that arises in choosing suitable instantiations in a semantic tableau or G system tree deduction. A cleverer approach interleaves substitutions and resolutions so that the minimum necessary substitutions are made before each resolution step. An accumulation of each of these individual substitutions is then used to compute an equivalent single-step substitution.

The process of making two atoms the same through substitution is called unification. Taking the simplest example first, $P(z)$ unifies with $P(w)$ after the substitution $\{w/z\}$ or with $P(c)$ after substitution $\{c/z\}$. Atoms with different predicate symbols cannot be unified and cannot therefore be resolved out of a clause, e.g. $P(x)$ and $Q(y)$ cannot be unified. Substitutions only apply to variables appearing as arguments in atoms so that, even when predicate symbols are identical, differences of constants prevent unification, e.g. $P(a)$ and $P(b)$ cannot be unified. Atoms with two arguments might require a double substitution before unification occurs, e.g. $Q(a,x)$ and $Q(y,b)$ are unified by the substitution $\{a/y, b/x\}$. Sometimes one substitution forces another; for example, the unification of $Q(x,x)$ and $Q(a,y)$ requires substitution a/x, but since x occurs twice in the first atom, a further substitution a/y is also necessary.

Functions occurring as arguments are handled in much the same way as simple constants, e.g. $Q(x, f(a))$ and $Q(g(b), y)$ are unified by the substitution $\{g(b)/x, f(a)/y\}$. In a slightly more complicated example, $Q(x, f(x))$ and $Q(g(b), y)$ are unified by the substitution $\{g(b)/x, f(g(b))/y\}$. Notice that ground atoms result from unification in both of these examples and there is no alternative substitution. In contrast, the atoms $Q(x, f(x))$ and $Q(y, f(z))$ may be unified in two ways:

a. By $\{c/x, c/y, c/z\}$ to give $Q(c, f(c))$.
b. By $\{x/y, x/z\}$ to give $Q(x, f(x))$.

The second example admits a further substitution that produces the same result as the first:

$$Q(x, f(x)) \{c/x\} = Q(c, f(c))$$

and is considered to be a more general unifier. In fact, this substitution is the most general unifier (mgu) possible for the atoms, leaving open the maximum possible number of subsequent substitutions. An mgu is obtained by avoiding the instantiation of constants wherever possible.

Atoms with more than two arguments are treated in exactly the same way as above, e.g. atoms $R(a, f(x), y)$ and $R(w, f(z), z)$ are unified in two ways:

a. By $\{a/w, a/x, a/y, a/z\}$ to give $R(a, f(a), a)$.

b. By $\{a/w, z/x, z/y\}$ to give $R(a, f(z), z)$.

The second method is the most general unifier for the two atoms. Notice that the most general unifier is not unique and $Q(a, f(x), x)$ or $Q(a, f(y), y)$ might have been obtained with a different strategy.

3.2.2   Robinson's algorithm

Unifications might be found by inspection, as in the examples above, but if the process is to be mechanised, they have to be discovered by a fixed algorithm. Robinson's algorithm for finding an mgu is fairly simple: just work from left to right through the arguments of a pair of atoms, making whatever substitutions are necessary to unify each individual argument. A composition of the substitutions then provides the unifier. The arguments in atoms $P(w, f(a), z)$ and $P(b,x,y)$ are unified as follows:

	$P(w, f(a), z)$	$P(b,x,y)$	
Arg 1	$P(b, f(a), z)$	$P(b,x,y)$	$\{b/w\}$
Arg 2	$P(b, f(a), z)$	$P(b, f(a), y)$	$\{f(a)/x\}$
Arg 3	$P(b, f(a), z)$	$P(b, f(a), z)$	$\{z/y\}$

When the last pair of arguments has been unified, the atoms themselves have been unified and, provided no unnecessary constants have been introduced, this procedure generates the most general unifier for the two atoms. A single equivalent substitution is obtained from the composition of individual substitutions

$$\{b/w\} \circ \{f(a)/x\} \circ \{z/y\} = \{b/w, f(a)/x, z/y\}$$

Here the single unifier is the sum of the individual substitutions, but this might not always be the case. A variable substituted into a term might itself be removed in a later substitution and this chaining of replacements has to be reflected when individual steps are combined. Such a problem occurs when atoms $Q(x, f(y,a))$ and $Q(z, f(z,z))$ are unified by Robinson's method:

	$Q(x, f(y,a))$	$Q(z, f(z,z))$	
Arg 1	$Q(z, f(y,a))$	$Q(z, f(z,z))$	$\{z/x\}$
Arg 2	$Q(z, f(z,a))$	$Q(z, f(z,z))$	$\{z/y\}$
Arg 3	$Q(a, f(a,a))$	$Q(a, f(a,a))$	$\{a/z\}$

An allowance has to be made for the fact that x and y were initally replaced by z, but this variable was then itself replaced by constant a, so the net effect is that all variables are replaced by constant a:

$\{z/x\} \circ \{z/y\} \circ \{a/z\} = \{a/x, a/y, a/z\}$

A final and larger example unifies atoms $S(x, g(f(z), v, a))$ and $S(f(y), g(x, h(x), y))$, demonstrating the approach when argument functions themselves contain functions:

	$S(x, g(f(z)), v, a))$	$S(f(y), g(x, h(x), y))$	
Arg 1	$S(f(y), g(f(z)), v, a))$	$S(f(y), g(f(y), h(f(y))), y))$	$\{f(y)/x\}$
Arg 2	$S(f(y), g(f(y)), v, a))$	$S(f(y), g(f(y)), h(f(y))), y))$	$\{y/z\}$
Arg 3	$S(f(y), g(f(y)), h(f(y))), a))$	$S(f(y), g(f(y)), h(f(y))), y))$	$\{h(f(y))/v\}$
Arg 4	$S(f(a), g(f(a)), h(f(a))), a))$	$S(f(a), g(f(a), h(f(a))), a))$	$\{a/y\}$

and the unifying substitution is obtained from the sum of individual steps:

$\{f(y)/x\} \circ \{y/z\} \circ \{h(f(y))/v\} \circ \{a/y\} = \{f(a)/x, a/z, h(f(a))/v, a/y\}$

EXERCISES 3.2

1. Convert each of the following valid formulas into negation normal form and convert the resulting formula to its dual form:

   a. $\forall x P(x) \wedge \forall x Q(x) \rightarrow \forall x(P(x) \vee Q(x))$

   b. $\exists x(P(x) \wedge Q(x)) \rightarrow \exists x P(x) \vee \exists x Q(x)$

   c. $\forall x(P(x) \rightarrow Q(x)) \wedge \exists x(R(x) \wedge P(x)) \rightarrow \exists x(R(x) \vee Q(x))$

   d. $\forall x(P(x) \rightarrow Q(x)) \leftrightarrow \neg \exists x(P(x) \wedge \neg Q(x))$

   e. $\exists x(P(x) \wedge \forall y(Q(y) \rightarrow R(x,y))) \wedge$
      $(\forall x P(x) \rightarrow \forall y(S(y) \rightarrow \neg R(x,y))) \rightarrow \forall x(Q(x) \vee \neg S(x))$

2. Produce refutation trees similar to that shown in Figure 3.6 for each of the dual formulas obtained in the previous exercise.

3. Skolemise out any existentially quantified variables in the NNF dual formulas obtained from Exercise 1, convert the resulting formulas to clausal form and show they are unsatisfiable in a refutation diagram.

4. Produce unifying substitutions for the following pairs of atoms or explain why unification is not possible:

   $P(a)$ and $Q(x)$
   $R(f(a))$ and $R(f(b))$
   $Q(x)$ and $Q(f(a))$
   $Q(x)$ and $Q(f(y))$
   $R(x, f(x))$ and $P(f(a), y)$
   $R(x, f(a))$ and $R(g(b), f(y))$

5. Use Robinson's algorithm to unify the following pairs of atoms and so produce unifying substitutions:

   $P(w, f(a), z)$ and $P(b, x, g(x))$
   $R(x, z, f(a))$ and $R(y, g(b), x)$
   $Q(x, x, a)$ and $Q(y, f(z), z)$

3.3 HORN CLAUSES AND FORWARD CHAINING

Resolution might show that a collection of clauses is unsatisfiable by showing that successive removal of clashing literals from pairs of disjunctions leads to an empty clause. The technique can be applied to sets of clauses containing arbitrary numbers of literals with and without negation symbols. In order to convert logic statements into a form that may be animated, clauses have to be restricted to the Horn clause form described below. Statements in Horn clause form are equivalent to a logic program that may be used to answer questions on the basis of a number of axioms called facts and rules. This section is concerned with the generation of all theorems or *true* statements from program axioms through the process of forward chaining. The following section uses a technique called backward chaining to decide whether a specific statement is *true* in the environment created by a particular program.

3.3.1 Horn clauses

A Horn clause is a disjunction of literals containing at most one positive literal. Clauses containing this one allowed positive literal are called definite clauses whereas those without such a literal are called negative clauses. Definite clauses have the general form

$$R \vee \neg A \vee \neg B \vee \neg C \vee \ldots$$

but one application of the generalised De Morgan rule to the negated atoms in this formula introduces the following alternative formulations:

$$R \vee \neg(A \wedge B \wedge C \wedge \ldots)$$
$$R \leftarrow A \wedge B \wedge C \wedge \ldots$$

Notice that in logic programming it is convenient to write an implication from right to left and to read the reversed implication statement as "if". Thus R is *true* if A and B and C ... are *true*. A reverse implication of this sort is related to disjunction through a variation of the familiar identity

$$Y \vee \neg X \cong Y \leftarrow X$$

A definite clause must contain one positive literal, but need not contain a negative literal, so a single positive literal is also a Horn clause. Such a clause is usually shown in the form $R \leftarrow$ or more simply as just R.

A definite program is a collection of definite clauses written in both resolution form and as a logic program:

1. $p \wedge$ p
2. $q \wedge$ q
3. $r \vee \neg t \vee \neg s \wedge$ $r \leftarrow t, s$
4. $r \vee \neg q \vee \neg t \wedge$ $r \leftarrow q, t$
5. $t \vee \neg p \qquad \wedge$ $t \leftarrow p$
6. $t \vee \neg q \vee \neg s$ $t \leftarrow q, s$

The meaning or interpretation of a propositional definite program is a valuation of the atomic statements in the program, usually expressed as the set of those statements that are *true*. Thus an interpretation in which none of the program statements is *true* is shown as an empty set:

$$I0 = \{ \ \}$$

but this cannot be a model for the program. A first pass through the program reveals that statements p and q occur as facts and any valuation that acts as a model must include them among its *true* statements. The next attempt at a model might therefore be the set

$$I1 = \{p, q\}$$

but this too proves to be inadequate. Passing down the program a second time, armed with the knowledge that elements p and q are *true*, we encounter the clause $t \leftarrow p$ and deduce by resolution that t must also be *true*. This leads to a further improved attempt:

$$I2 = \{p, q, t\}$$

but another pass through the program, starting with $I2$, establishes r as a consequence of the clause $r \leftarrow q, t$, forcing us again to expand the interpretation:

$$I3 = \{p, q, t, r\}$$

Further passes through the program do not produce any new *true* statements, so $I3$ is a "fixed-point" interpretation for the program. The meaning of a program is clearly obtained by forward chaining in repeated passes through the program, generating greater numbers of *true* statements until the fixed point is reached. The distinctive advantage of definite programs over arbitrary clauses is that a fixed point of this kind is always obtained.

Clauses derived from first-order logic formulas carry implicit universal quantifications and might be better shown as

$$\forall (R \leftarrow A \wedge B \wedge C \wedge \ldots)$$
$$\forall (R \leftarrow)$$

Once again, these clauses are equivalent to the axioms of a formal system, so the program is a theory. An interpretation that is a model for each of these axioms is also a model for the theory.

Unfortunately there exist an infinite number of possible interpretations when a program includes predicates, and some way of expressing every possible interpretation in a single form is required. One way of doing this is suggested by the Herbrand and Skolem–Herbrand–Gödel theorems of Chapter 2. It was shown there that quantified formulas are proven or refuted if and only if special kinds of quantifier-free formulas appearing in the midsequent are proven or refuted. The deduction trees used to demonstrate validity or contradiction use one particular interpretation to characterise the properties of an infinite number of other interpretations. In effect, a Herbrand interpretation uses the formal symbols themselves to characterise every possible interpretation. Thus, predicate symbols P, Q, ... are represented by the letters P, Q, ... and term symbols a, b, c, ..., f, g, h, ... are also represented by their own characters. Existentially quantified variables will have been replaced in refutation mode by Skolem functions and universally quantified variables will not introduce further constants into a definite program. As a result, the domain of a Herbrand interpretation is restricted to a special set called the Herbrand universe (sometimes called the Herbrand domain). This restriction on domain elements limits the number of possible interpretations of each predicate to a set called the Herbrand base; the set that can be constructed from objects in the Herbrand universe. A small definite program with predicates is now provided as an example:

$P(a)$

$Q(b)$

$P(x) \leftarrow Q(x)$

$R(y) \leftarrow P(y)$

This program contains no functions and thus has the simple Herbrand universe $\{a, b\}$ with just two constants. Its Herbrand base contains all the atoms of the program in every possible ground state, and since there are two constants and three arity-one predicates, this amounts to a set of six ground atoms:

$\{P(a), P(b), Q(a), Q(b), R(a), R(b)\}$

Herbrand interpretations of programs with predicates differ only in their valuations of atoms in the Herbrand base. An interpretation is usually described by the set of atoms mapped to *true*, all other atoms being assumed *false*. Clearly the simplest possible Herbrand interpretation ($I0$) for the above program is the empty set of base atoms

$I0 = \{\ \}$

but this is not a model for the program. No base atom evaluates to *true* in this interpretation, but the program requires that $P(a)$ and $Q(b)$ are *true* because these are facts in the program. Any interpretation capable of acting as a model for the program must at least contain these two atoms, so a next attempt might be

$I1 = \{P(a), Q(b)\}$

Here the two atoms shown are evaluated to *true* and the remaining atoms to *false*. Although this interpretation acts as a model for the first two clauses of the program, it fails on the third. Interpretation $I1$ evaluates atom $Q(b)$ as *true* and the program contains formula $P(x) \leftarrow Q(x)$, making atom $P(b)$ *true* by resolution A Herbrand interpretation without this atom cannot act as a model for the program, forcing us to expand the previous attempt to

$$I2 = \{P(a), Q(b), P(b)\}$$

Similar reasoning based on the fourth clause demands a further expansion of the interpretation to include $R(a)$ and finally to Herbrand interpretation $I3$, which does act as a model for the program:

$$I3 = \{P(a), Q(b), P(b), R(a)\}$$

It should be clear that the method used to arrive at this interpretation is the forward-chaining procedure described earlier. An interpretation containing the least number of elements is always obtained when it is generated in this way, and any other interpretation that is a model for the program must contain all the elements of this set. Although they are models, interpretations taking further atoms from the Herbrand base, including interpretations taking the base itself, are less useful than the minimum model. In fact, the set of atoms obtained as the fixed point of forward chaining through a definite program defines the meaning of the program: it is a statement of all the atoms that may be proven *true*. Thus the least Herbrand model defines the semantics of a program.

As a second example of a logic program, consider the definite formulas describing the linkages shown in Figure 3.9. This diagram contains an example of a directed acyclic graph, directed because the arrows limit movements in one direction only, acyclic because it is not possible to return to the same point in the graph. An alternative representation of the information in the diagram is possible through the following facts:

$Path(a,b)$, $Path(b,d)$, $Path(d,e)$, $Path(a,c)$, $Path(c,e)$

Suppose now that we want to describe every pair of points that are connected by paths in the graph, listing all allowed routes in the graph. The simplest routes are the links themselves and this observation could be formalised by the rule

$Route(x,y) \leftarrow Path(x,y)$

There are also a number of routes passing over more than one link. For example, a route from b to e via d is possible and this may be expressed in the clause

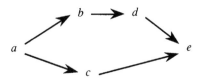

Figure 3.9   A directed acyclic graph

Route(b,e) ← *Path(b,d)*, *Path(d,e)*

Routes over increasing numbers of intermediate points may be described by introducing variables into similar clauses:

Route(x,z) ← *Path(x,y)*, *Path(y,z)*
Route(w,z) ← *Path(w,x)*, *Path(x,y)*, *Path(y,z)*

A route might pass overy many links in a larger graph and different rules would have to be used for routes with different numbers of intermediate stages. A more elegant solution than this encapsulates routes with differing numbers of intermediate points in a single rule:

Route(x,z) ← *Path(x,y)*, *Route(y,z)*

There is a route from x to z if there is a path from x to some intermediate point y and a route from there to z. The final program then has the form

1. *Path(a,b)*
2. *Path(a,c)*
3. *Path(b,d)*
4. *Path(c,e)*
5. *Path(d,e)*
6. *Route(x,y)* ← *Path(x,y)*
7. *Route(x,z)* ← *Path(x,y)*, *Route(y,z)*

and it would be of interest to find the least Herbrand model of this program. First of all, the Herbrand universe of this program is the set $\{a, b, c, d, e\}$ and the Herbrand base contains the two predicates in every possible ground state:

{*Path(a,a)*, *Path(a,b)*, *Path(b,a)*, ...
Route(a,a), *Route(a,b)*, *Route(b,a)*, ... }

There are five constants in the Herbrand universe and thus $25 = 5 \times 5$ pairs of arguments that might appear in either of the two predicates, producing a Herbrand base of 50 atoms. An interpretation $I0$ in which none of these base atoms is assigned *true* is shown as the empty set

$$I0 = \{ \}$$

but this is certainly not a model for the program. In order to find the minimal interpretation required for the least Herbrand model, a series of interpretations based on forward chaining through the program is explored. Interpretation $I1$ contains those base atoms known to be true from the facts of the program alone:

$$I1 = \{Path(a,b), Path(a,c), Path(b,d), Path(c,e), Path(d,e)\}$$

A second attempt adds the *Route* ground atoms generated by clause 6:

$$I2 = I1 \cup \{Route(a,b), Route(a,c), Route(b,d), Route(c,e), Route(d,e)\}$$

A further pass uses clause 7 to generate interpretation *I3*, containing routes with one intermediate point in addition to the atoms of *I2*:

I3 = *I2* ∪ {*Route(a,d)*, *Route(a,e)*, *Route(b,e)*}

and a final pass generates the one route spanning two intermediate points:

I4 = *I3* ∪ {*Route(a,e)*}

but this adds nothing new because *Route(a,e)* already occurs in *I3*. No more ground states can be added in this way, so a fixed-point interpretation has been obtained. The model *I3* obtained by forward chaining to the fixed point is called the least Herbrand model of the program and is a characteristic feature of a definite program, defining the meaning of the program. Different models may be obtained by adding further base elements to the least Herbrand model, but such models would not be particularly helpful or informative.

Both of the examples above have a finite universe, making the enumeration of the least Herbrand model a practical proposition, but the presence of functions makes this impossible. Interpretations for functions are considered in more detail in Chapter 6, so we just note the problem of an infinite Herbrand universe here. A formal system defining the natural numbers is provided by the constant *zero* and the successor function *succ* as follows

zero, *succ(zero)*, *succ(succ(zero))*, etc.

and a program to add such numbers may be written as follows:

Add(x, zero, x)
Add(x, succ(y), succ(z)) ← *Add(x,y,z)*

Adding *x* to *zero* gives *x* and adding *x* to *succ(y)* gives *succ(z)* if adding *x* to *y* gives *z*. The series of constants above is usually interpreted by the numbers 0, 1, 2, ..., but a Herbrand interpretation takes the strings themselves as the interpretation. Hence the Herbrand universe of this program is an infinite but denumerable series of constants; attempts to define a fixed-point interpretation, as we have done earlier, will therefore not succeed.

3.3.2   Soundness and completeness

Logic programs are syntactic statements in a simplified form of first-order logic: they are collections of axioms from which further statements may be deduced according to a set of deduction rules. Since they consist entirely of definite clauses, only positive statements may be derived. At the same time, the least Herbrand model represents a particular interpretation of the program, equivalent to the intended interpretation. This representation is generated by a production rule that gradually increases the number of known *true* facts until a fixed point is obtained. Now if a given ground fact is derived from program *P* by proof theoretic reasoning, we write

$P \vdash F$

and if that fact is *true* in the least Herbrand interpretation (M_P) we write

$M_P \vDash F$

But the least Herbrand model is a collection of all the facts that can be derived from the program, so logical consequence must follow from derivability. A predicate that is derived from the program must be *true* and the method of deduction is therefore sound; conversely, the *true* statements are those that may be derived, so the method is complete.

3.3.3   The Datalog language

A forward-chaining strategy such as that described in connection with the least Herbrand model may be used as the basis of a logic language. Programs are divided into two parts: an extensional part containing factual information and an intensional part consisting of rules from which further ground states are derived. Such programs are seen as databases that store some of their information in the form of production rules but most of it in the form of an extensional database of facts. When presented with a query, the extensional database is first checked; if this check fails and there are rules that may be applied, further ground facts are produced. Repeated applications of the rules produce more ground facts until the fixed point is reached; if the desired predicate has not been found by this time, it will never be found. There are many different languages of this kind, but all of them are included in a general area described as Datalog languages. If we have a specific query that can be presented to a definite Datalog program, the question arising is, can this predicate be derived from the facts and rules of the program? Suppose we wish to know if *Route(a,d)* follows from the program *P* above, we are asking if it can be proven from the program that

$P \vdash Route(a,d)$

or, in terms of the least Herbrand interpretation M_P, if this atom is contained in the fixed point obtained by forward chaining:

$\{ \ldots , Route(a,d), \ldots \} \vDash Route(a,d)$

The basic principles of Datalog programs are clearly quite simple: just forward chain through the program until the desired result is obtained. If a fixed point is obtained without finding the result, it is assumed to be untrue.

A Datalog program has fairly simple semantics: its meaning is revealed by forward chaining to the fixed point and is therefore exactly that of the least Herbrand model. Intensional database rules may be applied in any order, but the same defining fixed-point set of predicates is always obtained. Forward chaining generates duplicate copies of the same predicate, and implementations have to ensure that such duplicates are removed at each stage. Even so, the method generates many predicates that are of no interest to a user, and its attractive semantics is to some extent offset by problems in implementation. Much of the work in this area is carried out in connection with the set-oriented relational databases described in Chapter 10.

EXERCISES 3.3

1. Obtain the least Herbrand interpretation of the following definite program by forward chaining until a fixed point is obtained:

    p
    $s \leftarrow p$
    $s \leftarrow r, v$
    $r \leftarrow s$
    $t \leftarrow u, s$
    $v \leftarrow p, r$

2. Write down the Herbrand universe, Herbrand base and least Herbrand interpretation for the following program:

    $P(a)$
    $Q(b)$
    $R(x) \leftarrow Q(x)$
    $S(x) \leftarrow P(x), R(x)$

3. Write down the Herbrand universe, Herbrand base and least Herbrand interpretation for the following program:

    $R(a)$
    $P(a,b)$
    $P(b,c)$
    $Q(x,y) \leftarrow P(y,x)$
    $S(x) \leftarrow Q(x,y), R(y)$

3.4   BACKWARD CHAINING AND SLD RESOLUTION

Backward chaining does not require the generation and storage of large numbers of intermediate predicates because it works backwards from the goal using only the rules it needs. This technique is based on the simple observation that if a statement S can be derived from a program, i.e.

   $Program \vdash S$

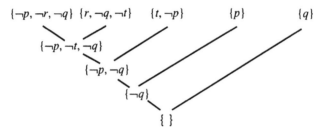

Figure 3.10 Backward chaining from a goal clause

a conjugation of the program and negated statement S must be inconsistent. To show that S follows from the program, we have to show that the formula *Program* $\wedge \neg S$ is inconsistent, or in terms of the interpretation, that it is a contradiction. To show that *Route(a,d)* can be derived from our earlier program P, we have to show that

$$\{P\} \wedge \neg Route(a,d)$$

must be a contradiction. Thus the production of a contradiction between the negated query and the program refutes the statement and indirectly shows the query to be *true*. This is of course the refutation style discussed earlier, so backward chaining is essentially a refutation argument.

The definite program given at the beginning of the previous section may be written in clausal form as

$$\{p\}, \{q\}, \{r, \neg t, \neg s\}, \{r, \neg q, \neg t\}, \{t, \neg p\}, \{t, \neg q, \neg s\}$$

Forward chaining revealed that this program is equivalent to the clausal form $\{p\}, \{q\}, \{t\}, \{r\}$. In other words, the meaning of the program may be expressed as $p \wedge q \wedge t \wedge r$ and a question like "is $p \wedge q \wedge r$ *true*?" is easily answered by checking that propositional statements in the query appear in the Herbrand model.

Adopting the backward-chaining approach, we show that proposition $p \wedge q \wedge r$ is *true* by showing that the negation of this query is inconsistent with the program. The dual of the query is $\neg p \vee \neg q \vee \neg r$ and this is expressed as a negative Horn clause $\{\neg p, \neg q, \neg r\}$. Figure 3.10 shows how this goal is resolved against succesive program clauses until the empty clause is obtained, proving that the negated query is inconsistent with the program. Goals are resolved against definite clauses to produce subgoals until the empty clause is obtained, refuting a conjugation of the negated clause with the program.

Such a procedure obviously has to begin with the goal clause, but there remains a choice of literals within the goal that might be selected for resolution and a choice of clauses against which the selected literal might be resolved. The method shown in Figure 3.10 selects the middle literal of the initial goal and resolves this against an appropriate clause:

$$\{\neg p, \neg r, \neg q\} \wedge \{r, \neg q, \neg t\} \rightarrow \{\neg p, \neg q, \neg q, \neg t\}$$

but the duplicated $\neg q$ literal is removed after resolution. Next the third literal of a modified goal is selected for resolution against an appropriate clause, then the first and finally the only remaining one. This ad hoc selection of literals has to be replaced by a fixed selection rule when the process of resolution is automated and a simple selection rule that always selects the leftmost literal is usually chosen. The process of resolving a goal with a set of definite clauses using a fixed selection rule is called SLD resolution, the acronym arising from Linear resolution for Definite clauses with Selection function. If the leftmost goal literal is always selected for resolution, the process is called normal SLD resolution and the result of resolution is described as a normal resolvant.

Not all the available clauses were used to produce the above refutation and it is clear that different initial choices might lead nowhere, i.e. they might fail to produce the empty clause. On the other hand, there might be other ways of producing an empty goal, allowing multiple refutations. Clauses are usually chosen for resolution in the order in which they appear in the logic program text, on a top-to-bottom basis when the program is written as

$$p$$
$$q$$
$$r \leftarrow t \wedge s$$
$$r \leftarrow q \wedge t$$
$$t \leftarrow p$$
$$t \leftarrow q \wedge s$$

Actually the choice of literals to be clashed in Figure 3.10 was based on the desire to produce a neat resolution diagram. An automated search using normal SLD resolvants traces out a rather less tidy path that can be displayed in the form of an SLD tree. A tree beginning with the goal $\neg(r \wedge q \wedge t)$ following the program above is shown in Figure 3.11. Here leftmost goal literals are chosen for resolution against program clauses and the first available clause in the program is taken for resolution. Following the leftmost branch of this tree to its leaf, we see that atom s needs to be resolved against a clause, but there is no appropriate clause in the program. At this point, the search has failed and has to backtrack to an earlier point where an alternative clause can be used. A second resolvant is possible for literal t, but though this is tried it also leads to a leftmost literal that cannot be resolved. The whole process continues in a very mechanical way, leading to an empty clause (shown as a box) and a further failed attempt.

Note that the SLD tree is explored from left to right so that two branches have been tried and failed before the empty clause is obtained. Furthermore, the SLD mechanism continues to explore alternative ways of showing the goal to be inconsistent with the program, even after it has already done so. This method of searching is described as depth-first because it descends to the tips of each branch before searching alternatives to the right.

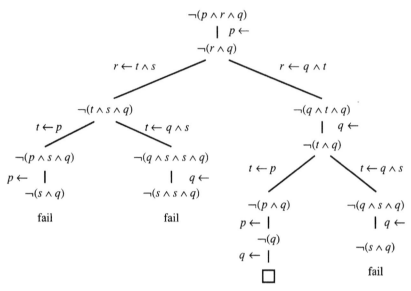

Figure 3.11   An SLD tree

3.4.1   SLD resolution for first-order formulas

Resolution is essentially a feature of propositional logic, so predicate literals are treated as simple statements. There exists, however, the extra complication that terms might have to be unified through substitutions before resolution is possible, and such substitutions have to be made throughout both goal and clause. Figure 3.12 shows how a goal and clause containing predicates are resolved through a most general unifier μ_1 to give a substituted negative clause for further resolution. A series of normal resolutions of this kind $\mu_1, \mu_2, \ldots, \mu_n$ applied to an initial goal G0 might eventually lead to an empty clause. If so, the substitutions made would then be the composition of a series of most general unifiers:

$$\mu = \mu_1 \circ \mu_2 \circ \mu_3 \circ \ldots \circ \mu_n$$

Consider the route procedure with the following path data:

C1 $Route(x,y) \leftarrow Path(x,y)$
C2 $Route(x,y) \leftarrow Path(x,z) \wedge Route(z,y)$
C3 $Path(a,b)$
C4 $Path(b,c)$

and take as a goal the predicate $Route(a,c)$. Normal resolution produces the SLD tree shown in Figure 3.13 with one successful refutation and two failed paths, so we deduce $Route(a,c)$. Each resolution step on the way to the empty clause required

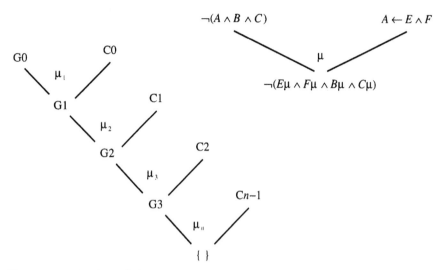

Figure 3.12 Backward chaining with substitutions

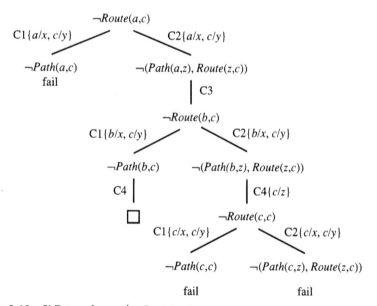

Figure 3.13 SLD tree for goal ¬Route(a,c)

a substitution and the composition of all such unifiers records a complete set of substitutions. However, these substitutions are of no interest because the goal contains no variables. In this case a refutation is itself the answer.

Suppose we begin the SLD tree with the goal containing two variable arguments, *Route(v,w)*, and apply clauses of the same program to produce the tree shown in

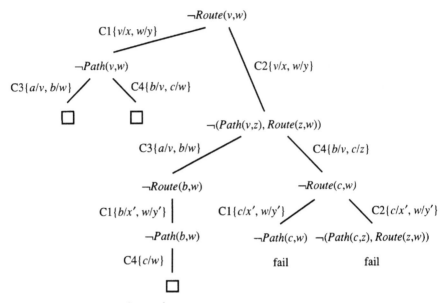

Figure 3.14   SLD tree for goal ¬Route(v, w)

Figure 3.14. This produces three successful refutation paths followed by two failed paths as the SLD mechanism attempts to find a route from point *c*. In this case the composition of unifiers required to achieve the empty clause is important: it provides the instantiated constants that cause refutation. Thus the first instantiation to produce a result is the substitution

$$\sigma = \{v/x, w/y\} \circ \{a/v, b/w\}$$
$$\sigma = \{a/v, b/w\}$$

Simplifications are possible here because *v* and *w* are substituted for *x* and *y* but the substituted variables are themselves subsequently replaced by *a* and *b*. Composition of these changes leads to a simpler substitution. Similarly, the series of substitutions required for the third refutation reduces to a much simpler single-stage substitution:

$$\rho = \{v/x, w/y\} \circ \{a/v, b/w\} \circ \{b/x', w/y'\} \circ \{c/w\}$$
$$\rho = \{a/v, c/w\}$$

The order of predicates within the body of a rule and the order of the clauses themselves may be changed to give a modified form of the program:

C1   Route(x,y) ← Route(z,y) ∧ Path(x,z)
C2   Route(x,y) ← Path(x,y)
C3   Path(a,b)
C4   Path(b,c)

If we now grow an SLD tree from the goal *Route(a,c)*, we obtain Figure 3.15. Normal resolution combined with the top-to-bottom selection of clauses now produces

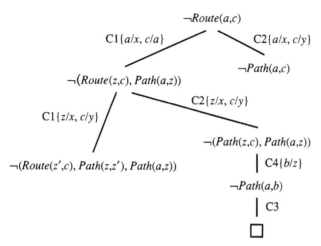

Figure 3.15 An SLD tree with an infinite branch

a path that neither fails nor succeeds, but instead creates an infinite series of increasingly large goals. Every attempt to resolve $Route(z,c)$ with the first program clause results in the creation of a fresh variable z' and a further attempt to resolve $Route(z',c)$. Backtracking from this hopeless endeavour and resolving $Route(z,c)$ against the second clause leads fairly quickly to a refutation that is never obtained.

An SLD tree appears to have three different types of path:

a. Successful paths that produce the empty goal and provide the constant instantiations required in the original goal.

b. Failing paths that terminate because the leftmost literal in the goal does not have a matching literal in a program clause.

c. Infinite paths that never produce a result.

Unfortunately, the mechanism we have described is equivalent to a depth-first search of the SLD tree, meaning that paths in a tree are explored to the maximum depth before any alternative to the right is considered. If, as in the above example, an SLD tree contains an infinite path to the left of a potentially successful path, the more productive path is never attempted. The technique fails to produce a result when one would have been expected and is therefore incomplete. An alternative breadth-first approach resolves the leftmost literal of a goal with every clause before proceeding to deeper levels and can be made complete. Unfortunately, the adoption of a breadth-first approach makes the implementation of backward-chaining systems rather more difficult.

We saw that forward chaining produces a large number of ground relations that will never be required, so backward chaining seemed an attractive alternative. Now we discover that a simple backward-chaining system depends on the order in which clauses occur in a program script. All of these problems can be avoided when more sophisticated algorithms are used.

EXERCISES 3.4

1. The clausal form of the definite program given in Exercise 1 of Exercises 3.3 is

   $$\{p\}, \{s, \neg p\}, \{s, \neg r, \neg v\}, \{r, \neg s\}, \{t, \neg u, \neg s\}, \{v, \neg p, \neg r\}$$

   Show that proposition $s \wedge v$ is true by resolving the dual of this expression in clausal form against the program clauses above. Similarly show that $r \wedge p$ is true.

2. Produce an SLD diagram tracing out the paths of attempts to prove propositions $p \wedge v$ and $s \wedge r \wedge v$ *true* in the definite program of Exercise 1 in Exercises 3.3.

3. A relation *Couple* has arguments naming a man and a woman; a relation *Mother* has arguments mother and child. A rule named *Father* relates fathers to their children through the *Couple* and *Mother* relations:

   Couple(a,e)
   Couple(d,f)
   Couple(b,c)
   Mother(f,g)
   Mother(e,b)
   Mother(f,c)
   Father(x,z) ← *Couple(x,y), Mother(y,z)*

   Draw SLD diagrams for the goals *Father(d,g)*, *Father(d,x)* and *Father(x,y)*.

CHAPTER FOUR

Prolog

4.1 PROLOG BASICS

At its simplest level, a Prolog system works by comparing facts in a database with a query called a goal presented at the prompt. Consider as an example some facts holding information about depositors and borrowers in a building society. A depositor fact contains an account number followed by the customer name and balance, whereas a borrower fact contains a loan number followed by a name and the loan amount:

```
depositor(123,smith,500).
depositor(234,brown,200).
depositor(345,patel,700).

borrower(735,jones,2000).
borrower(674,patel,6000).
borrower(865,evans,5000).
```

Collections of facts with the same name are called procedures or relations, and the individual instances are called clauses. Each fact consists of an identifier name followed by a number of arguments contained in brackets together with a terminating full stop. Prolog distinguishes between atomic and numeric constants by requiring atomic constants to begin with a lower case letter and numeric constants to begin with a digit. Thus, depositor, borrower and the names smith, brown, etc., are symbolic constants whereas the numbers are numeric constants. A string of characters beginning with a capital letter represents a variable, but when enclosed in single quotes, e.g. "Jones", the string is taken as an atomic symbol. Prolog will accept facts in which numeric and symbolic arguments have been entered inconsistently because it is not a typed language, so a great deal of care is required.

A database of information such as the facts above may be written into a text file then a Prolog system is instructed to "consult" that file. After consultation, Prolog is ready to answer queries presented at the query prompt. For example, a query might ask if the depositor relation contains an entry with the following specific arguments:

```
?-depositor(123,smith,500).
yes
```

Here the user supplies a goal at the question-mark prompt, and to achieve this goal, Prolog systematically attempts to match the goal name with a procedure name then to match the goal arguments with database arguments. This form of matching is a particularly simple form of a process called unification that checks goals against information in the database. If a goal can be unified with a clause in the database, the answer "yes" is obtained; otherwise the response is "no".

In practice the user is more likely to want to find information from a query rather than confirm known facts; this program finds the name and balance corresponding to a particular account number:

```
?-depositor(123,Name,Balance).
Name = smith
Balance = 500
yes;
no
```

Here a goal contains numeric constant 123 together with two variables distinguished from symbolic atoms by leading capital letters. Prolog again attempts to unify the goal with a fact in the database and, as before, matches the relation name and the first argument with constants. Since a variable can take any constant value, a unification is possible by setting Name = smith and Balance = 500 and this satisfying instantiation of the two variables is reported. Any further depositor facts for account number 123 will be shown when the goal is resatisfied by typing a semicolon after the first result. As there is none, the system simply responds with the word "no".

Attempts at unification take place in order from the top to the bottom of the text file containing the clauses and satisfactory unifications are reported to the user in this order. A query with three variables, e.g. the query depositor(X,Y,Z), would return all three arguments in the depositor clauses, producing three satisfactions in the order in which they occur in the text file.

Prolog can satisfy goals requiring more than one procedure, allowing questions like, "Is there anybody who is both a borrower and a depositor?"

```
?-depositor(A,N,B),borrower(L,N,S).
N = patel
```

A comma between the two parts of the goal acts as a logical "and", requiring truth in both relations: there must exist a triple A, N, B in the depositor relation and a triple L, N, S in the borrower relation. Since N is the same variable in both relations, it is said to join the two procedures and only situations where the same name occurs in both are reported. One problem with the query above is that, in addition to reporting the name patel, Prolog also provides substitutions for A, B, L and S even though they are probably not required. A goal is only ever matched with facts having the same number of arguments, so arguments cannot simply be left out of goals. However, if some arguments are of no interest, they can be replaced by underscores:

```
?-depositor(_,N,_),borrower(_,N,_).
N = patel
```

and only instantiations of the named variables are reported. Underscores represent anonymous variables and might be seen as don't care or wild card variables. A semicolon represents logical "or" in a similar way to the logical "and" above, and we can discover if a named person is a customer, either a depositor or a borrower, with the following query:

```
?-depositor(_,smith,_);borrower(_,smith,_).
yes
```

In reality this goal is equivalent to two separate subgoals, one for depositor and one for borrower. It is true if depositor can be unified with a fact in the database or if borrower can be unified with a fact in the database. It is also true when both these subgoals are unified with clauses in their appropriate procedures, i.e. it is not an exclusive-or.

Rules may be added to the text file to provide a more permanant formulation of queries. For example, a rule to supply the balance for a depositor with a specific account number might be added to the facts in a database:

```
balance(AcctNo,Bal) :- depositor(AcctNo, _ ,Bal).
```

This type of clause is divided into a head on the left and a body on the right by the "if" symbol (:-) and the head of a rule is true if the body is true. When a text file of facts and rules is modified, the file must be "reconsulted" before the modification is incorporated. If the above rule is added to the initial database, the following query is possible:

```
?-balance(123,X).
X = 500
```

In practice this is very little help, except to demonstrate the use of a rule. A slightly more useful rule is possible for finding clients who are both depositors and borrowers:

```
both(Name) :- depositor(_,Name,_),borrower(_,Name,_).
```

which, after reconsultation, allows the following interaction:

```
?-both(X).
X = patel
```

Rules become more useful as queries become more complex. In particular, their usefulness increases when the heads of existing rules are used in the bodies of further rules, building up a series of references to rules.

Prolog contains a number of built-in predicates (BIPs) to carry out standard procedures such as numerical comparison. The "greater than" BIP may be used to find those depositors with balances greater than a certain value, e.g.

```
:- depositor(X,Y,Z), Z > 500.
X = 345, Y = patel
```

No introduction to Prolog would be complete without mentioning the relation parent and some of its family connections. Databases that include parent might contain the following facts and some comments distinguished by the leading % sign:

```
parent(anne,bob).     %examples of the parent relation
parent(john,jane).
female(anne).         %some gender relations
male(john).
```

They might also include rules to derive information from these simple facts, such as

```
mother(X) :- parent(X,Y), female(X).
```

indicating that a mother is at once a parent and a female. A variable X must be instantiated with the same value within a rule, but the value used in this rule has no connection with the use of the same variable name in another rule. Similar rules might be written for father, son and daughter.

Relation grandparent can be formed by conjugating parent:

```
grandparent(X,Z) :- parent(X,Y), parent(Y,Z).
```

A single variable Y now joins clauses in procedure parent to other clauses in the same procedure. A goal grandparent(fred,tom) generates subgoal parent(fred,Y) and Prolog systematically attempts to unify this subgoal with every fact in the procedure. Each time it instantiates Y to a constant, it searches the same procedure from top to bottom for the clause parent(Y,tom) and might report "yes" zero or more times.

A rule such as this can be used in the body of a further rule as follows:

```
grandma(X,Y) :- grandparent(X,Y), female(X).
sibling(X,Y) :- parent(Z,X), parent(Z,Y).
```

EXERCISES 4.1

1. A small library maintains the book number, author, title and price of its stock items in two Prolog relations such as

```
fiction(123,smith,dreaming,14.54)
non-fiction(467,jones,databases,20.30)
```

Enter six clauses for each relation into an editor and make Prolog consult the resulting file. Invent data for the relations, guided by the requirements of the following queries, then carry out the exercises at the prompt.

a. Find the price of any non-fiction book written by `patel`.

b. Show the author and title of all fiction books costing more than 20 currency units (cu).

Add rules to the file defining the following relations:

`books(B,A,T,P)`, describing all books, both fiction and non-fiction

`cheap(B,A,T,P)`, describing all books costing less than 10 cu

`authors(A)`, listing the names of all authors

`common(B1,B2)` where B1 and B2 are fiction and non-fiction book numbers of books with the same title

Use these rules to show the following information:

c. Names for the authors of all books costing less than 10 cu.

d. Author and title of books priced between 10 and 15 cu (inclusive).

e. Book numbers of fiction/non-fiction pairs with the same title when either one of them costs more than 30 cu.

4.2 FLAT TABLES

A flat table is a relation containing only simple atomic objects as opposed to structured objects such as functions and lists. Tables of this sort are used in relational databases together with a number of characteristic operations that define new tables or procedures from existing ones. For example, tables describing undergraduates, courses and their links can be written in Prolog as follows:

```
ugrad(123,wendy,f).          %students
ugrad(234,bill,m).
ugrad(345,norma,f).

course(c204,lisp,2,15).      %courses
course(c213,database,1,15).
course(c234,prolog,2,8).

link(123,c204,12).           %the connections
link(345,c213,10).
link(345,c234,11).
```

A ugrad relation contains arguments describing student number, name and gender, whereas a course relation has arguments for course number, title, semester (1 or 2) and credit value (15 for a full course, 8 for a half-course). A link relation contains student and course numbers from the previous two relations together with a grade point result (a figure between 0 and 16) for that combination of student and course. In relational database language the first two procedures are called entity relations and the third is called a relationship relation because its purpose is to connect other relations. Each of the procedures ugrad, course and link is equivalent to a base table of information in a relational database and is sometimes called the extensional database in Prolog.

A projection operation extracts arguments from one procedure to form a new procedure of fewer arguments. For example, a procedure of student names may be formed from the ugrad relation with the following rule:

```
names(Sn) :- ugrad(_ , Sn , _).
```

so that a user can find the names of all undergraduates by typing names(X). A very important point follows from this query: a user would never know whether the information obtained by typing names(X) had been obtained directly from facts or indirectly through rules. Instead of adding the rule above, we could have added a new procedure called names that contained only name facts. A virtual database obtained by adding rules in this way is called an intensional database.

A selection operation chooses tuples from a procedure on the basis of the values of its tuple arguments. Thus, instances of female undergraduates can be extracted from the ugrad procedure with the following rule:

```
f_ugrad(S,N,f) :- ugrad(S,N,f).
```

and the resulting f_ugrad relation has the same number of arguments but might have fewer instances. Since the third argument of f_ugrad must be f, it makes sense to combine the projection and selection operations, selecting females and projecting just the student number and name in one rule:

```
f_ugrad2(S,N) :- ugrad(S,N,f).
```

Only those tuples in which the third argument of ugrad is equal to f appear in the f_ugrad2 relation. A selection based on a relation other than equality has to be made explicitly in the rule instead of placing the value in an argument position. For example, student number and course number combinations with grade points greater than 12 are revealed by the following rule:

```
high_marks(S,C) :- link(S,C,P),P >12.
```

4.2.1 Cartesian products and joins

The Cartesian product of two relations is a further relation containing ordered combinations of the arguments in the smaller relations. A Cartesian product can be formed from the ugrad and link relations through the following rule:

```
cprod(S1,N,G,S2,C,P) :- ugrad(S1,N,G),link(S2,C,P).
```

Remembering that Prolog works on a top-to-bottom and left-to-right basis, we should expect the ugrad variables' subgoal to be unified initially with the first ugrad fact appearing in the script file. The link subgoal is similarly unified with the first link fact appearing in the script, leading to a first satisfaction of the initial goal. Prolog then resatisfies the link subgoal as many times as possible before moving on to further instantiations of ugrad. Since there are three facts of each kind (in this example), the Cartesian product contains $3 \times 3 = 9$ entries, the first three of which are equivalent to

```
cprod(123,wendy,f,123,c204,12).
cprod(123,wendy,f,345,c213,10).
cprod(123,wendy,f,345,c234,11).
```

In practice a Cartesian product produces many more instances than are useful in any application. Two of the instances above contain information on different students, 123 and 345, and are unlikely to be useful. Placing a common variable in the student number positions of both subgoals produces a special subset of the Cartesian product:

```
cprod2(S,N,G,S,C,P) :- ugrad(S,N,G),link(S,C,P).
```

but we now recognise that the duplicate copy of the student number in this relation is not necessary. When relations are joined through one or more attributes and duplicate copies of these attributes are removed from the resulting relation, a natural join is obtained. A join based on the student number is written as

```
join(S,N,G,C,P) :- ugrad(S,N,G),link(S,C,P).
```

A combination of this rule with the extensional database is equivalent to

```
join(123,wendy,f,c204,12).
join(345,norma,f,c213,10).
join(345,norma,f,c234,11).
```

but the rule is far more flexible. If the content of an extensional database changes, the rule uses modified data.

Joining operations are often accompanied by selections or projections. For example, the student numbers and names of female students who achieved more than 11 grade points in any course can be found with the rule

```
fover11(S,N) :- join(S,N,f,_,P),P > 11.
```

A join of the three relations in the extensional database may be written as

```
join2(S,N,G,C,P,T,L,V) :-
join(S,N,G,C,P),course(C,T,L,V).
```

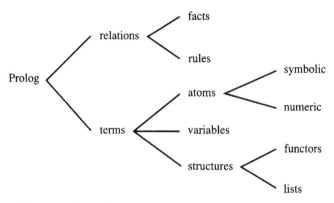

Figure 4.1　The parts of a Prolog program

A joined table can then be used to answer questions where information is spread over all three relations. For example, given a course title, provide the names of all students following that course:

```
members(Title,Name) :- join2(_,Name,_,Title,_,_,_,_).
```

Such a rule could have been written directly in terms of the extensional database relations with just enough variables to link the subgoal relations and produce the required results:

```
members2(Title,Name) :- course(C,Title,_),link(S,C,_),
ugrad(S,Name,_).
```

Prolog has the general form of first-order logic described in Chapter 2, but this form is restricted as described in Chapter 3 to give the language its operational features. Figure 4.1 shows that the objects making up a Prolog program are derived from the logic structure and are subdivided in much the same way. A program is composed of terms and relations; terms are subdivided into constants, variables and functions. Notice, however, that term constants are atoms in Prolog parlance and are further subdivided into symbolic and numeric forms. Functions are called structures and are subdivided into functors and lists. Functors look much the same as the functions described earlier and lists are a special functional notation. Terms are not evaluated and replaced by their denotations, as they would be in a functional language, so functors and lists have the more limited role of binding together other objects. Thus, the value of a function such as `square(4)` cannot be computed and its denotation `16` used to replace the function, because Prolog has a simple syntactic definition of equality. Nevertheless, functors are useful for binding together collections of objects into a single object, as in the date of birth functor `dob(12,june,1967)` or in the list structures `[1,2,3]` or `[mary,john,4]`. Since Prolog is not a typed language, a list may contain arbitrary atomic or structured objects. Similarly, any term may occur as an argument in a clause, but since we are limited to first-order logic, no clause can appear as an argument in another clause.

4.2.2   Tables with complex terms

Relational database systems accept the limitation to atomic terms in flat tables
because this allows efficient implementation. Prolog allows more complex terms
and therefore more expressive relations, but is rather less efficient in execution.
However, some progress has been made in implementing databases that allow more
complex terms and such systems could become commercially viable in the future.
Consider as an example an extensional database containing information on winners
of the Wimbledon men's singles tennis competition, with entries such as

```
mens_singles(player(stefan,edberg,dob(19,1,1966)),
[1988,1990],[becker,becker]).
```

Here a relation called `mens_singles` contains three arguments: a functor describing the player, a list of the years in which he won the title and a list of the
defeated finalists in those years. A player functor contains the first name, surname
and a further functor recording the date of birth of the player. Both lists are of variable length, depending on the number of times the player has won the competition, but
the two have the same length. Entries only occur in the database when players have
won the competition, so these lists cannot be empty. The `mens_singles` relation is still composed of symbolic and numeric atoms, but these atoms are gathered
together into structures that allow them to be treated as a single entity when it would
be useful to do so. For example, a simple query to the above database might be

```
?-mens_singles(X,Y,Z).
X = player(stefan,edberg,dob(19,1,1966))
Y = [1988,1990],
Z = [becker,becker]
```

and we see that complex terms rather than atoms have now been substituted for the
variables. Complex terms might equally be substituted for anonymous variables, as
in the following query that finds the years in which Borg won the men's singles
competition:

```
?-mens_singles(player(_,borg,_),X,_).
X = [1976,1977,1978,1979,1980]
```

If we wish to know who won the competition exactly three times, we might write

```
?-mens_singles(player(Fname,Sname,_),[_,_,_],_).
```

Built-in predicates such as "greater than" may be included in a query to find surnames for all title winners born after 1950:

```
?-mens_singles(player(_,Sname,dob(_,_,Yr),_,_),Yr>1950.
```

Obviously the use of complex terms makes the language far more flexible and
expressive in comparison with relations limited to atomic terms.

Prolog terms may be tested for equality with the special built-in equality predicate, represented by the equals sign (=), e.g.

```
?-person(tom,13) = person(tom,13).
yes
```

If two terms can be unified, the appropriate substitution is made and reported:

```
?-player(stefan,edberg,X) = player(stefan,edberg,
dob(19,1,1966)).
X = dob(19,1,1966)
yes
```

Essentially the equals sign represents a special relation that is true when its two arguments are the same string of symbols or can be made the same by instantiation. A special strict equality is available (==) and this makes no attempt to unify the two terms; if they are not the same without unification, it fails.

EXERCISES 4.2

1. A small library contains the details of its stock and loans in the following relations:

```
book(123,smith,dreaming,14.54).
reader(894,palmer,finance).
serial(123,894,date(12,5,97)).
```

Book details remain as in Exercise 4.1 and the reader relation contains a reader number, reader name and reader department. Any book out on loan is connected to a reader number through the serial relation and is due back by the date shown in that relation.

Enter six clauses for each relation into a file through an editor and make Prolog consult this extensional database. Check the database by carrying out the following queries at the prompt:

a. Show names of all readers who currently have a book out on loan.

b. Show the book numbers and return dates of books on loan to jones.

Go back to the editor and define a relation that joins book and reader relations through the serial relation, then use this rule to answer the following queries:

c. Show title and price for all books currently on loan.

d. Show title for books currently on loan by evans.

e. Show title and return date for books on loan to sales_dept.

Define a relation called later that has two date arguments and is true if the second date is later than the first. Thus the goal later(date(29,3,94), date(1,4,94)) elicits a "yes" response from the program.

f. Write a rule that allows a user to input a date and receive in return the reader names and titles of books on loan but due back by that date.

4.3 RECURSIVE QUERIES AND OPERATORS

The simple route diagram from the previous chapter is shown again in Figure 4.2 and used here as an example to illustrate recursive rules. Paths between various locations are shown in the form of a directed acyclic graph, a diagram of one-directional paths without any loops. Exactly the same information may be stored in a Prolog database as follows:

```
path(a,b).
path(a,c).
path(b,d).
path(d,e).
path(c,e).
```

and a query of the type "where can I go from d?" is an easily answered goal:

```
?-path(d,X).
X = e
```

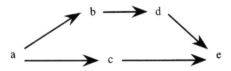

Figure 4.2 A directed acyclic graph

Single-step queries of this kind are not likely to be very useful. More often the user will want to know if a journey can be made between two points, perhaps with intermediate stages. Imagine that a user wants to know if a journey from b to e is possible and makes the following first attempt:

```
?-path(b,e).
no
```

followed by

```
?-path(b,X),path(X,e)
X = d
```

in which satisfaction is obtained. It might have taken many attempts with increasing numbers of intermediate points before a given goal succeeded. But some help could be provided by route rules such as

```
routeA(Start,Finish) :- path(Start,Finish).
routeB(Start,Finish) :- path(Start,X),path(X,Finish).
routeC(Start,Finish) :- path(Start.X),path(X,Y),
path(Y,Finish).
```

so that a user might try each rule in turn until one succeeds:

```
?-routeB(b,e).
yes
```

A more general approach follows from observing that a route consists of one path alone or one path followed by a further route, properties that are expressed in the rules

```
route(Start,Finish) :- path(Start,Finish).
route(Start,Finish) :- path(Start,X),route(X,Finish).
```

Suppose that the query ?-route(d,e). is presented to Prolog with these rules and the above database. Goal route(d,e) is unified with the first clause of the route procedure, instantiating variables Start and Finish to constants d and e. Thus route(d,e) is true if path(d,e) is true and a systematic attempt to unify this subgoal with a database clause begins. Attempts to match goal against database fact proceed from the top of the text file and eventually succeed, causing Prolog to respond with the word "yes".

Suppose, however, that a query for a route with intermediate stages such as ?-route(b,e). is presented. This goal is again unified with the head of the first rule and a systematic attempt to match subgoal path(b,e) with a database clause begins. This attempt fails, so variables Start and Finish in the second rule are instantiated to b and e, producing the following instantiation:

```
route(b,e) :- path(b,X),route(X,e).
```

Two subgoals now have to be satisfied, and Prolog works from left to right through the body of the rule attempting to unify subgoals with database clauses. Working from top to bottom through the text file, several attempts at unification are required before fact path(b,d) is unified with goal path(b,X) by instantiating X to d. This instantiation is transmitted to the following subgoal, and systematic attempts to unify route(d,e) with a database clause begin. Searching again begins at the top of the text file, leading to the first route rule and an instantiation of d and e for Start and Finish. A search for path(d,e) takes place and success is reported.

The second of the two route rules is said to be recursive because the head of the rule appears also in the body, causing it to make references to itself until a terminating condition occurs. Note that fresh variables are used each time a recursive reference occurs, even though the rule has a single name for each variable. The scope of variables in the head of the rule only extends to the body of that rule, not to other clauses used recursively by the procedure.

4.3.1 Operators and functors

Clauses might contain atoms, variables or functors as arguments, but Prolog functors serve a quite different purpose compared to the functions of a functional programming language. Although the two forms look the same, they behave differently because equality in Prolog means syntactic equivalence rather than denotational equivalence. Two terms are equal in Prolog if they are represented by the same string of symbols, whereas they are equal in a functional language if they can be reduced to the same canonical value. However, it is possible to define operators and provide Prolog rules that allow Prolog to discover canonical terms for complex terms expressed as relational arguments. As a particularly simple example, consider the fact

```
val0(and(true,true),true).
```

in which a fact of a relation called val0 contains a functor and its denotation as first and second arguments. There is no difference in the form of a relation and a functor, so Prolog has to distinguish the two by their positions, thus in the example above, the and atom must be a functor because it occurs as an argument within a clause. Three more relations could be added to the one above, and the resulting procedure would completely define the effect of the and functor on two Boolean atoms. A particular functor may then be evaluated as

```
?-val0(and(true,false),X).
X = false
```

but queries that can be evaluated are limited to the four defined facts. However, four facts defining functor and in terms of constants may be replaced by just two rules using variables and taking advantage of Prolog's built-in operations, as in the val relation:

```
val(and(X,Y),true) :- val(X,true),val(Y,true).
val(and(X,Y),false) :- val(X,false);val(Y, false).
```

These rules express what we already know about the meaning of conjunction: the function and(X,Y) is true if X and Y are both true, but false if either X or Y is false or if both are false. If a database contained the rules above in a file together with facts

```
val(p,true).
val(q,false).
```

the following query response would be obtained:

```
?-val(and(p,q),X).
X = false
```

Relation val has the advantage over val0 that it allows recursive references to decompose subterms within goal relations. A query in which a functor appears as an argument in another functor is possible:

```
?-val(and(p,and(q,r)),X).
X = false
```

allowing the evaluation of arbitrary Boolean expressions. Although this notation is perfectly correct, it suffers from two problems: the prefix use of and can become cumbersome in large expressions and it does not provide the usual precedence rules for propositional operators, i.e. it does not give conjunction priority over disjunction. Prolog allows users to define functions to be operations through operator definitions and, in the case of conjunction above, we could define an operator labelled & as follows:

```
:- op(600,xfy,&).
```

An operator declaration, sometimes called a directive, must precede any attempt to use the operator in a program. It consists of the atom name op with three arguments, the last of which is a symbol for the operator being defined.

The first argument is a number (usually between 1 and 1200) that defines a precedence level for the operator, lower numbers representing operators that bind most tightly to their arguments. For example, a Boolean expression $p \vee q \mathbin{\&} r$ is assumed to represent $p \vee (q \wedge r)$. To ensure that the & operation is applied first, it is defined with a lower precedence number (giving it a higher precedence) than the $\vee$ operation.

The second argument of the operator definition defines the position of the operation symbol in relation to its own arguments. Operator arguments are represented by the letters x and y, and the operator itself is represented by the letter f. Prefix, infix and postfix operators are then defined with the notations fxy, xfy and xyf. Argument x has a lower priority than y, so an operator defined in this way associates to the right when the arguments are themselves functors. Notice that an operator definition tells us nothing about the "meaning" of an operator, i.e. what it denotes, so this information has be be added with rules:

```
val(X & Y,true) :- val(X,true),val(Y,true).
val(X & Y,false) :- val(X,false);val(Y,false).
```

Except for the replacement of the prefix and symbol by an infix & symbol, these rules are the same as those above, but now the abbreviated symbol can be used at the prompt:

```
?-val(p & q, Z).
Z = false
```

Operator definitions for negation, disjunction and implication can be made in the same way:

```
:- op(500,fy,~).
:- op(700,xfy,v).
:- op(800,xfy,->).
```

Since all these symbols have to be typed on a normal keyboard, they are slightly different from equivalent symbols used earlier. Conjunction is represented by the symbol & because the usual ∧ is not available on keyboards, though it would be possible to define ∧ with two keystrokes. A negation function is represented by the tilde ~, disjunction by a lower case letter v and implication by a combination of a minus sign with the chevron ->.

Rules can be written for disjunction and implication using the operators defined above:

```
val(X v Y,true) :- val(X,true);val(Y,true).
val(X v Y,false) :- val(X,false),val(Y,false).
val(X -> Y,true) :- val(X,false);val(Y,true).
val(X -> Y,false) :- val(X,true),val(Y,false).
```

The valuation of a disjunction is true when either X or Y is true; it is false only when both arguments are false. Implication is slightly more difficult to follow; its valuation is true when the first argument (the antecedent) is false or when the second (the consequent) is true, or when both situations occur together. Only a true antecedent with a false consequent makes an implication false. Negation is expressed as a simple inversion:

```
val(~X, true) :- val(X,false).
val(~X, false) :- val(X,true).
```

Having entered these rules in the database, it is instructive to follow the evaluation of a query. Suppose that the following goal is presented to the database:

```
?-val((p v ~q) & (~p v q),true).
```

This proposition was written earlier as $(p \vee \neg q) \wedge (\neg p \vee q)$ and its semantic tableau is shown in Figure 1.3. A trace of the way in which Prolog attacks this problem follows the form of the semantic tableau and provides some insight into its search mechanism. The goal above is matched with the head of the true & rule, so that both subgoals have to evaluate to true in order to make the goal itself true. Since both have to be true, they are shown one directly below the other, leftmost first, in Figure 4.3. It is important that the leftmost subgoal of the rule appears highest in the diagram because subgoals are discharged in order from top to bottom. The goal in line 2 is now matched with the head of the true v rule, creating two further subgoals that have to be satisfied. A split in the diagram indicates that only one of these subgoals has to be satisfied in order to satisfy the parent goal. Now subgoal val(p,true) has to be satisfied, but it cannot be unified with a rule head, so the following possibilities arise:

a. No matching fact occurs in the database, so Prolog "backtracks" to its parent clause in order to check alternatives, in this case it would try val(~q,true).

b. A matching fact does occur and Prolog continues with the current sequence of satisfactions, in this case unifying the subgoal in line 3 with a rule.

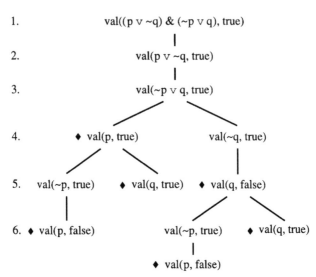

1.   val((p v ~q) & (~p v q), true)

2.   val(p v ~q, true)

3.   val(~p v q, true)

4.   ♦ val(p, true)   val(~q, true)

5.   val(~p, true)   ♦ val(q, true)   ♦ val(q, false)

6. ♦ val(p, false)   val(~p, true)   ♦ val(q, true)

                              ♦ val(p, false)

Figure 4.3   A Prolog search tree: backtracking points are marked with a diamond

Each backtracking point is marked with a diamond in the diagram; they are the make or break points where Prolog either finds a suitable fact in its database or it does not. Hopefully, `val(p,true)` and `val(p,false)` would not occur together in the database, so Prolog would have to backtrack from one of them. If the database contains both `val(p,true)` and `val(q,true)`, the bottom of the search tree is reached and the original goal is satisfied.

Whenever a branch occurs in a diagram such as Figure 4.3, it is the left-hand side that is explored first. If the system is unable to match a goal with the head of a rule or a fact, it backtracks to the point where it branched and tries the alternative route. This is called a depth-first strategy because the tip of the leftmost branch is reached before any alternative routes are explored. If the database contained facts `val(p,true)` and `val(q,true)`, the tableau would be explored to the left-hand tip, but `val(p,false)` would fail, causing backtracking to line 4 and an attempt to match the subgoal `val(q,true)` with a fact, which succeeds. Prolog reports this success, but continues to look for further matches, backtracking at each of the marked points.

An exclusive-or operation labelled @ might be defined by the following program instructions:

```
:-op(700,xfy,@)
val(X @ X,true).
val(X @ Y,false) :- X \== Y.
```

EXERCISES 4.3

1. Create a database of parent facts of the type `parent(john,mary)`. Write a procedure called `ancestor` that succeeds if the person in the first argument

position is ancestor of the person in the second argument position. Add a relation female to the database that includes all the females in either argument positions of the parent relation. Write a modified version of ancestor called maternal that relates a person in the second argument position through a series of female parents to a female in the first argument position.

2. Declare operator symbols and write procedures that implement the *nand* (|), *nor* (↓) and *imp* operations described in Chapter 1. Enter atomic valuations val(p,true), val(q,false) and val(r,false) into the database, then evaluate the following expressions, in which ⊕ is *niff* (exor) and ¬ is *not*; both will have to be translated to keyboard symbols.

$$p \mid q \oplus r \mid r$$
$$p \mid q \downarrow \neg p \mid r$$

3. Draw diagrams similar to Figure 4.3, showing the search path when the following goals occur at the prompt:

```
val(p & ~q v ~p & q,true)
val((p & ~q) -> r ,true)
```

4.4 OPERATORS AND ARITHMETIC

In the logical expressions above, we chose to write function and(X,Y) in the form X & Y, having defined an infix operator & with a specific precedence level. Remember that the operator definition did not explain how the result of the operation is deduced from its arguments. Similar considerations apply to the arithmetic operators used in Prolog except that both the operator definitions and their meanings are predefined in a standard environment.

Armed with the knowledge that the necessary operator definitions are built into the Prolog system, a naive user might attempt the following calculation at the prompt:

```
?- X = 2 + 3 * 4.
X = 2 + 3 * 4
```

Such a user might have hoped that Prolog would evaluate the expression on the right then report an equivalent value for X. Unfortunately, the concept of equality in Prolog is that of simple syntactic equivalence, not of denotational equivalence, and in this light the response above is perfectly correct. The user has asked Prolog what sequence of symbols a variable X would need to represent in order to be equal to 2 + 3 * 4 and the system has obliged with the appropriate sequence. Prolog recognises arithmetic symbols as syntactic infix operator symbols and instantiates variables to make expressions equivalent:

```
?-X + 2 = 3 + Y.
X = 3
Y = 2
```

Arithmetic operations are so useful that they are allowed and activated by special symbols. In particular, the calculation intended above could be carried out with the is operator at the ? prompt:

```
?-X is 2 + 3 * 4.
X = 14
```

Operator is represents a form of denotational equality that causes the evaluation of the arithmetic expression on its right-hand side and the substitution of the result into the variable X. In fact, the is keyword evaluates the expression then unifies the result with the term on its left. If the other atom is a variable, the unification amounts to a simple substitution, as in the example above; but if it is a numeric constant, the operation amounts to an equivalence test. For example, the following query results in a successful unification:

```
?- 14 is 2 + 3 * 4.
yes
```

All atoms in a numerical computation must be numeric atoms. The available range of arithmetic operations varies between implementations but always includes the familiar operations: +, −, *, /, mod, div. Arithmetic operators associate from left to right, so the expression 4 − 3 − 2 evaluates as (4 − 3) − 2 rather than 4 − (3 − 2). This is a direct consequence of the x and y arguments in the operator definition of the subtraction symbol:

```
op(500,yfx, -).
```

The keyboard symbol for a minus sign is a hyphen (−). Arguments x and y can themselves be expressions but the principal functor of x must have a lower precedence than f, whereas the principal functor of y might be either lower or equal in precedence to f. This means that only left association is allowed. Precedence numbers also ensure the usual evaluation priorities, i.e. an expression of the form 2 + a * b is understood to represent 2 + (a * b).

4.4.1   Relational operators

An intended numerical comparison of the type

```
?-4 * 3 = 2 * 6.
no
```

again fails because the strings of symbols are different. Prolog is concerned with syntactic equality, so it does not recognise the fact that 4 * 3 and 2 * 6 denote the same value. However, numerical comparisons of arithmetic expressions are so useful that they too are included in the language by adding some special relational symbols. Operations of this kind employ a different equality symbol:

```
?- 4 * 3 =:= 2 * 6.
yes
```

This new symbol causes the numerical evaluation of the two sides before a comparison is made. Several other numerical relation operators are defined such that they force the evaluation of two arguments then perform the numerical comparison, reporting "yes" and "no" as though the answer were a Boolean result:

> greater than
< less than
=< less than or equal to
>= greater than or equal to
=\= numerical inequality
=:= numerical equality

Built-in relational operators are very useful in writing a procedure to find the larger of two numbers X and Y:

```
max(X,Y,X) :- X >= Y.
max(X,Y,Y) :- Y > X.
```

allowing the following interaction at the prompt:

```
?-max(2,5,B).
B = 5
```

Although Prolog is a syntactic reasoning language "without equality", it uses a suprisingly large number of different equality symbols and we need to be sure of their meaning. Predicates = and \= represent syntactic equality or inequality respectively, allowing substitutions to achieve a result. Predicates == and \== represent strict equality and inequality respectively; they do not permit substitutions in order to obtain a result. Finally, Prolog's numerical comparisons force evaluations of the arguments then compare the values denoted by the arguments.

4.4.2 Arithmetic in recursive procedures

Distances could be incorporated into some facts derived from Figure 4.3 as follows:

```
path(a,b,8).
path(b,d,7). etc.
```

A rule could then be written to show not only that routes are possible, but also to provide the distance of a given journey:

```
route2(X,Z,D) :- path(X,Z,D).
route2(X,Z,D) :- path(X,Y,D1),route2(Y,Z,D2),D is D1 + D2.
```

Procedure route2 works in the same way as route itself, but adds the path distance of each individual step to the distance of the remaining route.

The factorial of a given natural number is the product of that number with all natural numbers smaller than itself; factorial 5 is equal to $5 \times 4 \times 3 \times 2 \times 1 = 120$. In order to express a factorial in recursive form, we note that the factorial of any number n is equal to n multiplied by the factorial of $n - 1$. From this simple observation comes the following recursive Prolog program:

```
fac(1,1).
fac(X,Y) :- X1 is X - 1,fac(X1,Y1),Y is X * Y1.
```

and factorial 1 is easily found to be 1 by pattern-matching the goal fac(1,R) with the first clause. Goals containing larger integers such as fac(4,R) can only be matched with the second clause, the number being instantiated into variable X and the result R sharing with rule variable Y. It is instructive to follow the steps required to produce a result from the goal ?-fac(4,R) when it is unified with the rule head:

```
fac(4,R) :- 3 is 4 - 1,fac(3,Y1),R is 4 * Y1
fac(3,Y1) :- 2 is 3 - 1,fac(2,Y2),Y1 is 3 * Y2
fac(2,Y2) :- 1 is 2 - 1,fac(1,Y3),Y2 is 2 * Y3
fac(1,Y3) :- fac(1,1)
```

at which point the series of recursive references is terminated. The first arithmetic subgoal is satisfied and produces a decremented integer that is shared with an argument in the second subgoal, a recursive call to the factorial procedure. Fresh variables are introduced in each step but they cannot be assigned values until the final terminating stage is reached. Even then it is only the last variable (Y3) that is assigned a value of 1. This allows Y2 to be calculated, then Y1 and finally R as follows:

```
fac(2,2) :- 1 is 2 - 1,fac(1,1),2 is 2 * 1
fac(3,6) :- 2 is 3 - 1,fac(2,2),6 is 3 * 2
fac(4,24) :- 3 is 4 - 1,fac(3,6), 24 is 4 * 6
```

An alternative approach to the traditional factorial computation is provided by the following accumulator procedure:

```
fac2(N,R) :- faux(N,1,R).
faux(1,Y,Y).
faux(N,A,S) :- N1 is N - 1,A1 is N * A,faux(N1,A1,S).
```

in which an auxiliary procedure faux has an argument that accumulates the value of the final result as it proceeds, avoiding the need to return to previously unsatisfied subgoals. Again it is instructive to follow the steps required to find factorial 4:

```
fac2(4,R) :- faux(4,1,R).
faux(4,1,R) :- 3 is 4 - 1,4 is 4 * 1,faux(3,4,R)
```

```
faux(3,4,R) :- 2 is 3 - 1,12 is 3 * 4,faux(2,12,R)
faux(2,12,R) :- 1 is 2 - 1,24 is 2 * 12,faux(1,24,R)
faux(1,24,24)
fac2(4,24)
```

Euclid's method for finding the greatest common divisor of two numbers is implemented by the following Prolog procedure and is by nature an accumulating algorithm:

```
gcd(X,X,X).
gcd(X,Y,Z) :- X < Y,Y1 is Y - X,gcd(X,Y1,Z).
gcd(X,Y,Z) :- X > Y,X1 is X - Y,gcd(X1,Y,Z).
```

If the two numbers are the same, then the largest number that divides into both without remainder is the number itself. If the numbers are different, the larger number is reduced by the value of the smaller number until the two are equal, and the greatest divisor is that number. The accumulative nature of this procedure is shown in the following trace:

```
gcd(12,15,R) :- 12 < 15, 3 is 15 - 12,gcd(12,3,R)
gcd(12,3,R) :- 12 > 3, 9 is 12 - 3, gcd(9,3,R)
gcd(9,3,R) :- 9 > 3, 6 is 9 - 3, gcd(6,3,R)
gcd(6,3,R) :- 6 > 3, 3 is 6 - 3, gcd(3,3,R)
gcd(3,3,3)
```

EXERCISES 4.4

1. Define a procedure that takes a pair of numbers and returns a number expressing the first as a percentage of the second, e.g.

   ```
   ?-percent(3,4,X)
   X = 75.00
   ```

2. Write a procedure that accepts the radii of two circles on the same centre and calculates the area of the space between the two circles.

3. Simple and compund interest are calculated from the formulas $p(1 + ry/100)$ and $p(1 + r/100)^y$ in which p is the principal (the amount of money invested), r is the percentage annual rate of interest and integer y is the number of years of the investment. Write Prolog procedures to calculate the simple and compound interest of money invested. Use both procedures to calculate the value of 500 currency units invested at 5.5% per annum for seven years. (The ISO standard symbol for the exponential in Prolog is **.)

4. Define procedures div60 and mod60 that reveal the number of times 60 will divide into a given integer and the remainder when this is done. (The standard symbols for mod and div are mod and //.) The interaction at the prompt should appear as follows:

```
?div60(150,X)
X = 2

?mod60(150,X)
X = 30
```

5. Define a procedure that converts a whole number of seconds into a triple of hours, minutes and seconds:

```
?-convert(4350,X)
X = hms(1,12,30)
```

6. Define an infix, arity-two operator symbol # that always yields the smaller of its two arguments:

```
?- val(4 # 7,X).
X = 4
```

7. A directed acyclic graph such as that described in Section 4.3 might carry cost information as follows:

```
path(a,b,20).
path(a,c,35).
path(b,d,43).
path(d,e,26).
path(c,e,44).
```

Write a Prolog procedure that finds the total cost of each possible route from one point to another in the graph. Test this routine by finding the costs of two possible routes from a to e.

4.5   LISTS

Lists are structures provided to hold sequences of data objects, though in Prolog these objects do not have to be of the same type. Prolog is not a typed language, so a single list might contain any mixture of atomic and structured objects. An empty list appears simply as a pair of square brackets [ ]; lists with increasing numbers of elements are represented in one of these forms:

```
[ ]          [ ]
[a]          .(a,[ ])
[b,a]        .(b,.(a,[ ]))
[c,b,a]      (c,.(b,.(a,[ ])))
```

regular form   cons form

Lists are commonly used in the regular form shown in the left column, so it is not immediately obvious that they consist of a series of functors applied to an empty list. A list of one element is really that one element bound to an empty list by the constructor (cons) functor, shown as a dot in the prefix position. Larger lists consist of further elements each added by an application of cons so that every list expressed in regular form has an equivalent functor form. A small goal presented to the system confirms the equality of the regular and cons forms of a given list:

```
?-[a,b] = .(a,.(b,[ ])).
yes
```

This small query shows not only that Prolog accepts both forms of the list as equivalent, but also that it can test pairs of lists for syntactic equality, because the query

```
?-[a,b] = [b,a].
no
```

is equivalent to the comparison of two complex functors

```
?- .(a,.(b,[ ])). = .(b,.(a,[ ])).
```

Variable substitutions are allowed to achieve a unification

```
?-[2,Y,6] = [X,4,Z].
X = 2 Y = 4 Z = 6
yes
```

Lists are often processed by repeatedly removing the leftmost element, the head, for examination or computation, reversing the action of the cons operator. This process is aided by a special notation $[H|T]$ in which the head element H is shown separated from a list of all the remaining elements by a vertical bar. Two relations

```
hd([H|T],H).
tl([H|T],T).
```

could be placed in the database and would allow the following queries:

```
?-hd([4,6,3],X).
X = 4

?-tl([mary,john,tex],X).
X = [john,tex]
```

Notice that the head is an element whereas the tail of a list is itself a list. The sum of all the elements in a numeric list is computed by the following recursive procedure:

```
addup([ ],0).
addup([H|T],X) :- addup(T,X1),X is X1 + H.
```

which implements two obvious truths: the sum of the elements in an empty list add up to 0; the sum of any other list is found by adding the value of the head element to the sum of its tail elements. The following trace of an invocation might help to show the recursive nature of this procedure:

```
addup([3,4,5],R) :- addup([4,5],R1),R is R1 + 3
addup([4,5],R1) :- addup([5],R2),R1 is R2 + 4
addup([5],R2) :- addup([ ],R3),R2 is R3 + 5
```

at which point the repeated calls are terminated because addup([ ],R3) can be unified with the first clause, setting R3 to 0. Variables R1, R2 and R3 are fresh variables created for each recursive call, and they acquire values as the process returns to the top level:

```
addup([5],5) :- addup([ ],0),5 is 0 + 5
addup([4,5],9) :- addup([5],5),9 is 5 + 4
addup([3,4,5],12) :- addup([4,5],9),12 is 9 + 3
```

A similar but simpler procedure can be used to count the number of elements in a list:

```
len([ ],0).
len([_| T],X) :- len(T, X1),X is X1 + 1.
```

Any empty list has a length 0 whereas every non-empty list has a length one greater than the length of its tail. The second clause is applied until the list is empty, incrementing a counter every time a head element is removed, then the recursive procedure is terminated by the first clause. A goal could then be presented at the ? prompt:

```
?-len([tom,dick,34,harry],X).
X = 4
```

A specific element is a member of a list if it is the head element of that list or it occurs in the tail, leading to the following pair of rules:

```
member(X,[X |_]).
member(X,[_|Y]) :- member(X,Y).
```

Conversely, a list is free of a certain element if that element is not the head element and the element does not occur in the tail:

```
free(X,[ ]).
free(X,[H|T]) :- X \== H,free(X,T).
```

A procedure such as addup can be written in an alternative accumulator .form described earlier in connection with the factorial evaluation. The new procedure includes an auxiliary accumulator relation addacc:

```
addup2(L,N) :- addacc(L,0,N).
addacc([ ],A,A).
addacc([H|T],A,N) :- A1 is A + H,addacc(T,A1,N).
```

Using this procedure, the trace of our addition example is

```
addacc([3,4,5],0,N) :- 3 is 0 + 3, addacc([4,5],3,N)
addacc([4,5],3,N) :- 7 is 3 + 4, addacc([5],7,N)
```

```
addacc([5],7,N) :- 12 is 7 + 5, addacc([ ],12,N)
addacc([ ],12,12)
```

Two lists can be checked for a common element by systematically checking whether elements of the first list are members of the second:

```
common([X|L],M) :- member(X,M).
common([X|L],M) :- common(L,M).
```

Prolog allows more than one element to be placed on the left of the vertical bar so that the lists [c,b|[a]] and [c|[b,a]] are equivalent. This feature is useful in a procedure to discover whether two given symbols occur side by side in a list:

```
next(X,Y,[X,Y|T]).
next(X,Y,[H|T]) :- next(X,Y,T).
```

4.5.1 List-producing procedures

Each of the above procedures produces a single number or Boolean result from the inspection of a list of items. Now we examine a number of procedures that both accept and produce lists. First of all, an operation called append combines (concatenates) two lists into one through the following procedure:

```
append([ ],L,L).
append([X|L1],L2,[X|L3]) :- append(L1,L2,L3).
```

Given two lists, append concatenates them together as follows:

```
?-append([a,b,c],[p,q,r],R)
R = [a,b,c,p,q,r]
```

but it will also accept a list in the third argument position and return each of the possible sublists that could be concatenated to produce that list:

```
?-append(L1,L2, [a,b,c,d]).
L1 = [a], L2 = [b,c,d];
L1 = [a,b], L2 = [c,d]; etc.
```

Non-deterministic behaviour of this kind is sometimes seen as a major feature of the Prolog language, but in practice not many procedures behave in this way.

Operation append may be used as a subrule in a procedure to reverse the elements of a list:

```
rev([ ],[ ]).
rev([X|L],M) :- rev(L,N),append(N,[X],M).
```

Elements are repeatedly detached from the head of a list and appended to the right of a reversed tail list. An accumulator approach that does not require the use of append might have been used to achieve the same result.

Two important procedures called `map` and `filter` are used in Prolog in the same way that they are used in many other languages: `map` repeatedly applies some operation to every element of a list; `filter` selects specific sublists from an initial list. An operation called `oper` might simply multiply numbers by 3 as in

```
oper(X,Y) :- Y is X * 3.
```

then procedure `map` applies this operation to every element in a list:

```
map([],[]).
map([H1|T1],[H2|T2]) :- oper(H1,H2),map(T1,T2).
```

Similarly, a filtering condition might simply choose values over 12:

```
cond(X) :- X > 12.
```

then a sublist of elements that satisfy this condition is selected by procedure `filter`:

```
filter([],[]).
filter([H|T1],[H|T2]) :- cond(H),filter(T1,T2).
filter([H|T1],T2) :- filter(T1,T2).
```

4.5.2   Ordering and sorting list elements

List sorting has to be based on some defined element order, but it is desirable to write sorting procedures independently of the test for element order. Thus a simple relation called `less` might be defined as the simple numeric relation

```
less(X,Y) :- X < Y.
```

or perhaps as an ordering based on two date of birth functors:

```
less(dob(D1,M1,Y1),dob(D2,M2,Y2)) :- Y1 < Y2 ;
                                      Y1 = Y2,M1 < M2;
                                      Y1 = Y2,M1 = M2,D1 < D2.
```

It is possible to imagine many different procedures for ordering pairs of functors based on combinations or sums of argument values, but such procedures should be separated from list-sorting procedures themselves. As a result, the sorting procedures described below are generic, i.e. they work for elements of any defined type, provided an ordering such as the one above is available.

Elements from a numerical list can be divided into two sublists according to whether they are greater or less than a given number. Thus, numbers less than 12 and greater than 12 are separated by a procedure `split`:

```
?-split(12,[9,16,3,14,7],X,Y)
X = [9,3,7] Y = [16,14]
```

and the definition making this result possible is as follows:

```
split(N,[ ],[ ],[ ]).
split(N,[H|T],[H|A],B) :- less(H,N),split(N,T,A,B).
split(N,[H|T],A,[H|B]) :- less(N,H),split(N,T,A,B).
```

An empty list divides into two empty sublists whereas a non-empty list shares its head element with one of the two sublists; the choice of sublist depends on the relation of the head element to number N. Repeated applications of the two recursive clauses eventually produces a tail depleted to an empty list and the first clause then applies.

This split procedure clearly goes some way towards sorting a list of elements and could be used as an auxiliary definition to partially sort elements in a single list. The two sublists obtained from split could be rejoined with append to give a rule called partsort:

```
partsort([H|T],R) :- split(H,T,A,B),append(A,[H|B],R).
```

If the original head element was either the largest or smallest element in the list, then the result of partsort is the same as the original one, so nothing will have been achieved. In all other situations some degree of sorting will have occurred, though the elements of the two sublists remain in the same order as in the original. If partsort is used on a list similar to the one above, we obtain

```
?-partsort([12,9,16,3,14,7],X)
X = [9,3,7,12,16,14]
```

so the original head element separates elements smaller and larger than itself. If unsorted lists either side of the head element are themselves partsorted in this way, and the algorithm repeated for further sublists until empty lists are obtained, a fully sorted list is obtained. This technique of sorting lists is called a quicksort and is defined in Prolog as follows:

```
qsort([ ],[ ]).
qsort([H|T],R) :-split(H,T,A,B),qsort(A,A1),qsort(B,B1),
                                  append(A1,[H|B1],R).
```

A procedure called divide produces two sublists of equal or nearly equal size from a list in the first argument position:

```
?-divide([a,b,c,d,e],X,Y).
X = [a,c,e]
Y = [b,d]
```

and the fact that the resulting sublists contain alternating elements from the original list indicates how the procedure has been defined:

```
divide([ ],[ ],[ ]).
divide([X],[X],[ ]).
divide([X,Y|L],[X|M],[Y|N]) :- divide(L,M,N).
```

The first two elements of a list become the head elements of two result lists, and the rest of the initial list is divided between the two sublists. This recursive removal of pairs of elements eventually generates a call to divide with an argument list containing either one or no elements and the series of recursive calls is terminated.

Suppose we have two ordered lists that have to be merged into a single ordered list as follows:

```
?-merge([2,5,8],[3,7,9]),W).
W = [2,3,5,7,8,9]
```

so the lists in the first and second argument positions are merged to give the ordered list in the third position. Five defining clauses seems generous:

```
merge([ ],L2,L2).
merge(L1,[ ],L1).
merge([X|L1],[X|L2],[X|L]) :- merge(L1,[X|L2],L).
merge([X|L1],[Y|L2],[X|L]) :- less(X,Y),merge(L1,[Y|L2],
L).
merge([X|L1],[Y|L2],[Y|L]) :- less(Y,X),merge([X|L1],L2,
L).
```

but the first two just define the result of merging an empty list with another list. The other three clauses are related to the three ways in which head elements X and Y may be related:

a. If the head elements of the two lists to be merged are the same, one copy of the element is "consed" onto the result list and the other is passed to the second argument in a recursive call.

b. If the head element of the first list is less than the head element of the second list, it is "consed" onto the result list and its tail is merged with the whole of the second list.

c. If the head element of the second list is less than the head element of the first list, the head of the second list is taken and its tail is merged with the first list.

The ability to merge two ordered lists into a larger ordered list could be used as the basis of a list-sorting routine. Lists containing just one element are certainly in order, so merging two such lists must produce an ordered list of two elements. These lists may in turn be merged to give ordered lists of four elements, and so forth, until a list of any desired size is obtained. The procedure to sort a list with this approach is quite simple: just break down a given list into single-element lists by repeatedly using divide, then merge the resulting single-element lists:

```
msort([ ],[ ]).
msort([X],[X]).
msort([X,Y|L],M):-divide([X,Y|L],L1,L2),
                   msort(L1,M1),msort(L2,M2),
                   merge(M1,M2,M).
```

Two clauses specify the obvious truth that single- or zero-element lists are already sorted. A third clause contains an argument [X,Y|M] that can only be unified with a goal argument containing at least two elements, which explains why this style of list description is used in the head of the rule. A list presented as a goal is divided into sublists until each sublist has fewer than two elements, then merge is invoked.

4.5.3   Sets implemented as lists

Sets are powerful, high-level constructs but they are difficult to implement in programming languages. One solution to the difficulty is to use lists to carry a representation of the set, disregarding the order of the elements in the list. Although list [a,b,c] is strictly different from list [b,c,a], we can write procedures that are independent of the ordering of the elements. However, sets should not contain multiple occurrences of the same element and, as a first step towards defining set operations, we need a procedure to delete every occurrence of a given element from a list:

```
delete(X,[ ],[ ]).
delete(X,[X|T],Z) :- delete(X,T,Z).
delete(X,[H|T],[H|Y]) :- X \== H,delete(X,T,Y).
```

Deleting a specified element from an empty list leaves an empty list. If the list does contain elements then either the element to be deleted occurs as the head element or it does not. In one case the list element is included in the result list and in the other it is not.

Armed with a procedure that deletes all copies of a specified element from a list, we then use it to delete all duplicate copies of the head element in a given list:

```
mkset([ ],[ ]).
mkset([H|T],[H|X]) :- delete(H,T,Y),mkset(Y,X).
```

Here the head element of a list presented as the first argument is made the head element of the second list, but all further occurrences of this element in the tail are deleted to produce a new list Y. The head of this list is in turn subjected to the same procedure to produce list X. Recursive applications terminate when every head element has been treated in this way. In use this procedure is very simple:

```
?-mkset([a,b,a,c],X).
X = [a,b,c]
```

Set union is an operation that produces a result set containing every distinctive element from two set operands, but with only one copy of any element that occurs in both operands. In the following procedure two lists in the first and second argument positions have a union given by the list in the the third position:

```
union([ ],S2,S2).
union([X|S1],S2,R) :- member(X,S2),union(S1,S2,R).
union([X|S1],S2,[X|R]) :- free(X,S2),union(S1,S2,R).
```

Each head element from the first argument list is made the head element of the third list, unless it is also contained in the second list, in which case it is left off the third list. One head element is removed from the first list with each recursive call until that list becomes empty, then all elements of the second list are transferred to the third list. An interaction at the ? prompt might now proceed as follows:

```
?-union([a,g,w,y],[w,a,d,f],X).
X = [g,y,w,a,d,f]
```

and the order of the elements in this resulting list can be related to the procedure above. Elements of the first list that do not occur in the second list will appear first, followed by all the elements from the second list.

Intersection is a set operation that extracts just the common elements from two set operands; it may be implemented as follows:

```
intersect([ ],S2,[ ]).
intersect([X|S1],S2,[X|R]) :- member(X,S2),intersect(S1,
S2,R).
intersect([X|S1],S2,R) :- free(X,S2),intersect(S1,S2,R).
```

Members of the first set are now included in the result set only if they also occur in the second set, and it is clear from the first clause that the second set itself is not copied over when the procedure terminates.

EXERCISES 4.5

1. Write a Prolog procedure that relates a list of individual character symbols and a number indicating the number of symbols in the list that are vowels. The program may give further irrelevant answers after giving an initial correct response.

2. Write a Prolog procedure that accepts a list containing both positive and negative numbers and returns a list of absolute numbers obtained from the signed numbers.

3. Define a procedure that relates a list of positive and negative integers to another list containing the same integers, but in which all positive numbers appear in the list before any negative number. Both positive and negative sublists should retain the order of the numbers in the original list.

4. Write a Prolog procedure that accepts a list of lists and returns a list of numbers indicating the lengths of each sublist in the original list.

5. Write a procedure that takes a list of integers and produces an average value for the list.

6. A functor contains the name of a child, his or her date of birth and a list of scores out of 10 for the workbooks completed. A list of such functors is contained

in a relation called `kids` and identified by the first argument as a list of details for a first group of childen, `group1`:

```
kids(group1, [f(tom,dob(14,3,89),[4,7,5]),
f(lee,dob (7,12,88),[3,6]), ... ])
```

Create a relation `kids` containing the details of six children and define procedures that produce the following lists:

a. Functors containing name and date of birth, without the grades.

b. Functors containing name and number of workbooks completed for each child name.

c. Functors containing the name and average mark for each child.

d. Functors containing name and age of each child when the current date is included in the query.

e. Names of children who are older than the average of the list.

f. Names of children in increasing order of total marks in the list.

Create a second relation that contains information for a second group

```
kids(group2, [(jill,dob(14,12,87),[8,3,5,7]), ... ])
```

g. Use the quicksort procedure to produce a list of girls in order of date of birth.

h. Define a procedure that produces a single list of both groups in order of date of birth.

i. Define a procedure that produces a list of names of children who have completed a specific workbook.

4.6 PROCEDURAL MATTERS

Prolog programs are statements in a restricted form of first-order logic; viewed in this way, they are said to have declarative semantics. A program defines the relationship of data objects to each other without committing objects to be either input or output. Ideally a logic-programming system would be presented with a relation containing both known and unknown objects and would report suitable values for the unknown objects. Prolog does indeed do this for many simple relations, but for reasons connected with practical implementation, it is not generally the case. Worse still, we find that a particular order of clauses in a file or an order of subgoals in a rule body might prevent a result being obtained at all. Prolog operates in a top-to-bottom, left-to-right direction through text files, and the outcome of a particular query is heavily dependent on this procedural behaviour. As a result, the language has a procedural semantics that depends on the layout of facts and rules in a text file. It is sometimes helpful to think of declarative semantics as the true specification and procedural semantics as the result actually obtained by a particular ordering.

To explore the difference between declarative and procedural semantics, we consider again the problem of finding routes through the directed acyclic graph of Figure 4.2. Recall that procedure `route` decides if there is a route between two points:

```
route(Start,Finish) :- path(Start,Finish).
route(Start,Finish) :- path(Start,X),route(X,Finish).
```

Now we define procedure `route2`; it is similar to `route` except that the route and path conditions in the body of the rule are interchanged:

```
route2(Start,Finish) :- path(Start,Finish).
route2(Start,Finish) :- route2(Start,X),path(X,Finish).
```

The original version first found a path from a starting-point to position X, then called the route procedure to find a route from that point to the finish. Now a route is found to X and the database is searched to find a final completing step. The existence of a route between points a and d in the graph is confirmed by the query

```
?-route2(a,d).
yes
```

but when presented with a query about a route that does not exist, such as

```
?-route2(e,a).
```

the procedure fails to produce the expected negative result or indeed any result at all. The first clause initiates a search for `path(e,a)` that results in failure, then the second clause makes an immediate recursive call to `route2(e,X)`. Since there is no fact in the database with arguments that could unify with `path(e,X)`, this clause fails and a further successful unification occurs with the head of the second clause. This cycle never terminates, so the system eventually runs out of memory.

If the order of the rules themselves is changed in addition to this reordering of the conditions, the following procedure results:

```
route3(Start,Finish) :- route3(Start,X),path(X,Finish).
route3(Start,Finish) :- path(Start,Finish).
```

This version places the recursive relation first in the body of the first clause, so the first thing the procedure does is to make a recursive call to itself. If we now pose the same query `?-route3(a,d).` that worked previously for `route2`, no result is obtained. An initial goal `route3(a,d)` results in a subgoal of `route3(a,X)`, initiating a series of non-terminating recursive calls.

These revised versions of `route` have the same declarative semantics as the original, but each one has a procedural semantics that prevents termination in some cases. It would of course be possible for two programs to have the same declarative semantics and different procedural semantics, but to produce the same result. It is the procedure for generating the results that decides the procedural semantics rather than the result obtained. Changing the order in which clauses or conditions appear

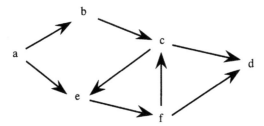

Figure 4.4 A directed cyclic graph

does not change the declarative semantics and does not therefore change any result that is obtained. What it can do is to prevent any result being obtained at all, i.e. it might prevent program termination.

Even when we accept that `route` has to be written in a particular way to get a result, the earlier working version has a number of deficiencies. This procedure applies only to directed acyclic graphs, and we might wish to find routes through directed graphs that include cycles or even through undirected graphs. Rather than extend the original procedure, we first look at a different way of holding the graph information as a list of path functors:

```
graph(one,[p(a,b),p(b,e), ... , ]).
```

This style of presentation has the advantage that it names a particular graph, so a database could contain several graphs, allowing references to be made to any required graph. A path exists between two points X and Y in a list of paths L if it is a member of the list

```
path(X,Y,L) :- member(p(X,Y),L)
```

and a further procedure may be defined to use the path relation

```
route4(S,F,L) :- path(S,F,L).
route4(S,F,L) :- path(S,Z,L),route4(Z,F,L).
```

then a search is related to a particular graph through the rule

```
findrt(X,Y,G) :- graph(G,L),route4(X,Y,L).
```

Procedure `route4` does much the same job as `route` and is equally restricted to directed acyclic graphs. The existence of a cycle in a graph such as Figure 4.4 causes the routine to follow a path in a circle without ever reaching the finishing-point.

One way of avoiding termination problems is to accumulate a list of nodes as they are encountered and to check this list as the route is extended. A check of this kind is easily carried out with the `free` (non-member) procedure described earlier. One advantage of accumulating a trail of used nodes for checking in this way is that the list itself may be produced, informing the user not only of the existence of a route, but also its intermediate stages. If L is a graph expressed in the list form above, S and F are starting and finishing nodes and T is a trace of the route between S and F, these objects are related as follows:

```
route5(L,S,F,T) :- racc(L,S,[F],T).
racc(L,S,[S|T],[S|T]).
racc(L,S,[Y|Sofar],R) :- member(p(X,Y),L),free(X,Sofar),
                         racc(L,S,[X,Y|Sofar],R).
```

Unlike the previous version, this procedure takes the finish as its starting-point and attempts to work backwards towards the start of the route. As a first step, the parameters above are transferred to procedure `racc`, converting variable F to a list at the same time. If the head of this third argument is identical to the starting-point, a route has been found and is transferred to the fourth argument. If not, a path `p(X,Y)` capable of extending the route backwards from the finish is chosen from the list of paths L, and node X is checked to see if it has already been used. If it is indeed free, the node is added to the accumulating list in the third argument position of the recursive rule. A route may then be found in any graph with the rule

```
findroute(G,S,F,T) :- graph(G,L),route5(L,S,F,T).
```

A surprisingly small modification of this program allows routes to be found between nodes in an undirected graph, since the main problem of avoiding the repeated use of a single node has already been solved.

4.6.1   Backtracking and the cut

The order of evaluation in Prolog is evident on running the following program:

```
const(true).
const(false).
pair(X,Y) :- const(X),const(Y).
```

with the query `?-pair(A,B)`. Variable X (shared with A) is instantiated first because it is the leftmost predicate in the body of the rule and value `true` is taken because this is the first matching fact, working from top to bottom. Variable Y is then also instantiated to `true` because attempts to match this subgoal work separately from top to bottom. Since both subgoals have succeeded, Prolog reports A = `true`, B = `true`. Backtracking now takes place from right to left, so the most recent instantiations are undone and new ones attempted. Another search of the database starting from a position just below the previous success reveals that Y can be instantiated to `false`, a second satisfaction of the body is obtained and Prolog reports X = `true`, Y = `false`. A further search fails to find another value for Y and the predicate fails, causing backtracking to the previous subgoal. X is instantiated to `false` and the database is searched from the top for a match with `const(Y)`, resulting in the same two instantiations as before.

The pair rule might be extended to three subgoals:

```
triple(X,Y,Z) :- const(X),const(Y),const(Z).
```

producing eight sets of instantiated variables. Again the order of the facts in the database decides the order of the triplets, so `(true,true,true)` is followed by `(true,true,false)` as backtracking first resatisfies the rightmost subgoal.

A special predicate called cut is provided to give Prolog programmers control of the backtracking mechanism and is shown by the `!` symbol as in the following example:

```
pairb(X,Y) :- const(X),!,const(Y).
```

Cut acts as a valve that allows satisfactions to proceed from left to right, but prevents any attempt to backtrack from right to left over the cut symbol. Instantiated variables on the left of a cut symbol are committed to those values when the cut symbol itself is satisfied, but those on the right can be resatisfied in the usual way. A pair rule as modified above produces only two satisfactions, both of which have X instantiated to `true`. Moving the cut symbol to the right as in

```
pairc(X,Y) :- const(X),const(Y),!.
```

results in just one satisfaction with both X and Y instantiated to `true`.

A suitably placed cut can make a program run much more efficiently by preventing unnecessary work. Earlier we saw that the valuation of an implication is `true` if the antecedent is `false` or the consequent `true`, but only one of these conditions needs to occur. If both conditions occur, the rule succeeds on two counts and the time spent evaluating the consequent is wasted. A suitably placed cut prevents a further attempt at satisfaction after the first attempt succeeds:

```
val(X -> Y,true) :- val(X,false),!;val(Y,true).
```

If the first subgoal is satisfied, the cut is also satisfied and no further attempt is made to satisfy the `val` relation.

Multiple reports of success might be a problem in other situations. For example, the familiar member definition finds satisfactions every time the required item occurs in the list. A cut following the first satisfaction prevents any attempt to find alternative satisfactions:

```
member(X,[X|_]) :- !.
member(X,[_|L]) :- member(X,L).
```

Programs can also be made more efficient in situations where a number of mutually exclusive possibilities occur. For example, the max procedure given earlier requires the use of two separate comparisons, though only one can be true:

```
max(X,Y,X) :- X >= Y.
max(X,Y,Y) :- X < Y.
```

A cut placed after the first comparison will be satisfied if the comparison itself is satisfied, and no attempt will be made to instantiate the second clause. But if the first comparison fails, it may be assumed that the second will succeed:

```
max(X,Y,X) :- X >= Y, !.
max(X,Y,Y).
```

If the first comparison succeeds, the cut also succeeds and the following clause is not attempted; but if the comparison fails, the second clause is the only other option.

4.6.2 Input–output predicates

Interactions with the Prolog system have so far consisted of queries at the prompt that are answered by a simple "yes" or "no" together with a possible instantiation of variables. Thus, a database of the form

```
mother(jill,bob).
mother(lucy,john).
mother(mary,carol).
```

could tell us the mother of a particular child through the following query:

```
?-mother(X,bob).
X = jill
```

An alternative interactive method of obtaining the same information is possible through read and write predicates:

```
go :- write('input child's name>>'),
      read(Child),nl,
      mother(Mother,Child),
      write('The mother of'),write(Child),
      write('is'),write(Mother).
```

This rule consists of a head without arguments and a body containing a number of relations that are, as always, satisfied from left to right. First of all, a write predicate is satisfied when the text contained as an argument is written to the standard output device, usually the screen. A read predicate is then satisfied when a term is provided by the standard input device, usually the keyboard, and this term is taken as the value of the Child variable. A further built-in predicate nl then causes a new line in the output device, so the text telling the user the mother of a child appears on a fresh line. Between reading the name of the mother and writing the output, relation mother is accessed to provide the required information. Notice that the write predicate substitutes values for variables if they are instantiated at the time, whereas text contained between quotes is printed literally. Instead of exchanging information between the head and the body of a rule, a direct exchange between the relations and input/output devices occurs. This rule is achieving its result through the side-effects of read and write relations in the same way as an imperative language.

EXERCISES 4.6

1. Cost informaton may be included in a list of paths in much the same way as in the facts of Exercise 7 in Exercises 4.4:

   ```
   graph(five,[p(a,b,20),p(a,c,35),p(b,d,43),p(d,e,26),
   p(c,e,44)])
   ```

   Define a procedure that calculates the cost of each possible route from one point to another in a directed acyclic graph. Test the procedure by calculating the costs of the two routes between nodes a and e.

2. Translate the graph shown in Figure 4.4 into a labelled list of edges similar to that shown in the text for the earlier acyclic graph. Use the procedure route5 to find every possible route from node a to node d.

3. Cost information might also be included in directed graphs containing cycles, e.g. Figure 4.4. Extend the list of edges in the previous exercise to include cost information, and define a Prolog procedure that finds the cost of every route between two possible points in the graph.

4. An undirected graph allows moves between nodes in either direction, but only one direction is included in the list of edges. As a result, the presence of an edge p(a,b) implies the existence of a further edge p(b,a). A path between two nodes is possible as follows:

   ```
   path(X,Y,G) :- member(p(X,Y), G);member(p(Y,X),G)
   ```

   Modify the route-finding procedure shown in the text so that it finds all routes through undirected graphs.

5. The delete procedure of Section 4.5 requires relation X \== H in the third clause to prevent both the second and third clauses being satisfied when the head element is the element to be deleted. Redesign the procedure using a cut rather than this relation.

6. Remove relation free from the union and intersection procedures as defined in the text and test the new procedure that results. Use a cut to remove the problem that now arises when the procedure is used.

7. Write a small procedure without cuts that relates times of the day before 1200, 1700 and 2400 hours to the symbols good_morning, good_afternoon and good_evening. An interaction at the prompt should then appear as follows:

   ```
   ?greet(14.00,X).
   X = good_afternoon
   ```

   Show that a more efficient procedure is possible when cuts are added.

8. Write a procedure using `read` and `write` predicates that prompts a user for a starting-point and then for a finishing-point in a directed acyclic graph such as Figure 4.2. Advise the user whether a route exists between the two points.

4.7 PROGRAMS FOR PROPOSITIONS

In this section the Prolog language is used to manipulate the syntactic form of a proposition and to decide the truth of propositions in some or all valuations. As a first step in this direction, a small routine to check that a proposition is correctly formed is provided, then a further program converts an arbitrary proposition to negation normal form. An implementation of the Wang algorithm allows propositions to be tested as tautologies then a truth table program allows the evaluation of contingent propositions.

A proposition may be a constant symbol f, one of a number of statement symbols p, q, r, s or the application of a logical connective to other propositions. Section 4.3 explained how the connectives ~, &, v, and -> are defined in the Prolog operator notation, providing the usual precedence rules for propositional operators. Given that those definitions have been made, the following program checks a string to see if it is a proposition:

```
check(F)  :- member(F,[p,q,r,s,f])
check(~F) :- check(F).
check(F)  :- (F = X & Y;F = X v Y;F = X -> Y),check(X),
check(Y).
```

Correctly formed formulas could then be checked at the prompt:

```
?-check(~p -> ~q & r).
yes
```

An extension of the above program informs the user if a proposition is one of the three Hilbert axioms. Only a proposition having the form of the first axiom could match with the functor pattern in the head of the following rule:

```
axiom1(X -> Y -> X)  :- check(X),check(Y).
```

Provided X and Y are correctly formed, a proposition that matches this pattern is an axiom. Similar rules may be written for the other two axioms.

4.7.1 Finding negation normal forms

Negation normal forms of propositions contain a restricted number of logical connectives, specifically the set {v, &, ~} in the notation used above. More important, every occurrence of the negation symbol must stand directly before an atom, so the scope of the operator is limited to that one atom. A conversion of NNF generally proceeds in two stages: unwanted connectives are first replaced by equivalent forms, then negation symbols are driven into the atoms by repeated applications of De Morgan's rule. Any unwanted connective may be removed in this way, but most commonly it is the implication and mutual implication connectives that have to be discarded; this is achieved by the following program:

```
impout ((A <-> B), ((A1 & B1) v (~A1 & ~B1))) :-
                              impout(A,A1), impout(B,B1).
impout ((A -> B),(~A1 v B1)) :- impout(A,A1),impout(B,B1).
impout ((A & B),(A1 & B1)) :- impout(A,A1),impout(B,B1).
impout ((A v B),(A1 v B1)) :- impout(A,A1),impout(B,B1).
impout ((~A),(~A1)) :- impout(A,A1).
impout (A,A) :- member(A,[p,q,r,s,f]).
```

Unwanted logical connectives are replaced by acceptable ones, and functor arguments A and B are replaced by arguments A1 and B1, free of such connectives. Once consulted, the above procedure allows the following interaction:

```
?-impout ((p -> q) -> r).
~ (~p v q) v r
```

returning a result free of implication symbols, but not yet in negation normal form. Negation symbols with scope greater than a single atom are then moved inwards by these mutually recursive procedures:

```
nnf ((A & B),(A1 & B1)) :- nnf(A,A1),nnf(B,B1).
nnf ((A v B),(A1 v B1)) :- nnf(A,A1),nnf(B,B1).
nnf (~A,A1) :- dual(A,A1).
nnf (A,A) :- member(A,[p,q,r,s,f]).

dual ((A & B),(A1 v B1)) :- dual(A,A1),dual(B,B1).
dual ((A v B),(A1 & B1)) :- dual(A,A1),dual(B,B1).
dual (~A,A1) :- nnf(A,A1).
dual (A,~A) :- member(A,[p,q,r,s,f]).
```

which may be combined in a single rule that converts a formula F to its equivalent negation normal form R.

```
transform(F,R) :- impout(F,X),nnf(X,R)
```

4.7.2   The Wang algorithm

Wang's algorithm is essentially an implementation of the propositional part of the Gentzen G proof system described earlier; it therefore depends on the reduction of a sequent of form

antecedent $\Rightarrow$ succedent

to axioms. Although both antecedent and consequent are sets of propositions, a Prolog program implements these sets as lists to be accessed from left to right. An axiom is a sequent with a common atom contained in both antecedent and succedent, a feature very easily recognised by the common procedure given earlier. G system rules are fairly easily translated into Prolog rules and are applied to the sequent until axioms are obtained or until no further applications are possible.

The first step in deciding if a formula is a tautology, i.e. is universally valid, is to make that list the succedent of a sequent and to take an empty list as the initial antecedent. These two lists are then made the arguments of a seq body:

```
valid(Formula) :- seq([ ],[Formula]).
```

A sequent is true if its lists contain a common element or if applications of the rules produces such sequents:

```
seq(Left,Right) :- common(Left,Right).

seq(Left,Right) :- member(~A,Right),
                   delete(~A,Right,Newright),
                   seq([A|Left],Newright).

seq(Left,Right) :- member(~A,Left),
                   delete(~A,Left,Newleft),
                   seq(Newleft,[A|Right]).

seq(Left,Right) :- member(A -> B,Right),
                   delete(A -> B,Right,Newright),
                   seq([A|Left],[B|Newright]).

seq(Left,Right) :- member(A -> B,Left),
                   delete(A -> B,Left,Newleft),
                   seq(Newleft,[A|Right]),
                   seq([B|Newleft],Right).

seq(Left,Right) :- member(A & B,Right),
                   delete(A & B,Right,Newright),
                   seq(Left,[A|Newright]),
                   seq(Left,[B|Newright]).

seq(Left,Right) :- member(A & B,Left),
                   delete(A & B,Left,Newleft),
                   seq([A,B|Newleft],Right).
```

These rules just implement the G system rules of Figure 1.10 and are easily recognised from the arguments of the member subgoal. A proposition is easily tested for validity as follows:

```
?-valid((~A -> ~B) -> (B -> A)).
yes
```

and application of rules is easily followed. First an application of the right -> rule produces the sequent

```
seq([~A -> ~B],[B -> A])
```

then a further application of the same rule produces

```
seq([B,~A -> ~B],[A])
```

Obviously there was a choice of rule at this point; a left implication was used because it occurs before the right implication in the program text, not because it avoids splitting the sequent. Now the left -> rule generates two subsequents:

```
seq([B],[~A,A])
seq([B,~B],[A])
```

and applications of the right and left negation rules then produce axioms.

4.7.3   Printing truth tables

Combinations of the Boolean values true and false are generated by the pair and triple relations given earlier:

```
const(true).
const(false).
pair(X,Y) :- const(X),const(Y).
triple(X,Y,Z) :- const(X),const(Y),const(Z).
```

and these relations may be used to generate the inputs to the val relation described in Section 4.3. Used in this way, the val relation requires two terminating clauses in addition to pairs of clauses required for the evaluation of expressions with each connective. Showing only the implication relation, this gives us

```
val(true,true).
val(false,false).
val(X -> Y,true) :- val(X,false),!;val(Y,true).
val(X -> Y,false) :- val(X,true),val(Y,false).
```

A cut has been added to the implication relation to prevent val(false -> true, true) being satisfied twice, and similar cuts would also have to be inserted in the disjunction and conjunction relations. Once Prolog has consulted these modified definitions, a query at the prompt could tell the user the result of evaluating an expression for every input combination as follows:

```
?-triple(X,Y,Z),val(X -> Y -> Z,R).
X = true, Y = true, Y = true, R = true; and so forth
```

This works well enough, but the output style obscures any patterns that might emerge from the computation and it would be much more helpful to see the familiar Boolean table. Output of this kind is possible with table:

```
table :- triple(X,Y,Z),val(X -> Y -> Z,R),line(X,Y,Z,R),fail.
line(A,B,C,D) :- write(A),tab(3),write(B),tab(3),
                 write(C),tab(3),write(D),nl.
```

The first two subgoals of `table` generate values for X, Y, Z and R in just the same way as if they were used at the prompt, but in `table` they are passed to procedure `line` for printing. Input and output predicates are only satisfied once on each left-to-right pass, so a built-in predicate called `fail` is added to force back-tracking. Predicate `fail` is simply a built-in predicate that always fails, causing Prolog to backtrack and thus resatisfy the triple predicate. A `tab` predicate outputs a number of spaces indicated in its argument and a newline predicate `nl` causes output to continue at the beginning of the next line, giving us the expected tabular output.

We might add headings to each of the columns with a customised header predicate as follows:

```
header :- write('X'),tab(3),write('Y'),tab(3),
write ('Z'),tab(3), write('Result'),nl.
```

The table, complete with header, might be printed through the rule

```
show :- header,table.
```

Prolog systems have a built-in predicate that allows order comparisons between terms, and this feature allows alphabetical comparisons between symbolic atoms. Thus, queries at the prompt proceed as follows:

```
?-false @< true.
yes

?-false @< false
no
```

Relational operations normally cause their two numerical arguments to be computed before a comparison is made, but these special predicates compare individual characters from left to right until a difference is obtained. Strings are tested for alphabetical order in the same way that numbers are tested by the more familar relations. Minimum and maximum relations on symbol strings may be defined analogously to those defined on numbers:

```
mins(X,Y,X) :- X @=< Y,!.
mins(X,Y,Y).

maxs(X,Y,X) :- X @>= Y,!.
maxs(X,Y,Y)
```

If these two relations are restricted to the arguments `true` and `false`, they exactly reproduce the behaviour of conjunction and disjunction operations. This allows the valuation rules for these operations given earlier to be written simply as

```
vals(A & B,V) :- vals(A,A1),vals(B,B1),mins(A1,B1,V).
vals(A v B,V) :- vals(A,A1),vals(B,B1),maxs(A1,B1,V).
```

and an implication can be written in terms of the equivalent disjunction

```
vals(A -> B,V) :- vals(~A,A1),vals(B,B1),maxs(A1,B1,V).
```

As before, it would be necessary to add terminating clauses to the relation:

```
vals(true,true).
vals(false,false).
vals(~X,true) :- vals(X,false).
vals(~X,false) :- vals(X,true).
```

Procedure `vals` produces the same results as procedure `val`, but has the advantage that it may be used for the ternary logic described in Chapter 7 without change.

EXERCISES 4.7

1. Write procedures `axiom2` and `axiom3` that test propositions to see if they match Hilbert axioms 2 and 3. The style of these procedures should follow the style of `axiom1` in this section.

2. Write a routine that converts propositions containing the symbols ~, v, & and -> to a proposition containing only negations and implications.

3. Enter and consult the first three sequent rules shown in the text then test that they are working with the following query:

   ```
   ?-seq([],[a,~a])
   yes
   ```

   Remember that the appropriate operator declarations have to be made. Add the two implication rules, reconsult and test with the following formula:

   ```
   (p -> q) -> (~q -> ~p)
   ```

   Write left and right v rules in the style of the others shown in the text, then use them to demonstrate the following tautologies:

   ```
   p v q -> q v p
   (p v (q & r)) -> ((p v q) & (p v r))
   ```

4. Show that the `vals` procedure described in this section works equally well for the ternary logic described in Chapter 7. Modify the constant facts to include a null element, then produce truth tables for the ternary expression

$(p \wedge q) \vee (\neg p \wedge r)$

5. Write rules in the Wang style for the intuitionistic form of logic explained in Chapter 9. Neglect the "thin" rule, even though this means the algorithm sometimes fails to produce a result.

6. Write a procedure based on the Wang algorithm that produces either CNF or DNF forms from a deduction tree.

PART TWO

Logic with equality

CHAPTER FIVE

Logic with equality

Chapter 1 emphasised a clear distinction between the syntactic forms of propositions and the semantic functions that provide interpretations for the propositional symbols. Syntactic forms are decided by the order in which symbols appear in a string of symbols whereas the semantics of that string of symbols is decided by the interpretation, meaning or denotation given to the symbols. Many different interpretations may be given to strings defining formulas and we have to be sure that the denotations given are consistent with the syntactic form. This distinction between syntactic and semantic forms might at first seem unfamiliar, but it has been with us since our earliest days in primary school. If a child were asked whether 6×7 is equal to 42, he might reasonably reply that it is not. The symbols 6, $\times$ and 7 on the left are quite clearly different from the 4 and the 2 on the right, so the two expressions are not the same. Two expressions are syntactically the same if they consist of the same symbols in the same order. Later the child will learn that, although the expressions are syntactically different, they denote the same value and are interpreted as equivalents.

As a result of our early training, we accept a denotational or algebraic meaning of equality. We place an equality symbol between two syntactically different expressions if they denote equivalent values, and we feel free to replace arithmetic expressions with equivalent values. In our daily lives we use the equality symbol (=) to mean denotational equality. Although the Prolog language contains several versions of an equality symbol, the preceding chapters have repeatedly warned that it is a language based on logic without denotational equality. Equality in Prolog means syntactic equality, i.e. two Prolog expressions are equal when they are syntactically identical. In the following chapters we shall see that a denotational form of equality allows a different style of computation from the SLD mechanism of logic languages. From now on, we shall use the word *equality* to indicate algebraic equality. First of all we need a clearer idea of what equality involves and how the concept extends the logic without equality described in the first four chapters.

5.1   EQUIVALENCE AND EQUALITY

Boolean expressions have the syntactic forms and semantic functions described in Chapters 1 and 2. From a very early stage in Chapter 1, we used the concept of equivalent Boolean expressions in much the same way that we use the idea of equivalent arithmetic expressions. In fact, we have already employed the denotational meaning of equality in the earlier evaluations of compound Boolean expressions. For example, if statements p and q are interpreted respectively as *true* and *false*, a compound formula $\neg p \vee q$ may be interpreted by the expression *or(not true, false)*. This expression is in turn evaluated by reference to the truth tables contained in Chapter 1:

$$or(not\ true,\ true) = or(false, true)$$
$$= true$$

Clearly a meaning or semantics for each of the classical Boolean connectives is contained in the truth table for that connective. Although this might seem quite a trivial example, it is worth reminding ourselves of the justifications for each step. First of all, the expression *not true* is replaced by the equivalent value *false*, then the resulting expression *or(false, true)* is replaced by the equivalent value *true*. The fragment *not true* denotes the same value as *false* and we are justified in replacing one by the other. Similarly the fragment *or(false, true)* denotes the same value as *true* and whenever the former expression occurs it may be replaced by the latter.

Two expressions denote the same value when they produce the same result in all interpretations. For example, the equivalence

$$p \rightarrow q \cong \neg p \vee q$$

means that the two expressions denote the same value whatever the interpretations of p and q. However, denotational equality signifies more than just equivalence: it includes a justification for replacing any expression by a different but equivalent expression. Fragments within expressions are usually replaced by equivalent simpler forms until the simplest possible form is obtained. In principle there is no reason why fragments within expressions should not be replaced by increasingly large equivalent expressions, it is just less likely that this would be useful. The procedure of substituting equivalent terms is called term rewriting and leads us to a new method of computation based on term-rewriting systems (TRSs)

Boolean expressions must always reduce to one of the primitive values *true* or *false*, so every Boolean expression is equivalent to one of these constants. If we consider just the interpretations *true, false* and *imp* then every correctly formed expression constructed from these constants must be equivalent to either *true* or *false*. This simple observation allows us to partition all such expressions into two equivalence sets:

{*true*, *imp(true,true)*, *imp(false,true)*, *imp(false,false)*, ... }

{*false*, *imp(true,false)*, *imp(imp(true,true),false)*, ... }

Here the first set contains all expressions equivalent to *true*, the second those equivalent to *false*. Since every element in a given equivalence set denotes the same value, any one expression may be used to replace another expression from the same set. In practice a computation consists of a gradual reduction in the size of expressions until one of the two simplest possible expressions is obtained. The Boolean expression above was evaluated by replacing subexpressions with simpler equivalents until no further simplification was possible. The two equivalence sets are characterised by these so-called canonical values, so the equivalence sets might equally well be written as

[*true*] and [*false*]

Sometimes the elements in an equivalence class are said to be congruent or to belong to a congruence class. As a result, the shorthand notations [*true*] and [*false*] are also said to represent congruence classes.

5.1.1 Numerical equivalence

The process of evaluating arithmetic expressions by rewriting terms is already familiar and needs no further explanation. This familiarity with the method perhaps prevents us from seeing it as a term-rewriting system that might be extended to more general computations outside the field of arithmetic. Looking again at the process, an expression 3 * 2 + 4 * 5 is evaluated by systematically rewriting terms until a canonical value is obtained:

```
3 * 2 + 4 * 5
  6   + 4 * 5
  6   +   20
      26
```

Terms 3 * 2 and 4 * 5 are first replaced by the values they denote, then the resulting term 6 + 20 is substituted by an equivalent value. Each subterm is replaced by a simpler equivalent value until the simplest possible value, the canonical or normal value, is obtained. Each replacement is a term rewritten within a term-rewriting system defined by arithmetic tables.

Numerical expressions containing natural numbers and arithmetic operations belong to numerical equivalence classes in the same way that the earlier expressions belong to Boolean equivalence classes. There is, however, an infinite number of numerical equivalence classes corresponding to the infinite series of natural numbers 0, 1, 2, 3, ... and in the absence of any arithmetic operations these classes contain just the canonical values themselves

{0}, {1}, {2}, {3}, . . .

If, in addition to the fundamental values of this type, we define an addition operation that makes certain expressions equivalent, each class contains more than just the canonical value. For example, the standard definition of addition makes $7 + 2$ equivalent to 9 and this expression appears in the equivalence class containing the canonical value, i.e.

{9, 6 + 3, 7 + 2, 8 + 1, 3 + (3 + 3), . . . }

Every numerical expression in this class denotes the same value and any one could be replaced by another without changing the value of an expression in which it occurs. One of the major advances in computer science in recent years is the recognition that types such as the natural numbers are more than just the fundamental or canonical values. Operations defined on the fundamental values are equally important and have to be included in a definition of the type.

Many other equivalence classes may be defined, such as the infinite number of equivalence classes of natural numbers with multiplication:

{42, 6 × 7, 3 × 14, . . . }

If both addition and multiplication are defined in a type, then the number of equivalent expressions is increased to include terms such as $3 + 4 * 3$.

Fractions form similar equivalence classes and a series of expressions is clear from the equivalents of numbers with division:

{1/2, 2/4, 3/6, . . . }

Any one value in this equivalence class may be used to replace another in a larger expression, but usually we are interested in reducing an expression to its simplest possible value.

5.1.2 Automated reasoning

Logic languages do use an equality symbol, but its meaning in that context is quite different from denotational equivalence described above. For example, the following interaction might occur at a logic language prompt:

```
?- 6 + 3 = 9
no
```

and an unaware user might be surprised at this response. Logic languages use the equality symbol to represent syntactic equality, so the system is being asked if the syntactic string $6 + 3$ is equivalent to the symbol 9. Clearly it is not, and the language responds accordingly. If an apparently similar question is put to a language using a denotational form of equality, the interaction is

```
?6 + 3 = 9
true
```

Now the question being asked is, does the string 6 + 3 denote the same value as 9? In other words, do these two expressions belong to the same equivalence class? The obvious answer is quickly returned. If an arithmetic expression alone is presented to a term-rewriting language, it is evaluated and its denotation is returned:

```
?6 + 3
9
```

A logic language based on logic without equality should not be capable of doing arithmetic, but in practice logic languages such as Prolog always have built-in arithmetic features as "impure" additions to the language.

In order to compare the different approaches, a simple computation will be carried out in two different ways, using the SLD logic-programming method and using a term-rewriting approach. Programs are given for the evaluation of the Boolean expression $(p \rightarrow q) \rightarrow r$ for any valuation of the atoms p, q and r. It is convenient in this example to express an individual implication in the prefix form as $imp(x,y)$, so the expression above is written as $imp(imp(p,q),r)$. A double implication is then evaluated by the following logic program:

C0 $Dimp(p,q,r,x) \leftarrow Eval(imp(imp(p,q),r),x)$
C1 $Eval(imp(a,c),false) \leftarrow Eval(a,true),Eval(c,false)$
C2 $Eval(imp(a,c),true) \leftarrow Eval(a,false)$
C3 $Eval(imp(a,c),true) \leftarrow Eval(c,true)$
C4 $Eval(true,true)$
C5 $Eval(false,false)$

An individual implication evaluates to *false* if its antecedent is *true* and its consequent *false*; otherwise it evaluates to *true*. The last two lines of this program are especially interesting because they terminate the recursive calls and effectively transfer a value from left to right.

Suppose now that we want to find the value of an expression such as *imp(imp(true, false),true)* using the logic program above. A goal ?-*Dimp(true,false,true,x)* is presented and is backward chained through the series of steps shown in the SLD tree of Figure 5.1. This process proceeds by finding every possible binding for the arguments in the goal, leading to two failed branches and two successful branches that each report an x value of *true*.

A logic program embeds the term to be evaluated in a relation and includes in that relation a variable term that becomes unified with the result of the evaluation. A goal containing variables might be instantiated in several different ways to produce a variety of possible answers. As a result, logic languages possess a strange ability to start with an answer and find all possible questions that might lead to that answer. For example, the goal *Dimp(p,q,r,true)* could be presented as a goal and the SLD mechanism would find all possible combinations of p, q and r that could fit this pattern. This bidirectional nature follows from the fact that logic languages are built from relations as opposed to functions and are capable of producing multiple results for a single set of input arguments. Indeed there is no clear distinction

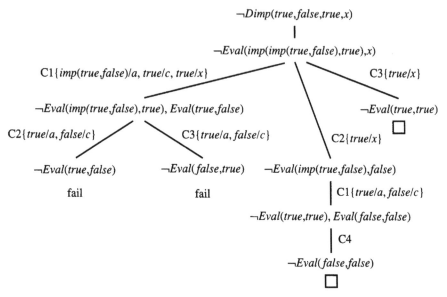

Figure 5.1   An SLD tree

between arguments as input or output, and Prolog expressions are said to be non-deterministic.

Computation by term rewriting requires a program that amounts to statements of equivalences and our earlier example requires the following equivalences:

E0 $dimp(p,q,r) \cong imp(imp(p,q),r)$
E1 $imp(true,false) \cong false$
E2 $imp(false,c) \cong true$
E3 $imp(a,true) \cong true$

To carry out the computation of $imp(imp(true,false),true)$ appropriate argument values are now placed in $dimp(p,q,r)$ and a series of terms are rewritten according to the program equivalences:

$dimp(true,false,true)$
$imp(imp(true,false),true)$ E0
$imp(false,true)$ E1
$true$ E2

Each step in this evaluation replaces one term in the expression by another one that the program defines to be equivalent. Notice that each replacement uses the equivalences from left to right, simplifying the expression until the simplest (canonical) value is obtained. In principle these equivalences can be used in either direction, but in practical term-rewriting systems they will usually be used in the direction that ensures simplification.

A term-rewriting system uses only terms, substituting equivalent fragments within an expression according to a program until the simplest possible value is obtained. Most important, a term-rewriting system produces just one answer and there is a very clear distinction between the initial input arguments and the final value denoted by the expression, the result. If there is only one result, the computation is inherently functional and term rewriting quickly converges on that single result. On the other hand, the exhaustive searching mechanism of a logic language goes on searching for further satisfactions because nothing in the language tells it that a particular expression only has one result. A major difference between the two approaches is that a term within a logic program relation is never replaced by an equivalent value as the computation proceeds. The concept of replacing one term by another of equivalent value simply does not exist in languages such as Prolog. A functional language, on the other hand, does little else except compute equivalent values and replace subexpressions by their denotations until a canonical value is obtained.

It would be wrong to assume that term rewriting is in some way better than logic programming because the above computation is more compactly achieved as a series of term rewrites. Some queries naturally lead to multiple answers, particularly in the area of databases, and logic-programming techniques are then advantageous.

5.2 EQUALITY IN DEDUCTION TREES

The discussion above suggests that two forms of equality may be defined: the first arising as a syntactic equivalence, the second as a semantic or denotational equivalence. Logic languages such as Prolog are essentially animated forms of the logic described in the first two chapters and admit the first form of equivalence, but not the second. Since we generally accept equality to mean denotational equality, the logic of the first four chapters (including the logic of Prolog) is described as "logic without equality". From the brief discussion above it is clear that a denotational concept of equality is a very useful property, providing us with the ability to replace terms by the values they denote, hence reducing an expression to its simplest form. As a result, we now define an extension of the earlier logic that incorporates equivalence, giving us a "logic with equality".

In fact, the extension of the earlier logic to include equality is straightforward in principle, but makes constructions such as semantic tableaux very large in practice. All that is required is the addition of three equality axioms that may be added to a tableau or deduction tree at any point:

$x = x$

$x_1 = y_1 \land x_2 = y_2 \land \ldots \land x_n = y_n \rightarrow f(x_1, x_2, \ldots, x_n) = f(y_1, y_2, \ldots, y_n)$

$x_1 = y_1 \land x_2 = y_2 \land \ldots \land x_n = y_n \land P(x_1, x_2, \ldots, x_n) \rightarrow P(y_1, y_2, \ldots, y_n)$

Thus, if a term c occurs anywhere in a tableau or G system proof we are permitted to add the formula $c = c$, asserting that a term denotes the same value as itself. This first equality formula is sometimes called the reflexive axiom. Each of the axioms above should be read with an implicit universal quantification for each variable, so the reflexive axiom should be interpreted as the formula

$$\forall x(x = x)$$

The second and third axioms contain conjunctions of equal terms, x_i and y_i, that justify the equality of the same function with different arguments or the same predicate with different arguments. Specifically, the second equality axiom tells us that a function f applied to equivalent arguments denotes an equivalent value. Suppose we have an arity-two function max that denotes the maximum of two numbers; this axiom might take the form

$$2 * 8 = 16 \wedge 3 * 5 = 15 \rightarrow max(2 * 8, 3 * 5) = max(16, 15)$$

If a function is applied to syntactically different but equivalent arguments, it returns the same value. Since 16 denotes the same value as $2 * 8$ and 15 denotes the same value as $3 * 5$, function $max(2 * 8, 3 * 5)$ denotes the same value as function $max(16, 15)$.

Axiom three states that if a certain predicate P is *true* for one set of arguments x_i, it must be *true* for an equivalent set y_i. The quantifiers for this axiom can be made explicit in specific examples such as the application to an arity-two predicate P:

$$\forall x_1 \forall x_2 \forall y_1 \forall y_2 (x_1 = y_1 \wedge x_2 = y_2 \wedge P(x_1,x_2) \rightarrow P(y_1,y_2))$$

An interesting special case of this last formula arises when the predicate P is equality itself:

$$\forall x_1 \forall x_2 \forall y_1 \forall y_2 (x_1 = y_1 \wedge x_2 = y_2 \wedge x_1 = x_2 \rightarrow y_1 = y_2)$$

Making x_1, x_2 and y_2 the same as x and renaming y_1 simply as y, we obtain the formula

$$\forall x \forall y(x = y \wedge x = x \wedge x = x \rightarrow y = x)$$

or removing the duplicated equality, we obtain the axiom

$$\forall x \forall y(x = y \wedge x = x \rightarrow y = y)$$

This axiom, together with the reflexive axiom, is shown by the Gentzen-style proof in Figure 5.2 to entail the statement

$$\forall x \forall y(x = y \rightarrow y = x)$$

usually called the symmetric condition of equality. This proof shows that the symmetric property of equality follows from two of the equality axioms given earlier. Remember that equality is a special case of a predicate symbol. If each equality symbol in Figure 5.2 is replaced by predicate symbol P, so that $x = y$ becomes $P(x,y)$, the proof looks much more like those given in Chapter 2.

$$\forall x \forall y (x = y \wedge x = x \rightarrow y = x),\ \forall x (x = x) \Rightarrow \forall x \forall y (x = y \rightarrow y = x)$$

$\forall x \forall y (x = y \wedge x = x \rightarrow y = x),\ \forall x (x = x) \Rightarrow a = b \rightarrow b = a$	2 right $\forall$

$a = b \wedge a = a \rightarrow b = a,\ \forall x (x = x) \Rightarrow a = b \rightarrow b = a$	2 left $\forall$

$a = b \wedge a = a \rightarrow b = a,\ a = a \Rightarrow a = b \rightarrow b = a$	left $\forall$

$a = b,\ a = b \wedge a = a \rightarrow b = a,\ a = a \Rightarrow b = a$	right $\rightarrow$

$a = b,\ b = a,\ a = a \Rightarrow b = a$	left $\rightarrow$
$\times$	

$$a = b,\ a = a \Rightarrow (a = b \wedge a = a),\ b = a$$

$a = b,\ a = a \Rightarrow a = b,\ b = a$	$a = b,\ a = a \Rightarrow a = a,\ b = a$	right $\wedge$
$\times$	$\times$	

Figure 5.2 Proof of the symmetric property

A third well-known characteristic of equivalence is called the transitive property. To demonstrate this, we again take the special case of the third equality axiom where predicate P is equality itself:

$$\forall x_1 \forall x_2 \forall y_1 \forall y_2 (x_1 = y_1 \wedge x_2 = y_2 \wedge x_1 = x_2 \rightarrow y_1 = y_2)$$

We now set variables x_1 and x_2 to x, relabel y_1 as y and y_2 as z, obtaining a further axiom

$$\forall x \forall y \forall z (x = y \wedge x = z \wedge x = x \rightarrow y = z)$$

Now we want to show that, together with the reflexive axiom $\forall x (x = x)$, this formula entails the transitive axiom

$$\forall x \forall y \forall z (x = y \wedge y = z \rightarrow x = z)$$

If these three formulas are labelled as Axiom1, Axiom3 and Trans, the entailment that we wish to prove is

Axiom1, Axiom3 $\vDash$ Trans

meaning that Trans is true whenever Axiom1 and Axiom3 are true. A semantic tableau proves this entailment by demonstrating that the formula Axiom1 $\wedge$ Axiom3 $\wedge \neg$Trans is a contradiction; the detailed proof is shown in Figure 5.3. First of all, a right universal rule is used to generate three constants a, b and c in a self-generated (Herbrand) universe. Since the resulting formula has no quantifiers, it is then broken down into subformulas using the familiar proposition rules. After this has been done, the constants already generated are used to instantiate the left universal formulas of lines 1 and 2, resulting in further unquantified formulas that can also be decomposed by propositional rules. A trace of the branches of the tableau then shows that every branch has a pair of conjugated formula, so the tableau is closed and the original entailment is confirmed. As a consequence, the transitive condition of equality is proven.

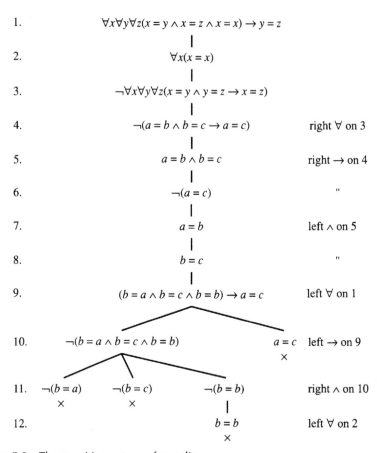

1. $\forall x \forall y \forall z (x = y \land x = z \land x = x) \rightarrow y = z$

2. $\forall x (x = x)$

3. $\neg \forall x \forall y \forall z (x = y \land y = z \rightarrow x = z)$

4. $\neg (a = b \land b = c \rightarrow a = c)$ right $\forall$ on 3

5. $a = b \land b = c$ right $\rightarrow$ on 4

6. $\neg (a = c)$ "

7. $a = b$ left $\land$ on 5

8. $b = c$ "

9. $(b = a \land b = c \land b = b) \rightarrow a = c$ left $\forall$ on 1

10. $\neg (b = a \land b = c \land b = b)$ $a = c$ left $\rightarrow$ on 9
                                                        $\times$

11. $\neg (b = a)$ $\neg (b = c)$ $\neg (b = b)$ right $\land$ on 10
         $\times$ $\times$

12. $b = b$ left $\forall$ on 2
                                                $\times$

Figure 5.3   The transitive nature of equality

5.2.1   Using equality axioms in a proof

The proofs so far have only derived modified axioms from the three original equality axioms. Now we want to use the original axioms to prove formulas that include equality predicates.

Imagine that we have a relation P that associates football players with the teams in which they play. Thus $P(jones,redskins)$ tells us that *jones* is a player for the *redskins* team. At the same time, we have a function f that maps teams to their captains; if *smith* is captain of the *buffaloes*, then $f(buffaloes) = smith$. Since the captain of a team must always be a player in that team, the relation $\forall x P(f(x),x)$ must always be *true*. If now we find that the captain of team a is player b, i.e. $f(a) = b$, it follows that b plays for a. Expressing this in the form of a proof, we might write

$\forall x P(f(x),x) \land f(a) = b \rightarrow P(b,a)$

1. $\Rightarrow \forall x(P(f(x),x) \wedge f(a) = b \rightarrow P(b,a)$

2. $\forall x(P(f(x),x) \wedge f(a) = b \Rightarrow P(b,a)$ right $\rightarrow$

3. $\forall x(P(f(x),x), f(a) = b \Rightarrow P(b,a)$ right $\wedge$

4. $P(f(a),a), f(a) = b \Rightarrow P(b,a)$ left $\forall$

5. $f(a) = b \wedge P(f(a),a) \rightarrow P(b,a), P(f(a),a), f(a) = b \Rightarrow P(b,a)$ EqAx 3

6. $P(b,a), P(f(a),a), f(a) = b \Rightarrow P(b,a)$ left $\rightarrow$
                                     ×

7. $P(f(a),a), f(a) = b \Rightarrow P(b,a), f(a) = b \wedge P(f(a),a)$

8. $P(f(a),a), f(a) = b \Rightarrow P(b,a), f(a) = b$ | right $\wedge$

9.   × $P(f(a),a), f(a) = b \Rightarrow P(b,a), P(f(a),a)$
                                                  ×

Figure 5.4 A Gentzen proof using an equality axiom

Figure 5.4 shows a Gentzen-style proof for this formula that starts with three familiar inference rules to produce the following sequent in line 4:

$$P(f(a),a), f(a) = b \Rightarrow P(b,a)$$

Intuitively this might seem quite obvious, but the proof is only terminated when identical atoms occur on both sides of the sequent. To achieve this, we have to introduce the following version of equality axiom 3 into the antecedent of the proof:

$$f(a) = b \wedge P(f(a),a) \rightarrow P(b,a)$$

Two further propositional steps are then required to produce axioms and thus prove the original formula.

As a final example, we use a semantic tableau to validate the following formula involving equality:

$$P(f(y)) \rightarrow \forall x(x = f(y) \rightarrow P(x))$$

In words, if $f(y)$ satisfies predicate P and all instantiations of x denote the same value as $f(y)$, then all x values satisfy predicate P. As usual, the tableau proof follows from a demonstration that the negated formula is a contradiction, leading to a tableau in which every branch contains a clashing pair of atoms. Although the formula is fairly simple, its semantic tableau proof is large because the equality axioms introduce new formulas that require further decomposition. These axioms are introduced in the three positions indicated in Figure 5.5, each of the equality axioms being used once.

A manual approach to the proofs of Figures 5.4 and 5.5 would be guided by some insight into the form of the axioms necessary to conclude a proof. A mechanical theorem prover on the other hand would have to try every possible axiom in the relentless pursuit of a conclusion. It would be possible to add equality axioms to a

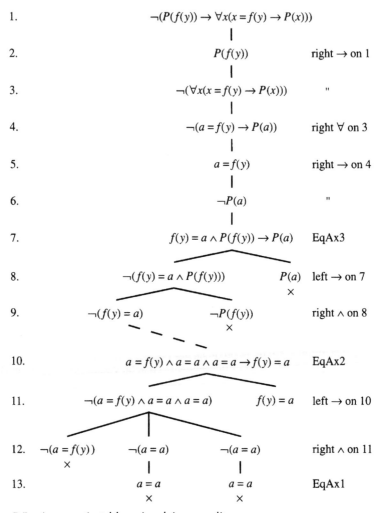

Figure 5.5   A semantic tableau involving equality

logic language like Prolog, but this would result in a massive increase in the search space and an unacceptable loss of efficiency. This is why logic languages avoid equality as though it were the plague.

EXERCISES 5.2

1. Repeat the proof of Figure 5.4 using the semantic tableau notation.

2. Repeat the proof of Figure 5.5 using Gentzen G system notation.

3. Show the following to be valid:

   a. $F(a) \rightarrow \exists x(x = a \wedge F(x))$

   b. $\forall x(P(x) \rightarrow Q(x)) \wedge P(a) \wedge a = b \rightarrow Q(b)$

4. If a and b are the only objects having property P then, for all objects x, the truth of $P(x)$ implies that x is either a or b. A further hypothesis is that there exists at least one object having both properties P and Q. From these two statements we reason that either object a or b has property Q as follows:

$$\forall x(P(x) \rightarrow x = a \vee x = b), \exists x(P(x) \wedge Q(x)) \vdash Q(a) \vee Q(b)$$

Prove this to be valid with a semantic tableau or with a G system diagram. Remember that a new constant (say c) must be introduced when the left existential rule is applied and this could be reused for the left universal rule. Once this has been done an equivalence axiom may be used, leading to a closed tableau.

5. Use a semantic tableau to demonstate the following theorem

$$P(a), \forall x \forall y(Q(x) \wedge P(y) \rightarrow P(f(x,y))),$$
$$\forall x(Q(x) \rightarrow f(x,a) = x) \vdash \forall x(Q(x) \rightarrow P(x))$$

5.3   ABSTRACT TYPES

We now examine a system of "abstract" types introduced by Birkhoff in 1935 to describe semantics through equivalences. In this context the semantics is also called the algebra and the whole subject area established by Birkhoff is called universal algebra. The importance of this work for computing was first recognised during the early 1970s by several disparate individuals and groups, but the defining work in the area seems to have been produced by Joseph Goguen and other members of the mysteriously named ADJ group. The approach taken by the ADJ group has become standard in computing and is adopted in the following examples. In particular, the ADJ notation has many advantages over Birkhoff's original notation, particularly for the examples of the following chapter.

    Abstract types are abstract in the sense that they take away the detail of specific instances, leaving just a bare structure of the objects being described. Taking an informal analogy, we might think of a motor car as an abstract type because the concept itself conveys a great deal of information without indicating a particular vehicle. An object would be an acceptable interpretation of the abstract type motor car if it had four wheels, a metal body, windows and so forth. In short, if it looked like the abstract picture of a motor car that is contained in our minds. An abstract type defines a class of objects and any one of these objects might have features in excess of that required by the abstract type. Thus a motor car with electric windows and four-wheel steering remains an object in the same class of objects because the extras do not change its basic nature.

    Abstractions are important in describing software systems because they capture the essence of what is required without the detail of how it is to be achieved.

Abstract types may be used to specify the requirements for a particular piece of software, then the specification can be checked for consistency and completeness. If all is well, the specification is then implemented in some programming language, preferably one which has built-in features that implement objects, i.e. one that is object-oriented. A language such as Miranda, which is both declarative and object-oriented, can be used to implement the abstract type directly. Machine-oriented languages such as C++ require a careful transformation of the abstract type into the machine-oriented code.

An abstract type may be "animated" in order to test that the operations specified do in fact behave as required and this is the basis of the OBJ language described in the next chapter. OBJ may be seen as a fairly inefficient declarative language capable of acting as a test bed for software specifications. In this role it is often described as a prototyping language. Computer scientists working on large-scale projects have developed the idea of abstract type definitions, prototyping and program transformations to provide powerful software production environments.

Chapters 1 and 2 showed how a meaning or semantics was given to defined syntactic forms with the aid of specific interpretations, often supplied in the form of a truth table. In what follows we shall see that this meaning is encapsulated in the syntactic form of an abstract type and that it is the concept of equality that makes this possible. It is the equations in the syntactic form of an abstract type that impose on the type the same behaviour as the truth table. However, we should avoid thinking of the equations as an interpretation or as the semantics because the equivalence statements are purely syntactic in their nature. Abstract types do not have to include equations and a small example without them provides a good introduction to the concept.

The simplest syntactic form or theory that we can describe is the abstract type describing the two constants of propositional logic. An abstract type labelled bool0 is defined as follows:

bool0 =
   sorts
      bool
   opns
      $\bot, \top : \to$ bool

Here a user-defined name introduces an abstract type bool0 by describing the sorts and the operations (opns) of the type. This particular type has one sort called bool and two zero-arity operations, $\bot$ and $\top$, both of sort bool. Within the specification, an opns line $\bot, \top : \to$ bool defines these symbols to be of zero arity by not showing a sort on the left of the arrow. This definition does no more than the syntactic definitions at the beginning of Chapter 1, it just introduces two constants. Every operation in a one-sorted abstract type must denote an object of that sort, hence Birkhoff described them as homogeneous algebras. Many-sorted types have two or more sorts defined under the appropriate heading and were described by Birkhoff as heterogeneous algebras. Operations in a many-sorted type may denote any sort of the type, i.e. the result of applying the operation is one of the sorts defined in the type. In a one-sorted type, such as the example above, the distinction between type and sort is unecessary, but in many-sorted types it is essential. ADJ notation is used here for consistency and in the knowledge that it provides elegant specifications for many-sorted types.

Having defined the complete but very simple theory or specification bool0, we now have to find interpretations for it. These interpretations might also be called representations or, more commonly in computing, objects in the class of the abstract type. A first object, which we label obj1, can be written as follows:

obj1 = ({*false, true*}, $\perp$ = *false*, $\top$ = *true*)

This notation first shows a set of domain elements {*false, true*} that carry the interpretation followed by a pairing of abstract type operations with interpretation functions. In this particularly simple case, there are two domain elements that each interpret one of the operations of the abstract type. Equality symbols may be left out of this notation, so the interpretation obj1 might sometimes appear as

obj1 = ({*false, true*}, *false*, *true*)

In this notation the order of functions and relations in the interpretation is taken to be the same as for operations and predicates in the abstract type. Three other interpretations may be written as follows:

obj2 = ({0, 1}, $\perp$ = 0, $\top$ = 1)
obj3 = ({*true*}, $\perp$ = *true*, $\top$ = *true*)
obj4 = ({0, 1, 2}, $\perp$ = 0, $\top$ = 1)

Object obj2 feels similar to obj1 in that the two different constants of the theory bool0 are mapped to two distinct domain elements, but interpretation obj3 maps the two distinct theory constants to a single domain element. Although obj3 is a perfectly legal interpretation, it is unlikely to reflect the intended semantics of the theory. An interpretation in which distinct constants of the abstract type are mapped to a single domain element is said to involve "confusion". A different problem arises in interpretation obj4, where there are more domain elements than constants in the theory. When both constants are mapped to distinct domain elements, a spare domain element (2) remains. This remaining element is called "junk" because it can have no purpose in implementing the intended meaning of the theory. We shall see that obj1 and obj2 are initial interpretations or, put another way, they provide an initial semantics for the theory bool0; this is connected with the fact that obj1 and obj2 are free of junk and confusion.

Every abstract type contains a signature defining the sorts and operations defined by the type, and this information also defines the Herbrand universe of the type. In addition to the signature there is usually a collection of equations defining equivalences between expressions in the universe. In a sense the equations build into a syntactic form the semantics previously provided by an interpretation, but we should avoid thinking of the equations as the semantics. Instead we should think of the abstract type as a syntactic form that enforces its behaviour on all interpretations. To illustrate the effect of equations, we expand the specification bool0 to give the larger definition bool1:

bool1 =
    sorts
        bool
    opns
        $\bot, \top : \rightarrow$ bool
        $\neg$: bool $\rightarrow$ bool
        $\wedge$: bool, bool $\rightarrow$ bool
    eqns
        $x \in$ bool
        $\neg \top = \bot$
        $\neg \neg x = x$
        $x \wedge \top = x$
        $x \wedge \bot = \bot$

Two operations have been added. Their arities are different, one and two, but both operations are of sort bool because this is the only sort declared. By following the information given in the signature above, we can build syntactically correct expressions in the same way as we did from the formation rules in Chapter 1. Thus $\bot$ and $\top$ are elements of sort bool and any syntactically correct application of functions $\neg$ and $\wedge$ results in further expressions in the Herbrand universe. Any examples of correctly formed formulas in the universe are exactly those that might be deduced from the formation rules in Chapter 1, e.g.

$$\bot \quad\quad \neg\bot \quad\quad \neg(\neg\bot \wedge \top) \quad \text{etc.}$$

Abstract type equations not only define equivalences, but also provide authority for the replacement of one expression by another. This is a consequence of the substitutive nature of equality mentioned earlier. If the fragment $\neg\neg\top$ occurred in an expression, it could be replaced by the equivalent term $\top$. As a result, the equations of an abstract type may be used in a series of term rewrites to give a simpler canonical or normal term. For example, the expression $\neg(\bot \wedge \top) \wedge \neg\bot$ may be reduced as follows:

$\neg(\bot \wedge \top) \wedge \neg\bot$
$\neg(\bot) \wedge \neg\bot$ eq 3
$\neg\neg\top \wedge \neg\bot$ eq 1   (used right to left)
$\top \wedge \neg\bot$ eq 2
$\top \wedge \neg\neg\top$ eq 1   (used right to left)
$\top \wedge \top$ eq 2
$\top$ eq 3

Any expression can be reduced to either $\top$ or $\bot$ with the aid of the equations, allowing us to partition all propositions in the Herbrand universe defined by bool1 into two equivalence classes:

trueclass = { $\top$, $\neg\bot$, $\neg\neg\top$, $\top \wedge \top$ }

falseclass = { $\bot$, $\neg\top$, $\neg\neg\neg\top$ }

Every element in trueclass is equivalent to $\top$ and is reduced to this canonical value using equations of the abstract type. Since every expression in the class is equivalent, only one of them has to be named in order to characterise the class. As a result, the two classes above may be represented by the congruence classes [$\top$] and [$\bot$], and these two elements are said to represent the quotient algebra.

Two different objects might be offered as interpretations of bool1 as follows:

obj1 = ({*true, false*}, $\bot$ = *false*, $\top$ = *true*, $\neg$ = *not*, $\wedge$ = *and*)
obj2 = ({0, 1}, $\bot$ = 0, $\top$ = 1, $\neg$ = *flip*, $\wedge$ = *min*}

and it would be useful to know how the operations of each representation behave in relation to the abstract type. Take as a simple first example the equation $\neg\top = \bot$ and replace each symbol in this equation with the symbol allocated in each object to give the two equations

not true = *false*
flip 1 = 0

Two symbols on the left of the abstract equation are replaced by their interpretations and, when reduced, produce a result that represents the right-hand symbol. Thus the behaviour of each operation in an interpretation is dictated by the equations of the abstract type. Similarly, the abstract type equation $\neg\neg\top = \top$ leads to two interpretation equations

not not true = *true*
flip(*flip*(1)) = 1

Moving on to the arity-two operation, we convert the abstract type equation $\top \wedge \bot = \bot$ into the interpretations

and(*true,false*) = *false*
min(1,0) = 0

Suppose now that we want to simplify the expression $\neg(\neg\top \wedge \neg\bot)$, according to the equations of the abstract type. The simplification proceeds as follows:

$\neg(\neg\top \wedge \neg\bot)$
$\neg(\bot \wedge \neg\bot)$ $\neg\top = \bot$
$\neg(\bot \wedge \top)$ $\neg\bot = \top$
$\neg\bot$ $x \wedge \top = x$
$\top$ $\neg\bot = \top$

Notice that the equation $\neg\bot = \top$ does not occur explicitly in the abstract type and has to be obtained from equations $\neg(\neg\top) = \top$ and $\neg\top = \bot$. A representation of this proposition in obj1 has the form *not(not true and not false)* and might be simplified as follows:

> *not(not true and not false)*
> *not(false and not false)*   *not true = false*
> *not(false and true)*   *not false = true*
> *not false*   *x and true = x*
> *true*   *not false = true*

At each step, equations of the abstract type have been recast in the form of the interpretation, allowing a series of reductions to the interpreted equation. The important point to be observed is that whenever an abstract expression evaluates to $\top$, an interpretation of that expression in obj1 must evaluate to *true*. Similarly, an abstract expression that evaluates to $\bot$ must have a representation in obj1 that reduces to *false*. A cynical observer might note that all we are doing here is using different symbols or names for the same things, and this would be perfectly correct. Initial representations are intended to capture an underlying structure, so the exact symbols used to represent that structure are unimportant. It does not matter whether we simplify an expression before converting it to a specific representation or after; the same answer is always obtained. A similar chain of reasoning allows us to deduce that the canonical value of a related expression in the second object *flip(flip 1 min flip 0)* is the value 1.

Both interpretations of bool1 provided above are initial interpretations because they define one domain element or domain operation for every operator in the abstract type. The words used to describe the abstract type are unimportant; it is the underlying structure defined by the operations and equations that matters. Every initial object in a class defined by an abstract type is said to be isomorphic – from the Greek meaning the same shape – because it has the same basic internal structure.

A non-initial interpretation in which both $\top$ and $\bot$ are mapped to *true* may be written as follows:

$$obj3 = (\{true\}, \bot = true, \top = true, \neg = not, \wedge = and)$$

but every expression now evaluates to *true*. This is an acceptable interpretation in the formal sense, but is unlikely to reflect the intention of the original specification. It allows a total collapse of the domain space and is an example of a final interpretation as opposed to an initial interpretation, which allows no collapse of the domain space. Initial and final semantics are the limiting forms of interpretations; anything in between is described as loose semantics. We will only be concerned with initial semantics.

5.3.1 Inheriting an existing specification

Since the intended interpretation of a Boolean theory is Boolean algebra, we would obviously like to add operations that would be interpreted as the usual Boolean connectives. One way of doing this would be to write down a new theory with the extra operations included, but a better option is to recognise that all the previous theory is included in the new one and only the additions need to be described. An abstract type can inherit all the operations and equations of a preceeding definition simply by including the name of the previous type in the new heading. Thus, an extended Boolean type bool2 includes bool1 as follows:

bool2 = bool1 +
    opns
        $\vee$: bool, bool $\rightarrow$ bool
        $\rightarrow$: bool, bool $\rightarrow$ bool
    eqns
        $x, y \in$ bool
        $x \vee y = \neg(\neg x \wedge \neg y)$
        $x \rightarrow y = \neg x \vee y$

Theory bool2 includes all of bool1 and this is indicated in the opening line bool2 = bool1 +, then the extra operations and their equations are given in a style similar to the original. This form of addition to an existing abstract type is called an enrichment and is obviously a time-saving device. Since our intended interpretation is Boolean algebra and negation and conjunction connectives are an adequate set for the algebra, we should expect that every other connective can be expressed in terms of these two. The added equations do not have to be defined in terms of the previous ones, so we could have chosen to define operation $\vee$ directly as

$x \vee \top = \top$
$x \vee \bot = x$

In summary, an abstract type – sometimes called a theory, a presentation or a specification – has the following general form:

name =
    sorts s
    opns
        $f : s^n \rightarrow s$
        $p : s^n$
    eqns
        variable declarations
        $L = R$

First of all, a name is given to the theory so that it becomes an identifiable unit binding together a number of operations and their properties into useful modules. Large specifications might consist of collections of such theories. Keyword sorts opens the theory, listing the sorts or types of objects being defined in the abstract type. In this chapter we are concerned only with single-sorted, homogeneous abstract types and this line only occurs because it is necessary in the many-sorted, heterogeneous theories of the next chapter. Next we have keyword opns followed by one line for each of the operations or predicates being defined in the abstract type. These lines describe the sorts of the arguments required by each function or predicate and the sort resulting from the evaluation of an operation. By definition a single-sorted theory has only one sort, so in this case the lines tell us just the arity, i.e. the number of arguments, required by the function or predicate. Constants are seen as zero-arity operations, so they appear as follows:

$$c : \to s$$

Each operation name has to be different from every other operation and predicate name in the abstract type. The top part of the definition, consisting of sorts and opns declarations, is called the signature of the abstract type and might be followed by a number of equations. If there are equations, they define equivalences between strings of symbols in a Herbrand universe constructed according to the signature.

EXERCISES 5.3

1. Use the abstract type bool2 to reduce the following expression to its simplest (canonical) value:

   $$\neg(\neg(\top \wedge \bot) \vee \neg\top)$$

2. An operation called *max* may be defined on symbols 0 and 1 as follows:

   x max 1 = *x*
   x max 0 = 0

   and this operation has the same relation to $\vee$ as that of *min* to $\wedge$ in bool2. Evaluate the following expression:

   flip(*flip*(1 *min* 0) *max* 0)

3. Define an abstract type called booln with a signature consisting only of the constants $\top$, $\bot$, $\neg$ and $\to$. Add equations to the abstract type that force objects of the type to behave as indicated by the interpretations of *true*, *false not* and *implication* as described in Chapter 1.

4. Define an abstract type called boolm as an enrichment of booln. The enrichment should include the operation $\leftrightarrow$ with the meaning defined in the truth tables of Chapter 1. It should also include operations $\wedge$, $\vee$ with the meanings defined above.

5.4   A NATURAL THEORY

A first attempt at a theory to describe numbers begins with a fundamental abstract type called nat0 as follows:

```
nat0 =
    sorts
        nat
    opns
        zero : → nat
        suc  : nat → nat
```

Any theory that consists of a signature without any equations is said to be funda-mental because it generates all possible strings of symbols without defining any equivalences between the strings. In this particular case the signature contains an arity-zero operation called *zero* and an arity-one operation called *suc*. These oper-ators generate the following infinite series of expressions:

zero, suc(zero), suc(suc(zero)), suc(suc(suc(zero))), . . .

in the Herbrand universe of the type. As usual, the elements of this universe are all those strings of symbols constructed in accordance with the arity rules of the abstract type. The only well-formed applications of these operators are the constant *zero* itself or successive applications of the *suc* function beginning with *zero*. The Herbrand universe is sometimes called the Herbrand domain, but in the context of abstract types it is often also called the word algebra. Since there are no equations in this theory, every element is distinct and we obtain an infinite number of one-element equivalence classes.

One very obvious interpretation for the possible elements of the abstract type nat0 is the series of denary numbers {0, 1, 2, 3, . . . }, setting *zero* equal to 0, *suc(zero)* equal to 1, and so forth, but it is not the only possible choice. Number systems may be developed from any base number in just the same way that the denary system is developed on the base number 10, and the binary and hexadecimal systems based on numbers 2 and 16 are widely used in computer science. The relationship of these possible interpretations with increasingly large strings of the word algebra are then shown as follows:

Word algebra	Denary	Binary	Hexadecimal
zero	0	0	0
suc(zero)	1	1	1
suc(suc(zero))	2	10	2
suc(suc(suc(z)))	3	11	3
suc(suc(suc(suc(z))))	4	100	4
suc(suc(suc(suc(suc(zero)))))	5	101	5
⋮			
suc^{20}(zero)	20	10100	14

Each term in the word algebra corresponds to distinct terms in each of the other three interpretations, so there is no confusion. At the same time, there are no junk elements in any of the interpretations, i.e. there are no symbols that do not correspond to an element of the word algebra. Since there is no junk or confusion, each of the three interpretations can be considered an initial interpretation of the abstract type.

Fundamental abstract types have no equations hence no method of making strings of symbols equivalent. The following extended presentation is a first step towards a more useful theory:

nat1 =
    sorts
        nat
    opns
        zero :   → nat
        suc : nat → nat
        add : nat, nat → nat
    eqns
        $x, y \in$ nat
        add(*zero*,*x*) = *x*
        add(*suc*(*x*),*y*) = *add*(*x*,*suc*(*y*))

An extra operation called *add* has been added, increasing the word algebra to include strings such as *add*(*zero*, *suc*(*zero*)), but the equivalences relating to this operation allow it to be simplified through term rewrites. Consider a term *add*(*suc*(*suc*(*suc*(*zero*))), *suc*(*suc*(*zero*))) and a series of term rewrites following the abstract type equations above:

    add(*suc*(*suc*(*suc*(*zero*))), *suc*(*suc*(*zero*)))
    add(*suc*(*suc*(*zero*)), *suc*(*suc*(*suc*(*zero*))))   eq 2
    add(*suc*(*zero*), *suc*(*suc*(*suc*(*zero*))))   eq 2
    add(*zero*, *suc*(*suc*(*suc*(*suc*(*zero*)))))   eq 2
    suc(*suc*(*suc*(*suc*(*suc*(*zero*)))))   eq 1

A series of term rewrites using equation 2 of the abstract type gradually moves *suc* operators from the left to the right argument. Eventually the left argument becomes zero, equation 1 becomes applicable and the series terminates with a canonical value. It is clear from this reduction that the original expression is equivalent to the term *suc*(*suc*(*suc*(*suc*(*zero*))))). Otherwise stated, the term belongs to this equivalence class. Of course, additions may be applied to any pair of expressions and the one-element equivalence classes of the fundamental type are increased to include these expressions:

    {*zero*, *add*(*zero*,*zero*), *add*(*zero*,*add*(*zero*,*zero*)), . . . }
    {*suc*(*zero*), *add*(*zero*,*suc*(*zero*)), *add*(*suc*(*zero*),*zero*)}
    {*suc*(*suc*(*zero*)), *add*(*zero*,*suc*(*suc*(*zero*)), *add*(*suc*(*zero*),*suc*(*zero*))}
    etc.

Denary, binary and hexadecimal numbers equipped with an addition operation provide initial interpretations for the specifications above. As a result, we defined the three interpretations

obj1 = ({nat} *zero* = 0, *add* = +)
obj2 = ({bin} *zero* = 0, *add* = ◊)
obj3 = ({hex} *zero* = 0, *add* = ♦)

in which {nat}, {bin} and {hex} each represent an infinite series of natural numbers expressed in the appropriate base. The usual + symbol represents denary addition, and in common practice this symbol would also be used for binary and hexadecimal addition. Since we are interested in comparing the operations, and the base will not always be obvious from the context, two new symbols (◊ and ♦) are used to represent binary and hexadecimal addition. Note carefully that operator *add* in the abstract type is defined as a prefix operation whereas we shall use each of the others in the more familar infix style.

The result of the term rewrites above confirms the following equivalence:

$$add(suc(suc(suc(zero))),suc(suc(zero))) = suc(suc(suc(suc(suc(zero)))))$$

and when the operations of this equation are mapped onto the three interpretations, the following representations are obtained:

    3 + 2 = 5
    11 ◊ 10 = 101
    3 ♦ 2 = 5

When the appropriate addition operator is applied to the arguments of a particular representation, the result is the image of that obtained in the abstract equation. Each of the three interpretions above is initial, so each reflects exactly the operations of the abstract type. More importantly, the three interpretations are isomorphic and are in effect three different notations for a common underlying structure. If two denary numbers are added together using denary addition and the result converted to binary, the result is the same as if the numbers had first been converted to binary then subjected to binary addition. It is the isomorphism between the representations that permits this form of interconversion.

5.4.1 Homomorphisms between objects

We now wish to extend the abstract type nat1 with just one additional equation to give new type called mod3:

    mod3 = nat1 +
        eqns
            $suc(suc(suc(zero))) = zero$

The effect of this extra equation is to reduce the infinite number of equivalence classes of nat1 to just three, because large strings now reduce to much simpler ones; for example

$suc(suc(suc(suc(zero)))) = suc(zero)$
$suc(suc(suc(suc(suc(zero))))) = suc(suc(zero))$

Every string of symbols in the Herbrand universe then falls into one of the three equivalence classes

$\{zero,\ suc(suc(suc(zero))),\ \ldots\}$
$\{suc(zero),\ suc(suc(suc(suc(zero)))),\ \ldots\}$
$\{suc(suc(zero)),\ suc(suc(suc(suc(suc(zero))))),\ \ldots\}$

This abstract type should be recognisable as an abstraction of the natural numbers modulo 3, more familiar in the interpretation

$obj1 = (\{0,\ 1,\ 2\},\ add = \oplus)$

The single equation of the abstract type may be stated in the form $3 = 0$ and the derived equations below as $4 = 1$ and $5 = 2$, but representations of numbers greater than 2 are not necessary in the interpretation. Modulo 3 additions never produce numbers larger than 2, for example

$2 \oplus 2 = 1$
$3 \oplus 5 = 2$

One way of working out a modulo 3 result is to perform the calculation in denary, then convert the result according to Figure 5.6. We just divide by three and take the remainder.

The relationship between denary and mod3 numbers revealed in Figure 5.6 is quite different from that between the three representations of nat1 given earlier. Given a number in any one of the three representations, denary, binary and hexa-decimal, it is possible to find the unique equivalent number in either of the other representations. Given a denary number it is possible to find a unique equivalent modulo 3 number from the graph of Figure 5.6, but the reverse process is imposs-ible. For example, the modulo 3 number 1 could be traced back to any infinite series

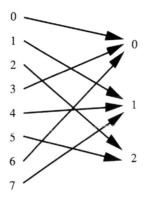

Figure 5.6   Mapping denary to mod 3

of denary numbers 1, 4, 7, ... rather than to a unique number. This is an example of the confusion property mentioned earlier. A relationship of this kind is called a homomorphism.

A homomorphism is a structure preserving mapping from one object or algebra to another in one direction only. If we write down a small denary expression

$$5 + 6 = 11$$

this could be easily be converted to the mod3 equivalent

$$2 \oplus 0 = 2$$

However, it would not be possible to first convert the denary numbers to mod3, carry out the addition in mod3, then convert the answer back to denary. The result 2 could be mapped to any one of an infinite series of numbers. On the other hand, it is possible to carry out a denary addition first then convert the result to mod3, as opposed to first converting to mod3 then applying the mod3 addition.

Generally, if h is the homomorphism function that maps the domain elements of one interpretation onto another and if f is some operation, then

$$h(f(a_1, a_2, \ldots, a_n)) = (f'(h(a_1), h(a_2), \ldots, h(a_n)))$$

For example, a homomorphism mapping the calculation from denary to mod3 is

$$h(3 + 2) = h(3) \oplus h(2)$$
$$= 0 \oplus 2$$
$$= 2$$

but there is no homomorphism in the reverse direction. An isomorphism essentially consists of homomorphisms working in both directions.

A relational operation may be added to a specification in order to allow comparisons between elements of the type. For example, the specification nateq (natural with equality) allows comparisons between naturals:

nateq = nat1 + bool1 +
    opns
        eq : nat, nat $\rightarrow$ bool
    eqns
        $x, y \in$ nat
        $eq(zero, zero) = true$
        $eq(zero, suc(x)) = false$
        $eq(suc(x), zero) = false$
        $eq(suc(x), suc(y)) = eq(x, y)$

This extension simply says that the successors of two numbers are equal to each other when the numbers, x and y, are themselves equal. Thus strings with equal numbers of successor functions are equal, whereas those with differing numbers of successor functions are unequal. A similar set of equations might be used to define the less than (lt) relation as follows:

$lt(zero, suc(x)) = true$
$lt(zero, zero) = false$
$lt(suc(x), zero) = false$
$lt(suc(x), suc(y)) = lt(x,y)$

EXERCISES 5.4

1. An abstract type may be defined as follows:

   integer =
       sorts int
       opns
           $zero$:   → int
           suc : int → int
           $pred$: int → int
       eqns
           $x, y \in$ int
           $pred(suc(x)) = x$
           $suc(pred(x)) = x$

   a. List the equivalence classes of this specification.

   b. Simplify the expression $suc(pred(pred(suc(zero))))$.

2. Children sometimes do multiplications by repeated addition, i.e. to work out
   8×4 they compute $8 + (8 + (8 + 8))$. Use this technique to define multiplication in terms of an addition operation called *add*. Remember that any number multiplied by 0 is 0.

CHAPTER SIX

Many-sorted abstract types

Before proceeding with a definition of a type, we need to understand a simple construction called a set comprehension. Suppose that we wanted to write down the set of all integers between 20 and 30 inclusive. One way of doing this would be the direct way of listing the elements:

{20, 21, 22, 23, 24, 25, 26, 27, 28, 29, 30}

but this could become impractical as the range of numbers increased. A set comprehension allows the same information to be declared without an explicit listing of the elements:

$\{x \mid 20 \leq x \wedge x \leq 30\}$

The vertical bar here might be read as "such that" and this comprehension represents the set of elements x such that x is greater than or equal to 20 but less than or equal to 30. Comprehensions are very powerful and easily implemented in languages such as Miranda that have a list comprehension facility. Set comprehensions of the general form $\{x \mid P(x)\}$ define the elements x of a set in terms of some qualifying predicate P such as the greater-than or smaller-than predicates. Thus, the set of odd numbers may be written in this notation as $\{n \mid Odd(n)\}$ whereas an explicit description of the infinitely many odd numbers is impossible. An object c is a member of a set defined through a comprehension if and only if it has the property required for set membership:

$c \in \{x \mid P(x)\} \leftrightarrow P(c)$

If we define the set of all woodpeckers through the comprehension $\{x \mid Wood-pecker(x)\}$ then an individual bird called *woody* is a member of the set if and only if he has the property of being a woodpecker:

$woody \in \{x \mid Woodpecker(x)\} \leftrightarrow Woodpecker(woody)$

Woodpeckers are divided into classes such as lesser spotted and greater spotted, so the woodpecker set has a number of recognisable subsets, each of which might be described by a comprehension similar to that above. If *bill* is a lesser spotted woodpecker, we may write

$bill \in \{x \mid Lesser\text{-}spotted(x)\}$

and is a member of the set because he has all the properties of a lesser spotted woodpecker. If *helmut* and *john* are both members of the set of greater spotted woodpeckers, we could write membership relations similar to those above for each one. Given that both of these birds are members of the greater spotted set, it seems reasonable to consider a set containing the two of them as a member of the set of all greater spotted woodpeckers:

$\{helmut, john\} \in \{x \mid Greater\text{-}spotted(x)\}$

A certain set of woodpeckers might then be written in the form $\{woody,\ bill,\ \{helmut, john\}\}$, with a subset indicating a common species or type of bird.

Unfortunately, allowing subsets to be members of sets in the same way as individual objects leads to the problem now described. If subsets are allowed to be members of sets, might it then be argued that the set of all woodpeckers is a member of itself? The question of self-membered sets led Russell to examine the set R of sets s that do not contain themselves, i.e. the set of sets described by the comprehension

$R = \{s \mid s \notin s\}$

A particular subset k belongs to set R if and only if it is not a member of itself:

$k \in R \leftrightarrow k \notin k$

but the set R itself qualifies and we might substitute it for k in the above mutual equivalence to give

$R \in R \leftrightarrow R \notin R$

and we are immediately led into a contradictory statement, now known as the Russell paradox.

One way of avoiding the problem is to place restrictions on the elements allowed as members of sets by introducing type classifications. Russell's work at the turn of the century was the beginning of the branch of computing now known as type theory. Type systems introduce a hierarchy of types that allow objects in one level to be members of the next highest level. Returning to the example used above, we might write a particular collection of woodpeckers in a typed system as

$\{\{woody\},\ \{bill\},\ \{helmut, john\}\}$

placing the other birds in one-element sets. Alternatively, we could convert the set of two elements to individual elements, giving

{*woody, bill, helmut, john*}

Types are associated with set membership, so the two sets above consist of individual woodpeckers or they consist of sets of woodpeckers. According to Russell's type theory, all the members of a set must be of the same type, prohibiting mixtures of individual objects and sets of objects. The same principle holds for more deeply nested levels of set membership, so the set

$$\{\{\{a, b\}, \{d, e\}\}, \{\{e\}\}\}$$

is acceptably typed whereas $\{\{\{a, b\}, \{d, e\}\}, \{e\}\}$ does not meet the criteria.

Programming languages usually implement sets in the form of lists, replacing the { } brackets above with the familiar [ ] form. Untyped languages such as Prolog and Lisp allow mixtures of primitive objects, and lists to be elements of a list. As a result the list $[a, [b], [[c]]]$ is quite acceptable in these languages. Strongly typed languages such as Miranda reject attempts to define such lists. Typing has a number of practical advantages in computer science. Most importantly, it allows software translators to check the consistency of a program submitted by a programmer. If a programmer has applied an arithmetic operation to a person's name, he or she has probably made a mistake and a translator should refuse to implement the instruction.

We noted in the previous chapter that types are only really meaningful when we have more than one of them. In this chapter we extend the abstract type to the many-sorted case by declaring more than one type or sort under the sorts keyword.

6.1 LISTS

One of the advantages of the ADJ notation for abstract types is that the transition from the one-sorted situation to the many-sorted situation is quite simple. A fundamental two-sorted specification of a list may be written as follows:

```
list0 =
    sorts
        element, list
    opns
        a, b, c, . . , z :              → element
        nil             :              → list
        cons       : element, list → list
```

Now there are two sorts of objects: elements and lists. Constants $a, b, c, . . , z$ are the elements of some alphabet that is to be contained in a list and are of the type element whereas the constant *nil* represents the simplest form of list, a list that contains no elements. Lists that do contain elements are constructed with an arity-two *cons* operator that attaches one element at a time to the left-hand side of an existing list. Specification list0 is a fundamental abstract type, defining the members of a particular Herbrand universe or word algebra to be a set of strings constructed in accordance with the arity rules. Thus, increasingly large lists of elements are constructed through repeated applications of the *cons* operator

   cons(a,nil)
   cons(b,cons(a,nil))
   cons(c,cons(b,cons(a,nil)))

Obviously the order in which elements are added is important, and different lists are produced when the same set of elements is added in a different order. Just as important, we note that a list containing one element is different from the element itself, i.e. element *e* is not the same as *cons(e,nil)* because the use of the *cons* operator changes the sort of the expression. Sometimes the *cons* operator is described as a "make" operator since it makes a list from a single element. Although specification list0 defines what a list is, it says nothing about the things we might want to do with a list, and this deficiency is now corrected by introducing some useful operations and defining the results of those operations through equations.

    A fundamental specification such as list0 contains only constructor operations, allowing the construction of increasingly large lists of alphabet elements. Since there are no equations defined in the type, there are no equivalences between any of these strings, so each one sits alone in its equivalence class. The elements of a fundamental type are of little use on their own; it is the equivalences defined in the equations that allow term rewriting and make the abstract type useful. One of the useful things we can do with lists is concatenate two of them together into a single list. This feature is added to the previous specification in the form of an operation called *append*:

   list1 =
      sorts
         element, list
      opns
         a, b, c, .., z :   → element
         nil   :   → list
         cons   : element, list → list
         append   : list, list   → list
      eqns
        xs, ys ∈ list, *el* ∈ element
        append(nil,xs) = xs
        append(cons(el,xs),ys) = cons(el,append(xs,ys))

Symbols *xs* and *ys* represent any list objects, perhaps even the same object; *el* represents an element object. When the append operator is applied to argument lists *cons(c,cons(d,nil))* and *cons(a,nil)* the result is *append(cons(c,cons(d,nil))*, *cons(a,nil))*, but this is equivalent to a simpler form obtained through a series of term rewrites based on equivalences in the type. Applications of theory equations reduce this expression to an even simpler form that cannot be further simplified, the so-called canonical or normal form:

$append(cons(c,cons(d,nil)),cons(a,nil))$
$cons(c,append(cons(d,nil),cons(a,nil)))$ equation 2
$cons(c,cons(d,append(nil,cons(a,nil))))$ equation 2
$cons(c,cons(d,cons(a,nil)))$ equation 1

Equations in the abstract type list1 allow the Herbrand universe of specification list1 to be partitioned into equivalence classes. For example, the canonical term obtained in the reduction above is the canonical term in just one equivalence class:

$\{cons(c,cons(d,cons(a,nil))), append(cons(c,cons(d,nil)),cons(a,nil)), \ldots \}$

6.1.1 Selector operations on lists

So far we have provided operations for adding elements to a list and for joining lists together, both of which create increasingly large lists. We have seen that equivalences in the abstract type allow the reduction of appended lists to canonical lists. In addition to these constructor operations, there is also a need for selector functions that extract information from the list, so the head and tail operations are defined below. A head operation applied to a list denotes the most recently added, leftmost element of that list as follows:

$hd(cons(el,xs)) = el$

whereas a tail operation denotes the list of elements remaining after the head element has been removed:

$tl(cons(el,xs)) = xs$

where el is the most recent element to be added by the *cons* operation and xs is any list, possibly an empty one. Notice carefully that the *hd* operation is of sort element whereas the *tl* operation is of sort list, i.e. the one denotes an element the other a list.

Selector operations introduce a problem not encountered in the previous constructor examples: the problem that they might not apply to every argument of the correct type. What, for example, might be the intended meaning when these operations are applied to an empty list?

$hd(nil) = ?$
$tl(nil) = ?$

An empty list has no head element but it is of sort list, as required by the head operator, and we might reasonably expect the operation to produce a result of the appropriate sort. There are three possible ways of coping with this problem:

a. First of all, we could simply leave the denotation of *hd(nil)* undefined so that the matter is left open. More generally, the operations are then said to be partial operations or functions, leading to partial abstract types or partial algebras.

b. Alternatively, we could choose a distinct element value of the appropriate domain for this special case. If the theory is to be interpreted as lists of numbers, it might be appropriate to define the head of an empty list as *zero*, i.e. define *hd(nil)* = *zero*. This technique might be appropriate in some cases, but is not likely to be generally useful.

c. Finally, we could define a special element of the correct sort to denote the application to an empty list. Since this application of the function will usually be interpreted as a mistake, the special symbol can be taken to be *error*, so *hd(nil)* = *error*.

Computer scientists have generally avoided partial algebras because they leave the specification incomplete and this has generally been considered unsatisfactory. Options b and c are quite similar in that they assign a distinctive element of the appropriate domain whenever applications of this kind arise. This gives total functions with a result defined for every possible argument of the correct type. The real problem is that the head and tail operations should never be applied to an empty list in the first place, making it more sensible to produce an error element than an arbitrary element of the domain. Taking this approach, we now define an enriched list2 that inherits the sorts and operations of list1. Instead of repeating the signature and equations for those operations already defined, we can present a new theory that adds operations *error*, *hd* and *tl* as follows:

list2 = list1 +
    opns
        error :   → element
        hd   : list → element
        tl   : list → list
    eqns
        xs ∈ list, *el* ∈ element
        hd(cons(el,xs)) = *el*
        hd(nil) = *error*
        tl(cons(el,xs)) = *xs*
        tl(nil) = *nil*

Unfortunately, both the assignment of a constant domain element such as *zero* or an error element to *hd(nil)* lead to further problems. If *xs* is some list, the following equality must hold:

$xs = cons(hd(xs),tl(xs))$

When the head of a list is *cons*ed back onto the tail, it must reproduce the original list; but if the head of an empty list is set equal to *error*, the following problem is observed:

$xs = cons(hd(xs),tl(xs))$
$nil = cons(hd(nil),tl(nil))$
$nil = cons(error,nil)$

By following the defined equations, we deduce that a list containing element *error* is equivalent to an empty list and we conclude that the reasoning is inconsistent. Taking *hd(nil)* = *zero* does not improve matters because a similar problem arises, this time resulting in *nil* = *cons(zero,nil)*, and it is clear that some other solution to the problem is required. The head operation should not be applied to an empty list, and once this occurs the application of further operations should not be allowed. In the example above, *error* has to be a member of the nat domain, but it would not be correct to treat this element in just the same way as any other number. When an error arises, further constructor applications should propagate the error, creating error elements of a different sort. Thus an attempt to *cons* a nat error onto a list should produce a list error shown as:

cons(error,x) = *error-list*

defining the addition of an error to a list to be a constant *error-list*. One consequence of this need to propagate errors through a series of term rewrites is a corresponding need to equip every sort with an error element. There are a number of problems in propagating errors in this way, and they are examined in the following section. For the rest of this section we neglect error propagation, taking the head of an empty list to be an error and the tail of an empty list to be a further empty list.

Many other useful operations can be defined on lists, but some of them require the use of other types such as bool and nat. The word enrichment is used only when new operations and equations are added to a given type. If new sorts are added to an existing abstract type, the resulting type is said to be an extension of the previous one. Extensions also include cases where two abstract types with their own sorts are merged into a new type. Looking at this the other way around, an abstract type inherits the sorts and operations of two or more smaller types. Viewed in this way the process might be described as multiple inheritance. We now define theory list3 to be an extension of two previous specifications, each containing distinctive sorts:

list3 = list2 + nateq +
    ops
        is_empty : list → bool
        member : element, list → bool
        length   : list → nat
    eqns
        $e_1, e_2 \in$ element $xs \in$ list
        is_empty(cons(e_1,xs)) = *false*
        is_empty(nil) = *true*
        member(e_1,nil) = *false*
        member(e_1,cons(e_2,s)) = e_1 = e_1 ∨ *member(e_1,xs)*
        length(nil) = *zero*
        length(cons(e_1,xs)) = *suc(length(xs))*

This is in fact something of an overkill because many unwanted Boolean and natural operations have been drawn into the extension; but if a theory is built with a particular interpretation in mind, just the required subtypes can be defined. Although the above type is a syntactic, abstract form, it uses suggestive names that reflect an intended interpretation and might be criticised for this. As theories become larger, they tend to be directed towards specific interpretations and there is no great gain in using abstract operation names.

Implementations of the list structure usually represent an empty list as a pair of square brackets [ ]. A *cons* operator then adds elements to the left-hand side of the list, one after the other. Although the notation is different, the procedure is similar in the Prolog and Miranda languages:

nil	[ ]	[ ]
cons(a,nil)	. (a, [ ])	a : [ ]
cons(b,cons(a,nil))	. (b, . (a, [ ]))	b : a : [ ]
abstract type	Prolog	Miranda

In addition to the *cons* forms above, both Prolog and Miranda allow the programmer to write lists without explicit *cons* symbols. For example, the two-element list above would be written in the form [b, a].

EXERCISES 6.1

1. Define an abstract type named boolist that contains the bool and list sorts described in the text.

    a. Enrich abstract type boolist with an operation called flag that denotes *true* when applied to a list that contains element *true* at least once.

    b. Further enrich boolist with an operation extract that denotes a list containing all the *true* elements in a given list.

    c. Define a new abstract type called boolist2, consisting of an extension of boolist with nateq.

    d. Enrich boolist2 with an operation truecount that counts the number of times the element *true* occurs in a list.

6.2   STACKS AND QUEUES

Stacks and queues are familiar concepts that acquire a very precise definition in the form of abstract types. In both cases the underlying structure is exactly that of the list: an ordered sequence of elements applied to an initially empty structure of the correct sort. Consequently, the fundamental specifications stack0 and queue0 below are structurally identical to that of list0 given earlier. The differences between these structures and the list follow from the different operations that are applied to this fundamental structure. Operations are required to add and remove elements from one end of a stack in the same way that the *cons* and *hd* operations attach and detach elements from a list. In fact, we shall see that the *push* and *top* operations of a stack are structurally identical to the list *cons* and *hd* operations. On the other hand, there are some operations such as *append* that are only sensibly applied to lists. Queues differ from both lists and stacks in that elements are added at one end and removed from the other. We shall see that the *join* operation required for a queue is structurally identical to both the list *cons* and stack *push* operations, but that the operation required to remove elements from the queue is quite different.

As a first step, we write down just the constructor operations for a stack, again with a set of elements $a, \ldots, z$ in the following fundamental abstract type

stack0 =
   sorts
      element, stack
   opns
      $a, b, \ldots, z$:   → element
      nil   :   → stack
      push   : element, stack → stack

This definition differs from that of list0 in the different naming of some elements and sorts, but it is actually the same abstract type. Remember that an abstract type is defined not by the words used in its definition, but by the underlying structure when its operations are applied. Thus the use of the *push* operation exactly mirrors that of the *cons* operation, producing increasingly large stacks by adding to an initially empty stack. A Herbrand universe or word algebra of increasingly large expressions is constructed as follows:

push(b,nil)
push(a,push(b,nil))
push(c,push(a,push(b,nil)))

Two selector operations are usually defined on a stack: a *top* operation returns the element at the top of the stack whereas a *pop* operation returns the stack remaining when the top element is removed. Examples of these operations are

top(push(c,push(a,push(b,nil)))) = c
pop(push(c,push(a,push(b,nil)))) = *push(a,push(b,nil))*

Operations *top* and *pop* are abstractly equivalent to the head and tail operations in a list specification. However, we have already noted a problem concerning the application of these operations to an empty list, and a similar problem is now encountered with stacks. This time we go further and define the application of either of these operations to an empty stack to be an error:

top(nil) = *error*
pop(nil) = *error-stack*

but since the operations themselves are of different sorts, the errors have to be of different sorts. An abstract type incorporating these operations can be defined as an enrichment of stack0:

stack1 = stack0 +
    opns
        error   :   → element
        error-stack :   → stack
        top   : stack → element
        pop   : stack → stack
    eqns
        el ∈ element, *xs* ∈ stack
        top(push(el,xs)) = el
        top(nil) = error
        pop(push(el,xs)) = xs
        pop(nil) = error-stack

This abstract type differs from list2 not only in the introduction of a second form of error element but also in that it has not inherited an *append* operation, because such an operation is not required. Even with a second sort of error defined in this way, a major problem remains in expressions such as *push(top(nil),xs)*, i.e. take the element denoted by the top of an empty stack and push it on to some other stack. According to the above abstract type, an expression like this would give *push(error,xs)* and we would find ourselves building structures of error elements as though they were normal domain elements. When an error occurs, it must be treated differently from the fully defined elements of its domain. If an operation of another sort is applied to an error element, it must propagate the error to produce an error element in the new domain. As a result, we need further equations of the following kind:

push(error,xs) = error-stack
push(el,error-stack) = error-stack
top(error-stack) = error
pop(error-stack) = error-stack

Now an attempt to push an element error on to a stack results in a stack error and an attempt to read or remove an element from an error-stack results in an element error. In this way an error is propagated through an expression as desired, but these new equations have an unfortunate and unwanted consequence when used in conjunction with the earlier ones. By combining two of the above error equations, we obtain

top(push(el,error-stack)) = error

but from the previous equations we have

top(push(el,xs)) = el

and since *error-stack* is of type stack it can be used in argument position *xs*. The net effect of this is that all the domain elements are set equal to *error* and the whole element domain collapses into one equivalence class. Since both normal and error propagation equations are essential, some way of preventing the two running into each other is required; the first step towards this is an operation that picks out normal (ok) expressions. Before this can be done, we have to find some way of distinguishing between error domain elements by defining equations such as

ok-stack(nil) = *true*
ok-stack(push(el,xs)) = *ok-elem(el)* ∧ *ok-stack(xs)*
ok-stack(error-stack) = *false*

A stack is ok if none of its components represents an error, so successive removals of the top element eventually lead to an empty stack. Similar tests also have to be applied to the element, using the *ok-elem* operation, to check that it too is not an error element. Conditional equations also have to be defined so that different actions can be taken, depending on whether or not error arguments are encountered. With the aid of such equations, the selector operations can be redrafted as follows:

top(nil) = *error*
top(error-stack) = *error*
top(push(el,xs)) = *if(ok-elem(el)* ∧ *ok-stack(xs))*
                     then *el*
                     else *error*
pop(nil) = *error-stack*
pop(error-stack) = *error-stack*
pop(push(el,xs)) = *if(ok-elem(el)* ∧ *ok-stack(xs))*
                     then *xs*
                     else *error-stack*

The inclusion of error propagation makes the abstract type quite complex, but such a complete treatment might not always be essential. In practical term rewriting it might be satisfactory to terminate the rewriting process as soon as an error appears. The really important point to arise from Goguen's work is that abstract types must include abstract errors. If the person specifying software does not make clear what action is to be taken in the event of an error, another person implementing that specification might do anything. We shall see that Goguen's OBJ language rewrites terms as far as possible without propagating the errors.

6.2.1 Queues

A simple queue has only two constructor elements, an empty queue which we will call *nil* and a *join* operation that adds domain elements to the queue as follows:

```
queue0 =
    sorts element, queue
    opns
        a, b, .. , z :                    → element
        nil          :                    → queue
        join         : element, queue → queue
```

This is of course the same abstract type as list0 and stack0 already described and queues are constructed in the same way as lists and stacks, so *join(c,join(b,nil))* looks much the same as the earlier examples. Two selector operations have to be defined, one to read the element at the front of a queue, the other to remove that element. Since the *join* constructor adds elements to the left, the front of a queue is the rightmost element and we are faced with the problem of finding this element in a queue of arbitrary length. In fact, the strategy is simple: just look along a string until an argument pair *(el,nil)* is found, at which point *el* is the front element. This leads to the recursive equation for *front* shown in the following abstract type extension:

```
queue1 = bool + queue0 +
    opns
        error        :                         → element
        remove       :                 queue → queue
        front        :                 queue → element
        is-empty     :                 queue → bool
        if_then_else_ : bool, queue, queue → queue
    eqns
        el ∈ element, qx, qy ∈ queue
        front(nil) = error
        front(join(el,qx)) = if is-empty(qx)
                                then el
                                else front(qx)
        remove(nil) = nil
        remove(join(el,qx)) = if is-empty(qx)
                                  then nil
                                  else join(el,remove(qx))
        is-empty(nil) = true
        is-empty(join(el,qx)) = false
        if true then qx else qy = qx
        if false then qx else qy = qy
```

Notice how underscores are used in the signature of operation *if_then_else_* to show the argument positions of each sort. This notation might be equally useful to show that an arity-two operation is to be used in the prefix style rather than as an infix operation. For example, a signature declaration in a stack might contain *push_ _* rather than *_push_* to show that it is prefix rather than infix.

EXERCISES 6.2

1. There is an alternative specification of a list that follows directly from Birkhoff's classic work in universal algebra. The following heterogeneous abstract type is a two-sorted version of a homogeneous type called the monoid:

```
listm =
    sorts
        element, list
    opns
        a, b, c, .. , z :          → element
        nil             :          → list
        [_]             : element → list
        _ ++ _          : list, list → list
    eqns
        xs, ys, zs ∈ list
        nil ++ xs = xs
        xs ++ nil = xs
        (xs ++ ys) ++ zs = xs ++ (ys ++ zs)
```

A list is now formed, not by a *cons* operation onto an empty list, but by a special conversion operation that appears to have no name. Remember though, that operation names are only symbols and the two square brackets in the signature [_] are the name and an underscore indicates the position of the argument. Thus, b is an element, but $[b]$ is a list. Once lists have been formed in this way, they may be joined to other lists with an append operation, represented here by an infix double-addition symbol (++). Two lists might be appended as follows:

$$[b, d, e] ++ [a, c] = [b, d, e, a, c]$$

a. Extend the abstract type above to include head and tail operations. Introduce two types of error, one for each sort, to cope with exceptional conditions.

b. Further extend this abstract type to include the operations *is-empty*, *member* and *length*. The meaning of these operations should be equivalent to that defined by list3 in the text.

c. Again extend the type to include two operations called *last* and *leading*, denoting in one case the rightmost element of the list and in the other all elements except the rightmost. For example

$$last[a, b, c] = c$$
$$leading[a, b, c] = [a, b]$$

These operations are, in a sense, a reverse form of the head and tail operations.

6.3   BINARY TREES

Each of the specifications so far described contains a linear structure to which data elements are added at one end and removed from positions characteristic of the particular structure. In lists and stacks, data elements are removed from the side on which they are added; they are removed from the opposite side in a queue. Elements do not in fact have to be added to one end of a linear structure and it is posssible to write equations that specify the insertion of elements at positions along a list or a queue. This might be useful if data elements are to be placed in some order characteristic of the elements themselves. Unfortunately, the correct position has to be found before an element can be inserted, and this requires many more applications of the equations than simply attaching the element to one end. Perhaps these are arguments about the efficiency of an implementation rather than the elegance of a specification, but it may be wise to write a specification that can be easily animated. Tree structures offer more flexibility when inserting data; the ordered insertion of elements in the following binary search tree is quite straightforward.

Trees in computer science have the same root, branch and leaf structure that appeared in our childhood drawings, but we now choose to draw them with their roots uppermost. A generalised tree may be defined to contain any number of branches, but a binary tree with just two branches emanating from each node has some especially attractive properties. Such a tree may be constructed with the aid of a new tree constructor *tcons*:

btree =
    sorts
        element, btree
    opns
        a, b, c, .. , z :   → element
        nil   :   → btree
        tcons   : btree, element, btree → btree

A binary tree is constructed incrementally from a set of elements $a, b, \ldots, z$ and an empty tree *nil* in much the same way as a list is built from smaller components:

nil
tcons(nil,b,nil)
tcons(tcons(nil,b,nil),a,nil)
tcons(tcons(nil,b,nil),a,tcons(nil,c,nil))

Every new addition to the tree occurs by replacing one of the *nil* trees by a new node such as *tcons(nil,e,nil)*, extending the tree away from its root. The shape of a tree depends on the positions at which new elements are added. If additions are always made to the leftmost *nil* subtree or to the rightmost *nil* subtree, the binary tree degenerates into a list. If, on the other hand, new elements are added evenly by replacing every *nil* element in a given tree, a balanced tree is obtained. The abstract type defined above is fundamental in that it does no more than construct increasingly large binary trees. Since this abstract type has no equations, there are no equivalences between the terms constructed, so each one resides in an equivalence class of its own. Unfortunately, a simple binary tree of this kind offers little advantage over the list structure because it is as difficult to find a particular element in the tree as in a list.

A binary search tree modifies the specification of the binary tree by positioning elements in a tree according to their values. Elements are added to a position in the tree that depends on the value of the added element in relation to those already in the tree. More specifically, elements are added to the left subtree or the right subtree according to whether they are below or above the value that appears at a node in the tree. Eventually the left or right subtree must be a *nil* tree and the element is attached in this position. A binary search tree of natural numbers is specified as follows:

> bstree = natlt + bool +
> > sorts
> > > bstree
> > opns
> > > *nil*   : $\rightarrow$ bstree
> > > *tcons* : bstree, element, bstree $\rightarrow$ bstree
> > > *insert* : num, bstree $\rightarrow$ bstree
> > eqns
> > > *n, root* $\in$ nat *ltree, rtree* $\in$ bstree
> > > *insert(n,nil)* = *tcons(nil,n,nil)*
> > > *insert(n,tcons(ltree,root,rtree))* =
> > > > *if n = root*
> > > > *then tcons(ltree,root,rtree)*
> > > > *else if root < n then*
> > > > > *tcons(ltree,root,insert(n,rtree))*
> > > > > *else tcons(insert(n,ltree),root,rtree)*

Further operations test if a particular element is contained in the tree using a *member* operation and test if a given tree is empty using the *empty* operation:

> *member(n,nil)* = *false*
> *member(n,tcons(ltree,node,rtree))* =
> > *if n = node then true*
> > *else if n < node then member(n,ltree)*
> > > *else member(n,rtree)*
> *empty(nil)* = *true*
> *empty(tcons(ltree,node,rtree))* = *false*

Removing an element from a binary search tree is a particularly difficult operation because the element to be removed might be at any position in the tree. Since every subtree within a binary search tree hangs on a node in the tree, the removal of an internal node leaves a subtree that has to be reattached to the tree. The complexities of this process are well explained in a chapter of Bratko's book dealing with Prolog implementations (see bibliography). A Miranda implementation is included in Chapter 8 of this book.

EXERCISES 6.3

1. Extend the binary tree specification (not the binary search tree) to include operations *left*, *right* and *member*. The first two of these operations take a binary tree as their argument and return the left subtree in one case and the right subtree in the other. A *member* operation takes an element and a binary tree as its arguments and returns a Boolean result, indicating whether that element is a member of the tree. The binary search tree operation cannot be used because elements are not necessarily in an ordered position in the tree.

2. An in-order traversal takes elements from a binary search tree in a leftmost depth-first order. Define an operation *in-order* that accepts a binary search tree argument and returns an ordered list containing the elements of the tree.

6.4   PARAMETRISED SPECIFICATIONS

We have seen how specifications are written describing lists, stacks, queues and binary trees of elements, either taking an arbitrary alphabet a, b, c, ... or by inheriting some element specification. Each of these structures is defined for some previously defined sort by including that sort in the initial declaration of the abstract type. However, we might reasonably feel that these structures exist independently of the elements within them, because the basic nature of a list remains the same regardless of whether it is a list of Boolean constants or a list of complex records. List operations are characteristic of lists and independent of the sort contained in the list. Recognising this, it would be useful to have a specification system that describes a structure without committing the specification to a particular element type. Such a specification has to be written using a formal parameter that might be replaced with any abstract type, the so-called actual parameter. This suggests a parametrised form of list, in which a specification such as plist takes the formal parameter data and can replace it by an actual parameter such as bool, nat or any appropriate sort. Each of the operations and equations is then defined in terms of this replaceable parameter as follows:

```
plist(data) = data +
    sorts list
    opns
        nil     :                 → list
        cons    : data, list  → list
        append  : list, list  → list
```

eqns
$xs, ys \in list, d \in data$
$append(nil,xs) = xs$
$append(cons(d,xs),ys) = cons(d,append(xs,ys))$

This specification differs from that of list1 given earlier in that the sort "element" defined within list1 is replaced by formal parameter "data". When the formal parameter is replaced by an actual parameter, all of the operations of the actual parameter are included in the larger sort.

Problems might arise when a parametrised specification has to produce an element belonging to the sort of its parameter, but which is not included in the parameter sort. For example, a parametrised stack would have to define a result for the operation $top(empty)$ independently of the actual parameter that might be used. As a result, the only acceptable parameters are those sorts having a suitable distinguished error element.

Consider as a further example the parametrised abstract type set(data) with operations that insert and remove data elements to and from a set. Set construction does not permit a second insertion of a given element, so an operation is required to compare an element with those already inserted. Equally, the same operation is required to check if a given element is the one to be removed. Since the parameter has to be extended in this way, we examine a specification set(nateq) in which the formal parameter of set(data) has been replaced by an actual parameter. This is an actualised specification and has the additional advantage that it is clearer.

set(nateq) = nateq +
    sorts set
    opns

nil	:	$\rightarrow$ set
insert	: nateq, set	$\rightarrow$ set
member	: nateq, set	$\rightarrow$ bool
empty	: set	$\rightarrow$ bool
if_then_else_	: bool, set, set	$\rightarrow$ set
remove	: nateq, set	$\rightarrow$ set

    eqns
$i, j \in nateq, xs, ys \in set$
$insert(i,insert(j,xs)) =$
    $if\ eq(i,j)\ then\ insert(i,xs)$
    $else\ insert(j,insert(i,xs))$

$member(i,nil) = false$
$member(i,insert(j,xs)) =$
    $if\ eq(i,j)\ then\ true$
    $else\ member(i,xs)$

$empty(nil) = true$
$empty(insert(i,xs)) = false$

remove(i,nil) = nil
remove(i,insert(j,xs)) =
     if eq(i,j) then remove(i,xs)
     else insert(j,remove(i,xs))

if true then xs else ys = xs
if false then xs else ys = ys

Set terms can be constructed in much the same way as the earlier abstract types, so increasingly large terms might be obtained as follows:

insert(3,nil)
insert(2,insert(3,nil))
insert(3,insert(2,insert(3,nil)))

Nothing prevents the construction of a term with a second insertion of the same element, but applications of the *insert* equations show that a term with duplicated elements is equivalent to a smaller term. For example, the set *insert(3,insert(2,insert (3,nil)))*, containing two instances of the number 3, is formed in accordance with the constructor rules. However, the equations show that it is equivalent to a set without the repeated element:

insert(3,insert(2,insert(3,nil))) =
          if eq(3,2) then insert(3,insert(3,nil))
          else insert(2,insert(3,insert(3,nil)))

Clearly *eq(3,2)* evaluates to *false* and the *else* part of this equation becomes relevant, giving the result *insert(2,insert(3,insert(3,nil)))*. A further application of the same rule to the subterm gives

insert(3,insert(3,nil)) = if eq(3,3) then insert(3,nil)
                                      else insert(3,insert(2,nil))

and we derive the following equivalence:

insert(3,insert(2,insert(3,nil))) = insert(2,insert(3,nil))

Thus applications of the *insert* equations remove duplicate copies of any element, eventually producing an equivalent but smaller term.

The fact that the order of insertion is unimportant in sets is revealed by the application of the same equation to the final result:

insert(2,insert(3,nil)) = if eq(2,3) then insert(2,nil)
                                    else insert(3,insert(3,nil))

showing the equivalence

insert(2,insert(3,nil)) = insert(3,insert(2,nil))

The *member* operation is almost identical to that given earlier for a list, except that it is formulated in terms of the *if_then_else_* operation. Similarly, the empty operation differs only in the variable symbols used in its description. This suggests that the underlying structures of the list and the set have much in common: an *insert* operation constructs sets in much the same way as a *cons* operation constructs lists. These operators differ in that equivalences are defined for *insert* but not for *cons*. As a result, many apparently different sets collapse into the same equivalence class whereas lists remain distinct.

A selector operation such as *remove* might have been partially defined if the specification had not included the equation *remove(i,nil)* = *nil*, defining the application of this operation to an empty set. This equation terminates a series of term rewrites when an attempt is made to remove an element from a set that does not contain that element. The problem here is exactly that encountered earlier in the specifications of lists, stacks, queues and trees. A *remove* operation should never be applied to an empty list and any attempt to do this should be regarded as a mistake. However, we cannot simply replace this equation by *remove(i,nil)* = *error-set* because the operation in its current form is required as the terminating step in correct removals. Consider the steps required to *remove* data element 2 from the set *insert(3,insert(2,nil))*:

remove(2,insert(3,insert(2,nil)))
= *if eq(2,3) then remove(2,insert(2,nil))*
else insert(3,remove(2,insert(2,nil)))

Clearly 2 is not equal to 3, so the *else* part of the *if_then_else_* statement is evaluated as follows:

insert(3,remove(2,insert(2,nil))) =
insert(3,if eq(2,2) then remove(2,nil)
else insert(2,remove(2,nil)))

This time the equality holds and the equation *remove(2,nil)* = *nil* may be applied to give the final result *insert(3,nil)*. An abstract type that handled errors appropriately would require an operation that first checked whether an element was a member of a set before attempting its removal. If the element were a member of the set, the removal would proceed as above, otherwise an error would be returned.

EXERCISES 6.4

1. The cardinality of a set is a natural number equivalent to the number of elements in a set. Extend the abstract type above to include an operation *card* that denotes the cardinality of a set argument.

2. Extend the set abstract type above by defining two operations *union* and *intersection*. Both of these operations combine two sets into a single set. Operation *union* denotes a set containing every element that occurs in either of its argument sets whereas *intersection* denotes a set containing just those elements that

occur in both argument sets. Some inspiration may be obtained from the implementations of these operations in the Prolog and Miranda chapters.

6.5   TERM-REWRITING SYSTEMS

Each of the previous sections of this chapter contained examples of compound expressions based on particular abstract types being reduced to their simplest forms. In each case this is achieved by substituting equivalent terms in accordance with the equations of the abstract type. Since every term rewrite replaces a fragment of the expression with an equivalent term, the resulting simplified expression is equivalent to the expression from which it was derived. Since this is largely a mechanical process, it should be amenable to some form of automation, i.e. given a description of the abstract type, the process of rewriting terms to produce canonical values could be mechanised. Birkhoff's equational term rewriting treats the equations of an abstract type as axioms from which further theorems are derived in the style of the Hilbert calculus. Thus, a set of equations E is used to deduce a theorem e and this is represented in the usual notation

$$E \vdash e$$

As a consequence, term rewriting may be treated in syntactic manner as a series of rewrites directed by the structure of the terms.

As soon as computer scientists recognised the importance of abstract types to the development of software, they began to produce automated term-rewriting systems. Many of these early attempts failed because the underlying work on abstract types was not sufficiently well developed. However, the work by Joseph Goguen and other members of the ADJ group was carefully developed and led to the very succesful OBJ automated system described below. Much better term-rewriting systems have been produced since OBJ and they have become the basis of very sophisticated software production methodologies. However, OBJ is attractive because it is relatively simple and demonstrates the important principles involved in term-rewriting systems.

A term-rewriting system is based on the initial interpretation of an abstract type, hence it defines a class of objects, but just one object is defined to be typical of the class. This one object is defined in OBJ in a style almost identical to that of the abstract types described earlier. When this has been done, OBJ accepts expressions constructed from operators defined in the object and reduces them to their simplest normal or canonical form. Since the abstract type or object is considered as a specification, the OBJ system is sometimes described as an executable specification language. As a result, the animation of specifications through term rewriting can be seen as a form of programming language: an arbitrary expression is given to an evaluator that uses stored equations to reduce the expression and return a canonical result.

The animation of high-level specifications is often described as rapid prototyping, because a working but perhaps inefficient version of the final system is available for testing. This form of immediate animation has the advantage that any errors or misconceptions in a specification are revealed before the later stages of project development are reached, saving time and money. OBJ is a strongly typed system and every expression submitted has a sort that can be checked by the system. OBJ also allows a software developer to check if particular applications give the expected result. Each object represents one module of the system being developed, leading to a very natural decomposition of the overall system. Development in OBJ is interactive in the sense that immediate feedback in the development process is provided as work proceeds.

OBJ has three built-in objects: integers with the usual arithmetic operations, Booleans with their operations and identifiers. User-defined objects are introduced with the keyword OBJ then the subheadings of the object follow those of the abstract types described earlier. There is, however, one significant difference in the layout of objects in OBJ in comparison to the abstract types. OBJ divides operations into OK-OPS and ERR-OPS instead of placing both under a single operations heading. The equations are similarly divided into OK-EQNS and ERR-EQNS, the first group containing those equations that produce acceptable results, the second those that produce errors. The following factorial object provides an easy example:

```
OBJ FACTORIAL /INT BOOL
OK-OPS
      FAC       : INT -> INT
ERR-OPS
      NEG-ARG : -> INT
VARS
      N : INT
OK-EQNS
      (FAC(0) = 1)
      (FAC(N) = N * FAC(N - 1) IF(N > 0))
ERR-EQNS
      (FAC(N) = NEG-ARG IF(N < 0))
```

An introductory OBJ FACTORIAL names this object then the fragment /INT BOOL indicates that it uses two other previously defined objects, in this case the built-in objects INT and BOOL. Two operators of sort INT are defined: an OK arity-one FAC operation and an arity-zero error operation NEG-ARG. In fact, the definition used in OK-EQNS is identical to that used in the stack recursive Miranda example of Chapter 8. A particular instance of the object is animated as follows:

```
RUN FAC(3) NUR
AS INT : 6
```

An expression to be evaluated is sandwiched between RUN and NUR then the sort and a simplified form is returned by the OBJ system. The error equation becomes effective if a factorial with a negative argument is submitted, e.g.

```
RUN FAC(3) + FAC(3 - 5) NUR
AS INT: >>ERROR>> 6 + F(NEG-ARG)
```

Notice that OBJ evaluates as much as it can before a result is produced. It does not propagate errors through applications because this might not help the person developing a system.

OBJ uses equations as term-rewriting rules, but there is a difference between equations and rules: equations are symmetric whereas rules are applied from left to right. There is no reason in principle why an abstract type equation should not be used for term rewriting in both directions, and this property can be useful. If this were permitted in an automated system, an endless sequence of backwards and forwards rewrites would be possible, so the OBJ system rewrites in only one direction. There is still a danger of non-terminating sequences from equations such as OP(X, Y) = OP(Y, X) and OBJ avoids this by refusing to evaluate an identical term twice. Evaluation begins when OBJ unifies a submitted expression with the left-hand side of one of its equations. In this example FAC(3) is unified with FAC(N) by setting N equal to 3, then this value is substituted for N in the right-hand side of the equation and the evaluation proceeds.

This factorial example is essentially a one-sorted example because the second, Boolean sort is used only to decide whether the argument is greater than 0. A stack, on the other hand, is many-sorted by its nature and provides a good comparison with the abstract type given earlier:

```
OBJ STACK /BOOL
SORTS STACK ELEM
OK-OPS
      NIL   :                   -> STACK
      PUSH  : ELEM, STACK -> STACK
      POP   : STACK       -> STACK
      TOP   : STACK       -> ELEM
      EMPTY : STACK       -> BOOL
ERR_OPS
      ERR-STACK -> STACK
      ERR-ELEM  -> ELEM
VARS
      N : ELEM
      S : STACK
OK-EQNS
      (POP PUSH(N,S) = S)
      (TOP PUSH(N,S) = N)
      (EMPTY NIL = T)
      (EMPTY PUSH(N,S) = F)
ERR-EQNS
      (TOP NIL = ERR-ELEM)
      (POP NIL = ERROR-STACK)
JBO
```

Again the object name follows keyword OBJ and the fact that this object uses a previously defined object is indicated by the switch /BOOL. Unlike the previous example, a stack introduces two new sorts and these are listed following the keyword SORTS. Operations and equations for the type are then written in the OBJ notation, but the relationship with the abstract type is quite obvious. One feature of the specification that is perhaps not so obvious is that it represents a parametrised object. OBJ contains a facility that allows element ELEM to be replaced by any other object such as the built-in objects INT and BOOL. At the same time, the object itself may be renamed to STACK-OF-INT or to STACK-OF-BOOL. Of course ELEM could equally well be replaced by a user-defined object. Parametrised modules encourage the reuse of software because the same basic structure may be used in many different instantiations.

EXERCISES 6.5

1. Write an accumulator version of the factorial object, taking the basic algorithm from the Miranda example in Chapter 8.

2. Define an object for the common divisor of two numbers, again taking the basic algorithm from the Miranda example in Chapter 8.

3. Define an object called QUEUE, following the abstract type queue1 in the text.

CHAPTER SEVEN

The included middle

7.1 SEMANTIC DOMAINS

It became clear in the previous chapter that a term-rewriting system has to cope with exceptional and unwanted events such as an attempt to read the head element of an empty list. It became equally clear that once such an event had occurred, it was necessary to propagate the error through a whole series of term rewrites, eventually returning an error of the correct type. As a consequence, every domain involved in the computation has to be equipped with an error element of the correct type. For example, a Boolean domain of just two constants has to be extended to a larger domain that includes an error element *error* $\in$ *Bool2* to give a new set

Bool2 = {*true, false, error*}

A Boolean error might result if one of the arguments in a Boolean function were itself an error in the domain of that argument. This procedure works well enough, but it gives the error element in any domain exactly the same status as every other element of the domain. We might instinctively feel that an error element is rather less useful or perhaps less defined than the acceptable, fully defined answers in a domain and might therefore wish to distinguish between the two forms of element.

Scott's domain theory provides a model for syntactic objects in the lambda calculus in much the same way that initial semantics provided models for the abstract types of Chapters 5 and 6. To cope with undefined objects, Scott introduces a "bottom" element into each domain to act as the undefined element of the domain, lifting every other element to a more highly defined level. Each lifted domain has its own bottom element but we can use the symbol *null* for all domains because the type will be obvious from the context. For example, a lifted Boolean domain *Bool*$^+$ contains the elements

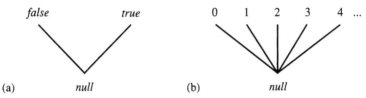

Figure 7.1   Hasse diagrams

$$Bool^+ = \{false,\ true,\ null\}$$

but the third element here has a lower status than the other two. The *null* element is said to be "less defined" than the other two fully defined elements, a situation represented by the following special notation:

null $\sqsubseteq$ *false*
null $\sqsubseteq$ *true*

This difference in status is best shown by the Hasse diagram of Figure 7.1a in which the Boolean *null* element sits below the more defined elements. Lines connecting these elements indicate that a *null* element might evolve to become either one of the two defined elements, but one defined element cannot evolve into another. It is perhaps best to think of the *null* element as the result of a computation that has not yet terminated and might never terminate; but if it does, the result must be one of the defined elements. The *null* represents a certain level of ignorance that might or might not be resolved as matters proceed, but if it is resolved, the only acceptable answers are *true* and *false*. Movements upwards along the lines of a Hasse diagram correspond to increasing levels of "definedness" along a coherence line. A *null* is said to be coherent with both *true* and *false* because it is capable of developing into either one, whereas the two fully defined values are themselves incoherent. Once an element has become fully defined, its value is fixed.

Natural numbers can be lifted in the same way as Booleans, giving the Hasse diagram of Figure 7.1b. A lifted domain of naturals has each of its elements in the usual order, but in addition has a *null* element representing an undefined natural. This unknown number might become known and thus move along a line in the Hasse diagram to a higher state of "definedness". A *null* value in this domain represents any one of the more defined elements of the domain and could not, for example, represent a Boolean value. It follows that *null* values in Boolean and natural domains are different objects even though the same symbol is used to represent both. However, this causes no problems because the domain to which a *null* relates is usually obvious from the context in which it appears.

These *null* values are widely used in computing to represent unknown states that might be missing attributes in tuples or programs that have not yet terminated, and the word *null* is widely used in relational database work. Electronics engineers working in very large scale integrated (VLSI) circuit design have to use Boolean *null* values to model the third, uncertain state of field-effect transistors. Traditionally they have used 1 and 0 to represent *true* and *false* states and have then used either the symbol × or 1/2 to represent the null state. Mathematicians often follow the original notation of domain theory in using a symbol $\perp$ to represent bottom together with other symbols that take the theory beyond the needs of this text. The symbol *null* is simple, easy to write and is therefore used to represent bottom in the following sections.

According to Scott's interpretation, primitive domains such as $Bool^+$ and Nat^+ act as building blocks from which the following three compound domains may be constructed:

a. product domains

b. sum domains

c. function domains

More complex patterns of definedness arise in these structures and we can choose to add further null elements for each structure. Scott's work shows that these domains adequately provide models for any lambda calculus expression and are therefore the basis of a complete programming language.

7.1.1   Product domains

Product domains are the Cartesian products of a number of domains P, Q, ... shown in the usual way as $P \times Q \times \ldots$. Thus the product $P \times Q$ represents the set of all pairs (p,q) in which element p belongs to domain P and q belongs to domain Q. This requirement is neatly expressed in the form of a set enumeration, defining elements of the new product set

$$P \times Q = \{(p,q) \mid p \in P, q \in Q\}$$

Domains P and Q in a product might be different and the product of Boolean and natural domains gives rise to an infinite number of elements such as

$$(false, 42) \in Bool^+ \times Nat^+$$

However, nothing forces the product domains to be different and the enumeration is equally compatible with a product of two Boolean domains and the following elements:

$$(false, null) \in Bool^+ \times Bool^+$$

In fact a pair of lifted Boolean domains consists of $3 \times 3 = 9$ possible pairs and these are displayed in the Hasse diagram of Figure 7.2. The lowest and least defined tuple in this diagram is the pair $(null, null)$ and either one of the *null* elements might become more defined, leading to one of the four pairs to which it is directly connected in the lattice. These partially defined elements might then become even more defined to one of the fully defined tuples of the top row, but only along a coherence

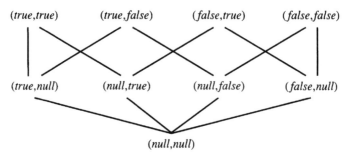

Figure 7.2   A Hasse diagram for Boolean pairs

line in the lattice. This means that the partially defined tuple (*null,true*) can become more defined to either (*true,true*) or (*false,true*), but it cannot evolve to either of the other fully defined tuples because they are not connected by a coherence line. Elements along a coherence path in a Hasse diagram differ in their level of definedness and the paths trace out the ways in which a partially defined state could become more defined. Two of the coherence paths in Figure 7.2 are

$(null,null) \sqsubseteq (null,true) \sqsubseteq (true,true)$
$(null,true) \sqsubseteq (null,true) \sqsubseteq (false,true)$

The symbol $\sqsubseteq$ should properly be read as "is less or equally defined than" and the truth of such a statement is decided by the positions in a Hasse diagram.

More generally, a pair (*a,b*) is less or equally defined than another pair (*a',b'*) if and only if both elements of the first tuple are less or equally defined than corresponding elements in the second tuple. Expressed more briefly

$(a,b) \sqsubseteq (a',b')$ iff $a \sqsubseteq a'$ and $b \sqsubseteq b'$

It is clear from Figure 7.2 that two partially defined tuples might have coherence paths to the same more defined tuple, e.g. tuples (*null,true*) and (*false,null*) might both become more defined to the tuple (*false,true*). This common more highly defined tuple is called the least upper bound (l.u.b.) of the other two tuples because it is the least defined state into which either of them could evolve. The set of tuples {(*true,null*), (*null,false*), (*false,null*)} does not have a least upper bound since there is no coherence line from these elements to a single more defined tuple. A set of tuples from more than one level might have an l.u.b., as in the following example:

l.u.b.{(*null,false*), (*false,null*), (*null,null*)} = (*false,false*)

and in other examples the least upper bound of a set of elements might already be a member of the set, as in the following example:

l.u.b.{(*null,true*), (*true,null*), (*true,true*)} = (*true,true*)

The symmetrical concept of the greatest lower bound (g.l.b.) is used to describe the most defined tuple from which a given set of tuples could have evolved along different coherence lines. Thus the g.l.b. of the set {(*true*,*true*), (*false*,*true*)} is the tuple (*null*,*true*) because either member of the set could be obtained from this element. Of course the two elements could also have been obtained from the less defined tuple (*null*,*null*), but this is not the greatest lower bound. On the other hand, the g.l.b. of set {(*false*,*true*), (*true*,*false*)} is the undefined tuple (*null*,*null*) because these elements have no common partially defined tuple. The greatest lower bound of a set might itself be a member of the set, as in the following example:

g.l.b.{(*true*,*false*), (*false*,*false*), (*null*,*false*)} = (*null*,*false*)

Products of more than two domains contain *n*-tuple elements, so the product domain $P \times Q \times R$ has elements (*p*,*q*,*r*) defined in the enumeration

$$P \times Q \times R = \{(p,q,r) \mid p \in P, q \in Q, r \in R\}$$

A triple of lifted Boolean domains $Bool^+ \times Bool^+ \times Bool^+$ is a set of $3 \times 3 \times 3 = 27$ tuples whereas a 4-tuple is a set of $3 \times 27 = 81$ tuples and it is clear that the number of allowed tuples quickly becomes very large. The bottom element of a triple of lifted Booleans is obviously (*null*,*null*,*null*) and three levels of definedness sit above this element with coherence paths similar to those shown in Figure 7.2.

7.1.2   Sum domains

A sum domain, sometimes described as the disjoint union or the discriminated union, labels the elements of two or more domains in order to merge them into a single domain. A constructor takes elements of each individual domain and "tags" them to show their origin so that the original elements can later be reclaimed with a case or select statement. A sum domain constructed from individual domains P, Q, ... is shown as the single domain $P + Q + \ldots$. In the case of a disjoint union of two domains $P + Q$, elements $p \in P$ and $q \in Q$ are "tagged" with the constructors *inl* and *inr* to make them members of the union. Thus p and q are elements of the separate domains P and Q, but *inl p* and *inr q* are elements of a single compound domain $P + Q$, the abbreviations *inl* and *inr* standing for "in left" and "in right". This means that values from the component domains are tagged to make them into values of the new sum domain. As a result, the set of values in the sum domain is given by the enumeration

$$P + Q = \{inl\ p \mid p \in P\} \cup \{inr\ q \mid q \in Q\} \cup null$$

Notice that an extra *null* element has been added so that, in addition to the tagged undefined element in each component domain, *inl null* and *inr null*, there is a more general level of undefinedness. This is reasonable because the tags *inl* and *inr* themselves define something about the objects whereas a simple untagged *null* represents a greater degree of ignorance.

Consider as an example a sum domain $Bool^+ + Nat^+$ built from Boolean and natural domains by prefixing constructors *inl* and *inr* to elements of the individual

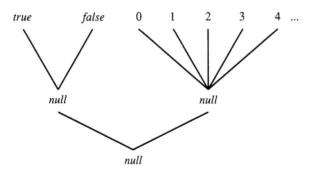

Figure 7.3   A disjoint union

domains. Thus, values *true* and 8 are elements of *Bool⁺* and *Nat⁺* respectively, but *inl true* and *inr* 8 are elements of the sum domain *Bool⁺ + Nat⁺*. Elements of the original domains can be reclaimed with the following selector operations:

> *selectb* ∈ *Bool⁺ + Nat⁺ → Bool⁺*
> *selectb(inl b) = b*
>
> *selectn* ∈ *Bool⁺ + Nat⁺ → Nat⁺*
> *selectn(inr n) = n*

Thus the tags convert individual domains into elements of a single sum domain and select operations extract individual domain elements from the sum.

    Figure 7.3 shows a Hasse diagram for the sum domain *Bool⁺ + Nat⁺*, and from it we discern the following orders of definedness:

> *null ⊑ inl null ⊑ inl true*
> *null ⊑ inr null ⊑ inr 3*

A tagged *null* element is more defined than a simple *null* element because more is known about the *null* value: it can only evolve into a value appropriate for its tag. Operations can be defined to check if an element of the sum domain is of a particular type:

> *isnum* ∈ *Bool⁺ + Nat⁺ → Bool⁺*
> *isnum(inr x) = true*
> *isnum(inl x) = false*

allowing the following deductions:

> *isnum(inr null) = true*
> *isnum(inl null) = false*
> *isnum(null) = null*

A sum domain element with a label *inr* clearly represents a number, even if that number is undefined, but an element with an *inl* label is not a number and can never become one. If the argument is absolutely undefined, the application of such a test is also undefined: the unknown element might or might not be a number.

Triples of sum domains $P + (Q + R)$ might be defined in the same way, leading to doubly tagged elements. The sum domain $Q + R$ has elements *inl q* and *inr r*, so the triple has elements *inl p*, *inr(inl q)* and *inr(inr r)*, which may be expressed as an enumeration:

$$P + (Q + R) = \{inl \ p \mid p \in P\} \ \cup \ \{inr(inl(q)) \mid q \in Q\} \ \cup$$
$$\{inr(inr(r)) \mid r \in R\} \ \cup \ null$$

Compound domains composed of both product and sum domains are common in practice. A domain $(P \times Q) + R$ has elements *inl(p,q)* and *inr r*, following the patterns described earlier. Thus a domain $(Bool^+ \times Bool^+) + Nat^+$ has elements such as *inl(true,false)* and *inr 5*.

7.1.3 Complete partial orders

A coherent series of elements in a domain D is said to form a chain if every element in the series is equally or more defined than the preceding element. Thus elements d_i of D form the chain

$$d_1 \sqsubseteq d_2 \sqsubseteq \ldots \sqsubseteq d_i \ldots$$

and these elements become more defined with increasing subscript number. A domain is complete if every chain has a least upper bound, so every element below the l.u.b. is seen as an approximation of that value. The examples so far are clearly complete because every chain in the given lattices leads to an increasingly defined element and eventually to a fully defined element. However, the definition of a chain allows chains of the following kind:

$$null \sqsubseteq null \sqsubseteq null \sqsubseteq \ldots \qquad false \sqsubseteq false \sqsubseteq \ldots$$

in which equally defined elements are repeated, but these examples are not of great interest. Infinitely long chains of values do arise in the recursive structures considered later. For the moment, we simply note that a domain is required to be a complete partial order.

EXERCISES 7.1

1. Following the example of Figure 7.2, draw a Hasse diagram for the product domain $Bool^+ \times Bool^+ \times Bool^+$.

2. A lifted domain $Flag^+$ is defined as follows:

   $$Flag^+ = \{red, white, blue, null\}$$

   and *null* is an undefined element capable of evolving into any one of the three defined elements. Draw a Hasse diagram to show the connections between all elements of the product $Flag^+ \times Flag^+$.

3. Find least upper bounds for the following sets of elements in the domain $Bool^+$ $\times Bool^+ \times Bool^+$:

> $\{(null, false, false),\ (null, false, null),\ (null, null, null)\}$
> $\{(null, true, null),\ (false, null, false)\}$

4. Find greatest lower bounds for the following sets of elements:

> $\{(true, null, false),\ (null, true, false),\ (null, false, false),\ (true, true, false)\}$
> $\{(true, false, true),\ (false, true, true)\}$

5. Following the example of Figure 7.3, draw a Hasse diagram for the sum domain $Bool^+ + Flag^+$ when $Flag^+$ is defined as above.

6. Describe informally or more formally with an enumeration such as that used in the text the elements of the following compound domains:

   a. $(P + Q) + R$
   b. $(P + Q) \times R$
   c. $(P \times Q) + R$
   d. $(P + Q) \times (R + S)$
   e. $(P \times Q) + (R \times S)$

7.2 FUNCTION DOMAINS

Much of our past experience persuades us that functions are different from data values. A data structure is often imagined to be an operand and a function is often pictured as an operator applied to the operand to produce a result. In this sense, functions have been second-class citizens, prevented from participating in many of the roles associated with data elements. Modern functional computing languages have emancipated the function domain so that it becomes a first-class citizen with similar rights and responsibilities to the product and sum domains. It may be assigned to variables, passed as a parameter to a subroutine or returned by subroutines. Conversely, it has imposed upon it the same restrictions as other domains so that, like other domains, it has to be complete.

Functions may be either partial or total, depending on whether they produce a result for every domain element used as an argument, but a function applied to a lifted domain is always total. An inappropriate argument is taken to be a *null* value and a function result can be defined for this value in the same way as for the more defined elements of the domain. Often the result of such an application will be a null element in the result domain of the function, but later we shall see that it might in some cases be a more defined element.

There are two general methods of expressing logical functions and relations: an extensional approach explicitly lists all the facts in the form of a graph whereas an intensional approach provides an algorithm from which a value is computed. For example, the squares of the natural numbers may be shown in an extensional style as

$graph(square) = \{(0,0), (1,1), (2,4), (3,9), \ldots \}$

or in an intensional style as

$square(x) = x * x$

In one case the values are provided explicitly; in the other case a formula is provided to compute them. Of course the general distinction between extensional and intensional information applies to all languages, including Prolog, where it may be seen as a distinction between facts and rules.

In order that function domains should be computable, they have to behave in the restricted way now described for some fairly simple examples. The simplest possible function, taking one argument from a lifted Boolean domain to give a result in the same domain, is represented by the type

$Bool^+ \rightarrow Bool^+$

but, somewhat surprisingly, there are $3 \times 3 \times 3 = 27$ possible functions of this type. The easiest way to demonstrate this is to begin to enumerate every possible combination of argument and result. To do this, we head a column with the three possible argument elements of $Bool^+$ then list the 27 different combinations of elements to which they could be mapped:

Functions	Arguments		
	true	*false*	*null*
$f1$	*true*	*true*	*true*
$f2$	*true*	*true*	*false*
$f3$	*true*	*true*	*null*
$f4$	*true*	*false*	*true*
$f5$	*true*	*false*	*false*
$f6$	*true*	*false*	*null*
$f7$	*true*	*null*	*true*
⋮	⋮	⋮	⋮
$f25$	*null*	*null*	*true*
$f26$	*null*	*null*	*false*
$f27$	*null*	*null*	*null*

Thus the first function, $f1$, maps each of the three possible arguments to *true* and this information might equally well be shown in the form of a graph:

$graph(f1) = \{(true,true), (false,true), (null,true)\}$

so that $f1$ *true* denotes the value *true* as indeed do $f1$ *false* and $f1$ *null*. The table above is obtained by varying the possible values most rapidly in the right-hand column and least rapidly in the left; by continuing this process, it would be a simple task to enumerate all 27 possibilities. Fortunately, further investigation shows that many of these potential functions are not in accord with the concept of definedness for Boolean domain elements. Consider the graph of function $f2$ represented as follows:

$graph(f2) = \{(true,true), (false,true), (null,false)\}$

in which the two fully defined elements are mapped to *true* whereas the undefined element is mapped to *false*. Remember also that the *null* argument might become more defined to either of the two fully defined values. Here we have the contradictory situation where a *null* element is mapped to *false*, but if it becomes more defined to either *true* or *false* it is mapped to *true*. The function is clearly unacceptable as it stands.

As a first attempt at removing such unacceptable functions, we might demand that any function with undefined or partially defined arguments should produce an undefined result. A "strict" regime like this solves the problem observed above by cutting out defined results when the function arguments themselves are not fully defined. Unfortunately, it also removes a property that might sometimes be useful: the ability of a function to produce defined results from partially defined inputs. A rather more sophisticated option is to exclude functions like the one above by insisting that function application preserves the order of definedness in arguments. Thus, if argument x is equally or less defined than argument y, result $f(x)$ must be equally or less defined than $f(y)$:

$x \sqsubseteq y \rightarrow f(x) \sqsubseteq f(y)$

Functions that behave in this way are said to be monotonic and this feature sometimes allows defined outputs to be obtained from partially defined inputs. A "nonstrict" regime replaces the strict insistence on fully defined inputs by an insistence on monotonic functions.

Function $f2$ in the Boolean example above maps arguments to results as follows:

$f2(true) = true$
$f2(false) = true$
$f2(null) = false$

and the problem is quite obvious. Argument *null* is less defined than arguments *true* or *false*, so an application of $f2$ must produce a result equally or less defined than those arguments. But *false* is not equally or less defined than *true* because these two fully defined elements do not lie on a single coherence line: one could not become the other. It would not make sense if function $f2$ *null* produced the result *false* then the *null* argument became more defined and the result changed to *true*. As a result, function $f2$ has to be discarded because it is not a monotonic function.

An even less acceptable example of a monotonicity failing is the function $f25$:

$graph(f25) = \{(true,null), (false,null), (null,true)\}$

in which both defined arguments produce an undefined result whereas the undefined argument produces a defined result. Far from being retained, the order of definedness in this function is actually reversed.

Of the original 27 possible functions, only the following 11 survive the monotonicity test:

Functions	Arguments		
	false	*true*	*null*
*f*1	true	true	true
*f*3	true	true	null
*f*6	true	false	null
*f*9	true	null	null
*f*12	false	true	null
*f*14	false	false	false
*f*15	false	false	null
*f*18	false	null	null
*f*21	null	true	null
*f*24	null	false	null
*f*27	null	null	null

One consequence of making functions first-class citizens is that they may be placed in an order of definedness in just the same way as other compound domains. As a result, the functions above can be placed along coherence lines in a Hasse diagram in much the same way as the earlier examples in product and sum domains. A function g is equally or less defined than a function h if it produces equally or less defined results for all arguments

$$g \sqsubseteq h \quad \text{iff} \quad \forall x (g(x) \sqsubseteq h(x))$$

Thus $f27$ is less defined than every other function in the example above because it produces the least defined results. Other functions have a level of definedness along the coherence lines in the Hasse diagram of Figure 7.4, but notice that only two functions produce fully defined results.

In fact, only one of the 11 monotonic functions ($f6$) is of interest to us because it looks like the familiar *not* function, but with an included middle element. When written in table form, it looks like an extension of the table given in Chapter 1:

x	*not x*
false	*true*
true	*false*
null	*null*

but this is quite different from the earlier interpretation of the $\neg$ symbol. Now an undefined *null* element acts as a middle from which either of the fully defined elements might evolve.

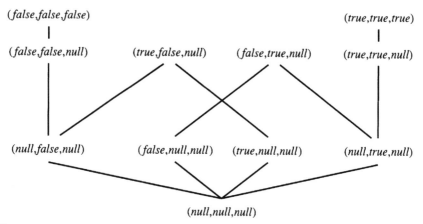

Figure 7.4 An order of definedness for functions

7.2.1   Functions from pairs of Booleans

A function taking a pair of elements from a lifted Boolean domain as its domain element and returning a single Boolean element has a result of the type

$$(Bool^+, Bool^+) \rightarrow Bool^+$$

Now there are nine distinct argument elements corresponding to all possible pairs of *true*, *false* and *null*, and each one of these nine may be mapped to any one of the three possible results. An amazing number of possible functions result, but most of them are not monotonic and very few of the remaining functions are of interest. Those that are of interest to us here are extensions of the simple truth functions given in Chapter 1. For example, the *and* function can be seen as an extension of the earlier simple function acting on the unlifted domain {*true*, *false*}. Four of the nine lines in this table are simply copied from the unlifted version:

X	Y	and(X,Y)	or(X,Y)	implies(X,Y)
true	true	true	true	true
true	false	false	true	false
true	null	null	true	null
false	true	false	true	true
false	false	false	false	true
false	null	false	null	true
null	true	null	true	true
null	false	false	null	null
null	null	null	null	null

An *and* function produces the result *false* when either one of its arguments is *false*, so the other argument is irrelevant. As a consequence, a non-strict evaluation of the function produces a defined result, even though one of the arguments is undefined:

and(false,null) = false
and(null,false) = false

Similarly, an *or* function produces the result *true* if either one of its arguments is *true*, allowing the following non-strict functions:

or(true,null) = true
or(null,true) = true

Now that we have a middle value, an interpretation of the expression $p \lor \neg p$ no longer has to evaluate to the fully defined value *true*. If p is interpreted as *null* then the expression may be evaluated:

or(null,not(null))
or(null,null)
null

and the law of the excluded middle is seen to fail. The evaluation of interpretations of symbolic expressions generally follows the pattern described in Chapter 1, but the non-strict tables are used instead of the tables in Chapter 1. For example, an expression $(p \land \neg q) \lor (\neg p \land r)$ is evaluated with the interpretations $p = true$, $q = false$ and $r = null$ as

or(and(true,not(false)),and(not(true),null))
or(and(true,true),and(false,null))
or(true,false)
true

Two interesting points arise here: (1) a defined result is obtained even though one of the arguments is undefined; (2) we really only needed to evaluate the first argument of the disjunction because, once this argument had been found *true*, the second argument became irrelevant. The first point is the characteristic feature of non-strict evaluation and the second leads to the lazy evaluation property described later.

It is useful to note that the conjunction and disjunction functions defined in the table are specialised cases of the *min* and *max* functions based on the lexical order *false < null < true*. As a result, intensional functions may be written as:

and(x,y) = x, if x < y
      = y, otherwise

or(x,y) = x, if x ⊃ y
     = y, otherwise

and the *implies* function might be written as a specialised disjunction:

implies(x,y) = or((not x),y)

These functions are used to generate tables for arbitrary propositions using Prolog in Section 4.7 and Miranda in Section 8.7.

The current generation of serial computers require that arguments are evaluated from left to right, so the leftmost argument has to be evaluated before the others are visible. As a result, the expression *and(false,null)* will be successfully evaluated from a partially defined argument, but *and(null,false)* has to be strictly evaluated, producing an undefined result. Similarly, the term *or(true,null)* evaluates to *true* whereas *or(null,true)* produces an undefined result. This form of serial non-strict evaluation is an intermediate stage between the non-strict and strict forms described earlier. Parallel-processing computers are now well advanced and their use in the future will allow fully non-strict evaluation and significant increases in processing speeds.

We have seen that monotonic functions preserve the order of definedness when applied to arguments, but this concept has to be extended a little to cope with the requirements of recursive functions. Earlier we saw that a chain of arguments is a directed sequence of increasingly defined objects that converges on a defined limit. A function is said to be continuous if it preserves that limit, i.e. if the function is applied to the most highly defined object, it produces the most highly defined result. Continuous behaviour extends the monotonicity property to recursive functions.

EXERCISES 7.2

1. A domain D contains just the one element *yes*, so the lifted domain becomes

   $D^+ = \{yes, null\}$

   List all the possible functions $D^+ \rightarrow D^+$ in this domain and extract those that are monotonic. Place the monotonic functions in order of definedness.

2. Show that the following functions of the domain $Bool^+ \rightarrow Bool^+$ are not monotonic:

f4	*true*	*false*	*true*
f23	*null*	*false*	*false*

3. A lifted domain is defined as $Flag^+ = \{red, white, blue, null\}$.
   How many $Flag^+ \rightarrow Flag^+$ functions are possible? Describe one monotonic and one non-monotonic function in this function domain.

4. Using interpretations in lifted Boolean domains, develop truth tables for the following expressions:

   a. $q \rightarrow (p \rightarrow q)$

   b. $(p \rightarrow q) \rightarrow (\neg q \rightarrow \neg p)$

   Notice that the result columns of these truth tables contain either defined *true* or undefined *null* entries.

5. Develop truth tables for the following three-variable propositions:

a. $(p \rightarrow (q \rightarrow r)) \rightarrow ((p \rightarrow q) \rightarrow (p \rightarrow r))$

b. $(p \vee (q \wedge r)) \rightarrow ((p \vee q) \wedge (p \vee r))$

Since each of them requires 27 rows, it would be wise to use the Prolog program described in Chapter 4 or the Miranda program described in Chapter 8.

7.3 EVALUATION STRATEGIES

Functional language expressions are constructed from

a. Variables x, y, ...

b. Constants such as the Boolean values *true* and *false* or the numbers 0, 1, 2, 3, ...

c. An abstraction that distinguishes a general expression with variables from a particular value. Abstractions are in fact the familiar function expressions such as

$$square(x) = x * x$$
$$plus(x) = x + x$$
$$f(x) = 2x + 4$$

in which variable x is bound in the function names *square*, *plus* and *f*.

d. An application in which bound variables, the formal parameters, are replaced by actual parameters through substitution:

$$f(3) = (2 * x + 4)\{3/x\}$$
$$= 2 * 3 + 4$$
$$= 10$$

An abstraction clearly amounts to a series of instructions for the term rewrites that are possible when the function is applied. An application involves the substitution of fragments within an expression by terms of equal value until a normal (canonical) value is obtained. An important property of such replacements is that the values of terms being evaluated are independent of any values outside the fragment being considered. This important feature is often described as the referential transparency property because there is no need to consider references outside the fragment being evaluated. This property follows from the substitutive property of equality, allowing us to substitute like for like without any concern for the context.

Functions might be defined in terms of previously defined functions as in the following example:

$$sqsum(x,y) = square(plus(x,y))$$

and the evaluation of this particular function is instructive. Consider the application *sqsum*(2,3):

$$sqsum(2,3) = square(plus(x,y))\{2/x, 3/y\}$$
$$= square(plus(2,3))$$
$$= square(5)$$
$$= 25$$

Here the innermost function is evaluated first then the outer function is applied to this inner result. An alternative strategy applies the outermost function before instantiating and evaluating the inner function as follows:

$$sqsum(2,3) = (square(plus(x,y))\{2/x, 3/y\}$$
$$= (plus(x,y) * plus(x,y))\{2/x, 3/y\}$$
$$= plus(2,3) * plus(2,3)$$
$$= 5 * plus(2,3)$$
$$= 5 * 5$$
$$= 25$$

At first sight, the outermost strategy appears to involve more work than the innermost strategy, but we shall see that the outermost approach has many advantages and the apparent extra work can be avoided by creating two pointers to a single expression. Outermost evaluation is sometimes called normal order reduction and innermost evaluation is sometimes called applicative order reduction. Outermost evaluation systems designed to avoid the extra computation arising from identical subexpressions are also described as lazy evaluators because they do the least possible work. This is in direct contrast to innermost evaluation systems such as OBJ that always evaluate arguments first and are sometimes called eager evaluators.

One major advantage of outermost or lazy evaluation becomes obvious when we build a compound equation with the following functions:

$$f(x,y) = f(y,x)$$
$$g(x) = 27$$

then evaluate the term $g(f(2,3))$ using the innermost strategy:

$$g(f(2,3)) = g(f(3,2))$$
$$= g(f(2,3))$$
$$= g(f(3,2))$$
$$= g(f(2,3)) \text{ etc.}$$

Obviously this evaluation never terminates, but the outermost evaluation immediately produces a result:

$$g(f(2,3)) = 27$$

Although a normal form exists for this expression, the particular evaluation strategy used might prevent that result from being obtained. This example shows that not all reduction strategies result in the normal form, even where one exists; but if it can be done, outermost will do it. As a result, the outermost strategy is said to be safe whereas an innnermost strategy is unsafe.

When they do terminate, different reduction strategies always produce the same normal form: the difference is whether or not they terminate. This is very similar to the effect of changing the order of clauses in a logic program, again affecting termination rather than the result obtained. Unlike a logic language, there is no backtracking in functional evaluation. Once a fragment has been evaluated and substituted, the original term from which it was derived may be discarded. The requirement that the same normal form must be obtained in any reduction strategy is called the Church–Rosser rule or sometimes the confluency property.

Lazy evaluation is a good method of avoiding unnecessary computation, even in situations where eager evaluation would have produced a result. Consider an evaluation of the following small Boolean function:

$$f(x,y,z) = or(x,and(y,not(z)))$$

for the application $f(true,true,false)$ to give the eager evaluation

$or(true,and(true,not(false)))$
$or(true,and(true,true))$
$or(true,true)$
$true$

but lazy evaluation recognises that the outcome may be decided by the first argument and jumps directly to the answer

$or(true,and(true,not(false)))$
$true$

Integrated circuits contain many thousands of switches whose states are represented by lifted Boolean values, and the ability to discard very large expressions in this way is invaluable.

Current implementations of functional languages are serial non-strict, evaluating their arguments in a left-to-right direction. If the arguments in the expression above are reversed to give

$or(and(true,not(false)),true)$

the first argument is evaluated, even though it is not really required. An implementation of the fully non-strict regime described earlier would require the parallel evaluation of both arguments. If either argument produces the value $true$, the value of the overall function is decided and the computation of the remaining argument is abandoned.

This sort of saving is carried over into functions on more complex structures such as a test to find if two lists are identical. Recalling that a list is either the empty list nil or an element $cons$ed onto another list, a test function may be written as follows:

$same(nil,nil) = true$
$same(cons(a,xa),cons(b,xb)) = (a = b) \ \& \ same(xa,xb)$

If the first elements of the two lists turn out to be different, the fragment $a = b$ evaluates to *false* and lazy evaluation returns *false* for the whole function. Eager evaluation compares every pair of elements derivable from the lists, even when the different first element has decided the final result. Of course it would be possible to define extra conditional functions to achieve the same effect in an eager evaluator, but this would require extra work on the part of the programmer.

7.3.1 Infinite data structures

We have seen that lazy evaluation allows a result, even when some parts of an argument are not fully defined. For example, the head of an empty list is undefined and if this fragment is *cons*ed onto another list, we obtain

  cons((hd nil),cons(3,cons(4,nil)))

If we now attempt to extract the tail of this list with the *tl* function:

  tl(cons((hd nil),cons(3,cons(4,nil))))

an innermost, eager evaluator would first attempt to produce a normal form for the fragment *hd nil*. Since this application is undefined, the whole expression is then undefined. An outermost, lazy evaluator recognises from the definition of *tl* that only the tail of the list is required and does not therefore attempt to reduce the head to normal form, producing instead the direct answer *cons(3,cons(4,nil))*. Exactly the same reasoning may be used for the application of the head operation to a list with a partially defined tail:

  hd(cons(3,cons(4,cons(hd nil,nil))))

producing, in this case, the element 3.

The fact that a defined result is produced from a list with a partially defined tail suggests that some operations applied to infinite lists might still produce a defined result. A list containing just one number repeated an infinite number of times may be defined recursively as follows:

  onenum n = cons(n,onenum n)

When expanded out, the application *onenum* 4 becomes

  cons(4,cons(4,cons(4,cons(4, ...))))

An eager evaluator attempting to reduce the application

  hd(onenum 7)

fails because it first attempts to evaluate the infinitely recursive *onenum* 7. A lazy evaluator recognises that only the head is required and therefore only reduces the argument to a head and a recursively defined tail

$hd(cons(7,onenum\ 7))$

In a similar style, a list of natural numbers starting from a specified number may be defined as

$from\ n = cons(n,from\ (n + 1))$

so that *from* 4 expands to become

$cons(4,cons(5,cons(6,cons(7,\ \ldots\ .))))$

Infinite lists such as those above are sometimes called streams because they create an endless stream of data for further evaluation.

7.3.2   Interactive programs

There are situations when a running program needs to halt in order to solicit information from the user or perhaps to return information to an interactive user. Traditional machine-oriented computing languages work as state machines in the sense that they modify the content of memory locations as a program proceeds. Certain instructions allow a user to input values that overwrite the content of memory locations or to copy out the current state of the machine to an output device. It might then seem improbable that a purely functional language could interactively accept data from users and output information at any point during computation, but this is indeed possible.

A purely functional language treats interactive input as a stream of data in much the same way as infinite lists are treated in the examples above. During an interactive session a user at the keyboard types a series of characters followed by a newline character, and this process may be repeated an infinite number of times. Lazy evaluation allows the first string of characters, essentially the head element, to be evaluated before any attempt is made to evaluate the tail. Subsequent inputs of information result from reading the head of a new tail list; when the interaction is completed, the partially defined tail list is discarded.

Outputs proceed in much the same way, so the head of a list is directed to some output device and the tail of the same list is partially defined, perhaps waiting for input from the user to become further defined.

7.3.3   Curried functions

Up to this point, functions of arity n have been shown as $f(a_1,a_2, \ldots ,a_n)$ so that the arity-two *and* function appeared in the form $and(x,y)$. However, it might be argued that all such functions are of arity one when the two arguments are seen as a single argument pair. Reasoning in this way, it would then be argued that all tuples are single arguments regardless of the number of elements in the tuple. An alternative form invented by logician Haskell Curry takes a series of individual arguments rather than a tuple, placing each argument in the same order after the function name. Thus the general form above becomes $f\ a_1\ a_2 \ldots a_n$ and a conjunction function equivalent to *and* is written *conj x y*. For comparison, the traditional tuple-oriented version and the Curried version of the conjunction function are written as

(Bool,Bool) → *Bool*
and(false,y) = *false*
and(true,y) = *y*

Bool → *(Bool* → *Bool)*
conj false y = *false*
conj true y = *y*

The real difference is obvious from the domains of each of these functions. Function *and* maps pairs of arguments to a single Boolean result whereas function *conj* maps a Boolean element to a function that itself maps Boolean to Boolean. Since function *and* takes a single argument, simultaneous substitutions are made:

and(x y){false/x, true/y}
and(false,true)
false

but function *conj* is partially applied in a first step

conj x y {false/x}
(conj false) y

to give a new function *(conj false)* that maps all Boolean elements to *false*

(conj false) y {true/y}
(conj false) true
false

A partial application *conj x y {true/x}* yields a different function *(conj true)* that maps Boolean elements to themselves, i.e. it acts as an identity function. A Curried function behaves like a little "munchie man" chewing through its arguments from left to right, changing its nature with each argument absorbed.

A similar distinction may be made between the Curried *mult* and the uncurried *times* operations with the following signatures:

times : *(Nat,Nat)* → *Nat*
mult: : *Nat* → *(Nat* → *Nat)*

Following the Boolean example above, a Curried multiplication may be partially applied as follows:

mult x y {3/x}
(mult 3) y

to give a new function (*mult* 3) that takes any natural number as an argument and multiplies it by 3.

A Curried function called *map* is defined to apply a function *f* to every element of a list and is defined as follows:

map f nil = nil
map f(cons(x,xs)) = cons(f x, map f xs)

So *map* is an example of a higher-order function because it takes a function *f* as one of its arguments. If a function *sqr* produces the square of a natural number, we can follow the evaluation of the expression:

hd(map sqr(from 4))
hd(map sqr(cons(4,(from 5))))
hd(cons(sqr 4,map sqr(from 5)))
sqr 4
16

Lazy evaluation recognises that only the head element is required, so the innermost expression is expanded by only one step rather than completely to normal form. Once this is done, the map operation is applied to bring the expression into a form from which the head element can be extracted. *Map* uses infinite lists to great advantage by taking just the elements required, in this case just one, but it could take any number of elements to produce a sublist.

Domain theory provides an interpretation for the syntactic forms of a functional language, and these languages might in turn be seen as "sugared" versions of the lambda calculus. High-level functional languages such as Miranda make the process of writing programs relatively easy by providing features such as pattern matching that do not appear in the calculus. Before a program is animated, it is first checked to confirm that there are no type mismatches and that queries can be unified with definitions. After several passes, the program is converted into a lambda calculus form, then this form is reduced to its simplest, canonical form. Many different methods are used to reduce lambda expressions, but the graphical method described later in this chapter is the most common method used in lazily evaluated languages. This method has the advantage that it can be extended to parallel evaluation. Before proceeding to graphical evaluation, the lambda notation is outlined in the following section.

7.4   LAMBDA CALCULUS

A functional expression such as *plus x* 1 is ambiguous in the sense that it represents different values according to the constant instantiated in the place of the variable *x*. Bertrand Russell resolved this ambiguity by distinguishing between two types of symbol: a symbol which represented a particular value and a symbol which abstracted the symbol to any value. A similar approach is adopted in the lambda calculus developed by Alonzo Church in the 1930s, although Church uses a λ symbol to "abstract" the value to a general expression. An expression such as *plus* x 1 becomes the "body" of a lambda expression $\lambda x.plus\ x$ 1, and the λx indicates that any appropriate value may be substituted for the variable x. Once a function has been abstracted into lambda calculus form, it may be applied to an appropriate number of arguments by substituting expressions for the head variables, the variables indicated by λ symbols.

A successor function might be expressed in terms of the *plus* function as follows:

$$suc\ x = plus\ x\ 1$$

meaning that the successor of a number is to be found by adding 1 to that number. An application of the function achieved by instantiating a particular value for the variable x, e.g.

$$suc\ 3 = plus\ x\ 1\{3/x\}$$
$$= plus\ 3\ 1 = 4$$

To find the value of *suc* 3, the argument 3 is substituted for variable x in the body of the function and a result computed. In lambda notation the abstraction appears as

$$suc = \lambda x.plus\ x\ 1$$

but now the function name *suc* is not essential and the ability to use anonymous expressions is a very useful feature of the lambda calculus. The evaluation of *suc* 3 again involves a substitution in the position indicated by variable x:

$$(\lambda x.plus\ x\ 1)\ 3 = plus\ x\ 1\{3/x\}$$
$$= plus\ 3\ 1 = 4$$

In many ways the head of this expression λx resembles the use of a universal quantifier with a variable in the fragment $\forall x$, allowing the instantiation of an appropriate constant. Similarly, variables in the body of the lambda expression, in this case *plus* x 1, are substituted just as variables in the body of a quantified statement are substituted. Although the lambda calculus was developed before digital computers were invented, it has become of great interest because the reduction of these expressions can be automated on a computer.

Pure lambda calculus expressions are constructed from just three components:

a. Variables $x, y, z, \ldots$.

b. Abstractions denoted by $\lambda x.p$ where p is a lambda expression called the body of the abstraction.

c. Applications denoted by $(p\ q)$ in which operator p is applied to operand q.

The example above is actually an impure expression because it uses the constants 1, 3, 4 and *plus* without defining them in the pure form, but for the moment we might accept them as abbreviations for pure expressions. Pure lambda calculus consists of strings of symbols that are manipulated by the reduction rules described below in much the same way that strings of logic symbols were manipulated by proof theory in the earlier chapters. It is the interpretation or semantics of the symbols that is of real interest to us, so it is convenient to use interpretations such as the numbers and their operations.

Variables in the body of an abstraction are bound if they are within the scope of the abstracted symbol. For example, variable x is bound in the abstraction $\lambda x.x\ y$, but variable y remains free. In the abstraction $\lambda x.\lambda y.x\ y$ both variables are bound by the symbols appearing in the head of the expression.

There is a term-rewriting rule, sometimes called the alpha reduction rule, that allows variables in an expression to be changed. For example, the identity function $\lambda x.x$ described below might equally well be written as $\lambda y.y$ or in any form derived by substituting another variable for x in the first expression. It is the structure of the expression that is important, not the specific variable names used in its formation. However, we have to be careful that variable substitution does not change the structure of an expression. For example, the variable y in expression $\lambda x.x\ y$ should not be substituted to give $\lambda x.x\ x$, changing the structure of the expression. The problem arises because the variable substituted in the body of the expression is captured as it is placed in the scope of the head symbol. Provided this bound variable is avoided, an alpha rewrite of the expression is straightforward, giving an expression such as $\lambda z.z\ x$.

Alpha rewrites do not reduce expressions to simpler forms, but are essential at certain points to avoid the clashing of symbols described above. The main term-rewriting rule used in the lambda calculus is called the beta reduction rule and this does indeed reduce expressions. A beta reduction is an application of an abstract expression to an argument, following which the argument is substituted for the abstracted symbol. The simplest example of such a reduction occurs when a single bound variable x is applied to some argument. This is the basis of a special lambda expression called the identity function which, when applied to any expression p, just returns that same expression:

$$(\lambda x.x)p = x\{p/x\} = p$$

On the other hand, the application of a similar expression with an unbound variable to an argument leaves the variable unchanged:

$$(\lambda x.y)p = y\{p/x\} = y$$

In order to apply this expression, every occurrence of variable x in variable y is substituted with expression p, but there are no such occurrences, so the variable remains unchanged.

If two variable symbols are abstracted in an expression applied to an argument, the pattern of substitution is as follows:

$$(\lambda y.\lambda x.p)q = \lambda x.p\ \{q/y\} = \lambda x.(p\ \{q/y\})$$

but some care is necessary here. Taking a simple example in which the expression is applied to variable z, we obtain

$$(\lambda y.\lambda x.y\ x)z = \lambda x.y\ x\ \{z/y\}$$
$$= \lambda x.(y\ x\ \{z/y\})$$
$$= \lambda x.z\ x$$

If this expresson is applied to variable x, we obtain

$$(\lambda y.\lambda x.y\ x)x = \lambda x.y\ x\ \{x/y\}$$
$$= \lambda x.(y\ x\ \{x/y\})$$
$$= \lambda x.x\ x$$

and the variable-capture problem arises. However, the problem is avoided if the substitution is preceded by a renaming of the remaining bound variable as in the following example:

$$(\lambda y.\lambda x.y\ x)x = \lambda x.y\ x\ \{x/y\}$$
$$= \lambda z.y\ z\ \{x/y\}$$
$$= \lambda z.x\ z$$

The risk of variable capture and the need to check variables and possibly to substitute for them is a major problem in automating functional evaluation using the lambda calculus.

The application of an expression in which the same variable is twice abstracted has no effect:

$$(\lambda x.\lambda x.p)q = \lambda x.p\ \{q/x\} = \lambda x.p$$

Argument q is only substituted for the free x variables in the body of the expression and, since this includes the inner λx, there are no such free variables.

Finally, a substitution in an application reduces to separate substitutions in the two parts of the application:

$$(p\ q)\ \{r/x\} = p\{r/x\}q\{r/x\}$$

In summary there are six clearly defined cases of these substitutions:

a. $x\{p/x\} = p$
b. $y\{p/x\} = y$
c. $\lambda x.p\{q/y\} = \lambda x.(p\{q/y\})$ x not free in q
d. $\lambda x.p\{q/y\} = \lambda z.(p\{z/x\}\{q/y\})$ z not free in p or q
e. $\lambda x.p\{q/x\} = \lambda x.p$
f. $(p\ q)\ \{r/x\} = p\{r/x\}q\{r/x\}$

7.4.1   Representing constants in the lambda calculus

At several points in this book we have distinguished between syntactic, proof theoretic reasoning and semantic, representational reasoning. At each point, a semantic domain provides a model for a syntactic theory in the sense that that model is a correct representation of the theory. Although the elements and operations of a semantic domain might look different from the syntactic forms, they behave in exactly the same way. Each syntactic construction has a semantic representation that exactly mimics its behaviour. The domain elements modelling syntactic behaviour are often more compact than the object they mimic and sometimes it is convenient to think of them as abbreviations for syntactic forms. This is certainly the case in the following representations of the Boolean constants *true*, *false* and *not* in pure lambda calculus form:

$true = \lambda x.\lambda y.x$
$false = \lambda x.\lambda y.y$
$not = \lambda x.x \; false \; true$

Notice that we have already departed from the pure form in using the constants *true* and *false* in the definition of the constant *not*. But the use of the first two constants as abbreviations has obvious advantages. Using this semipure form, we justify the interpretation *not true = false* as follows:

$$
\begin{aligned}
not \; true &= (\lambda x.x \; false \; true) \; true \\
&= true \; false \; true \\
&= (\lambda x.\lambda y.x) \; false \; true \\
&= (\lambda y.false) \; true \\
&= false
\end{aligned}
$$

Throughout this evaluation the constants *true* and *false* are used as abbreviations for the equivalent lambda calculus forms, but they could be replaced by their equivalent pure forms.

Lambda forms for disjunction and conjunction are written as follows:

$and = \lambda x.\lambda y.(x \; y \; false)$
$or = \lambda x.\lambda y.((x \; true) \; y)$

and we justify the interpretation *and true false = false* as follows:

$$
\begin{aligned}
\lambda x.\lambda y.(x \; y \; false) \; true \; false &= \lambda y.(true \; y \; false) \; false \\
&= (true \; false \; false) \\
&= (\lambda x.\lambda y.x) \; false \; false \\
&= (\lambda y.false) \; false \\
&= false
\end{aligned}
$$

Each constant of the natural numbers 0, 1, 2, . . . might be represented by a lambda expression as follows:

$0 = \lambda f.\lambda x.x$
$1 = \lambda f.\lambda x.f \; x$
$2 = \lambda f.\lambda x.f f \; x$

and the pattern of expressions with increasing numbers of f symbols becomes clear. This representation is similar to that used in Chapter 5 where the constant 0 is represented by symbol *zero* and succesive digits are represented by repeated applications of the *suc* function. Thus natural 2 is represented by *suc(suc(zero))*. Definitions of the various arithmetic operations such as addition may be formulated as lambda expressions then applied to the above constants. Again this procedure is similar to the use of the operation *add* defined in the abstract type nat1 of Chapter 5. It is possible to do arithmetic in the lambda calculus just as it is possible to do it using operations defined in an abstract type, but in neither case would this be a sensible way of proceeding. Computers have built-in arithmetic facilities which operate directly on binary representations that are easily converted to the familiar denary system.

7.4.2 Tuple forms

Each of the lambda expressions so far has used the Curried notation described earlier, so an operation such as *plus x y* has to be considered as *(plus x) y*. Operator *plus* is applied to operand *x* to form a new operator that is applied to a single operand *y*. However, within the lambda calculus we are free to define another addition operator called *add* whose operand is a pair and thus has the form *add(x,y)*. These two addition expressions denote the same value and must be interconvertible within the lambda calculus. In fact, the following operators *curry* and *uncurry* relate the two expressions:

$$curry = \lambda f.\lambda x.\lambda y.f(x,y)$$
$$uncurry = \lambda f.\lambda xs.f(fst\ xs)(snd\ xs)$$

The first of these expressions might then be used to show that the *plus* operation is equivalent to a Curried *add* operation:

$$
\begin{aligned}
plus\ a\ b &= curry\ add\ a\ b \\
&= \lambda f.\lambda x.\lambda y.f(x,y)\ add\ a\ b \\
&= \lambda x.\lambda y.add(x,y)\ a\ b \\
&= \lambda y.add(a,y)\ b \\
&= add(a,b)
\end{aligned}
$$

7.4.3 Combinators

In 1924 Moses Schonfinkel published a paper entitled "On the building blocks of mathematical logic", introducing a class of evaluators now known as combinators. Haskell Curry later extended Schonfinkel's work and showed that it is equivalent to Church's lambda calculus in the sense that every lambda expression can be translated into an equivalent combinator expression. Combinators remained an obscure mathematical area until in 1979 David Turner showed that lambda calculus expressions could be efficiently evaluated by first converting them to combinators then evaluating the resulting expression. In terms of the lambda calculus, a combinator is just a lambda expression that has no free variables. We have in fact already introduced several combinators such as $\lambda x.\lambda y.x$, $\lambda x.\lambda y.y$ and the identity expression $\lambda x.x$.

EXERCISES 7.4

1. Evaluate the following impure expressions, adopting the meaning for each function suggested by the name:

   a. $(\lambda x.\lambda y.\lambda z.mult\ x(plus\ y\ z))$ 2 3 4
   b. $(\lambda x.\lambda y.mult(plus\ x\ y)\ (plus\ x\ y))$ 2 3
   c. $(\lambda x.\lambda y.\lambda z.or\ (and\ x\ y)\ (and\ (not\ x)\ z))$ *false true true*
   d. $(\lambda w.\lambda x.\lambda y.\lambda z.and\ (and\ y\ w)\ (or\ x\ z))$ *false true false true*
   e. $((\lambda f.\lambda x.\lambda y.f\ x\ y)\ mult)$ 3 4
   f. $((\lambda f.\lambda g.\lambda x.\lambda y.f(g\ x\ x)\ (g\ y\ y))\ plus\ mult)$ 3 4

2. Using the lambda definitions in the text, show that *not false = true*.

3. Using the lambda definitions in the text, show that

   a. *and false true = false*
   b. *and true true = true*
   c. *or false true = true*

4. Using the lambda definition for *uncurry* in the text, show that *add(a,b)* is an uncurried form of *plus a b*.

7.5 GRAPH REDUCTION

Although different functional languages have similar semantics, the syntactic forms and methods of translating source code to running programs differ significantly. Some languages such as Lazy ML compile source code into machine language whereas others such as Miranda produce a semicompiled form that is then interpreted each time it is used. Compilation leads to levels of efficiency almost equivalent to that provided by machine-oriented languages such as Pascal and Ada, whereas interpretation allows a more elegant interactive presentation.

Whatever the approach, the first step is to create a syntax tree and then to carry out a type check on the submitted expressions. Robinson's unification algorithm, described in Chapter 2, is used to check functions submitted to the interpreter against descriptions already known. When this work is complete, the source code of the program is converted to an intermediate notation something like the lambda notation described above. This intermediate code is usually an enriched form of

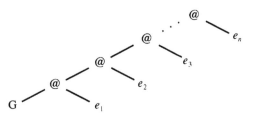

Figure 7.5   Graphs of expressions

lambda calculus, including some features that capture the intention of a high-level program while removing features that would be troublesome in evaluation.

Graph reduction is one method of reducing these intermediate expressions to canonical forms and has the advantage that it applies normal order reduction in a very natural way. A functional expression in a graph is one of the following three items:

a. A data object

b. A primitive function to be applied

c. A λ abstraction

If it is a data object, the evaluation is complete; but it it is either of the other two, there may be further work to do. A graph with a primitive applied function generally has the form shown in Figure 7.5, in which G is some function and the @ symbols are tags denoting applications. The highest tag is called the root node. Each tag points to an expression e_i that might itself be an unevaluated graph. The sequence of nodes running from the root node to the leftmost tip is called the spine of the graph and the process of traversing this path is called "unwinding the spine". A graph is reduced by unwinding its spine until a node other than a tag is encountered. If this node turns out to be a function of arity n, there must be at least n arguments attached to the spine, otherwise the function is partially applied, and in a computation this is regarded as an error. A strictness check is then applied to decide which expressions have to be evaluated and, if lazy evaluation is possible, the arguments essential to the computation are evaluated.

As a first example, we consider an evaluation of the expression

$(2 * 3) + (4 * 5)$

starting from the first graph in Figure 7.6. Operator + is the principal operator and is found by unwinding the spine from the root of the graph to this symbol. Arithmetic expressions are strict in both arguments, so both subgraphs of the addition function have to be evaluated and replaced by the values they denote. Evaluations of the subgraphs proceed by unwinding the spine from the node of each subgraph until a function is encountered. In this particular example, the multiplication operations are found and applied to their two constant arguments. When this has been done, the addition operation is applied and a final, single-node graph is obtained.

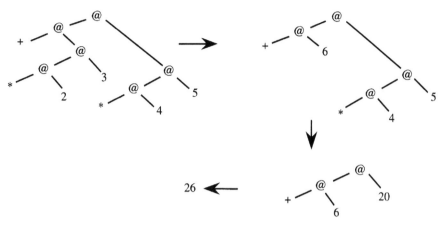

Figure 7.6 Evaluating an expression

An example of a lambda expression applied to an appropriate number of arguments is provided by the expression

$(\lambda x.\lambda y.and(or(x,y), not(and(x,y))))$ *false true*

This is recognisibly the exclusive-or function applied to two Boolean arguments from which we expect the denotation *true*. Figure 7.7 shows the graph for this expression, and from this graph we see that the first non-application node encountered on unwinding the spine is the λx node. When this lambda function is applied, the argument *false* is substituted at those positions in the graph marked with the variable x. This done, the tag leading up from the λy node becomes the root node and the procedure is repeated for the application of the remaining abstraction to the second argument. Once the abstractions have been removed, the spine unwinds to reveal the *and* function applied to two unevaluated values. The first of them, an *or* function, evaluates to *true* and this value is substituted in the appropriate argument position. Had this subexpression evaluated to *false*, the fact that *and false* always evaluates to *false* would have been recognised. A final result would have been obtained immediately and the second subgraph would never have been evaluated. In the event, this subexpression evaluates to *true* and the *not* application has to be evaluated, in turn forcing an evaluation of the innermost *and* function. Lazy evaluation can indeed be used on this innermost expression because the first argument is the value *false*, immediately yielding the result *false*. The whole expresson is eventually reduced to the single canonical value *true* and this value replaces the original expression. Graphical reduction carries out normal order reduction naturally, so it leads to a canonical form whenever one exists.

When written in textual form, a normal order reduction might appear to require more computational steps than applicative order reduction, but this extra work is avoided by sharing subexpressions in graphs. For example, variable x in Figure 7.7 is replaced in two places by the constant *false* and variable y is similarly replaced in

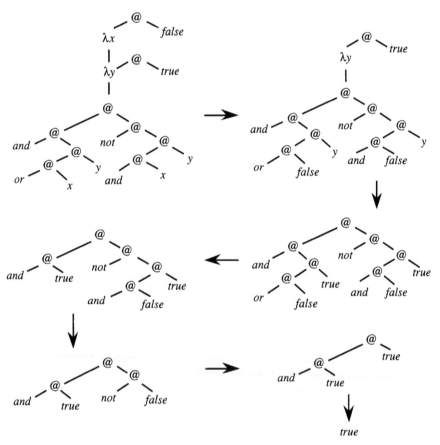

Figure 7.7 Evaluating an expression

two places by the constant *true*. Instead of writing copies of each constant in the variable positions, a pointer from the nodes could be directed to a single copy of each constant. If the arguments were themselves large reducible expressions, this would mean that the reduction of subexpressions would not have to be repeated each time the subexpressions were used.

Consider the simple example in Figure 7.8, representing the application

(λx.*mult x x*)(*plus* 2 3)

An inefficient approach to this evaluation would substitute separate copies of the fragment (*plus* 2 3) for each of the *x* variable arguments then separately evaluate both arguments. A cleverer approach substitutes pointers to one copy of this fragment on each of the *x* argument positions, as shown in Figure 7.8. As a result, the subgraph is evaluated only once and the result is shared between two arguments. Obviously the saving here is trivial, but in larger examples with many repeated subexpressions the efficiency gains are considerable.

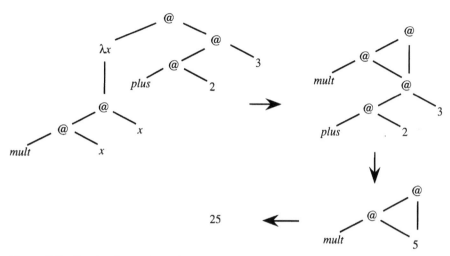

Figure 7.8 Sharing in a subgraph

Machine-oriented languages such as Pascal and Ada require explicit statements of the memory space required in declarations at the beginning of each program module. When the program is executed, the required space is allocated and reclaimed by the functional language system as each module is completed. Functional language systems automatically allocate memory space from a storage area as it is required, so functional programmers are free to concentrate on the problem rather than on its machine implementation. As a graph is evaluated, some of the allocated memory used for the graph is no longer required and needs to be returned from the functional language system to the evaluator. The preceding text makes several references to discarded subexpressions of graphs, but these expressions are contained in memory allocated by the operating system. A special routine called a garbage collector repeatedly checks to see if each part of the allocated memory is still in use, often by checking whether the memory is connected to a graph. Discarded memory cells are then periodically returned to the control of the operating system.

EXERCISES 7.5

1. Draw graphs for the following expressions and show the steps in the evaluation of each one:

   a. $(\lambda x.not\ x)\ true$

   b. $(\lambda x.\lambda y.plus\ x\ y)\ 5\ 6$

   c. $(\lambda x.plus\ x\ x)\ (mult\ 2\ 3)$

   d. $(\lambda x.and\ x\ x)\ (not\ true)$

CHAPTER EIGHT

Miranda

8.1 MIRANDA BASICS

Miranda is usually invoked by the system command `mira` and responds with a `Miranda` prompt, although in the following text this prompt is always shown as a question mark. An expression submitted at the prompt is evaluated and its canonical value returned on the following line. In the simplest case an irreducible value typed at the prompt is returned unchanged:

```
?42
42
```

but if reduction is possible, an expression presented at the prompt is reduced to its equivalent canonical value, e.g. in a subtraction:

```
?27 - 14
13
```

Other arithmetic operations use the familiar infix symbols and can be carried out at the `Miranda` prompt in the same way: the set of operators $\{+, -, *, /, \char`\^, \text{div}, \text{mod}\}$ represents addition, subtraction, multiplication, division, exponentiation, integer division and modulus operators. These built-in operations can be used to build larger expressions such as

```
?6^2 - 4*2*3
12
```

with the usual convention that multiplication and division have greater precedence than either addition or subtraction; exponentiation has the highest precedence of all. Thus the above expression is evaluated as $6^2 - (4*2*3)$ and explicit bracketing would be required if this were not the intended meaning. Each of these built-in

functions is contained in a standard environment loaded with the Miranda interpreter. A user could invoke Miranda, evaluate some expressions using standard
functions and then leave the interpreter by typing /quit at the prompt. The leading / symbol shows that this is a directive to the system rather than an expression
to be evaluated.

During a period of interaction, called a session, the standard environment can be
extended to include user-defined functions by adding function definitions to a file
called the current script. Typing /edit at the prompt invokes the default editor,
which is usually either the emacs or unix vi editor, and the user is then able to insert
function definitions into a default current script called script.m. If no previous
definitions have been made, the script will be empty and we might type the following definitions:

```
|| a first example - this is a comment
unit_cost = 13
total_cost x = unit_cost * x
```

in which a constant called unit_cost is defined to be equal to 13 and an arity-
one function with variable x is defined as the product of unit_cost and the
instantiated variable. Text following two vertical bars on any one line is treated as
a comment and is ignored by the interpreter. Correct function definitions are added
to the environment automatically on returning from the editor, so the following
queries are then possible:

```
?unit_cost
13

?total_cost 3
39
```

Further definitions could be added to the script through a series of /edit calls,
each addition being checked on return to the interpreter. At any point during a
session the environment consists of those functions in the standard environment
together with any functions defined in the current script.

A named script may be adopted as the current script by typing at the prompt

```
?/file filename
```

and any function definitions contained in filename are added to the environment.
If filename does not already exist, an empty script called filename.m is created
and a further /edit directive allows new functions to be added to the script. If the
current script is changed, the functions in the new script are checked and valid
functions are added to the environment but functions defined in the previous script
are no longer available. A reminder of the current script name is obtained by typing
/file without a file name and a list of identifiers in scope is obtained by typing a
question mark. An online manual is obtained by typing /man and a summary of
commands obtained by typing /help. Commands beginning with a ! symbol are

passed directly to the operating system, so the emacs editor could be used when it is not the default editor by typing

```
?!emacs costs.m
```

Provided the file taken into emacs is the current file, it will be checked automatically on returning to Miranda.

Each function in a script presented to the interpreter is first checked for correct syntax and then for type compatibility. Failure at either stage results in a rejection with an appropriate message. Miranda is a strongly typed language with three basic types: number, Boolean and character. Users have the option of providing type information for the interpreter, so an area function could be defined in a script as

```
area :: num -> num
area r = pi * r * r
```

informing the interpreter that the operand has to be of type num and that the correctly applied function denotes a num. In the absence of user-supplied type information, the interpreter uses an inference mechanism to deduce types. Without the type information supplied above, the interpreter would recognise that pi is a number (defined in the standard environment) and * is an operation applied to two number operands so that both r and the applied function must be of type num. The type num includes both integer and floating-point numbers without distinction and the interpreter recognises which is appropriate.

Boolean values are provided as a basic type with the following defined constants and functions:

Symbol	Arity	Meaning
True, False	0	Boolean constants
~	1	not
&	2	logical and
\/	2	logical or

Notice that constants True and False begin with a capital letter to distinguish them from variables and are built-in algebraic types of the kind described later. A logical "or" symbol consists of a combined backward and forward slash, representing the more familiar v symbol used earlier in the text.

Queries with boolean arguments can be presented in infix style at the Miranda prompt just as in numerical calculations:

```
?True & False
False
```

Boolean functions are not strict in both arguments and follow the serial lazy form described in the previous chapter, thus the following evaluations might occur:

```
?False & null
False

?null & False
error message
```

If `False` occurs as the first argument, the serial lazy evaluator deduces that the final result must be `False` and never attempts to evaluate the second argument; but if a null value occurs in the first argument position, the overall result is undefined. Similar considerations apply to the built-in disjunction function.

A script might contain functions built from the standard functions, e.g. an exclusive-or function is `True` when one of its operands is `True`, but `False` when both are `True`:

```
exor :: (bool,bool) -> bool
exor(x,y) = (x \/ y ) & ~(x & y)
```

According to this definition, the function `exor` is applied to a pair of Boolean values and the applied function denotes a Boolean value. When the above definition is contained in a current script, the following interaction could occur at the prompt:

```
?exor(True,True)
False
```

Relational comparisons between objects of any type are possible with the following arity-two relational operators:

>	greater than
<	less than
>=	greater than or equal to
<=	less than or equal to
=, ~=	equal, not equal

The exact meaning of these operations depends on the objects to which they are applied and, since they may be applied to compound structures, they have a much more powerful effect than in many other languages. For Boolean arguments the meaning is simply that indicated by the query

```
?False < True
True
```

Value `False` is defined to be "less than" `True`, not equal to `True` and of course equal to `False`.

Numbers can be compared at the prompt to give obvious Boolean results:

```
? 6 < 4
False
```

A script might contain function definitions with relational operations; for example, a function might be defined to show that a variable is a number between 6 and 9:

```
sixtonine :: num -> bool
sixtonine x = x >= 6 & x <= 9
```

8.1.1 Characters

Characters are placed between single quotes to distinguish them from variables and numbers. Thus x is a variable but 'x' represents the character x and 2 is a number while '2' represents the symbol 2 itself. Most machines store characters as ASCII values and these values are obtained with the aid of a standard function named code:

```
?code '2'
50
```

showing that the ASCII decimal representation for symbol 2 is 50. A small function to convert single-digit ASCII characters to integer numbers could be written

```
atoi :: char -> num
atoi x = code x - code '0'
```

For characters, "less than" means lower in the alphabet when 'a' is considered lowest and 'z' highest. Upper case letters are treated similarly but every upper case letter is lower than any of the lower case letters:

```
? 'a' < 'b'
True
```

This positioning is a consequence of the ASCII representation of characters used in most computers, and the ordering of any other character can be found from a table of ASCII values. Another built-in function called decode accepts a numeric argument and returns the character denoted by that number, reversing the above query as follows:

```
?decode 50
'2'
```

Function sixtonine could be rewritten for characters:

```
sixtonine2 :: char -> bool
sixtonine2 x = x >= '6' & x <= '9'
```

Similar functions can be written to check that a character is a lower case letter:

```
is_lcase x = x >= 'a' & x <= 'z'
```

Strings of characters are contained in double quotes, but quotation marks are not included in the output when a string is submitted for evaluation:

```
?"tom"
tom
```

In fact, the double quotes are a shorthand notation for a list of characters contained between square brackets, so that Miranda accepts the alternative form

```
?['t','o','m']
tom
```

Lists are an important topic in themselves; they are covered in Section 8.2.

8.1.2   Tuples

The basic data types num, bool and char are used to build increasingly complex structures using functions, tuples and lists. Functions describe the reduction path that allows computation. Tuples and lists are ordered sequences of elements, but tuples have a fixed number of elements of any type whereas lists have a variable number of elements of one type. The simplest tuple is a pair, two items contained between rounded brackets as in (1, 'a') or (True, "Mary"). Two functions are provided in the standard environment to project first and second values from a tuple:

```
fst(x,y) = x
snd(x,y) = y
```

so that the following interactions might occur at the prompt:

```
?snd(False,'r')
'r'

?snd(True,123)
123
```

Function snd is applied above to pairs of different types (bool,char) and (bool,num), producing char in one case and num in the other. Functions like this are said to be polymorphic because the data objects substituted for x and y in the function definitions above could be of any type. A special form of type declaration is used for polymorphic functions:

```
fst :: (*,**) -> *
snd :: (*,**) -> **
```

meaning that these functions map pairs of objects of type * and ** to individual objects of type * or **. Types * and ** might be the same.

Projection operations like fst and snd allow lazy evaluation to produce a result where eager evaluation would fail. For example, the projection

```
?fst(7,42/0)
7
```

produces a result because it never attempts to compute the non-terminating, null expression in the second argument position. This approach can be extended to tuples of any size; provided the argument in the required position is defined, the projection will succeed.

Triples and larger tuples may be provided with similar projection functions, but they have to be defined by the user. A function that projects out the third element of a triple is defined as follows:

```
proj3c :: (*,**,***) -> ***
proj3c(a,b,c) = c
```

And a function projecting out the second and fourth attributes of a tuple might be written as

```
proj4bd :: (*,**,***,****) -> (**,****)
proj4bd(a,b,c,d) = (b,d)
```

A consistent function name notation used here includes the tuple size and the positions of the elements projected, assuming that attributes are labelled a,b,c ... from the left of the argument tuple.

Relational operations can be applied to whole tuples and lists, treating them as single objects. For example, the following interaction is observed:

```
?(23, True) < (23, False)
False
```

in which the distinction is made on the second attribute of the tuple. Similarly, strings are ordered lexically:

```
?"maryland" < "maryville"
True
```

8.1.3 Patterns and guards

Pattern matching allows the use of different function bodies (the right-hand sides) depending on the form of function arguments. The simplest case arises when the function body is a constant, as in the following example:

```
not True = False
not False = True
```

mimicking the built-in negation function. A result is obtained by matching the function name and argument in a query with definitions in the environment. A pair of equations could also define the result of the disjunction operation:

```
vel(False,False) = False
vel anyother = True
```

but in this case the order in which the two equations are written is important. Variable anyother could mean any pair of Booleans, including the one argument pair

(False, False) that evaluates to False; so if this special case is to be caught first, its pattern must occur before the more general case. If pattern-matched arguments are not mutually exclusive, the order of presentation from top to bottom must be one of increasing generalisation.

Miranda performs an equality check when a given identifier is repeated in a pattern, a useful feature in the following implemention of a logical "if and only if" function, usually abbreviated to iff:

```
iff(x,x) = True
iff(x,y) = False
```

This function evaluates to True when invoked with identical arguments because iff(True, True) and iff(False, False) both pattern match the first equation after substitution. If no pattern match occurs, Miranda proceeds downwards to the next identically named function, so the order in which function definitions occur is again important. Without a more restrictive type declaration, the function written above is polymorphic and evaluates to True for pairs of identical arguments of any type. It could of course be restricted to Boolean arguments by including a suitable type declaration.

Guarded equations provide a further opportunity to invoke different function bodies, depending on some feature of the input. Again a group of equations evaluating to a constant provides a good example:

```
greet x = "Good Morning"      , if x < 12.00
greet x = "Good Afternoon"    , if x < 17.00
greet x = "Good Evening"      , if x < 24.00
greet x = "Check Your Clock"
```

Here a function called greet takes an argument number from a 24 hour clock and produces an appropriate greeting. Each of the first three equations has a guard introduced by the reserved word if and these guards are evaluated in order from the top. As soon as a guard evaluates to True, its function body is adopted to denote the application and any remaining guards or unguarded equations are ignored. Notice that the guards are not mutually exclusive in the above example because the range of time for afternoon appears to include that allocated for morning. Succeeding guards are only evaluated when preceding ones have failed, so they carry implied negations of the earlier guards. Implicit guards can be made explicit by extending the guard conditions.

Function names do not have to be repeated in guarded equations because an alternative form shown in the following example is provided:

```
checklet x = "upper case"    , if is_ucase x
           = "lower case"    , if is_lcase x
           = "not a letter" , otherwise
```

Here a single character is checked to show if it is upper case, lower case or not a letter at all. The first two guards in this case are mutually exclusive and the final default equation is given a pseudo-guard `otherwise` that always evaluates to `True`.

8.1.4 Curried functions

The following function takes a pair of numbers as an argument and denotes a number, specifically the larger of the numbers in its argument pair:

```
maxa :: (num, num) -> num
maxa (x, y) = x , if x >= y
            = y , otherwise
```

It might be used like this at the prompt:

```
?maxa (40, 55)
55
```

A similar function can be written in Curried form as follows:

```
maxb :: num -> (num -> num)
maxb x y = x , if x >= y
         = y , otherwise
```

and an interaction at the prompt now takes the form:

```
?maxb 40 55
55
```

In this form, the application `maxb x y` first applies `maxb` to x, creating a new and partially applied function `maxb x` that maps numbers to themselves if they are bigger than y or to y if they are not. Thus (`maxb 40`) maps numbers bigger than 40 to themselves whereas numbers smaller than this are mapped to the number 40. Curried functions are applied to their arguments in turn from left to right rather than to a whole tuple at a time. Use of the Curried form often gives neater, more readable programs.

8.1.5 Recursion

Recursive specifications are distinguished by the appearance of the same function name on both sides of an equality symbol. Each time such a function is invoked, a further application of the function occurs until some terminating condition is achieved. As an example, consider the following computation of a factorial.

The factorial of an integer is the product of that number with every integer greater than zero but smaller than itself, thus the factorial of 4 is $4 \times 3 \times 2 \times 1 = 24$. A function to achieve this multiplies number n by the factorial of $n - 1$, causing a recursive call to the function with an actual parameter $n - 1$. Repeated calls to the function decrement the argument until it reaches 1, at which point a pattern match with the first equation terminates the recursion:

```
fac 1 = 1                      || eq 1
fac n = n * fac (n - 1)  || eq 2
```

It is helpful to examine the stages of this evaluation:

```
fac 4 = 4 * fac 3              from eq 2
      = 4 * (3 * fac 2)        from eq 2
      = 4 * (3 * (2 * fac 1))  from eq 2
      = 4 * (3 * (2 * 1))      from eq 1
      = 4 * (3 * 2)            multiplication
      = 4 * 6                  multiplication
      = 24                     multiplication
```

The context of the calculation is stacked or suspended while the innermost factorial function is applied. Pattern matching ensures that equation 2 is used until the argument is reduced to 1, at which point the first equation terminates recursion. Unstacking then begins as the built-in definition of multiplication is repeatedly used until a canonical value is obtained.

A function denoting the same value can be written in a style that carries out multiplications as the recursive calls are made, avoiding the need for stacking. Since this approach accumulates the resulting value as it proceeds, it is described as the accumulator recursive form to distinguish it from the stack recursive form. A factorial function facb is now defined in terms of an auxiliary function faux that takes the factorial argument together with an accumulator initialised to 1:

```
facb x = faux x 1

faux 0 prod = prod
faux n prod = faux (n-1) (prod*n)
```

To see how this function computes a factorial, we elaborate the evaluation of factorial 4:

```
facb 4 = faux 4 1
       = faux 3 (1 * 4)
       = faux 3 4
       = faux 2 (4 * 3)
       = faux 2 12
       = faux 1 (12 * 2)
       = faux 1 24
       = 24
```

This version of the program carries out the arithmetic operations as it proceeds, accumulating the final result as the second argument.

The greatest common divisor (gcd) of two numbers is the largest number that divides into both numbers without remainder so that, for example, the gcd of 12

and 15 is 3. Euclid's method for computing the gcd of two numbers simply sub-
tracts one number from the other until the two numbers are equal and is defined in
the following function:

```
gcd x y = x                    , x = y  || eq 1
        = gcd (x - y) y , x > y  || eq 2
        = gcd x (y - x) , y > x  || eq 3
```

An elaboration of the evaluation of gcd 12 15 shows how the result is obtained:

```
gcd 12 15 = gcd 12 3   eq 3
          = gcd 9  3   eq 2
          = gcd 6  3   eq 2
          = gcd 3  3   eq 2
          = 3          eq 1
```

The second and third equations are applied until both arguments are the same,
at which point the argument is pattern matched with equation 1 and the recursive
calls finish.

EXERCISES 8.1

1. Define a function that accepts a pair of numbers as a single argument and returns
   a number expressing the first as a percentage of the second, e.g.

   ```
   ?percent(3,4)
   75.0
   ```

   Define a second function called `percent2` that takes the arguments in Curried
   form but produces the same result as function `percent`. Include type definitions with each of the above functions.

2. Write a function that accepts the radii of two circles on the same centre and
   calculates the area of space between them.

3. Simple and compound interest are calculated from the formulas $p(1 + r \times y/100)$
   and $p(1 + r/100)^y$ in which p is the principal, the amount of money invested, r is
   the annual percentage rate of interest and y is the number of years of the investment. Express these formulas in a Miranda script and use them to calculate the
   value of 500 currency units invested at 5.5% for seven years. Include type
   information in the script.

4. Write three functions that each accept a number of seconds and produce the
   following results:

   a. An integer representing the number of complete hours in that number of
      seconds.

b. An integer representing the number of whole minutes remaining after the hours have been removed.

c. A final integer representing the seconds remaining after complete hours and minutes have been subtracted.

Use the three functions to define a further function that accepts a number of seconds and returns a triple of integers representing the number of whole hours, minutes and seconds in the input.

5. A function is required to accept an integer n and a lower case letter of the alphabet as its two arguments and to produce a single lower case letter as its result. The resulting letter should be n places further in the alphabet than the letter input and should be wrapped around to the beginning of the alphabet where necessary.

6. Miranda has no built-in definition for the logical implication operation, but a function imp(p,q) could be defined in terms of the equivalent ~p ∨ q. Implement this definition, check that it works then use it to define further functions capable of computing values for the expressions

```
(p -> q) -> r
p ->(q -> r)
```

7. Implement a version of the implication function without using built-in features in the style of the vel function in the text.

8. Negated forms of the and, or, imp and iff expressions are called nand, nor, nimp and niff. These functions may be implemented in terms of the built-in functions, e.g.

```
nand(p,q) = ~(p & q)
```

Write functions implementing the negated operations in this way and also implement them directly in the way that vel and imp are implemented in the text.

9. Write a function that accepts a single character and returns a message "It's a vowel" or "No, it's not a vowel" depending on whether the letter input is a vowel.

8.2 LISTS

Lists are collections of elements in which the ordering of the elements is significant. Thus, the set {1, 2, 3} is equivalent to set {3, 2, 1} but list [1, 2, 3] is not equivalent to list [3, 2, 1] because the elements occur in a different order. Lists may be contained between square brackets or shown as the result of repeated cons (:) operations that attach elements to an empty list (a nil list). Thus lists of numbers may be shown in two ways:

```
[ ]            [ ]
[1]            1 : [ ]
[2,1]          2 : 1 [ ]
[3,2,1]        3 : 2 : [ ]
```

regular form   cons form

Sometimes a mixture of the two notations is useful, for example the list 3 : [2,1] is equivalent to list [3,2,1] and might be used to distinguish the leftmost element (the head) from the rest of the elements in a list (the tail).

Miranda lists may only contain elements of one type, so the simplest lists are sequences of Miranda basic types:

```
numlist :: [num]
numlist = [3,4,5]

boollist :: [bool]
boollist = [True, False,True]

string :: [char]
string = "Frodo"  || or string = ['F','r','o','d','o']
```

List elements have to be of the same type, but this type can be a structure such as another list or a tuple, giving examples such as

```
dlistnum :: [[num]]
dlistnum = [[1, 2], [3, 4]]   || compare with numlist above

dlistchar :: [[char]]
dlistchar = ["Frodo", "Bilbo"]

stars :: [(num, [char], char)]
stars = [(123,"Donald Duck",'m') (345,"Snow White",'f')]
```

Relational operations can be applied to lists as a whole with queries such as

```
?[2,3,2] < [2,3,4]
True
```

in which the first differing element decides the ordering. Lists as a whole can also be tested for equality:

```
?"String" = "String"
True
```

Functions hd and tl are provided in the standard environment, so a list can be broken into head and tail, but the definitions required for this are very simple:

```
hd(x:xs) = x
tl(x:xs) = xs
```

Thus, functions hd and tl applied to list [2,3,4] produce 2 and [3,4] respectively. Note that function hd applied to list [*] yields a result of type * whereas tl yields a result of type [*], i.e. one yields an element and the other a list. Arguments can only be pattern matched with these definitions if they are lists of at least one element; if either function is applied to an empty list, the system reports an error.

Built-in functions are provided to find the sum of all elements in a number list, to find the number of elements in any list and to test whether a given element is a member of a list. These functions have similar definitions and the way in which they are evaluated is also similar. For example, the following addup function mimics the built-in sum function:

```
addup [ ] = 0                    || eq 1
addup (x:xs) = x + addup xs   || eq 2
```

Obviously, the sum of all elements of an empty list add up to 0 whereas the sum of any other list is obtained by adding the head element to the sum of the elements in the tail. The following trace of an evaluation shows each intermediate stage leading to the canonical value:

```
addup[3,4,5] = 3 + addup[4,5] eq 2
             = 3 + (4 + addup[5])        eq 2
             = 3 + (4 + (5 + addup[]))   eq 2
             = 3 + (4 + (5 + 0))         eq 1
             = 3 + (4 + 5)               addition
             = 3 + 9                     addition
             = 12                        addition
```

Pattern matching of the actual list argument with the two arguments in the formal definition means that equation 2 is used repeatedly until an empty list is obtained, then equation 1 terminates the recursion. At each recursive call, a previously obtained number is stacked and its addition to the remaining numbers suspended while recursion proceeds. When every number in the list has been used, an empty list remains and a pattern match with equation 1 terminates recursion. Then the previously suspended numbers are unstacked and added to complete this stack recursive evaluation.

A function specifying the number of elements in a list is similarly defined and evaluated in much the same way:

```
length [ ] = 0
length (x:xs) = 1 + length xs
```

In words, the length of an empty list is 0 and the length of any other list is one greater than the length of its tail. Another function of this kind is used to discover if a given element occurs in a list:

```
is_in [ ] w = False
is_in (x:xs) w = w = x V is_in xs w
```

The element w obviously cannot occur in an empty list and this equation terminates the recursive procedure. Termination also occurs when the element is discovered because lazy evaluation produces value True from the body (True ∨ is_in xs w) but the results still have to be unstacked. This function is called member in the standard environment.

Stack recursive functions are easily defined but the process of returning through a series of suspended operations might make these definitions inefficient in operation. An alternative approach accumulates the final answer as it proceeds, as in the following definition of the built-in sum function:

```
addupb numlst = aaux numlst 0          || eq 1
aaux [ ] tot = tot                     || eq 2
aaux (x:xs) tot = aaux xs (tot + x)    || eq 3
```

Function addupb takes the list of numbers to be added and passes it to an auxiliary function called aaux with a running total initialised to 0. Function aaux then takes each element in turn, adding it to the running total (the accumulator), until the removals produce an empty list. An example elaboration shows how this works:

```
addupb [3,4,5] = aaux [3,4,5] 0    eq 1
               = aaux [4,5] 3       eq 3
               = aaux [5] 7         eq 3
               = aaux [ ] 12        eq 3
               = 12                 eq 2
```

Two lists can be joined together by an infix append function ++ (two addition signs) provided in the standard environment:

```
?[1,2,3] ++ [8,9]
[1,2,3,8,9]
```

A user-defined prefix version of the function follows the style of the same operation definition for the list abstract type in Chapter 6:

```
append [ ] ys = ys
append (x:xs) ys = x : append xs ys
```

Elements of the the first list argument are consed onto a second list until the first list is empty. At this point, the append function returns just the second list.

8.2.1   List comprehensions

Suppose that we define a function capable of converting Celsius temperatures to equivalent Fahrenheit values:

```
ctof x = x *9/5 + 32
```

and that we have a list of temperatures expressed in Celsius:

```
ctemps = [14,25,54,36,15]
```

Miranda provides the following very neat method of expressing a list of equivalent Fahrenhiet temperatures:

```
ftemps = [ctof x | x <- ctemps]
```

This expression has the form `[f x | x <- xs]` and is an example of a list comprehension in which function `f` is applied to every element `x` taken in order from some generator list `xs`. If definitions `ctof`, `ctemps` and `ftemps` occur in a script, the following interaction is possible:

```
?ftemps
[57.2, 77, 129.2, 96.8, 59]
```

A list to be used as a generator might be defined as an argument to be passed to a comprehension. For example, a function to produce squares of every element in a list is easily written in terms of the standard `sqr` function:

```
sqlist :: [num] -> [num]
sqlist xs = [sqr x | x <- xs]
```

so that a particular invocation could replace variable `xs` by a specific list. Such a replacement might be initiated at the prompt:

```
?sqlist [2,3,4,5]
[4,9,16,25]
```

In fact, the standard environment contains a function called `map`, which is pre-defined as

```
map f xs = [f x | x <- xs]
```

This standard form allows a programmer to achieve the same effect more simply as

```
?map sqr [2,3,4,5]
[4,9,16,25]
```

Clearly, `map` applies function `f` to each element of a list `xs`, producing a modified list of equal length to the original. Returning to the temperature conversion, we might write at the prompt:

```
?map ctof ctemps
[57.2, 77, 129.2, 96.8, 59]
```

Multiple generators are allowed and are useful for forming tuples from separate lists of elements:

```
mkpairs xs ys = [(x,y) | x <- xs ; y <- ys]
```

allowing the following interaction:

```
?mkpairs [1,2,3] ['a','b']
[(1,'a'), (1,'b'), (2,'a'), (2,'b'), (3,'a'), (3,'b')]
```

This function is called `zip2` in the standard environment and similar functions for zipping together three or more lists are called `zip3`, `zip4`, `zip5` and `zip6`.

Lists of tuples can be combined by taking advantage of the pattern-matching feature:

```
combine xs ys = [(a,b,c,d,e) | (a,b) <- xs ; (c,d,e) <- ys]
```

producing a Cartesian product, a 5-tuple, from two argument lists, a pair and a triple.

Qualifiers may be added to a comprehension in order to filter the elements from one list into a new list. Suppose we want to filter out the odd numbers from a list of numbers. We first require a function to decide if a number is uneven; this will be the case when division by 2 leaves a remainder of 1:

```
odd :: num -> bool
odd x = x mod 2 = 1
```

and this Boolean-valued function is inserted into a comprehension as follows:

```
oddlist xs = [x | x <- xs ; odd x]
```

Only those elements x of `xs` for which `odd x` is `True` are included in the new list, so the function acts as a filter to produce the following effect:

```
?oddlist [5,8,56,7,17]
[5,7,17]
```

A function called `filter` is defined in the standard environment as

```
filter p xs = [x | x <- xs ; px]
```

and could be used to filter odd numbers from a list as follows:

```
?filter odd [1,2,3,4]
[1,3]
```

Functions `map` and `filter` are described as higher-order functions because they take an argument that is itself a function to be applied to further arguments.

Multiple generators can be used with the equality condition to extract the common elements from two lists:

```
common xs ys = [x | x <- xs ; y <- ys ; x = y]
```

One element is taken from list `xs` then all the elements of `ys` are examined; if any of them has the same value, it is included in the resulting list. All of the elements of a generator on the right are produced for the production of one element of a generator on its left, so a first list of 100 elements causes 100 passes through the second list. More efficient functions could be defined if efficiency became an important issue.

8.2.2   Ordering lists

A function that reverses the order of elements in a list is easily defined with the aid of the cons and append operations:

```
rev [ ] = [ ]
rev (x:xs) = rev xs ++ [ x ]
```

Pattern matching distinguishes between empty and non-empty arguments, so the head element of a list can be appended to the right of its own reversed tail. Repeated use of the second equation must eventually lead to an argument that is an empty list, hence to the termination of the recursive calls.

A quicksort divides a list into two sublists, one containing all those elements less than the head element, the other all those elements greater than or equal to (i.e. not less than) the head element. This doubly recursive strategy is neatly expressed in Miranda as follows:

```
qsort [ ]     = [ ]
qsort (x:xs) = qsort [u | u <- xs ; less u x] ++
               [x] ++
               qsort [u | u <- xs; ~less u x]
```

After repeated applications, qsort will be applied to an empty list and yield an empty list, terminating the series of recursive calls.

Function less might just be the familiar "less than" relation:

```
less u x = u < x
```

but might be a more complex definition. A list of tuples containing item number, description and cost might be written as follows:

```
stock = [(256,"chair", 56.34),(637,"bed",100.75), . . . ]
```

and definitions of less might then depend on whether the tuples are to be ordered on item number, description or cost. If an alphabetical ordering on description is required, the definition is

```
less (i1,d1,c1) (i2,d2,c2) = d1 < d2
```

Dates may be sorted by reversing the day–month–year format then using Miranda's built-in "less than" relation:

```
less (d1,m1,y1) (d2,m2,y2) = (y1,m1,d1) < (y2,m2,d2)
```

Two lists already individually in order can be merged into a single ordered list with the merge function:

```
merge [ ] ys         = ys
merge (x:xs) [ ]     = x : xs
merge (x:xs) (y:ys) = x : merge xs (y : ys) , if less x y
                    = y : merge (x : xs) ys , otherwise
```

Again a suitable definition of function less has to be present in the script and in this case might take the form of a "less than or equal to" comparison. In fact, merge is a standard environment function, so we could make the following query without a script definition:

```
?merge [3,5,8] [2,6,7]
[2,3,5,6,7,8]
```

Remember also that relational operations apply to compound elements and it would be possible to use both qsort and merge on lists of tuples or lists of lists without modification.

8.2.3   Sets

In Miranda, as in many other languages, sets are implemented as lists; special functions are applied to these lists in order to impose set requirements. The similarity of set comprehensions and the list comprehensions provided in Miranda makes the treatment of set properties especially easy. A function to remove all occurrences of a given element from a list provides a first step in converting lists to sets:

```
delete x [ ] = [ ]
delete x xs = [ y | y <- xs ; x ~= y ]
```

An arbitrary list is then made into a set when each head element is consed onto a list from which any further copies of that element have been deleted:

```
mkset [ ] = [ ]
mkset (x:xs) = x : mkset(delete x xs)
```

Although the order of elements in a set is unimportant in defining a particular set, it might be an advantage to keep elements in order so that more efficient algorithms can be used.

Set operations such as union, intersection and difference are easily implemented with the aid of list operations from the standard environment. Set union takes advantage of the append function:

```
union xs ys = xs ++ ys
```

but this might result in a list containing duplicate elements that could be removed with mkset:

```
?mkset(union [1,2,3] [2,3,4])
[1,2,3,4]
```

Functions intersect and difference have similar implementations; intersect takes those elements of one list that appear in another, difference takes those elements that do not appear in a second list:

```
intersect xs ys = [x | x <- xs ; member ys x]

difference xs ys = [x | x <- xs ; ~member ys x]
```

EXERCISES 8.2

1. Write a function that accepts a single list containing both positive and negative numbers and produces a result list in which all negative numbers occur before the positive ones, but in the same order as in the original.

2. Write a polymorphic function in stack recursive style that counts the number of times a given element occurs in a list.

3. Repeat the previous exercise in the accumulator style described in the text.

4. Write a function that accepts a character string and informs the user if that string is a palindrome. If the reversed string is identical to the original, the function returns "Yes, it's a palindrome" otherwise it returns "No, it's not a palindrome".

5. A database contains the names of children, their dates of birth and a list of scores out of 10 for the workbooks they have completed. For example, the table group1 begins with the tuples

```
group1 = [("tom",(14,3,89),[4,7,5]),("john",(7,12,88),
[3,6]), ... ]
```

The list of scores has no fixed length, but usually contains two to five entries. Define and execute functions that take the group1 list as an argument and produce the following lists:

a. Names of all Sagittarian children, i.e. those born between 23 November and 21 December inclusive.

b. Pairs showing the names of each child with the number of workbooks completed, i.e. the number of workbook scores.

c. Pairs containing the child name and the average grade obtained by that child.

d. Pairs containing the name and age of each child when the current date is accepted as a second argument.

e. Names of those children who are older than the average age of the class.

f. Children's names in order of the sum of the scores they have achieved.

A second list repeats the above information for a second group in the class in the same style as the group1 table:

```
group2 = [("jill",(14,12,87),[8,3,5,7]), ... ]
```

g. Use the quicksort function to accept the group2 list and produce the same list with the children in order of date of birth.

h. Define a function that produces a list of both `group1` and `group2` in order of date of birth.

i. Write a function that produces a single list of pairs containing the name and age in years for each child in both groups 1 and 2. The list should be ordered on age, but within a given age, `group1` children should always precede those `group2` children.

j. Devise a function that accepts a workbook number and returns the names of all children who have not completed that workbook.

8.3 FLAT TABLES

A flat table is one in which individual cells of the table are atomic, i.e. they consist of basic data types such as numbers, Booleans or characters. These tables are the basic structures used in relational database systems, and in this context the atomic cells include fixed-length strings of characters and dates. This section is intended to show that relational database operations can be emulated in a functional language and to suggest that the emulation is in many ways neater than the original formulation. Fixed-length strings of characters will be modelled by the variable-length strings possible in Miranda. Relational databases usually show a date as a triple in the style 25-MAR-85, but store it as an absolute number by counting the day from an arbitrary date in the past. As a result, the cell value is an integer and is therefore an atomic value. Dates in the following examples are expressed as Miranda triples such as (25,3,85) in a style similar to that of relational databases.

As an example, we consider two tables describing the videos held in a video store and the customers who hire the videos, plus a further table linking them together. These tables are equivalent to the relations of relational databases; the first two are entity relations and the third is called a relationship relation. Entity relations contain information about distinct objects such as items of stock, employees and locations, whereas a relationship relation is used to link entities together. The following sample database is used in the examples:

```
VIDEO
VNUM        TITLE       TYPE        PRICE
47          Ghandi      Drama       3.00
68          Cocoon      SciFi       2.00
84          Tootsie     Comedy      2.50

CUSTOMER
CNUM        FNAME       SURNAME
467         John        Smith
547         Bill        Clinton
668         Albert      Jones
```

```
LINK
VNUM            CNUM            RETDATE
47              467             (11,8,97)
47              668             (27,8,97)
68              668             (20,8,97)
```

The VIDEO table contains four columns, the first of which is a unique key that identifies a particular video; this is followed by the title of the film and its type, an indication of the movie content. A further column headed PRICE indicates the charge for a fixed-period loan. A customer relation contains a unique customer number that identifies each customer together with first name and surname. Finally, a LINK table connects videos on loan to the customers who have them and includes the date on which they should be returned. Single rows in the above tables can be represented in Miranda by tuples having the following type synonyms:

```
date == (num,num,num)
video == (num,[char],[char],num)
customer == (num,[char],[char])
link == (num,num,date)
```

and one particular video tuple might be defined as follows:

```
vrow :: video
vrow = (47, "Ghandi", "Drama", 3.00)
```

Individual items in a tuple are called attributes in this context and are projected out of a tuple by the projection functions described earlier. For example, the second attribute of a 4-tuple, in this case the title of a video, can be projected out with the following function:

```
proj4b(a,b,c,d) = b
```

and other attributes might be similarly projected. Since these projection functions may be polymorphic, and other similar functions may be required, it makes sense to adopt a consistent notation. Projection function proj4b indicates a projection of the second value of a 4-tuple. If this function and the tuple above were contained in a current script, the following query might occur:

```
?proj4b vrow
Ghandi
```

Collections of attributes can be projected from a video tuple into smaller tuples and the simple notation takes an obvious extension:

```
proj4ab(a,b,c,d) = (a,b)
```

allowing the following interaction:

```
?proj4ab vrow
(47,"Ghandi")
```

Whole tables can be represented as a list of tuples with the following type synonyms:

```
videotab == [video]
custtab == [customer]
linktab == [link]
```

so the VIDEO table above might appear in a script as

```
vtable :: videotab
vtable = [(47,"Ghandi","Drama",3.00),
          (68,"Cocoon","SciFi",2.00),
          (84,"Tootsie","Comedy",2.50)]
```

A defined set of attributes can be projected from a whole list of tuples using the following function:

```
project atts vlist = [atts tup | tup <- vlist]
```

so the first and second attributes of the VIDEO table are projected out as follows:

```
?project proj4ab vtable
[(47,"Ghandi"),(68,"Cocoon"),(84,"Tootsie")]
```

In fact, the project function defined here is just a specialised version of the map function provided in the Miranda environment, so

```
?map proj4ab vtable
```

gives the same result.

Sometimes it is necessary to select tuples from a list, the choice of tuples depending on the values of one or more attributes in the tuple. Qualifying tuples are chosen by a Boolean function such as this example, which denotes True if the price attribute is below 3.00:

```
cheap tup = proj4d tup < 3.00
```

Function proj4d projects out the fourth attribute of a video tuple (a 4-tuple) in the style of the above projections, and this attribute is compared with the number 3.00. Once the selection function has been defined in this way, it can be passed with the following select function to extract all cheap videos from the database:

```
select cond vlist = [tup | tup <- vlist ; cond tup]
```

allowing the following interaction:

```
?select cheap vtable
[(68,"Cocoon","SciFi",2.00),(84,"Tootsie","Comedy",2.50)]
```

Selection as defined above is in fact a specialised version of the filter function in the standard Miranda environment and we could write

```
?filter cheap vtable
```

to obtain exactly the same result.

Projections produce new lists containing exactly the same number of tuples, but the number of attributes in each tuple is reduced. Selections, on the other hand, might produce a new list with fewer tuples, but the attributes of each tuple in the new list are the same as those in the old. A combination of `select` and `project` operations is often required; perhaps we need to know the numbers and titles of all cheap films in the database. Using the functions above, we could present a query at the Miranda prompt:

```
?project proj4ab (select cheap vtable)
[(68,"Cocoon"),(84,"Tootsie")]
```

Notice that the selection is carried out before the projection, otherwise the projection would remove the attribute on which the selection was based; this is not necessarily the case in all examples.

Individual video and link tuples might be combined into a single tuple by the following function:

```
mktup4x3 (a,b,c,d) (p,q,r) = (a,b,c,d,p,q,r)
```

and lists of such tuples can be combined into a Cartesian product with the following higher-order function:

```
cprod mkf xs ys = [mkf x y | x <- xs ; y <- ys]
```

allowing a Cartesian product table to be built from the `VIDEO` and `LINK` tables:

```
videoxlink = cprod mktup4x3 vtable ltable
```

The resulting table contains nine rows (3 × 3) corresponding to every combination of rows in the `VIDEO` and `LINK` tables. The first three of these nine rows are as follows:

```
47      Ghandi      Drama 3.00      47      467      (11,8,97)
47      Ghandi      Drama 3.00      47      668      (27,8,97)
47      Ghandi      Drama 3.00      68      668      (20,8,97)
```

showing that one line of the `VIDEO` table is combined with each line of the `LINK` table. Clearly a Cartesian product gets very large very quickly: two tables with 100 rows each together produce a new table of 10 000 rows.

All of the table constructions above are said to be written in tuple-oriented form because the generator produces labelled tuples to which projections, selections and Cartesian products are applied. Variable x in a generator such as x <- xs stands for the whole tuple rather than for individual attributes of a tuple. An alternative, domain-oriented definition of relational database operations directly labels individual attributes (domains) of tuples, instead of labelling tuples as a whole. A domain-oriented version of the Cartesian product may be written as follows:

```
cprod4x3 vs cs = [(a,b,c,d,p,q,r) | (a,b,c,d) <- vs; (p,q,r)
<- cs]
```

and a query ?cprod4x3 vtable ltable produces exactly the same result as above.

Although Cartesian products are useful to merge tuples from separate tables into larger tuples, in practice they only provide part of what is required. Normally a user is interested only in those tuples of the Cartesian product that relate to a single object or person. In the context of the VIDEO × LINK example, a user is likely to be interested in those tuples that relate to the same video. Looking at the Cartesian product above, it is clear that of the three rows shown, only the first two will usually be of interest. since the other one combines information for video number 47 with details of the customer who has borrowed video number 68. A join (more correctly called an equijoin) produces only those rows of the Cartesian product in which certain attributes of the contributing tuples are equal, in this case the video numbers in each tuple:

```
join4x3 vs cs = [(a,b,c,d,q,r)| (a,b,c,d) <- vs; (p,q,r) <-
cs; a = p]
```

Since the video numbers of tuples selected are equal by definition, only one copy of this number is included in the resultant table. Database operations are always applied to sets of tuples and always denote sets of tuples, but in practice we model the sets as lists. A set of tuples derived from the base sets is often described as a view of the database because it presents a particular picture of the information in the database. Thus we might write

```
view1 = join4x3 vtable ltable
```

and obtain a new derived table as follows:

```
?view1
[(47, Ghandi, Drama, 3.00, 467, (11,8,97)),
 (47, Ghandi, Drama, 3.00, 668, (27,8,97)),
 (68, Cocoon,SciFi, 2.00, 668, (20,8,97))]
```

Projection and selection functions might be applied to this derived table in just the same way that they are applied to the base tables described earlier. Indeed, a user need not know whether a table is a base table or a view in order to apply functions to it.

A simple Cartesian product of the type VIDEO × LINK × CUST on the small base tables above produces a table with 3 × 3 × 3 = 27 rows and could easily be produced with a comprehension using three generators. Fortunately, the only product tuples of any interest are those produced from pairs where the video number is the same and pairs where the customer number is the same. Since we have already joined two lists on their video number, that view of the database could be used to construct a further view joined on the customer number as follows:

```
join3x6 cs xs = [(a,b,c,p,q,r,s,u) | (a,b,c) <- cs;
(p,q,r,s,t,u) <- xs; a = t]
```

and this function might be used to construct a further view

```
view2 = join3x6 ctable view1
```

allowing the keyboard interaction

```
?view2
[(467,"John","Smith",47,"Ghandi","Drama",3.0,(11,8,97)),
 (668,"Albert","Jones",47,"Ghandi","Drama",3,(27,8,97)),
 (668,"Albert","Jones",68,"Cocoon","SciFi",2.0,(28,8,97))]
```

Suppose that we want to produce a table showing each film title currently on loan, together with the first name and surname of the customer holding the video. All that would be required is a projection of the appropriate three attributes from the list of tuples in view2.

8.3.1 More complex structures

Flat tables only admit tuples with atomic values, either basic types or fixed-length strings of characters. Languages such as Miranda can accommodate more complex structures in which the elements of a tuple are themselves tuples or lists of arbitrary length. Consider as an example a list of tuples containing information about musicians and the instruments they play. Each tuple contains a tuple with the name, telephone number, and fee charged by an individual musician together with a list of the instruments that person can play:

```
oneman = (("John Smith","556565", 45), ["guitar","flute"])
```

Variables can represent tuples and lists in the same way as basic data types, so structures can be projected out by the expressions

```
player(x,y) = x
ilist(x,y) = y
```

A list of the instruments played by the person in oneman may be obtained as follows:

```
?ilist oneman
["guitar","flute"]
```

A database of such tuples could be constructed as a collection of these tuples in a list

```
artistes = [(("John Smith","556565", 45), ["guitar", "flute"]),
            (("Tom Jones","235346",55), ["drums","piano"])]
```

and a list comprehension used to extract parts of tuples such as the player details:

```
listplayers xs = [player tup | tup <- xs]
```

A simple extension of this comprehension produces a list of those artistes who play a certain instrument:

```
plays inst xs = [players tup | tup <- xs ; member (ilist tup)
inst]
```

allowing the following query:

```
?plays "flute" artistes
[("John Smith","556565", 45)]
```

EXERCISES 8.3

1. Create lists of 3-tuples or 4-tuples with entries defined as in the following schemata:

```
UGRAD(snum,sname,dateob,gender)
COURSE(cnum,title,semest,credits)
LINK(snum,cnum,grade)
```

In this example snum and cnum are numeric keys for the student and course entity tables. Attribute sname is the student name, and for the purpose of this exercise it might be just a surname; dateob is the student date of birth; gender is a single lower case letter, either 'm' or 'f'. A semest attribute is 1 or 2, representing either first or second semester, and title is the name of the course, e.g. Database. Attribute credits is either 8 or 15, representing half and full courses and the grade point is a number between 1 and 16 inclusive. Define functions to produce the following lists:

a. Names of all students born in 1980.

b. Names of all students born before 7 July 1977.

c. Title and semester number for all courses.

d. Course number and title of all full-credit second-semester courses.

Define a function that joins the UGRAD and LINK tables into a single table called VIEW1. Define functions on the joined table that produce the following tables:

e. Student name, course number and grade.

f. Names for all students who obtained 14 grade points or higher on any course.

Define a function that joins the COURSE and VIEW1 tables into a single table called VIEW2 then define and test functions to produce the following tables:

g. Student name, course title and grade for each combination.

h. Name and course title for all female students who achieved 11 grade points or higher in a first-semester course.

   i. A list of all students and the courses on which they got better grade points than the average over all students and courses.

2. The flat tables described above do not permit any attribute (except date) to be anything other than a simple object. Languages that permit more complex structures might hold the information in the following schemata:

```
UGRAD(snum,sname,dateob,gender,[(cnum,grade)])
COURSE(cnum,title,semest,credits)
```

Copy the database above into a new file and modify its structure to reflect the new schema. Repeat items (a) to (i) for the modified schema.

8.4 NEW TYPES

A new type is introduced by the special notation shown in the following example:

```
logish ::= Falsch | Wahr
```

in which a German programmer defines a type called logish with components equivalent to the English False and True. It is important to note that the "is defined to be" symbol (::=) introduces a new type and that this is not simply a type synonym. Elements of the new type, called constructors, are distinguished from variables by a leading capital letter and from strings by the absence of quotation marks. Constructor definitions for False and True are provided in the standard environment together with built-in operations on the Boolean constants. No operations are defined on the type logish except that relational operations can be applied in the usual way:

```
?Falsch < Wahr
True
```

and their result depends on the enumeration order in the type definition, i.e. Falsch is declared before Wahr so it is "less than". Functions equivalent to negation, conjunction and disjunction may be defined on the elements of type logish as follows:

```
nicht :: logish -> logish
nicht Falsch = Wahr
nicht Wahr = Falsch

und :: logish ->logish -> logish
und x y = x , if x <= y
        = y , otherwise

oder :: logish -> logish -> logish
oder x y = x , if x >= y
         = y , otherwise
```

Functions nicht, und and oder denote functions equivalent to the built-in ~, &
and \/ functions, except they operate on constants of type logish rather than on
Boolean constants. Perhaps less obviously, functions und and oder are also equivalent to the min and max functions described earlier, so that one of them (und)
returns the lower value of its two arguments whereas the other (oder) returns the
higher value. Function und only yields Wahr, the German word for "true", when
both of its arguments are Wahr, i.e. the minimum of the two arguments is Wahr.
On the other hand, function oder yields Falsch only if both of its arguments are
also Falsch and the maximum of its arguments is therefore Falsch. Such expressions are evaluated at the prompt in the usual way:

```
?und Wahr (nicht Falsch)
Wahr
```

yielding the expected result. Although the functions above have been defined in
prefix form, they can be used in the infix style if a $ symbol is attached to the
function name:

```
?Wahr $und (nicht Falsch)
Wahr
```

making it easier to program expressions already written in infix notation.

A recursive form of definition may be written to include the connectives themselves as constructors:

```
logish2 ::= Falsch | Wahr | Nicht logish2 | Und logish2 logish2
```

and any expression is then syntactically of type logish2. Thus the compound
expression Oder (Und Falsch Wahr) (Oder Falsch Wahr) consists, not of
operations on two constants, but a single entity of type logish2. This single
syntactic entity must be semantically equivalent to one of the canonical values
Falsch and Wahr. A function called val is required to evaluate such expressions
and is defined as follows:

```
val :: logish2 -> logish2
val Falsch = Falsch
val Wahr = Wahr

val (Nicht Wahr) = Falsch
val (Nicht Falsch) = Wahr

val (Und x y) = val x , if val x <= val y
              = val y , otherwise

val (Oder x y) = val x , if val x >= val y
               = val y , otherwise
```

Now a single arity-one function called val of type logish2 -> logish2 takes
arguments of type logish2 and denotes values of logish2. An expression in
this form is evaluated at the prompt as

```
? val (Nicht (Und (Nicht Wahr) ( Nicht Falsch)))
Wahr
```

A constructor labelled Oder might be added to the type declaration and a valuation provided similar to that for Und. Expressions written in this way may be evaluated as in the example above, revealing the denotation of the expression. Constructors allow the syntactic checking or proof theoretic procedures described in Section 8.7.

8.4.1 Explicit null values in logical statements

A three-valued logic system defined from the truth tables in Section 7.2 is widely used by electronics engineers in simulating semiconductor circuits; we can mimic these simulations in Miranda programs. Constants for such a system of logic could be defined by the following type enumeration:

```
tern ::= Zero | Null | One
```

in which Zero and One represent False and True while Null represents the unknown or undefined state. Ternary symbols may then be inverted with a pattern-matching function:

```
inv :: tern -> tern
inv Zero = One
inv One = Zero
inv Null = Null
```

Conjunction and disjunction are expressed in two functions defined on ternary arguments:

```
conj :: tern ->tern -> tern
conj x y = x , if x <= y
         = y , otherwise
disj :: tern -> tern -> tern
disj x y = x , if x >= y
         = y , otherwise
```

In fact, these two functions are again specialised versions of min and max applied to constants of type tern. If these functions are included in a script with type definition tern, the following interaction is possible:

```
?Zero $conj ((inv Null) $disj One)
Zero
```

8.4.2 Disjoint unions

Constructors can be accompanied by previously defined types to build structures of a new type. Thus a new type called key is introduced by definition from base types num and [char]:

```
key ::= Inl num | Inr [char]
```

so that constructors `Inl` and `Inr` (abbreviations for inject left and inject right) act as functions of type `key`, injecting two components into a single type:

```
Inl :: num -> key
Inr :: [char] -> key
```

The resulting type is a disjoint union of component types that are tagged by constructors. Thus the values 27 and "four" are of type num and [char] whereas values Inl 27 and Inr "four" are both of type key. A value incorporated into a new type through a constructor may be recovered through functions such as getnum:

```
getnum :: key -> num
getnum(Inl x) = x
```

8.4.3 Variant types

Any number of previously defined types might follow a constructor to give a structure similar to a tuple. A structure called man could be defined as follows:

```
man ::= Man [char] [char]
```

and the two lists of characters could contain first name and surname of a man. A tuple such as ("John", "Jones") might serve a similar purpose to the product type Man "John" "Jones", but there are important differences. The product type is more secure because special functions have to be written to manipulate their content whereas standard functions such as fst and snd might be applied to a pair. On the other hand, the tuple form is more compact and the ability to use standard functions might be an advantage. However, the product type allows variant records to be defined, i.e. records that might contain different numbers of attributes. A person type might be a man or a woman named as follows:

```
person ::= Man [char] [char] | Woman [char] [char] [[char]]
```

Every person record contains a first name and a surname, but a Woman record also contains a list of previous surnames that have been lost through marriage or remarriage. The current surname might be projected out as follows:

```
surname :: person -> [char]
surname(Man x y) = y
surname(Woman x y z) = y
```

Lists of such records may be formed in much the same way as lists of tuples are constructed.

8.4.4   A recursive definition of natural

A natural number is defined to be either constructor `Zero` or constructor `Succ` with a natural:

```
nat ::= Zero | Succ nat
```

formalising the concept that every natural is either zero or the successor of another natural. Constants might then be defined as follows:

```
one = Succ Zero
two = Succ(Succ Zero)
three = Succ(Succ(Succ Zero))
```

in a manner that could become tedious. Natural addition is then defined by two equations:

```
plus x Zero = x
plus x (Succ y) = Succ(plus x y)
```

and this operation can be applied to two `nat` arguments:

```
?plus two three
Succ(Succ(Succ(Succ(Succ Zero))))
```

This representation is obviously very close to the type `nat` defined in Chapter 5 and is of interest for this reason rather than for immediate practical use.

8.4.5   Lists

A built-in list definition adds elements to an initially empty list with a cons operation (`:`) but we could also use constructors to define such a structure. A list of numbers is defined by the following recursive form:

```
nlist ::= Nil | Cons num nlist
```

indicating that a list is either a `Nil` element or a constructor `Cons` binding an element to a list. Lists are therefore constructed incrementally from `Nil` as follows:

```
empty = Nil
onenum = Cons 8 Nil
twonum = Cons 4 (Cons 6 Nil)
```

producing structures of increasing length. Remember, however, that there is an infinite number of distinguishable lists of any particular size because the list contains non-finite elements. An operation called `append` may be defined on lists as follows:

```
append Nil right = right
append(Cons item left) right = Cons item (append left right)
```

This Miranda representation of a list and its `append` operation is again very similar to the abstract type defined in Chapter 6 and the evaluation mechanism is similar to the earlier description. Notice, however, that the definition above uses Curried arguments as opposed to the tuple form in the earlier chapter. Parametrised definitions similar to those discussed in Chapter 6 are implemented with the polymorphic type constructor

```
list * ::= Nil | Cons * (list *)
```

but are otherwise similar.

EXERCISES 8.4

1. Write a function to implement the logic of *implies* as defined in Chapter 1, using the `logish` type defined in the preceding section. Use this function to evaluate instances of the logical expressions $(p \to q) \to r$ and $p \to (q \to r)$. Use sufficient examples to show that these two expressions are not logically equivalent.

2. Repeat the previous exercise using the `logish2` type defined in this section.

3. Implement the ternary logical system described in the text and use it to check the non-strict results in the table of Chapter 7. Write a function that implements the proposition $(x \land y) \lor (\neg x \land z)$ using the functions defined in the text and test it with the following sets of values:

x	Zero	Zero	One	Null
y	One	Null	Null	Null
z	One	Null	Zero	Zero

   Write a function to implement the ternary logic of *implies* and check that it produces the results shown in Chapter 7.

4. Construct a list of the `person` objects as described in the text and define functions taking that list as an argument to produce the following lists:

   a. First name and surname of all women who have been married twice.

   b. Surnames of men and women who currently have the same surname.

   c. Current surnames of women who have in the past had the same surname as one of the men.

5. Define a multiplication function for naturals based on the `plus` function shown in the text. This function achieves its objective by repeated addition, i.e. to multiply 3 by 4 start with `Zero` then add 3 four times.

8.5 INFINITE LISTS

Miranda provides the special notation [m .. n] for a finite ordered sequence of integers from *m* to *n* and the meaning of this notation is clear at the prompt:

```
?[3..8]
[3,4,5,6,7,8]
```

Increments of 1 separate elements between the lower and upper bounds unless a step is specified by a second initial list element:

```
?[3,5..12]
[3,5,7,9,11]
```

Infinite lists are specified even more easily, the upper limit being dropped from the definition:

```
?[3.. ]
[3,4,5,6,7,8,9,10, Ctrl D
```

leaving an interactive user with a stream of numbers that can only be stopped by a Control D or C (keyboard interrupt) signal. Like the finite version above, an infinite list proceeds in defined steps when the first two numbers of the series are supplied by the programmer.

An infinite list can be an argument for higher-order functions such as map and filter, as in the following query which produces the squares of odd numbers above 1:

```
?map sqr [3,5..]
[9,25,49,81,121,169, Ctrl D
```

This interaction is particularly interesting because a result is being produced before the whole of the list argument has been constructed. Lazy evaluation allows the partially applied function map to apply its argument function sqr to the leading element of the list:

```
sqr 3 : map sqr [5,7,9,...
```

to evaluate the head element

```
9 : map sqr [5,7,9,...
```

and to continue along the list until interrupted. The important point here is that function sqr is applied to produce results one by one from the left before the whole argument list is formed. A lazy evaluator recognises that the application of a map function to a head element does not depend on other elements in the tail of the list, and it acts accordingly.

Lazily evaluated streams of data are of considerable importance in the inter-active use of programs at the keyboard. User input is treated as a list of strings or values with head elements that can be evaluated before the tail of the list has been entered at the keyboard. This has to be the case because any further user input might depend on an output response obtained from the program. As a result, the interaction takes the form of two lazily evaluated streams, one carrying the input and one carrying the output. The great advantage of this approach is that it allows the input and output of data within a purely declarative language. A lazy functional language such as Miranda never has to use the procedural read and write routines required in Prolog. Before looking at input control in detail, we look at the simpler case of output control.

8.5.1   Output control

The result of a Miranda evaluation is directed to the standard output device which, if the default setting has not been altered, will be the screen. If the output consists of a string of characters, a literal presentation of the characters occurs:

```
? "good night"
good night
```

Unix control characters can be embedded in a string so that formatting of the output is possible; for example, the newline (\n) and tab (\t) control characters have the following effect:

```
?"one\ttwo\nthree\tfour"
one     two
three four
```

An output device such as a teletype screen requires a stream of ASCII characters, so Miranda automatically converts the result of an evaluation to a string when this is not already the case. Thus, the constant pi evaluates to a number, but this is converted to a string of characters "3.14159265359" then directed to the screen. As a result, the following interaction occurs at the prompt:

```
?pi
3.14159265359
```

Although a string and a number can be separately converted and directed to the screen, an attempt to append one to the other leads to a problem:

```
?"the value of pi is" ++ pi
type error in expression
cannot unify num with [char]
```

and the obvious intention of this query is thwarted. A built-in function called show is used to convert objects of any type to a string and is invoked automatically to prepare the result of an evaluation for output. If an operation such as append is to be applied before output, the show function must be used explicitly to ensure compatible arguments:

```
?"the value of pi is" ++ show pi
the value of pi is 3.14159265359
```

A similar approach could be used to combine string output with other built-in or user-defined types, but care needs to be exercised when this function is used in scripts. An unwary user might have expected the following function to append its string to any type of variable:

```
display x = "Answer is >> " ++ show x
```

but on leaving the editor, the following message is observed:

```
type error in definition of display
use of "show" at polymorphic type *
```

The show function is really a collection of different functions with the same name; in order to select the correct function, the interpreter needs to know the argument type to be converted. Simply including the following type information in the script solves the problem:

```
display :: bool -> [char]
```

Functions such as show exhibit ad hoc polymorphism, i.e. an apparent form of polymorphism rather than the true polymorphism more characteristic of Miranda functions.

An interesting observation can be made when the following multiplication function is defined in a script:

```
times x y = show x ++"\t * \t "++show y ++" \t= \t"++show (x*y)
++ "\n"
```

without an explicit type declaration. This time, the inference mechanism is able to deduce that x and y are numbers because they are the objects of a multiplication operation elsewhere in the function. Thus the following interaction occurs:

```
?times 3 4
3 * 4 = 12
```

A program to produce any of the multiplication tables is easily written from the above times function:

```
table n = [times x n | x <- [1..10]]
```

but when used at the prompt, this function produces the following list of strings:

```
?table 3
["1 \t*\t 3 = 3\n", "2 \t* \t3 = 6\n", ...]
```

which is not quite what is required. Although each individual string in the list would have produced the desired output, the fact they are contained in a list means that each control character is printed literally. Fortunately, the standard environment contains a built-in function called `concat` that joins all the strings in a list together in a single list; when this function is added, we have

```
tableb n = concat [times x n | x <- [1..12]]
```

so the output now appears as follows:

```
?tableb 3
1 * 3 = 3
2 * 3 = 6
3 * 3 = 9 etc.
```

Another built-in function called `lay` concatenates lists in the same way but also inserts new lines following each sublist. This function is not required in the program above because a newline instruction had already been included in the `times` function.

A list of tuples describing the stock held in a shop is given the following type description:

```
item :: (num, [char], num, num)
stock :: [item]
```

then the list itself begins as follows:

```
stock = [(4271, "Chair", 14, 78.56), ...]
```

where the first number is a unique key for the item, followed by a brief description, the number in stock and the item cost. When output to the screen, this database would simply fill the screen width and wrap around to the next line. A simple format could be achieved with the following instruction:

```
?lay [show x | x <- stock]
```

causing a new line to be output following each tuple. A neater table layout is possible using the following formatting function for each tuple:

```
laytup :: item -> [char]
col n = "\t"++show n
laytup (w, x, y, z) = col w ++ "\t"++ x ++ col y ++ col z
```

The whole table can then be printed from the following comprehension:

```
table = [laytup xs | xs <- stock]
```

A heading might be defined and formatted to place titles at the head of each column:

```
heading = "\tcode\titem\tnumber\tprice\n\n"
```

then the table could be printed with headings by appending together the heading and table lists:

```
stocktable = heading ++ table
```

8.5.2 Output to files

Writing to the standard output device is just one particular example of a system message through which Miranda interacts with the Unix operating system. System messages are defined in a standard type:

```
sys_message ::= Stdout [char] | Tofile [char][char] | ..
```

and structures of type `sys_message` are directed to the operating system only when a list of them is presented for evaluation. If an evaluation is not "wrapped" in a system message, it defaults to the standard output device. These devices only accept ASCII strings, so the default wrapper automatically applies the `show` function to convert results that are not already strings into that form. Simply typing value `pi` at the prompt is equivalent to wrapping it in the system message:

```
?[Stdout (show pi)]
```

The second `sys_message` in the structure above is necessary when output is directed to a named file in secondary storage. To write a string to a file called `greeting`, the following list is required:

```
?[Tofile "greeting" "have a nice day"]
```

Provided a function evaluates to a string, its output could be directed to a named file, e.g. if a current script contained definition

```
stringlist = ["line one","line two","line three"]
```

the built-in function `show` could be used to convert this list to a single string of characters and the result could be output to a file called `threelines`:

```
[Tofile "threelines" (show stringlist)]
```

Afterwards the file `threelines` contains an exact copy of `stringlist`, including the quotes, commas and square brackets. A quite different effect is obtained by the following system message:

```
[Tofile "threelines2" (lay stringlist)]
```

following which a file `threelines2` contains the single string of characters `"line one\nline two\nline three"`.

A similar relationship exists between two files when a list defined by `numlist` = `[4,5,6]` is stored in two different ways. A direct ASCII representation of the list `[4,5,6]` is stored in file `threenums` following the directive

```
[Tofile "threenums" (show numlist)]
```

However, if these values are to be read back into the system, it is better to store them as a string of characters separated by newlines, i.e. as `"4\n5\n6\n"`, a layout that is achieved as follows:

```
[Tofile "threenums2" lay[ show x | x <- numlist]]
```

Several Tofile constructors for the same file can be included in the same list. The first opens the file and begins writing; subsequent instructions append to the same file. These messages can be interleaved by messages to Stdout:

```
go = [Tofile "results" funct(x,y), Stdout "ok"]
```

provided funct (x,y) evaluates to a string.

8.5.3   Input control

A built-in arity-one function called read denotes the content of a file named after the operator, e.g. read "filename" represents the string of ASCII characters contained in filename. Text stored in the two files above can be recovered by a built-in read command:

```
?read "threelines"
["line one","line two","line three"]

?read "threelines2"
line one
line two
line three
```

allowing us to observe the effect of the two different outputs. A built-in function called lines converts "layed" text back into standard list notation:

```
?lines (read "threelines2)
["line one","line two","line three"]
```

Files might contain representations of numbers or other types; if the standard read function is used to recover such data, it appears to produce the required result:

```
?read "threenums"
[1,2,3]
```

File threenums does actually contain a list, but it is the list [1,2,3], i.e. the string of ASCII characters representing the original number list including brackets and commas. To recover the list of numbers, there is a special function called readvals but it works on the file that has been "layed", not the file that has been shown. Like the show function, a readvals function is not truly polymorphic and has to be accompanied in a script by a type declaration:

```
numsback :: [num]
numsback = readvals "threenums2"
```

Two special symbols, $- and $+, are provided for read and readvals when the input is to be taken from the standard input device, usually the keyboard. To illustrate the behaviour of $- at the keyboard, simply type it at the prompt, hit return then type any string with a return:

```
?$-
one
one
two
two
Control D
```

The first string of each pair is echoed to the screen by the operating system and is subject to alteration by backspace deletion and overwriting, but the second is produced by Miranda itself: it is an evaluation of the input. This might be a little more interesting if it did more than reproduce the input, so we define a partially applied function mkcaps that converts all the lower case letters in a string to upper case, leaving other characters unchanged:

```
upcase x = decode (code x - 32) , x >= 'a' & x <= 'z'
         = x                      , otherwise

mkcaps = map upcase
```

Strings typed at the keyboard are then converted interactively as follows:

```
lay[ mkcaps xs | xs <- lines $- ]
Two
TWO
a3B2
A3B2
Control D
```

Values other than strings are similarly handled with $+ , allowing an interactive program to repeatedly take in a value and output an evaluation from that input. An interactive square root informer takes values from a user, outputs the result then prompts the user to input a further value:

```
start = "enter first number >>"
more = "\nanymore? (Ctrl D to finish) >>"
onesq x = "square root of"++show x ++"is"++show(sqrt x)++more
prog = start++concat[onesq x | x <- $+]
```

The program terminates when the user types Control D as the program input.

Finally a little program that starts when one person types a function name prog together with a number between 0 and 100, e.g. prog 79:

```
reply :: num -> num -> [char]
reply x y = "too low - try again>"  , x < y
          = "too high - try again>" , otherwise
scroll n = concat["\n" | x <- [1..n]]
```

```
start = scroll 25 ++ "Guess a number between 0 and 100 >"
end = " thats it!"
prog y = start++concat[reply x y | x <- takewhile(~= y) $+]
++ end
```

A screen echo of the function with its actual parameter is scrolled off the screen and a second person is invited to guess the number. Successive guesses result in high or low prompts, allowing the person to converge on the correct number. Input is terminated by the built-in `takewhile` function, allowing the program to proceed to its terminating message. A small modification to the program would allow it to reject inputs outside the desired range.

EXERCISES 8.5

1. Except for the number 1, only four natural numbers are equal to the sum of the cubes of their digits. The number 153 qualifies because

   $$1^3 + 5^3 + 3^3 = 1 + 125 + 27 = 153$$

   Write a Miranda program to search for the other three numbers in the range between 150 and 450.

2. Improve the output given as a result of Exercise 4 in Exercises 8.1 so that it responds as follows:

   ```
   ?conv 4937
   1 hours 22 minutes 17 seconds
   ```

   Improve it further so that it uses the singular form when appropriate.

3. Write a program that produces a table containing one column of Celsius temperatures between 0 and 100 degrees with a second column of equivalent Fahrenheit temperatures. Include a heading above each column.

4. Write the necessary functions to display the VIDEO table of Section 8.3 in columns with appropriate headings.

5. Electrical engineers use the following colour codes for numbers from 0 to 9:
   [black,brown,red,orange,yellow,green,blue,violet,grey,white].
   A resistance of $pq \times 10^r$ is then represented by the colour bands (p,q,r). For example, a resistance of 4700 ohm might equally well be written as 47×10^2 and its value represented on the resistor by the colour bands yellow, violet, red. In effect the letter r represents the number of noughts following the first two digits.
       Write a program that takes a colour triplet and outputs the numerical resistance value it denotes. Write an interactive program that prompts a user for the colour band input and returns a numerical value, repeatedly until a user has finished.

8.6 ABSTRACT TYPES

Abstract types may be implemented in Miranda in a variety of ways, but the algebraic definitions of Section 8.4 are particularly useful in this respect. Representations of this kind are much closer to the form of the abstract types described in Chapter 6 than those using built-in structures such as lists, so the difference between the pure abstract type and its representation is minimised. Representations of abstract types are called objects and it is considered good practice to prohibit any direct access to the data structure of an object. Abstract types defined by module specifications are made available to programmers, who are then able to manipulate data only through the defined operations of the abstract type. Parts of the object structure might remain hidden, leaving the applications programmer with a small number of defined operations. Miranda provides a built-in feature that allows a representation to be hidden, so access to data is only possible through operations defined in the abstract type.

Consider as a first example the following algebraic representation of a stack of numbers:

```
abstype stackn with
        nil  :: stackn
        push :: num -> stackn -> stackn
        top  :: stackn -> num
        pop  :: stackn -> stackn

algstack ::= Nil | Push num algstack
stackn == algstack

nil = Nil
push a s = Push a s
top(Push a s) = a
pop(Push a s) = s
```

First of all the keywords abstype ... with introduce the name of an abstract type for which a representation is to be supplied and binds specified operation names to an abstract type name. Each operation of the abstract type is then enumerated with its type description. Notice that the type description for push differs from the signature given in Chapter 6 because this version uses the Curried form more usual in lazy functional languages. A tuple-based implementation similar to that given in Chapter 6 would differ only in the signature given to the push operation, making it (num,stackn) -> stackn rather than the line shown above. Equally, the abstract type could be defined with Curried notation in the first place, but this is not the usual practice.

The signature is followed by a representation declaration; in this example the declaration is an algebraic structure, defining a stack as the constructor Nil or the constructor Push with number and stack as arguments. The structure algstack defined above is abstractly identical to a list structure defined through a Cons constructor. Miranda requires an abstype representation to be declared with a type synonym, so `stackn` is made synonymous with the previously declared algebraic stack. Type synonyms are optional in other situations and are included for clarity, but in the case of an abstract type representation they are mandatory. Each of the equations following the declarations is an implementation of the stack abstract type of Chapter 6, using one particular representation. Notice, however, that no action is defined in this implementation of operations that previously resulted in error operations, making this a partial abstract type.

If a script containing an abstype definition is compiled in the usual way, an expression can be submitted for evaluation:

```
?top(pop(push 3 (push 4 nil)))
4
```

Numbers can be added to and removed from the stack but a representation of this kind cannot be directly observed, as the following interaction shows:

```
?push 5 nil
<abstract ob>
```

If it is necessary to represent these abstract objects, a special `show` function has to be written for each abstract type.

A different representation of a given abstract type should produce exactly the same result for a given query; this is, after all, the purpose of an abstract type. The similarity between the algebraic definition of a stack and the definition of a list suggests that we should use the built-in list structure to represent a stack as follows:

```
abstype stackn with
          nil  :: stackn
          push :: num -> stackn -> stackn
          top  :: stackn -> num
          pop  :: stackn -> stackn

stackn == [num]

nil = [ ]
push a s = a:s
top(a:s) = a
pop(a:s) = s
```

Although the signature is the same as the algebraic stack, the representation is now carried by the built-in list structure.

Modern software practice often divides computing staff into module implementors, who design and implement modules, and applications staff, who use such predesigned modules. The person implementing a module tries to make it of general value so it can be applied in a wide variety of applications programs. Applications staff are then presented with a specification naming the functions available and defining the results to be expected for various arguments. A specification of this kind allows the module to be used without any knowledge of how information is represented in the module or of how module functions deduce results. There is an obvious advantage in writing an abstype representation in one script then making these definitions available to other users. A Miranda script can incorporate all the definitions contained in another script by using the `include` declaration. All the definitions in a script `stack2.m` can be included in a current script by adding the following directive at the head of the script:

```
%include "stack2"
```

8.6.1 Queues

Representations of queues of numbers, Booleans or any other type can be written as above, following the abstract type definition in Chapter 6 or by taking advantage of the underlying list structure. It is, however, a bit tedious to write different implementations for queues of each type: a queue is characterised by the behaviour of its operations, not by the objects in the queue. This is of course the basis for parametrised abstract types in Chapter 6 and Miranda implements such types through its polymorphic type system. Using an underlying algebraic representation, we obtain the following definition:

```
abstype queue * with
          nil     :. queue *
          join    :: * -> queue * -> queue *
          front   :: queue * -> *
          remove  :: queue * -> queue *
algque ::= Nil | Join * (algque *)
queue * == algque *

join x q = Join x q
front (Join x Nil) = x
front (Join x (Join y q)) = front (Join x q)
remove (Join x Nil) = Nil
remove (Join x (Join y q)) = Join x (remove (Join y q))
```

Again the Curried notation makes the signature here slightly different from that in Chapter 6, but the general layout of this implementation is remarkably similar to the abstract type itself. As usual, the symbol * in `queue *` represents any type, including complex structures, and this type is not bound to the queue until it is used. An alternative representation in terms of a list would use the same signature with the following definitions of representation and functions:

```
queue * = [ * ]

emptyque = [ ]
join q x = q ++ [x]
```

```
front(a:xs) = a
remove(a:xs) = xs
```

8.6.2   Binary search trees

Binary search trees grow downwards from a single node called the root through pairs of left and right edges to other nodes until terminating nil nodes are reached. Such trees are binary because each of their nodes has two descendants and they are search trees because the positions of values in the tree are arranged to facilitate the search procedure. New values are added in such a way as to preserve this ordered structure. A new node is added to the left of an existing node if its value is "less than" that node or to the right if it is "greater than" the existing node. A path is traced from the root of the tree, branching left or right at each intermediate node, until there is found the terminating nil node to which it should become attached. Once found, the value is substituted for the nil node then two further nil nodes are attached to the added node. New nodes are only ever attached to the terminating nil positions, often called leaf nodes.

An algebraic constructor approach defines a binary search tree or subtree of numbers to be either the empty tree `Nil` or a tree with a node value and two subtrees such a `Bin 6 Nil Nil`. Larger trees are formed as more numbers are added. If the list of numbers `[6,3,5,8,7]` is added in order from left to right, the tree constructed is

```
Bin 6 (Bin 3 Nil (Bin 5 Nil Nil)) (Bin 8 (Bin 7 Nil Nil) Nil)
```

but the structure of this tree is more visible in Figure 8.1. If the same numbers were added in a different order, a differently structured tree might result. The tree shown in Figure 8.1 has a symmetrical, balanced shape, but there is a danger that a tree might become unbalanced as new nodes are added. In the extreme case where numbers are added in ascending or descending order, the tree has the form of a list and is then totally unbalanced.

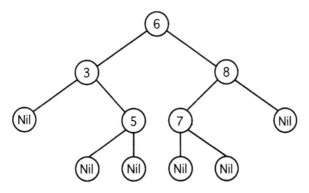

Figure 8.1   A binary search tree

A parametrised binary search tree may be defined by the abstype `bstree`:

```
%export bstree insert traverse delete

abstype bstree * with
        newtree  :: bstree *
        insert   :: * -> bstree * -> bstree *
        delete   :: * -> bstree * -> bstree *
        join     :: bstree * -> bstree * -> bstree*
        split    :: bstree * -> (*, bstree *)
        traverse :: bstree * -> [*]

algtree * ::= Nil | Bin * (algtree *) (algtree *)
bstree * == algtree *

nil = Nil

insert x Nil               = Bin x Nil Nil
insert x (Bin y left right) = Bin (insert x left) right , x < y
                           = Bin y left right , x = y
                           = Bin y left (insert x right) ,
                             otherwise

delete x Nil               = Nil
delete x (Bin y left right) = Bin y (delete x left) right ,
                             x < y
                           = join left right , x = y
                           = Bin y left (delete x right) ,
                             otherwise

join left right = right , left = Nil
                = Bin newroot newleft right , otherwise
              where (newroot,newleft) = split left

split (Bin x left right) = (x,left) , right = Nil
                        = (y, Bin x left newright) ,
                          otherwise
                          where (y,newright) = split right

traverse Nil              = [ ]
traverse Bin x left right = traverse left ++ [x] ++ traverse
                            right
```

This definition would be contained in its own script and accessed through a `%include` declaration in another script. An export definition is used here to limit access to the type itself and those functions insert, delete and traverse that characterise the type. Function insert is self-contained and either inserts a value into a new binary node or passes the value on to the left or right subtree. Notice that, in this definition, an attempt to insert a second copy of one value results in the copy being discarded. Function `traverse` is better described as an in-order traversal of the tree to produce an ordered list of elements in the tree.

Function `delete` is complicated by the fact that a node to be deleted might occur in the middle of a binary search tree and would then be a link to its own subtrees. As a result, a function called `join` is required to restore the left and right descendants of the lost node to the tree; this requires the auxiliary function `split`. Since `join` and `split` are only required within the abstract type, they are hidden from module users and do not therefore appear on the export list.

EXERCISES 8.6

1. Implement an abstype `listn` based on the description of list1 given in Chapter 6 but with the alphabet *a*, *b*, *c*, ... replaced by the built-in numbers of the Miranda system. The list should be implemented with the aid of algebraic constructors.

2. Extend the abstype `listn` to include head and tail operations, but leave these operations as partial functions, undefined on an empty list.

3. Extend the abstype again to include `isempty`, `member` and `length`.

4. Implement a polymorphic abstype based on the abstract type set given in Chapter 6.

5. Miranda has a built-in function called `foldr` that repeatedly applies a given function to each element of a list. However, `foldr` differs from `map` in that it applies the function like this:

    `foldr f a` $[x_1, x_2, \ldots, x_n]$ `= f` x_1 `(f` x_2 `(... (f` x_n `a)))`

    folding the elements of the list from the right into a single object. This might be used to construct a binary search tree of numbers as follows:

    `foldr insert nil [5,3,7]`

    to give a result equivalent to `insert 7 (insert 3 (insert 5 nil))`. Write a program that uses the abstype `bstree` to sort a list of integers by first constructing a binary search tree then doing an in-order traversal of the tree.

8.7 PROGRAMS FOR PROPOSITIONS

According to the definition in Chapter 1, a proposition may be either the value ⊥, a statement symbol *p*, *q*, *r*, *s* or a well-formed application of logical connectives to other propositions. Such a definition may be cast in the algebraic style of Miranda as follows:

```
prop ::= F | P | Q | R | S | Not prop | Imp prop prop | And prop
prop
```

though not all connectives are included here. A simple syntax checker can be
written to show that a given string is a proposition:

```
atoms = [F,P,Q,R,S]
```

```
check(Not x) = check x
check(Imp x y) = check x & check y
check(And x y) = check x & check y
check x = member atoms x
```

This function simply breaks down an expression until atoms are obtained:

```
?check (Imp (Not P) (And (Not Q) R))
True
```

A `True` result indicates a well-formed proposition. A function to evaluate canonical
values from such expressions is fairly easily written. Notice that if atoms other than
F,P,Q,R and S are used, the evaluation fails instead of producing the answer `False`.

A definition can be written to decide if a proposition conforms with Hilbert's
first axiom simply by pattern matching the form of that axiom:

```
axiom1(Imp x (Imp y z)) = check x & check y & x = z
axiom1 any = False
```

Comparable expressions for testing compliance with axioms 2 and 3 are possible
when the pattern adopted is that of the appropriate axiom.

8.7.1   The Wang algorithm

Wang's algorithm is essentially the propositional G algorithm described in Chapter
1 and decides systematically if a proposition is a tautology. The algebraic declaration of a proposition and definition of atoms is as follows:

```
prop ::= F | P | Q | R | S | Not prop | Imp prop prop | And prop
prop
atoms = [P,Q,R,S]
```

Before defining the algorithm itself, a small auxiliary function called new is defined to add items to a list:

```
new item list = list++[item] , member atoms item
              = item:list , otherwise
```

This function adds an item to the right or left of a list, depending on whether or not
it is an atomic statement. Remember that the G system deals with two sets of propositions standing either side of a sequent symbol:

```
antecedent ⇒ succedent
```

and that the procedure begins by placing a proposition in the succedent. Left and right inference rules are then applied to propositions in the sequent, building up a tree of subsequents. When every leaf subsequent in the tree has a common atomic proposition in both antecedent and succedent, the tautology is proven. If the antecedent and succedent lists are simply called `left` and `right`, the common function defined earlier reports when a subsequent represents a tautology:

```
seq(left,right) = common(left,right) > 0
```

This will not immediately be the case, so one of the following inference rules has to be applied:

```
seq(left, Not x:right) = seq(new x left,right)
seq(Not x left, right) = seq(left, new x right)

seq(left, Imp x y:right) = seq(new x left, new y right)
seq(Imp x y:left, right) = seq(left, new x right) & seq(new
y left, right)

seq(left, And x y:right) = seq(left, new x right) & seq(left,
new y right)
seq(And x y:left, right) = seq(new x (new y left) , right)
```

With these definitions in place, the following interaction to check the proposition $(p \rightarrow q) \rightarrow (\neg q \rightarrow \neg p)$ appears as

```
?seq([ ],[Imp (Imp P Q) (Imp (Not Q) (Not P))])
True
```

8.7.2 Printing truth tables

One of the major problems with a truth table approach to logic is that the tables rapidly become too large; this is especially true in the ternary logic described earlier. Even a three-variable example has $3 \times 3 \times 3 = 27$ lines, so automated methods of generating these tables become essential. Repeating the notation used in Section 8.4, a definition of the constants in this new type takes the form

```
tern ::= Zero | Null | One
```

then the functions `inv`, `conj` and `disj` are defined in the script exactly as before. This done, the proposition $(x \wedge y) \vee (\neg x \wedge z)$ is implemented by the expression

```
f x y z = disj (conj x y) (conj (not x) z)
```

and the three ternary elements might be contained in a list

```
lst = [Zero, Null,One]
```

Having completed these esssentials, the remainder of the program is concerned with the output and formatting of the table:

```
col :: tern -> [char]
col x = "\t"++ show x
row w x y z = col w ++ col x ++ col y ++ col z
header = "\tx\ty\tz\tfxyz\n"
prog = header++lay[row x y z (f x y z) | x <- 1st;y <- 1st;z <-
1st]
```

A small query now generates the whole table:

```
?prog
x        y        z        fxyz
Zero     Zero     Zero     Zero
Zero     Zero     Null     Null
Zero     Zero     One      One       etc.
```

An alternative method takes advantage of the lexical order of textual strings in the list:

```
txt = ["false","null","true"]
```

and the fact that Miranda is capable of direct string comparisons. As a result, the not function is defined like this:

```
not :: [char] -> [char]
not "false" = "true"
not "true" = "false"
not "null" = "null"
```

whereas the conjunction and disjunction functions have their signatures altered to

```
conj :: [char] -> [char] -> [char]
```

but remain otherwise the same. Since the items of the table are already strings, the formatting of the table is simplified:

```
tab x = "\t"++ x
line w x y z = tab w ++ tab x ++ tab y ++ tab z
table = lay[line x y z (f x y z) |x <- txt; y <- txt; z <- txt]
```

and a header might be added in much the same way as in the previous example.

EXERCISES 8.7

1. Write Miranda programs axiom2 and axiom3 that accept propositional expressions and inform the user whether the propositions follow the patterns of Hilbert axioms 2 and 3.

2. Design a program that accepts a proposition with implications and returns an equivalent proposition in which the implications are replaced according to the identity $x \rightarrow y \cong \neg x \vee y$. Check that the procedure works for propositions with multiple implications such as $p \rightarrow (q \rightarrow r)$ and for propositions without implications.

3. Design a program that converts a general proposition using only the conjunction, disjunction and negation connectives into negation normal form.

4. Combine the results of the previous two exercises into a program that converts arbitrary propositions into negation normal form.

5. Enter the implication and negation rules for the Wang algorithm and test that the procedure works for the proposition $(p \rightarrow q) \rightarrow (\neg q \rightarrow \neg p)$. Check the procedure for other propositions.

6. Add left and right *or* rules to the algorithm and check that it confirms the following tautologies:

   $(p \vee q) \rightarrow (q \vee p)$
   $(p \vee q \wedge r) \rightarrow (p \vee q) \wedge (p \vee r)$

7. Using the built-in Boolean constants and functions, write a program that prints out a truth table for any two-variable expression.

8. Extend the program of the previous exercise to work for a three-variable proposition.

CHAPTER NINE

Intuitionistic logic and types

9.1 INTUITIONISTIC LOGIC

Classical logic in its current form was established by Frege in the late nineteenth century, but there are fundamental assumptions within this logic that may be traced back to classical Greece, in particular to the philosophical school of Plato. One of the key assumptions of the Platonistic approach is that we may ascribe truth to a statement quite independently of our ability to demonstrate that truth. This is nowhere more obvious than in the statement of the excluded middle described in Chapter 1:

$p \lor \neg p = true$

This equivalence allows truth to be deduced from a statement p even when statement p is totally nonsensical. If, for example, p represents the statement "mermaids have magic powers" we have no method of demonstrating that this proposition is either *true* or *false*, yet the excluded middle proposition above still evaluates to *true*. There is an assumption in classical logic that somehow, somewhere one of the two familiar truth values can be bestowed on every possible statement. Intuitionistic logic on the other hand requires, in this particular case, that we either produce a mermaid with magic powers or we demonstrate that a mermaid cannot have magic powers. In either case we must make it clear which disjunct we have proven because the classical claim that it must be one or the other is no longer available.

At the time of its invention, Frege's formulation of classical logic was intended to fulfil a widely perceived need for a system that would underpin the whole of mathematics – to provide a foundation from which all other mathematical theories could be derived. Unfortunately, at the end of the nineteenth century, Bertrand Russell demonstrated a flaw in Frege's reasoning that became known as the Russell paradox, destroying the possibility of a consistent theory that would prop up the whole of mathematics. Russell was, of course, able to repair the problem in the way described in Chapter 6, introducing the concept of a "type" or "sort" into classical logic. Computer scientists have raised Russell's type theory to the status of a minor religion but mathematicians have generally been less enthusiastic, perhaps regarding it as sticking-plaster applied to a fundamentally flawed system. As a result, the many-sorted form of Frege's logic has become one of the foundations of computing but, though still a major subject area in mathematics, it is not the fundamental mathematical doctrine that Frege intended. Since the Russell paradox is a direct consequence of the classical assumptions, it does not occur in the intuitionistic version of logic but, as an unexpected bonus, the concept of types or sorts arises naturally in the newer system. Programs intended to satisfy intuitionistic specifications are inherently "strongly typed" in line with the best current programming practice.

Classical reasoning assumes that objects exist in some world independently of our knowledge, so that all statements are either *true* or *false*, allowing us to prove theorems relating to unproven statements. This amounts to a refusal to accept in our reasoning processes the concept that there are some things we just do not know and perhaps will never know. An alternative philosophy, initiated by Brouwer, took the view that the only acceptable proof is one that we are able to justify in our own minds, one which is intuitively acceptable. Such a proof must exhibit the objects about which it reasons, rather than appeal to their properties in some abstract world. Brouwer rejected grand plans to prop up the whole of classical mathematics, suggesting that the need for such a prop itself indicated weaknesses in classical reasoning. Instead he proposed that proofs should be individually justified by the production of objects having the properties claimed in the proof. These ideas were developed by Heyting into the intuitionistic logic system described below.

The distinction between intuitionistic and classical logic is most obvious in a proof of a disjunction. In a classical approach the proposition $A \vee B$ is proven if either disjunct is proven, leading to the Gentzen G system "right $\vee$" rule shown in Figure 9.1. The fact that both A and B appear as premises below the line allows either one to justify a conclusion above the line and it does not matter whether it is A or B that is proven. An intuitionistic proof of $A \vee B$ requires not just a proof of either A or of B but also a clear statement of which disjunct is being proven. One way of incorporating this requirement into a Gentzen-style proof system is to split the classical "right $\vee$" rule into the two separate rules shown in Figure 9.1. Now a single premiss below the line justifies a conclusion above the line and it is clear which half of the disjunct has been proven.

The new pair of "right $\vee$" rules shown in Figure 9.1 is just one component of a set of propositional rules for intuitionistic logic that we shall call the Gentzen I

$$\frac{X \Rightarrow Y, A \vee B}{X \Rightarrow Y, A, B} \qquad \frac{X \Rightarrow A \vee B}{X \Rightarrow A} \qquad \frac{X \Rightarrow A \vee B}{X \Rightarrow B}$$

Classical   Intuitionistic

Figure 9.1   Comparing "right $\vee$" rules

$$\frac{X, A \wedge B \Rightarrow C}{X, A, B \Rightarrow C} \qquad \frac{X \Rightarrow A \wedge B}{X \Rightarrow A \qquad X \Rightarrow B}$$

$$\frac{X, A \vee B \Rightarrow C}{X, A \Rightarrow C \qquad X, B \Rightarrow C} \qquad \frac{X \Rightarrow A \vee B}{X \Rightarrow A} \qquad \frac{X \Rightarrow A \vee B}{X \Rightarrow B}$$

$$\frac{X, A \rightarrow B \Rightarrow C}{X \Rightarrow A \qquad X, B \Rightarrow C} \qquad \frac{X \Rightarrow A \rightarrow B}{X, A \Rightarrow B}$$

$$\frac{X, \neg A \Rightarrow}{X \Rightarrow A} \qquad \frac{X \Rightarrow \neg A}{X, A \Rightarrow}$$

$$\frac{X, A \Rightarrow}{X \Rightarrow} \qquad \frac{X \Rightarrow A}{X \Rightarrow}$$

Left   Right

Figure 9.2 Propositional I system rules

system. Figure 9.2 shows that, apart from the modification described above, these rules look much the same as the earlier propositional G system of reasoning. There is, however, a major difference: sequents in the new I system are never allowed to contain more than one formula in any succedent, though this single formula might itself be a large expression. In right inference rules, this formula is the one being modified; but in left rules, the formula C shown in the quantifier rules might be any single formula. It is this restriction placed on the right-hand side of I system sequents that prevents many classically acceptable formulas being proven intuitionistically. Two extra rules, called the left and right thinning rules appear in Figure 9.2, but did not appear in the comparable classical rules of Figure 1.10. In fact, these rules could have been included in the G system, but they were not essential because that system allows any number of formulas in either its antecedents or succedents. Thinning rules, sometimes also called weakening rules, allow irrelevant formulas to be discarded as we work downwards from a conclusion to its premises. Succedent thinning is essential in the intuitionistic case because an unwanted and irrelevant formula might occupy a succedent and thus block a potential proof. However, only the right thinning rule is essential in the intuitionistic case and the left rule has the same optional extra status as in the classical case.

Although an I system axiom is allowed only one succedent formula, there may be many in its antecedent, so if X represents some set of formulas and C some atomic formula, the sequent $X, C \Rightarrow C$ represents an axiom.

Like the G system, the new system described here has the subformula property, meaning that every formula in a deduction tree is a subformula of some formula in the root sequent. Another feature in common with the previous work is that we shall derive trees in a top-down manner, working downwards from a root sequent. Having constructed the tree, we might equally well think about it in a bottom-up form, with axioms at the bottom of the tree combining to form a conclusion at the root.

A conjunction $A \wedge B$ is proven only when both A and B are separately proven, so the intuitionistic "right $\wedge$" rule conveys much the same message as its classical equivalent. An implication $A \rightarrow B$ is seen in intuitionistic logic as a construction that converts a proof of A into a proof of B whereas proposition $\neg A$ is seen as a statement that there will never be a proof of A. These requirements impose proof requirements quite different from the simple truth value interpretations of classical logic. One result of this difference is that propositions provable in classical logic might not be provable in intuitionistic logic. In fact, we find that the set of intuitionistic theorems is a subset of the set of classical theorems. One consequence of the more restrictive demands of intuitionistic logic is that some of the equivalences described in Chapters 1 and 2 no longer hold.

One widely used equivalence of classical logic is the identity often used to substitute a disjunction for an implication:

$$\neg A \vee B \cong A \rightarrow B$$

To demonstrate this equivalence in intuitionistic logic, we would have to show that an intuitionistic implication holds in both directions between these propositions, i.e. that a mutual implication holds. Taking first the implication

$$(\neg A \vee B) \rightarrow (A \rightarrow B)$$

we have to show that an intuitionistic proof of $\neg A \vee B$ leads to a proof of $A \rightarrow B$. If we can demonstrate there will never be a proof of A, we have proven $\neg A$ and the implication $A \rightarrow B$ is established, because anything might be implied by an unprovable statement. This is an extension of the classical reasoning that allows any consequent to be deduced from a *false* antecedent. But if we have a proof of B, the implication $A \rightarrow B$ is established because A becomes irrelevant. When the consequent is already proven in the general case, it does not additionally have to be proven from the statement A. It appears that if we have a proof of $\neg A$ or a proof of B and a clear indication which of these two is proven, we also have an intuitionistic proof of $A \rightarrow B$. This reasoning is confirmed by the I system proof of Figure 9.3. Turning our attention to the reverse implication

$$A \rightarrow B \rightarrow \neg A \vee B$$

we have to show that a construction for converting proofs of A into proofs of B can itself produce a proof of B or a demonstration that A will never be proven. Unfortunately, this is not possible. A proof of $A \rightarrow B$ is a construction that allows a proof of A to be converted to a proof of B and is therefore based on proofs of A. There is no way that a demonstration of the unprovability of A, i.e. $\neg A$ could be drawn from such a construction; this failure is reflected in the second deduction tree of Figure 9.3. After an initial right implication, it becomes clear there is no inference rule

$$\Rightarrow (\neg A \vee B) \to (A \to B)$$

$$\frac{}{\neg A \vee B \Rightarrow A \to B} \quad \text{right} \to$$

$$\frac{}{\neg A \vee B, A \Rightarrow B} \quad \text{right} \to$$

$$\frac{\neg A, A \Rightarrow B \qquad B, A \Rightarrow B}{} \quad \text{left} \vee$$
$$\qquad\qquad\qquad\qquad \times$$

$$\frac{\neg A, A \Rightarrow}{} \qquad\qquad \text{thin}$$

$$A \Rightarrow A \qquad\qquad \text{left} \neg$$
$$\times$$

(a)

$$\Rightarrow (A \to B) \to (\neg A \vee B)$$

$$\frac{}{A \to B \Rightarrow \neg A \vee B}$$

$$??$$

(b)

Figure 9.3 A classical equivalence lost

capable of producing axioms from the sequent. Figure 9.3 shows it is the modified "right $\vee$" rule which prevents the closure that was possible in the classical case. The intuitionistic version of this rule forces us to choose just one of the disjuncts $\neg A$ or B as the next succedent, but neither one alone is sufficient to produce a proof tree. Notice that the proof tree of Figure 9.3a contains a subsequent

$$\neg A, A \Rightarrow B$$

that would immediately be followed in a classical proof by a "left not" operation to produce an axiom. However, an intuitionistic "left not" may only be applied to a sequent with an empty succedent, otherwise there will be no room for the formula carried over from the antecedent. Since proposition B is unwanted, a thinning rule produces sequent $\neg A, A \Rightarrow$ and the "left not" rule may be legally applied to produce the leaf axiom $A \Rightarrow A$.

There is an equivalence between the $\neg$ and $\to$ symbols that carries over from classical logic, but was not discussed in the earlier chapters because it had no great significance at that point. If, as before, the symbol $\perp$ represents absurdity, the equivalence appears as

$$\neg A \cong A \to \perp$$

The relationship suggests that we have proven $\neg A$ only when we have shown that a proof of A translates to a proof of absurdity. Since we can never prove absurdity, we can never prove A itself. Thus, $\neg A$ is taken to mean there can never be a proof of A. Continuing in this vein, the proposition $\neg\neg A$ means we will never have a proof that we will never have a proof of A, but this does not imply a proof of A itself, as it does in classical logic. Although the proposition $\neg\neg A \to A$ is easily proven in the classical G system logic by making the formula the succedent of a G system proof tree, no intuitionistic proof is possible. Figure 9.4a shows what happens when the proof is attempted with the I system rules: after a first application of the "right $\to$" rule, there is no further rule that can be applied because an application of the "left $\neg$" would place two propositions in the succedent. Figure 9.4b shows that the converse expression $A \to \neg\neg A$ is a theorem in intuitionistic logic. If we

$$\Rightarrow \neg\neg A \rightarrow A$$

$\neg\neg A \Rightarrow A$　　right $\rightarrow$

???　　???

(a)

$$\Rightarrow A \rightarrow \neg\neg A$$

$A \Rightarrow \neg\neg A$　　right $\rightarrow$

$A, \neg A \Rightarrow$　　right $\neg$

$A \Rightarrow A$　　left $\neg$
×

(b)

Figure 9.4 An implication tried both ways

$$\Rightarrow (A \rightarrow B) \rightarrow (\neg B \rightarrow \neg A)$$

$A \rightarrow B \Rightarrow \neg B \rightarrow \neg A$

$A \rightarrow B, \neg B \Rightarrow \neg A$

$A \rightarrow B, \neg B, A \Rightarrow$

$A \rightarrow B, A \Rightarrow B$

$A \Rightarrow A$　　　$B, A \Rightarrow B$
×　　　　　×

(a)

$$\Rightarrow (\neg B \rightarrow \neg A) \rightarrow (A \rightarrow B)$$

$\neg B \rightarrow \neg A \Rightarrow A \rightarrow B$

$\neg B \rightarrow \neg A, A \Rightarrow B$

$A \Rightarrow \neg B$　　　$\neg A, A \Rightarrow B$

$\neg A, A \Rightarrow$

$A \Rightarrow A$
×

(b)

Figure 9.5 The intuitionistic contrapositive

already have a proof of A, it follows that we will never be able to prove that A is unprovable.

One consequence of the equivalence $\neg A \cong A \rightarrow \bot$ in both classical and intuitionistic logic is that the "left $\neg$" and "right $\neg$" rules are redundant because they may be seen as special cases of implication rules. For example, the "right $\neg$" rule may be expressed in terms of the sequent $X \Rightarrow A \rightarrow \bot$, then the "right $\rightarrow$" rule produces sequent $X, A \Rightarrow \bot$ and the sequent absurdity symbol may be dropped.

The contrapositive rules provide further examples of classical mutual equivalences that hold in only one direction in intuitionistic logic. Thus, the theorem

$$(A \rightarrow B) \rightarrow (\neg B \rightarrow \neg A)$$

is proven in the I system diagram of Figure 9.5a; an attempt to prove the reverse implication shown in Figure 9.5b leads to the subsequent

$$\neg B \rightarrow \neg A, A \Rightarrow B$$

from which no further progress is possible. A "left $\rightarrow$" inference generates subsequents $A \Rightarrow \neg B$ and $\neg A, A \Rightarrow B$, the first of which cannot become an axiom.

If a proof of A leads to a proof of absurdity, we may assume $\neg A$ in both classical and intuitionistic logic. In the intuitionistic case the statement $\neg A$ is read as "there will never be a proof of A". Classical logic also allows the deduction of absurdity from $\neg A$ to act as a proof of A, giving the following equivalence:

$$A \cong_c \neg A \to \bot$$

Statements in classical logic are interpreted as either *true* or *false*, and the excluded middle rule allows the falsification of one to justify the truth of the other. Intuitionistic logic rejects this converse argument: demonstrating that the impossibility of proving a certain statement implies a proof of absurdity in no way constitutes a proof of the statement itself. As a result, a convenient technique employed in classical reasoning is no longer available in the intuitionistic case.

Mutual implication is taken to be a construction that converts proofs in either direction, and the equivalence between this connective and separate directional implications is preserved in the intuitionistic form

$$A \leftrightarrow B \cong (A \to B) \wedge (B \to A)$$

9.1.1   Quantified formulas

Sequent quantifier rules are adapted for intuitionistic logic in exactly the same way as the propositional rules, by restricting succedents to one formula. Figure 9.6 shows that this formula might be any formula C in the left rules, whereas in the right rules it has to be the formula being instantiated.

An existentially quantified formula such as $\exists x P(x)$ might be proven in classical logic by demonstrating that $\neg \exists x P(x)$ leads to absurdity in some context, perhaps by showing that the equivalent formula $\forall x \neg P(x)$ is contradictory. This argument is again based on the excluded middle and does not therefore hold in the intuitionistic case. The only intuitionistically acceptable proof of $\exists x P(x)$ is an object a, capable of acting as a witness, together with a proof that the object does indeed satisfy the requirements of the predicate.

The following important mutual implication of classical logic remains acceptable in the intuitionistic case:

$$\neg \exists x P(x) \leftrightarrow \forall x \neg P(x)$$

and might be proven by separately proving a conjunction of implications:

$$(\neg \exists x P(x) \to \forall x \neg P(x)) \wedge (\forall x \neg P(x) \to \neg \exists x P(x))$$

$X, \exists x A(x) \Rightarrow C$	$X \Rightarrow \exists x A(x)$
$X, A(a) \Rightarrow C$	$X \Rightarrow A(a)$

$X, \forall x A(x) \Rightarrow C$	$X \Rightarrow \forall x A(x)$
$X, A(a) \Rightarrow C$	$X \Rightarrow A(a)$

Left	Right

Figure 9.6 I system quantifier rules

$$\Rightarrow \exists x\neg P(x) \rightarrow \neg\forall xP(x)$$

$$\frac{}{\exists x\neg P(x) \Rightarrow \neg\forall xP(x)} \quad \text{right} \rightarrow$$

$$\frac{}{\exists x\neg P(x), \forall xP(x) \Rightarrow} \quad \text{right} \neg$$

$$\frac{}{\neg P(a), \forall xP(x) \Rightarrow} \quad \text{left } \exists$$

$$\frac{}{\forall xP(x) \Rightarrow P(a)} \quad \text{left } \neg$$

$$\frac{}{P(a) \Rightarrow P(a)} \quad \text{left } \forall$$

$$\times$$

(a)

$$\Rightarrow \neg\forall xP(x) \rightarrow \exists x\neg P(x)$$

$$\frac{}{\neg\forall xP(x) \Rightarrow \exists x\neg P(x)}$$

???

(b)

Figure 9.7 Intuitionistic deduction trees

In fact, the proof of this formula proceeds exactly as in the classical G system because there is never more than one formula in the succedent. It is worth emphasising that intuitionistically provable formulas are a subset of classically provable formulas. As a result, any formula proven intuitionistically may also be proven classically, but not vice versa.

Some formulas with implications as their principal connectives are valid in both classical and intuitionistic logics, but the reverse implications are valid only in classical logic. For example, the formula

$$\exists x\neg P(x) \rightarrow \neg\forall xP(x)$$

is valid in both logics and an I system (or G system) proof of this claim is provided in Figure 9.7. Classical logic also accepts as valid the reverse implication

$$\neg\forall xP(x) \rightarrow \exists x\neg P(x)$$

but showing that a universally quantified formula will never be proven is not enough to assert the existence of an object with certain properties. Consequently, the formula is not valid in the intuitionistic case and it is interesting to see what happens when an I system proof is attempted. Figure 9.7b shows that, after the application of an initial "right →", we are unable to apply any further rules because a "left ¬" rule cannot be applied without a weakening that would discard an essential formula. Only "left ∃" and "right ∀" rules introduce constants, so no further progress is possible.

Two further implications may be quickly proven through a proof tree similar to that of Figure 9.7a:

$$\exists xP(x) \rightarrow \neg\forall x\neg P(x)$$
$$\forall xP(x) \rightarrow \neg\exists x\neg P(x)$$

but an attempt to prove the reverse implication of the first example leads us to the sequent

$$\neg\forall x\neg P(x) \Rightarrow \exists xP(x)$$

Again a "left $\neg$" inference rule cannot be applied unless the succedent has been weakened, but this will remove the subformula required to produce an axiom. Just as in the example above, a proof that we can never prove a universally quantified formula cannot assert the existence of an object in an existentially quantified formula.

One consequence of the more restricted intuitionistic rules is that it is not always possible to convert a given formula into the normal forms described in Chapters 1 and 2. In particular, the formation of prenex normal forms in classical logic depended on equivalences such as

$$\forall x(A(x) \rightarrow B) \cong \exists xA(x) \rightarrow B$$
$$\exists x(A(x) \rightarrow B) \cong_c \forall xA(x) \rightarrow B$$

but the second one is not an equivalence in intuitionistic logic. Although an implication holds in the left-to-right direction, the reverse implication is not a theorem. Most of the earlier equivalences do still hold, but the ones that fail mean that, unlike classical formulas, there are some intuitionistic formulas which cannot be converted to prenex form. Similarly, conversions to negation normal form are not always possible.

The I system outlined above is a syntactic proof system and it might be tempting to consider the Scott domains of Chapter 7 as the basis of a semantics for the system. In fact, the semantics of intuitionistic logic is a rather complex subject outside the scope of this text.

EXERCISES 9.1

1. Develop intuitionistic I system proofs for each of the following propositions involving only implications:

   a. $P \rightarrow (Q \rightarrow P)$
   b. $(P \rightarrow (Q \rightarrow R)) \rightarrow (Q \rightarrow (P \rightarrow R))$
   c. $(P \rightarrow Q) \rightarrow ((Q \rightarrow R) \rightarrow (P \rightarrow R))$
   d. $((P \rightarrow Q) \rightarrow (P \rightarrow R)) \rightarrow (P \rightarrow (Q \rightarrow R))$

2. Repeat Exercise 1 for the following propositions including conjunctions and implications:

   a. $P \rightarrow (Q \rightarrow (P \wedge Q))$
   b. $(P \rightarrow (Q \wedge R)) \rightarrow (P \rightarrow Q) \wedge (P \rightarrow R)$
   c. $(P \rightarrow (Q \rightarrow R)) \rightarrow (P \wedge Q \rightarrow R)$
   d. $(P \wedge Q \rightarrow R) \rightarrow (P \rightarrow (Q \rightarrow R))$

3. Repeat Exercise 1 for the following propositions that require a "right $\vee$" rule:

   a. $P \rightarrow (P \vee P)$
   b. $((P \vee Q) \rightarrow R) \rightarrow (P \rightarrow R)$
   c. $((P \vee (P \rightarrow Q)) \rightarrow Q) \rightarrow Q$

Notice that Proposition 3c is remarkably simple to prove in the classical G system, but requires more effort to prove in the intuitionistic I system. When faced with a sequent $A \Rightarrow B$, we are free to write $A, A \Rightarrow B$ because a repeated antecedent formula does not change the argument. Thinning can then be used to remove unwanted propositions.

4. Repeat Exercise 1 for some propositions that require a "left $\vee$" rule:

    a. $P \vee P \to P$

    b. $((P \to Q) \wedge (R \to Q)) \to (P \vee R \to Q)$

    c. $(P \vee (Q \wedge R)) \to (P \vee Q)$

5. Repeat Exercise 1 for some propositions including negations:

    a. $(\neg P \vee \neg Q) \to \neg (P \wedge Q)$

    b. $(\neg P \wedge \neg Q) \to \neg (P \vee Q)$

6. Prove the following sequents:

    a. $\neg\neg A, \neg\neg (A \to B) \Rightarrow \neg\neg B$

    b. $\neg\neg\neg A \Rightarrow \neg A$

7. Try to prove the following propositions:

    a. $\neg\neg(\neg\neg A \to A)$

    b. $\neg\neg(A \to \neg\neg A)$

9.2   NATURAL DEDUCTION RULES

In addition to the sequent systems so far described in this text, Gentzen invented another proof system that he called the natural deduction method of reasoning. Although this system has no particularly useful properties in classical logic, it plays an important role in helping to produce the proof objects required in the intuitionistic case. Natural deduction proofs are constructed from the elimination and introduction inference rules of Figure 9.8 in much the same way as sequent proofs are derived from the left and right rules of Figure 9.2.

Looking first at the introduction rules, we see they have much in common with the earlier right sequent rules. A conjunction $A \wedge B$ written above the line may be concluded if we can separately prove both A and B. Similarly, a disjunction written above the line is concluded if we prove either A or B, and from the form of the proof it is clear which one has been proven. In fact, these first two introduction rules look much the same as the succedent parts of the corresponding sequent rules.

A proof of the implication $A \to B$ may be concluded if a proof of B is shown to be derivable from a proof of A. This might appear quite different from the corresponding I system rule, which replaces sequent $\Rightarrow A \to B$ with subsequent $A \Rightarrow B$, but formula A carried over the sequent symbol can be seen as a hypothesis from which

$$
\frac{A \qquad B}{A \wedge B \qquad A \wedge B} \qquad \frac{A \wedge B}{A \qquad B}
$$

$$
\frac{C}{A \vee B \quad A \to C \quad B \to C} \qquad \frac{A \vee B \quad A \vee B}{A \qquad B}
$$

$$
\frac{B}{A \qquad A \to B} \qquad \frac{A \to B}{B}
$$

$$
\vdots
$$

$$
A
$$

$$
\frac{\bot}{A \qquad \neg A} \qquad \frac{\neg A}{\bot}
$$

$$
\vdots
$$

$$
A
$$

Elimination   Introduction

Figure 9.8 Natural deduction rules

formula B must be derived. We noted in the preceding section that in both classical and intuitionistic logic there is an identity relating the $\neg$ and $\to$ symbols:

$$\neg A \cong A \to \bot$$

If we are able to conclude absurdity from a proposition A, we can never have a proof of A and this is shown as $\neg A$. It follows that the form $\neg A$ in any proposition may be replaced by the equivalent $A \to \bot$ form and both I system and natural deduction proofs may be developed without $\neg$ rules. Nevertheless, it is useful and slightly more compact to handle these symbols directly in proofs, so the rule is included in Figure 9.8.

Natural deduction elimination rules are inverted in relation to the corresponding left sequent rules, so the order in which these rules are used in a proof is the reverse of that in a sequent proof. We might picture the propositions on the left of a succedent symbol as hypotheses from which propositions on the right of the symbol have to be derived. Since this distinction between left and right does not exist in natural deduction, the elimination rules are inverted to achieve the same effect. Using the left elimination rule, we may conclude a proof of A if we have a proof of $A \wedge B$, but of course we might equally well conclude a proof of B. Notice that we have not just inverted the corresponding sequent rule here, but divided it into two separate rules. Natural deduction rules only conclude one proposition.

Disjunction elimination might initially seem rather complicated because of the intuitionistic requirement that a proof object of the concluded proposition should be possible. If we have a proof of $A \vee B$, we cannot assume that it is based on either A or B. As a result, the premiss must also contain two propositions $A \rightarrow C$ and $B \rightarrow C$ capable of converting proofs of A and B to proofs of C. This means that, whatever proof object is produced for the disjunction, a proof of the proposition C results.

In contrast, implication elimination appears very simple: from a proposition A and implication $A \rightarrow B$ we may conclude B. If we have a proof of A and a method of converting it into a proof of B, we have a proof of B. Negation elimination follows the same pattern: given a proof of A and a method of converting this proof to a proof of absurdity, we may conclude absurdity.

Like the earlier sequent rule, these rules are written with a conclusion above one or two premisses. Although the final form of proof is from leaf hypotheses to a root conclusion in a bottom-up direction, the best way of constructing the tree is in a top-down manner from the proposition to be proven. At each stage of a proof, an inference rule is applied to the principal connective, but a natural deduction proof offers far fewer choices than the earlier sequent systems. Working upwards in the tree, introduction rules increase the number of connectives in a proposition whereas elimination rules reduce the number of connectives.

A natural deduction proof is developed by first writing down the formula to be proven and identifying the principal connective in the formula. If we want to prove the proposition

$$(A \rightarrow (B \rightarrow C)) \rightarrow ((A \rightarrow B) \rightarrow (A \rightarrow C))$$

the principal connective is the third implication symbol from the left. As a result, the whole proposition may be concluded if it can be shown that the consequent $((A \rightarrow B) \rightarrow (A \rightarrow C))$ is derivable from the hypothesis $(A \rightarrow (B \rightarrow C))$. This concluding step is called an implication introduction, but abbreviated in Figure 9.9 as $\rightarrow$ intro. Two further implication introductions in turn conclude $(A \rightarrow B) \rightarrow (A \rightarrow C)$ from hypothesis $(A \rightarrow B)$ and C from hypothesis A. At this point in the proof, the three hypotheses on which the final proposition is based might be shown as the equivalent of the left-hand side of a sequent

$$
\begin{array}{ll}
(A \rightarrow (B \rightarrow C)) \rightarrow ((A \rightarrow B) \rightarrow (A \rightarrow C)) & \rightarrow \text{intro} \\
\hline
(A \rightarrow B) \rightarrow (A \rightarrow C) & \rightarrow \text{intro} \\
\hline
(A \rightarrow C) & \rightarrow \text{intro} \\
\hline
C & \rightarrow \text{elim} \\
\hline
B \qquad\qquad B \rightarrow C & \rightarrow \text{elim} \\
\hline
A \quad A \rightarrow B \qquad A \quad A \rightarrow (B \rightarrow C) &
\end{array}
$$

Figure 9.9 A natural deduction tree

$$\dfrac{\dfrac{\dfrac{\dfrac{P \quad \dfrac{(P \to Q) \land (P \to R)}{(P \to Q)}}{Q} \qquad \dfrac{P \quad \dfrac{(P \to Q) \land (P \to R)}{(P \to R)}}{R}}{Q \land R}}{P \to (Q \land R)}}{(P \to Q) \land (P \to R) \to (P \to (Q \land R))}$$

$\to$ intro
$\to$ intro
$\land$ intro
$\to$ elim
$\land$ elim

Figure 9.10 An example including conjunctions

$$(A \to (B \to C)), (A \to B), A \Rightarrow C$$

and the proof concluded with left implication rules. This is where natural deduction becomes a little more difficult than sequent systems, because the elimination rules are inverted and are therefore applied in reverse order from the left sequent rules. We have to recognise that statement C is obtained by $\to$ elimination from B and $B \to C$, and these two propositions are themselves obtained by further $\to$ eliminations from the three hypotheses. Looking at the proof process from the bottom up, it is the adoption of these statements as antecedents in implication introductions that discharges the assumptions made at the leaf nodes. However, an antecedent statement adopted in this way is sometimes not used as a hypothesis or on other occasions may be used as an assumption on more than one leaf.

A larger example, using only implication and conjunction connectives, is provided by the formula

$$(P \to Q) \land (P \to R) \to (P \to (Q \land R))$$

and a natural deduction tree proving the validity of this formula is shown in Figure 9.10. Two applications of the $\to$ introduction rule remove two hypotheses $(P \to Q) \land (P \to R)$ and P that may then be used as assumptions at leaf positions in the tree. When used in this way, the implication introduction rule discharges such assumptions.

Starting from the larger hypothesis, we may conclude $(P \to Q)$ in one branch and $(P \to R)$ in the other, both by $\land$ elimination. Together with the smaller hypothesis P, these two implications are then used to conclude propositions Q and R in each of the branches. An application of the introduction rule then combines the two separately proven propositions into a single formula.

The following small example (Figure 9.11) leads to proof with both $\neg$ introductions and eliminations:

$$(P \land \neg Q) \to \neg(P \to Q)$$

The central implication symbol is clearly the principal connective and an implication introduction rule reduces this formula to its consequent. The antecedent $P \land \neg Q$ is then available as one hypothesis from which the consequent must be derived. A $\neg$

```
                    (P ∧ ¬Q) → ¬(P → Q)              → intro
                    ───────────────────
                          ¬(P → Q)                   ¬ intro
                    ───────────────────
                             ⊥                       ¬ elim
                    ─────────────────────────────
                Q        → elim        ¬Q            ∧ elim
          ───────────────          ─────────
          P     P → Q                 P ∧ ¬Q
          ───────────────
             P ∧ ¬Q
```

```
            (P ∧ (Q → ⊥)) → ((P → Q) → ⊥)            → intro
            ─────────────────────────────
                     ((P → Q) → ⊥)                   → intro
            ─────────────────────────────
                          ⊥                          → elim
            ──────────────────────────────
            Q        → elim        Q → ⊥             ∧ elim
        ──────────────          ───────────────
        P     P → Q   ∧ elim     P ∧ (Q → ⊥)
        ──────────────
           P ∧ (Q → ⊥)
```

Figure 9.11 A proof with negations

symbol is the principal connective in the next step and an introduction rule that concludes $\neg(P \to Q)$ is required. However, a negation introduction that concludes $\neg(P \to Q)$ is equivalent to an implication introduction that concludes $(P \to Q) \to \bot$ and is proven by showing that the consequent $\bot$ may be derived from hypothesis $P \to Q$. At this point, we have two hypotheses $P \wedge \neg Q$ and $P \to Q$ from which absurdity must be concluded, and since there is no principal connective to be introduced, attention turns to elimination rules. In particular, a $\neg$ elimination shows that if we can prove both Q and $\neg Q$ (or $Q \to \bot$), we may conclude absurdity. The literals P and $\neg Q$ are quickly derived by conjunction elimination from one premiss then literal Q is derived from the other hypothesis by implication elimination.

If the negation symbols are replaced by equivalent implication symbols, the proposition above becomes

$$(P \wedge (Q \to \bot)) \to ((P \to Q) \to \bot)$$

and the proof of this proposition involves only implication introduction and elimination. This revised proof provides a useful guide to the original form with negation symbols.

Figure 9.12 shows a natural deduction tree that includes an $\vee$ introduction and concludes the proposition

$$((P \vee Q) \to R) \to (P \to R) \wedge (Q \to R)$$

As a first step, we have to show that proposition $((P \vee Q) \to R)$ is a suitable hypothesis from which we are able to derive the formula

$$\frac{\frac{\frac{\dfrac{\dfrac{P \vee Q \quad (P \vee Q) \to R}{P}}{R} \quad \dfrac{\dfrac{P \vee Q \quad (P \vee Q) \to R}{Q}}{R}}{(P \to R) \quad (Q \to R)}}{(P \to R) \wedge (Q \to R)}}{((P \vee Q) \to R) \to (P \to R) \wedge (Q \to R)}$$

$((P \vee Q) \to R) \to (P \to R) \wedge (Q \to R)$	$\to$ intro
$(P \to R) \wedge (Q \to R)$	$\wedge$ intro
$(P \to R)$ $(Q \to R)$	$\to$ intro
R R	$\to$ elims
$P \vee Q$ $(P \vee Q) \to R$ $P \vee Q$ $(P \vee Q) \to R$	$\vee$ intro
P Q	

Figure 9.12 A tree with an *or* introduction

$((P \to R) \vee (Q \to R)) \to (P \wedge Q \to R)$	$\to$ intro
$P \wedge Q \to R$	$\to$ intro
R	$\vee$ elim
$((P \to R) \vee (Q \to R))$ R R	$\to$ elim
$P \quad P \to R \quad Q \quad Q \to R$	$\wedge$ elim
$P \wedge Q \qquad P \wedge Q$	

Figure 9.13 A tree with an *or* elimination

$(P \to R) \wedge (Q \to R)$

This leaves a conjunction as the principal connective, joining the two fragments $P \to R$ and $Q \to R$ through an $\wedge$ introduction rule. These propositions are themselves obtained by $\to$ introduction to the proposition R if propositions P and Q are taken as hypotheses or assumptions to be used in the tree. As a consequence of the $\to$ introduction steps, there are three hypotheses available for use in constructing the tree: P, Q and $(P \vee Q) \to R$. According to the natural deduction rules, we may conclude $P \vee Q$ from P or from Q, but we have to state very clearly which premiss is being used to establish the conclusion. This is achieved in Figure 9.12 by showing the $\vee$ introduction from P in one case and from Q in the other. This disjunction is then used with the remaining hypothesis to conclude R.

A disjunction elimination rule is required in the following example:

$((P \to R) \vee (Q \to R)) \to (P \wedge Q \to R)$

and the completed proof is shown in Figure 9.13. Two implication introduction rules identify the two hypotheses

$(P \to R) \vee (Q \to R)$
$P \wedge Q$

and these propositions are available as assumptions in the proof. At this point, we have two hypotheses from which we wish to derive the primitive statement R. The application of an $\lor$ elimination rule breaks this problem down into two separate subproofs. In one case we must derive statement R from the disjunct $P \to R$; in the other case we must derive it from the disjunct $Q \to R$. This step is indeed possible if we can separately prove statements P and Q then use implication eliminations to obtain R. Since $P \land Q$ is a hypothesis, it is clear that both statements are obtained by conjunction elimination from the leaf.

EXERCISES 9.2

1. Develop natural deduction proofs for Propositions 1a to 1d of Exercises 9.1.

2. Produce natural deduction proofs for Propositions 2a to 2d of Exercises 9.1.

3. Produce natural deduction proofs for Propositions 3a to 3c, 4a to 4c, and 5a and 5b of Exercises 9.1.

9.3   CONSTRUCTIVE LOGIC AND TYPES

A constructive approach is an explicit description telling us how to construct a particular object such as a computer program, whereas a non-constructive approach is an implicit description telling us what is required without actually producing the object itself. Constructivism is usually associated with intuitionism because intuitionistic logic requires that we are able to exhibit proof objects for every intuitionistic proof carried out. However, constructive proofs are also found in classical logic; the difference is that intuitionistic proofs have to be constructive whereas classical proofs are not so restricted.

Constructive type theory is based on a duality between the three main propositional connectives in the table and the three compound domain constructors described in Chapter 7. Since the earlier chapter associated element domains or programs with each type, we now have a direct correspondence between intuitionistic propositions and programs. This correspondence between constructive logic and domain elements is usually called the Curry–Howard isomorphism in honour of its principal inventors.

Domain	Proposition	Type	Program
Cartesian product	$A \land B$	$A \times B$	(a,b)
Disjoint union	$A \lor B$	$A + B$	$inl \; a \mid inr \; b$
Function	$A \to B$	$A \to B$	$\lambda x.f \, x$

Each propositional symbol is associated with a type construction symbol and therefore also associated with a program structure. Thus, a conjunction is associated with the product type $A \times B$ arising out of the construction of a pair (a,b) from two distinct objects a and b. A disjunction is associated with the construction of tagged objects $inl\ a$ or $inr\ b$ of type $A + B$, from either an object a of type A or object b of type B, but it is clear which was used in forming the disjoint union. Finally, an implication is associated with the function type, mapping an object x of type A to an object $f\ x$ of type B. In order to minimise the use of brackets the function $f(x)$ is shown above simply as $f\ x$ and this practice is adopted throughout the chapter. In this last case the $\rightarrow$ symbol is overloaded to represent both the propositional connective and the program type, but since the two are dual this is no bad thing.

A proof object p is associated with an atomic propositional statement P or equivalently with a primitive type statement P through a judgement with the form $p : P$ or $p \in P$. In words, program p is of type P or p belongs to the set of P objects. The second notation here emphasises the fact that p is a member of the set of objects of type P.

Judgements for compound types are derived by building up compound proof objects from primitive objects $p \in P$ and $r \in R$, etc., according to the proposition or the type. Thus the proposition $P \wedge (Q \wedge R)$ is associated with the type $P \times (Q \times R)$ hence with proof object $(p,(q,r))$. Since the type defines the form of the proof objects, we might prefer to express this as

$$(p,(q,r)) \in P \times (Q \times R)$$

emphasising the type of the proof object. Proposition $P \vee (Q \vee R)$ is similarly associated with the compound type $P + (Q + R)$ and with proof objects $inl\ p$, $inr(inl\ q)$ and $inr(inr\ r)$. It is simply a matter of building up the proof object according to the compound type (or proposition) in the way described in Chapter 7.

A proposition $(P \vee Q) \wedge R$ is identified with the type $(P + Q) \times R$, and if we have proof objects from the domains of the primitive types, we can again construct proof objects for the compound type. Proposition $P + Q$ has proof objects $inl\ p$ and $inr\ q$, so there are two possible kinds of proof objects:

$$(inl\ p,\ r)\ |\ (inr\ q,\ r) \in (P + Q) \times R$$

Proposition $(P \wedge Q) \vee R$ is similarly associated with the type $(P \times Q) + R$ and the pair (p,q) provides a proof object for the product $P \times Q$. Again there are two possible kinds of proof objects:

$$inl(p,\ q)\ |\ inr\ r \in (P \times Q) + R$$

Larger propositions just create larger proof objects, but no new principles are involved. For example, proposition $(P \vee Q) \wedge (R \vee S)$ corresponds to the type $(P + Q) \times (R + S)$ and gives rise to the following proof objects:

$$(inl\ p,\ inl\ r)\ |\ (inl\ p,\ inr\ s)\ |\ (inr\ q,\ inl\ r)\ |\ (inr\ q,\ inr\ s) \in (P + Q) \times (R + S)$$

because each of the disjuncts allows two possible proof objects and these may be combined into pairs in four ways.

Propositions that include implications correspond to proof objects that include functions and these objects are constructed in the same way as previous examples. For example, proposition $P \to Q$ corresponds to the type $P \to Q$ because we are using the same symbol for both implication and function types. If we have object p and function f as follows:

$$p \in P$$
$$f \in P \to Q$$

an application of the function has the following type:

$$f p \in Q$$

Notice that function application corresponds to the elimination of implication signs in a proposition, resulting in an object of the same type as the consequent. The reverse process of abstraction corresponds to implication introduction, and if this is applied to the above function, we obtain

$$\lambda p.f p \in P \to Q$$

Proposition $P \to (Q \to R)$ corresponds to the type $P \to (Q \to R)$ and this type maps objects of type P to a function that maps objects of type Q to objects of type R. Suppose that we have proof objects p and q together with function f as follows:

$$p \in P$$
$$q \in Q$$
$$f \in P \to (Q \to R)$$

An application of function f to p results in an object of type $Q \to R$:

$$f p \in Q \to R$$

but $f p$ is itself a function which, when applied to an object of type Q, produces an object of type R:

$$(f p)\, q \in R$$

If we now abstract over all objects p and q, the following abstracted object is obtained:

$$\lambda p.\lambda q.(f p)\, q \in P \to (Q \to R)$$

One final example to illustrate the occurrence of functions within larger proof objects is provided by the proposition $(P \to Q) \land (R \to S)$. Each implication leads to a function type

$$\lambda p.f p \in P \to Q$$
$$\lambda r.g\, r \in R \to S$$

and a single proof object for the whole type is obtained as follows:

$$(\lambda p.f p,\ \lambda r.g\, r) \in (P \to Q) \land (R \to S)$$

9.3.1 Proof objects and natural deduction

Section 9.2 explained how intuitionistic propositions are proven in the natural
deduction system, using a series of introduction and elimination rules. From what
has been said above, it is clear that every such proposition has an associated proof
object and that compound objects of this kind are constructed from primitive objects.
Now we want to merge these two lines of reasoning, using a natural deduction tree
to develop a proof object for the proven formula. This is achieved by associating
each of the introduction rules with a composition operation and each of the elimination rules with a decomposition operation.

Figure 9.14 shows how an ∧ introduction operation takes proof objects a and b
from the premises to produce a single proof object (a,b) for the conclusion. An →
introduction operation corresponds to the creation of an abstraction $\lambda x.f\,x$ when a
proof object $f\,x$ of type B is derived from an object x of type B. Implication introduction corresponds to a general method of mapping any object x of type A onto an
object $f\,x$ of type B, i.e. a function taking x as argument and yielding objects of type
B. A ¬ introduction operation creates the same form of proof object as an → introduction because of the equivalence relation between these two connectives.

A single object of type $A \wedge B$ is shown in Figure 9.14 as r, but might equally
well have been written as $(fst\ r,\ snd\ r)$ if we wanted to view it in terms of its components. An object $fst\ r$ of type A or an object $snd\ r$ of type B might be concluded
from the proof object of the conjunction. In this step, the elimination of the conjunction connective corresponds to the decomposition of the pair. A function f is
decomposed to produce a single proof object $f\,a$ of type B when it is applied to an

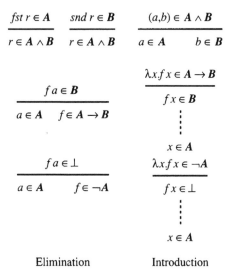

Elimination   Introduction

Figure 9.14 Proof objects for natural deduction: proof objects are in medium type,
propositions in bold type

object a of type A, and this corresponds to the elimination of an implication symbol. If the proposition $\neg A$ is written in the form $A \rightarrow \perp$, the $\neg$ elimination step is seen to be a form of the implication elimination rule.

Taking first an example containing only implication connectives, we develop a proof object for the formula proven in Figure 9.9:

$$(A \rightarrow (B \rightarrow C)) \rightarrow ((A \rightarrow B) \rightarrow (A \rightarrow C))$$

The natural deduction tree in Figure 9.9 shows how three implication introduction rules reduce this formula to the single symbol C. First of all, we label proof objects for each of the hypotheses removed:

$$f \in A \rightarrow (B \rightarrow C)$$
$$g \in A \rightarrow B$$
$$x \in A$$

These objects are then placed in a proof object tree at positions corresponding to the positions of their formulas in the natural deduction tree. Working back up through the tree, we note that proof objects f and g are both functions applied to x, producing objects with the types

$$f x \in B \rightarrow C$$
$$g x \in B$$

and these proof objects are placed in appropriate tree positions in Figure 9.15. Since gx is of type B whereas fx maps objects of type B to those of type C, the application of one to the other produces an object of type C:

$$fx(gx) \in C$$

An implication introduction now corresponds to the abstraction of this function to the general case for all objects x of type A.

$$\lambda x.fx(gx) \in A \rightarrow C$$

Two more implication introductions correspond to two further abstractions, producing a final proof object for the proposition above:

$$\lambda f.\lambda g.\lambda x.fx(gx) \in (A \rightarrow (B \rightarrow C)) \rightarrow ((A \rightarrow B) \rightarrow (A \rightarrow C))$$

$$
\begin{array}{ll}
\dfrac{\lambda f.\lambda g.\lambda x.fx(gx)}{} & \rightarrow \text{intro} \\[4pt]
\dfrac{\lambda g.\lambda x.fx(gx)}{} & \rightarrow \text{intro} \\[4pt]
\dfrac{\lambda x.fx(gx)}{} & \rightarrow \text{intro} \\[4pt]
fx(gx) & \rightarrow \text{elim} \\
\end{array}
$$

$$
\dfrac{gx \qquad\qquad fx}{\quad} \qquad \rightarrow \text{elim}
$$

$$\dfrac{\ }{x \quad g} \qquad \dfrac{\ }{x \quad f}$$

Figure 9.15   Constructing a proof object

Notice that the order in which the abstractions are applied is important and is directed by the proof tree.

9.3.2 Examples that involve conjunctions

Consider the following proposition as a conveniently small example:

$$P \wedge Q \rightarrow Q \wedge P$$

and, as a first step, we construct the natural deduction tree in Figure 9.16. Since the principal connective here is an $\rightarrow$ symbol, the appropriate introduction rule requires that we conclude $Q \wedge P$ by taking $P \wedge Q$ as a hypothesis. In a sequent proof this hypothesis is moved into the antecedent, but in natural deduction it is held aside and may be used as a leaf proposition at some point in the natural deduction tree. An implication introduction inference justifies the use of a leaf hypothesis in this way. Now we have to show how $Q \wedge P$ is proven from its components, by applying an $\wedge$ introduction rule to atomic propositions P and Q. Finally, these individual atomic symbols are derived from the hypothesis $P \wedge Q$ with the aid of conjunction elimination rules, completing the natural deduction tree in Figure 9.16.

Having built the natural deduction tree in this top-down fashion, we now derive a judgement of the proven formula by working back up through the tree, constructing an increasingly large judgement as we proceed (Figure 9.17). There is only one hypothesis in this example, and a proof object for the whole formula is constructed on the assumption that we have a proof object xs for that hypothesis:

$$
\begin{array}{c|c}
\dfrac{\dfrac{\dfrac{P \wedge Q \quad P \wedge Q}{Q \quad\quad P} \;\wedge\,\text{elim}}{Q \wedge P} \;\wedge\,\text{intro}}{P \wedge Q \rightarrow Q \wedge P} \;\rightarrow\text{intro}
&
\dfrac{\dfrac{\dfrac{xs \quad\quad xs}{snd\ xs \quad fst\ xs}}{(snd\ xs, fst\ xs)}}{\lambda xs.(snd\ xs, fst\ xs)}
\end{array}
$$

Figure 9.16 A proof including conjunctions

$$
\dfrac{\dfrac{\dfrac{\dfrac{xs}{x \quad fst\ xs} \quad \dfrac{xs}{x \quad snd\ xs}}{(fst\ xs)\ x \quad\quad (snd\ xs)\ x} \;\wedge\,\text{elim} \;\rightarrow\text{elim}}{((fst\ xs)\ x, (snd\ xs)\ x)} \;\wedge\,\text{intro}}{\dfrac{\lambda x.((fst\ xs)\ x, (snd\ xs)\ x)}{\lambda xs.\lambda x.((fst\ xs)\ x, (snd\ xs)\ x)} \;\rightarrow\text{intro}} \;\rightarrow\text{intro}
$$

Figure 9.17 Constructing a proof object

$xs \in P \wedge Q$

Applications of the elimination rules then produce the corresponding proof objects *snd xs* $\in Q$ and *fst xs* $\in P$. An $\wedge$ introduction rule then corresponds to the formation of a pair *(snd xs, fst xs)* $\in Q \wedge P$ from these separate objects. Finally, the $\rightarrow$ introduction rule corresponds to an abstraction on an object of the type introduced, providing the final judgement:

$\lambda xs.(snd\ xs, fst\ xs) \in P \wedge Q \rightarrow Q \wedge P$

A quick check will show that this function does actually convert objects of type $P \wedge Q$ into appropriate objects of type $Q \wedge P$. If P and Q are taken to be the natural and Boolean primitive types, we might expect an instance *(5,true)* $\in Nat \times Bool$ to be converted to an instance *(true,5)* $\in Bool \times Nat$. Thus the above function is applied:

$\lambda xs.(snd\ xs, fst\ xs)\ (5,true)$
(snd (5,true), fst (5,true))
(true,5)

and the expected result is obtained.

A larger example, again using only implication and conjunction connectives, is provided by the formula proven in Figure 9.10:

$(P \rightarrow Q) \wedge (P \rightarrow R) \rightarrow (P \rightarrow (Q \wedge R))$

Two applications of the $\rightarrow$ introduction rule to this proposition suggest initial proof objects of the following hypotheses:

$xs \in (P \rightarrow Q) \wedge (P \rightarrow R)$
$x \in P$

These proof objects are shown at positions in a tree corresponding to the positions of their formulas in Figure 9.10. Working back up through the left branch of the tree, an $\wedge$ elimination rule produces a proof object of the following type:

fst xs $\in (P \rightarrow Q)$

This function is then applied to an object $x \in P$ to produce the larger proof object

(fst xs) $x \in Q$

The right-hand branch is constructed in much the same way to produce the proof object

(snd xs) $x \in R$

An $\wedge$ introduction then joins these two components to produce the proof object

((fst xs) x, *(snd xs)* $x) \in Q \wedge R$

Finally the implication introduction steps abstract this expression over all constants of appropriate type to give

$$\lambda xs.\lambda x.((fst\ xs)\ x,\ (snd\ xs)\ x) \in (P \rightarrow Q) \wedge (P \rightarrow R) \rightarrow (P \rightarrow (Q \wedge R))$$

9.3.3 A negation example

Proof objects that are developed from propositions with $\neg$ symbols are easily understood when we remember the identity between this symbol and the implication connective, $\neg A \cong A \rightarrow \bot$. Figure 9.11 in the previous section shows how a proof of the proposition

$$(P \wedge \neg Q) \rightarrow \neg(P \rightarrow Q)$$

corresponds to a proof of the equivalent form

$$(P \wedge (Q \rightarrow \bot)) \rightarrow ((P \rightarrow Q) \rightarrow \bot)$$

One consequence of this equivalence is that a single proof object can be developed for both propositions. Taking the second form, Figure 9.11 shows how this proposition is constructed from two $\rightarrow$ introduction rules, allowing us to define the following proof objects:

$$xs \in P \wedge (Q \rightarrow \bot)$$
$$f \in (P \rightarrow Q)$$

A proof object for the whole proposition may then be constructed in accordance with the deduction tree of Figure 9.11. Taking the left branch first, we obtain $fst\ xs \in P$ through the action of a conjunction elimination on xs. Function $f \in (P \rightarrow Q)$ then acts on this argument through an $\rightarrow$ elimination rule to produce the proof object

$$f(fst\ xs) \in Q$$

Changing to the right-hand branch, we derive the judgement $snd\ xs \in Q \rightarrow \bot$ as a consequence of the conjunction elimination inference rule. This proof object of type $Q \rightarrow \bot$ may then be applied to the object of type Q from the left-hand branch to yield an object of type $\bot$:

$$(snd\ xs)(f(fst\ xs)) \in \bot$$

Two $\rightarrow$ introduction rules then abstract this judgement over all values of f and xs to give

$$\lambda f.(snd\ xs)(f(fst\ xs)) \in (P \rightarrow Q) \rightarrow \bot$$

$$\lambda xs.\lambda f.(snd\ xs)(f(fst\ xs)) \in (P \wedge (Q \rightarrow \bot)) \rightarrow ((P \rightarrow Q) \rightarrow \bot)$$

EXERCISES 9.3

1. Produce natural deduction proofs for Propositions 1a to 1d in Exercises 9.1 then show that the following expressions are proof objects for the root proposition:

    a. $\lambda x.\lambda y.x$

    b. $\lambda f.\lambda x.\lambda y.(fy)x$

    c. $\lambda f.\lambda g.\lambda x.(fx)gx$

    d. $\lambda f.\lambda x.\lambda y.f(\lambda z.y)x$

2. Produce natural deduction proofs and show that the following expressions are proof objects for Propositions 2a to 2d in Exercises 9.1:

    a. $\lambda x.\lambda y.(x,y)$

    b. $\lambda f.(\lambda x.fst \ (f \ xs), \ \lambda x.snd(f \ xs))$

    c. $\lambda f.\lambda xs.(f(fst \ xs)) \ snd \ xs$

    d. $\lambda f.\lambda x.\lambda y.f(x,y)$

9.4   PROOF OBJECTS FROM DISJUNCTIONS

We have a proof of $A \vee B$ when we have a proof of A or when we have a proof of B and a clear indication of which proof object is being offered. If we have proof objects $a \in A$ and $b \in B$, there are two possible proof objects for the disjunction, either $inl \ a \in A \vee B$ or $inr \ b \in A \vee B$, but only one of them is required. As a result, we have the two separate disjunction introduction rules shown in Figure 9.18; the choice depends on the premiss domain.

A small example including a disjunction may be written as follows:

$$Q \wedge R \rightarrow P \vee Q$$

and a proof of this proposition together with its proof objects is shown in Figure 9.19. Looking first at the natural deduction tree, the antecedent $Q \wedge R$ is removed through the $\rightarrow$ introduction rule and becomes available as a hypothesis in the tree. This leaves a disjunction $P \vee Q$ that is in turn obtained through an $\vee$ introduction rule applied to statement Q. Finally the hypothesis $Q \wedge R$ that was detached in the initial inference rule is used as a starting-point from which Q is derived with an $\wedge$ elimination rule. This tree has only one hypothesis or premiss, so the judgement

$$\frac{cases(r, f, g) \in C}{r \in A \vee B \quad f \in A \rightarrow C \quad g \in B \rightarrow C} \qquad \frac{inl \ a \in A \vee B}{a \in A} \quad \frac{inr \ b \in A \vee B}{b \in B}$$

Elimination   Introduction

Figure 9.18 Proof objects for disjunctions: proof objects are in medium type, propositions in bold type

$$\frac{\lambda xs.inr(fst\ xs) \in \pmb{Q} \wedge \pmb{R} \rightarrow \pmb{P} \vee \pmb{Q}}{\frac{inr(fst\ xs) \in \pmb{P} \vee \pmb{Q}}{\frac{fst\ xs \in \pmb{Q}}{xs \in \pmb{Q} \wedge \pmb{R}}}} \quad \begin{array}{l} \rightarrow \text{intro} \\[4pt] \vee \text{intro} \\[4pt] \wedge \text{elim} \end{array}$$

Figure 9.19 A proof involving a disjunction: proof objects are in medium type, propositions in bold type

$$xs \in Q \wedge R$$

acts as a starting-point from which a final proof object can be derived. Of course, the proof object xs represents a pair that might be written as ($fst\ xs$, $snd\ xs$). An $\wedge$ elimination rule then produces the statement Q and its associated proof object is $fst\ xs$. Statement Q is then injected into the right of the disjunction $P \vee Q$, so the proof object of Q is tagged to become $inr(fst\ xs)$. Finally, an $\rightarrow$ introduction rule abstracts the expression just obtained to give the function

$$\lambda xs.inr(fst\ xs)$$

According to the Curry–Howard isomorphism, the proposition above is isomorphic with the following compound type:

$$Q \times R \rightarrow P + Q$$

and we might demonstrate a use of the function by substituting primitive domains for the general symbols P, Q and R as follows:

$$Nat \times Bool \rightarrow Char + Nat$$

To show that the function does actually work, it is applied to object (5,*true*) of type $Nat \times Bool$:

$$\lambda xs.inr(fst\ xs)\ (5,true) = inr(fst\ (5,true)) = inr\ 5$$

confirming that a result $inr\ 5$ of type $Char + Nat$ is obtained when the function is applied.

A disjunction introduction rule was also used in Figure 9.12 in order to prove the proposition

$$((P \vee Q) \rightarrow R) \rightarrow (P \rightarrow R) \wedge (Q \rightarrow R)$$

There are three $\rightarrow$ introduction steps in the proof, generating three hypotheses and creating a requirement for proof objects of the following types:

$$x \in P$$
$$y \in Q$$
$$f \in (P \vee Q) \rightarrow R$$

These propositions might then appear as leaf elements in the tree. Looking first at the left-hand branch of the tree, we take object $x \in P$ to obtain proof object $inl\ x \in$

$P \vee Q$ as directed by the $\vee$ introduction rule. An application of function f now corresponds to a use of the $\rightarrow$ elimination rule, resulting in a new object $f(inl\ x) \in R$. An $\rightarrow$ introduction rule then corresponds to function abstraction, giving the proof object $\lambda x.f(inl\ x) \in P \rightarrow R$. A very similar sequence of rules in the right-hand branch produces the proof object $\lambda y.f(inr\ y) \in Q \rightarrow R$, then an $\wedge$ introduction combines the two into a pair

$$(\lambda x.f(inl\ x), \lambda y.f(inr\ y)) \in (P \rightarrow R) \wedge (Q \rightarrow R)$$

and a final $\rightarrow$ introduction corresponds to an abstraction of the function

$$\lambda f(\lambda x.f(inl\ x), \lambda y.f(inr\ y)) \in ((P \vee Q) \rightarrow R) \rightarrow (P \rightarrow R) \wedge (Q \rightarrow R)$$

9.4.1 Disjunction elimination

Disjunction elimination defined by the rule in Figure 9.18 at first looks quite forbidding, but is much simpler than it appears. A proof object $r \in A \vee B$ might be either *inl a* or *inr b* and we do not know in advance which one will occur in any particular proof. Consequently, a case statement has to be employed in the conclusion of this rule, catering for either possibility. A first attempt at an elimination rule might just recognise the tag, either *inl* or *inr*, and then extract the appropriate domain element, *a* or *b*. The problem with this approach is that the result of the inference rule might be in either one of two domains, depending on the premiss proof object. As a result, the premisses have to include methods of converting them to objects of a third, common type C. If the proof object of $A \vee B$ turns out to be *inl a*, the premiss function f is used to convert this to an object of type C. If it turns out to be *inr b*, the alternative premiss function g converts this to an object of type C.

A disjunction elimination is required in forming a natural deduction tree for the proposition

$$P \vee Q \rightarrow Q \vee P$$

and a proof tree with its proof objects is shown in Figure 9.20. An implication introduction rule supplies a hypothesis $P \vee Q$ from which the proposition must be derived, but there are two more hypotheses that are not so obvious.

In this particular example, objects $p \in P$ and $q \in Q$ act as hypotheses from which objects of type $Q \vee P$ are deduced in a step equivalent to implication introduction

$$
\frac{
\dfrac{
r \in P \vee Q \quad
\dfrac{inr\ p \in Q \vee P \quad inl\ q \in Q \vee P}{\substack{p \in P \qquad\qquad q \in Q}}
}{cases(r,\ inr\ p,\ inl\ q) \in Q \vee P} \quad \vee\ \text{elim}
}{\lambda r.cases(r,\ inr\ p,\ inl\ q) \in P \vee Q \rightarrow Q \vee P} \quad \rightarrow\ \text{intro}
$$

Figure 9.20   A proof with a disjunction elimination: proof objects are in medium type, propositions in bold type

rules. As a result, the *inl* and *inr* tags act as functions mapping objects of types P and Q to objects of type $Q \vee P$. Once it has been shown that objects of type $Q \vee P$ are produced from either disjunct, the disjunction itself can be eliminated and the two possible proof objects incorporated in a single case statement. Finally an implication introduction rule corresponds to an abstraction over all objects that might be instantiated for the disjuncts.

It should be clear that the proposition $P \vee Q \rightarrow Q \vee P$ corresponds to the type statement $P + Q \rightarrow Q + P$, representing a function that converts objects of type $P + Q$ to objects of type $Q + P$. This amounts to no more than exchanging the tag so that, for example, object *inl p* becomes *inr p*. An application of this function to an object *inl 7* of type *Nat + Bool* proceeds as follows:

$$\lambda r.cases(r, inr\ p, inl\ q)\ inl\ 7 = cases(inl\ 7, inr\ p, inl\ q)$$
$$= inr\ 7$$

and produces a result of the type *Bool + Nat*, as required. The instantiated object $r \in P \vee Q$ might be either *inl p* or *inr q*, and we have no way of knowing in advance which of them will arise. If it is *inl p* the first function is chosen; if it is *inr q* the second function is used.

Figure 9.13 shows a proof of the proposition

$$((P \rightarrow R) \vee (Q \rightarrow R)) \rightarrow (P \wedge Q \rightarrow R)$$

containing an implication elimination step. Two implication introduction rules identify two hypotheses and these might be assigned the following proof objects:

$$w \in (P \rightarrow R) \vee (Q \rightarrow R)$$
$$xs \in P \wedge Q$$

At this point, we have two hypotheses from which we wish to derive the primitive statement R. The application of an $\vee$ elimination rule breaks this problem down into two separate subproofs. In one case we must derive statement R from the disjunct $P \rightarrow R$; in the other case we must derive it from the disjunct $Q \rightarrow R$. This step is indeed possible if we can separately prove statements P and Q then use implication eliminations to obtain R. Since $P \wedge Q$ is a hypothesis, it is clear that both statements are obtained by conjunction elimination from the leaf.

Working back up through the proof tree adding proof objects, we first derive

$$fst\ xs \in P$$
$$snd\ xs \in Q$$

Then we have to allocate proof object symbols for each disjunct:

$$f \in P \rightarrow R$$
$$g \in Q \rightarrow R$$

and apply them in implication elimination rules to obtain two possible proof objects for R

$f(fst\ xs) \in R$
$g(snd\ xs) \in R$

Only one of them is required in any particular application, so the $\vee$ elimination step introduces the case statement

$cases(w, f(fst\ xs), g(snd\ xs))$

Finally this judgement is abstracted over the objects of the hypotheses to give a result

$\lambda w.\lambda xs.cases(w, f(fst\ xs), g(snd\ xs))$

EXERCISES 9.4

1. Produce natural deduction proofs and show that the following expressions are proof objects of Propositions 3a to 3c in Exercises 9.1:

   a. $\lambda x.inl\ x$

   b. $\lambda f.\lambda x.f(inl\ x)$

   c. $\lambda f.f(inr\ \lambda x.f(inl\ x))$

2. Produce natural deduction proofs and show that the following expressions are proof objects of Propositions 4a to 4c in Exercises 9.1:

   a. $\lambda d.cases(d,x,x)$

   b. $\lambda xs.\lambda xd.cases(xd, (fst\ xs)\ x, (snd\ xs)\ y)$

   c. $\lambda xd.cases(xd, inl\ x, inr(fst\ xs))$

3. Produce natural deduction proofs and show that the following expressions are proof objects of Propositions 5a and 5b in Exercises 9.1:

   a. $\lambda xd.\lambda xs.cases(xd, f(fst\ xs), g(snd\ xs))$

   b. $\lambda xs.\lambda xd.cases(xd, (fst\ xs)\ v, (snd\ xs)\ w)$

9.5 UNIVERSAL AND EXISTENTIAL TYPES

We have seen that three propositional connectives correspond to the three domain constructors described in Chapter 7 and that proof objects for the propositions are programs of the appropriate type. Formulas containing both universal and existential quantifiers may be proven in intuitionistic logic, and it follows that we must be able to produce proof objects for each proven formula. In fact, the proof objects arising for universally quantified formulas turn out to be the polymorphic functions described in Chapter 8, and those of the existential type turn out to be equivalent to the abstract types described in Chapters 5 and 6. The surprising conclusion is that

two of the most important founding areas in modern computing arise naturally in
intuitionistic logic.

An expression is said to be polymorphic or to be parametrised if that expression
is equally applicable to a variety of types. For example, a polymorphic language
allows the following type declaration and program definition:

```
fst :: (*,**) -> *
fst(x,y) = x
```

in which symbols * and ** represent two possibly different types. The program
definition projects out the first element of the pair

```
?fst(5,true)
5
```

and the function type is that of the first element. Functional languages have type
inference systems that allow programmers to use polymorphic code as though it
were an untyped notation.

We have already seen that a proof object for a proposition isomorphic to that
above is written in the lambda form

$$\lambda xs.fst\ xs \in A \wedge B \to A$$

but this is not a polymorphic expression. Propositions A and B are expressed here in
a general form, but these symbols stand for some fixed domain such as *Nat* and
Bool. A polymorphic version is obtained by quantifying over all types in the universe of types U, particularly $u \in U$ and $v \in U$ as follows:

$$\lambda u.\lambda v.\lambda xs \in (u,v).fst\ xs \in \forall u \forall v A(u) \wedge B(v) \to A(u)$$

Thus we abstract over types in exactly the same way as we abstracted over values,
and polymorphic proof objects may be obtained from a natural deduction proof tree
in much the same way as monomorphic proof objects.

Elimination and introduction rules for both the universal and existential quantifiers are shown in Figure 9.21. Concentrating first on the universal rules at the top

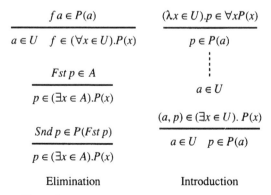

Figure 9.21 Quantifier rules

of this figure, we note a striking resemblance to the implication rules described earlier. If, from an arbitrary type a in the universe of types U, we can show that $P(a)$ is a type then, according to the universal introduction rule, we conclude this to be the case for all types. The difference between this and implication introduction is that now the resulting type depends on the initial type chosen as the hypothesis. Universal elimination performs the reverse task: it takes a specific type from the universe of types U together with a function that maps types to types and thus produces a new type.

As a first example of the use of natural deduction quantifier rules, we produce a proof for the formula

$$\forall u \in U.(P(u) \rightarrow Q(u)) \rightarrow (\forall u \in U.P(u) \rightarrow \forall u \in U.Q(u))$$

but, in order to make the proof more readable, we express this as

$$\forall u(P(u) \rightarrow Q(u)) \rightarrow (\forall uP(u) \rightarrow \forall uQ(u))$$

This abbreviated form removes the repeated assertions that type u belongs to the universe of types U, but this requirement is understood in the abbreviated formula. The fact this formula holds classically may be concluded from the semantic tableau proof of Figure 2.3. It would not be a difficult task to convert each of the steps in this tableau into I system proof steps and thus produce an intuitionistic I proof of the formula. Figure 9.22 shows a natural deduction proof for this formula, where the formulas in this proof are distinguished from their proof objects by bold type.

The first two rules used here are implication introduction rules equivalent to the right implication rules of an I system proof. When these rules have been applied, we are left with the formula $\forall uQ(u)$ and hypotheses $\forall u(P(u) \rightarrow Q(u))$ and $\forall uP(u)$ that we can use as leaf assumptions. An application of the $\forall$ introduction rule then allows us to conclude $\forall uQ(u)$ on the basis that formula $Q(a)$ has been established from the assumption that a is an arbitrary type from the universe of types U. If we prove $Q(a)$ for some specific but arbitrary type a then the formula must hold for all types, so we can add the quantifier. At this point, we have the three hypotheses mentioned above, from which we have to derive the formula $Q(a)$. This is achieved

$$
\frac{\dfrac{\dfrac{\dfrac{\dfrac{g\,a \in P(a)}{\quad} \qquad \dfrac{f\,a \in P(a) \rightarrow Q(a)}{\quad}}{(fa)ga \in Q(a)}}{\lambda u.(fu)gu \in \forall uQ(u)}}{\lambda g.\lambda u.(fu)gu \in ((\forall uP(u) \rightarrow \forall uQ(u))}}{\forall u(P(u) \rightarrow Q(u)) \rightarrow ((\forall uP(u) \rightarrow \forall uQ(u))}
$$

	$\forall u(P(u) \rightarrow Q(u)) \rightarrow ((\forall uP(u) \rightarrow \forall uQ(u))$	$\rightarrow$ intro
	$\lambda g.\lambda u.(fu)gu \in ((\forall uP(u) \rightarrow \forall uQ(u))$	$\rightarrow$ intro
	$\lambda u.(fu)gu \in \forall uQ(u)$	$\forall$ intro
	$(fa)ga \in Q(a)$	$\rightarrow$ elim
$g\,a \in P(a)$	$f\,a \in P(a) \rightarrow Q(a)$	$\forall$ elim
$a \in U \quad g \in \forall uP(u)$	$a \in U \quad f \in \forall u(P(u) \rightarrow Q(u))$	

Figure 9.22 Universal quantifiers in natural deduction: proof objects are in medium type, formulas in bold type

by using universal elimination rules on the hypotheses to obtain formulas instantiated with the arbitrary type a. An implication elimination rule then produces the desired formula. Notice again that the order in which the elimination rules are applied is the reverse of that in the sequent approaches.

A proof object for the formula is obtained by working back up through the tree, starting with the following proof objects for the hypotheses:

$a \in U$

$g \in \forall u P(u)$

$f \in \forall u(P(u) \rightarrow Q(u))$

Universal eliminations act in much the same way as implication eliminations except that they map types to formulas of variable type, rather than objects to formulas of fixed type. Thus the proof object of a universally quantified formula is a function mapping types to formulas. Given an initial type a from the universe of types U, the proof objects of the instantiated formulas are ga and fa in this example. An implication elimination then applies one of these proof objects to the other to produce the result

$(fa)ga \in Q(a)$

Since this proof object has been established without restriction on the type a, it can be abstracted to a variable u over all types to give the result

$\lambda u.(fu)gu \in Q(u)$

then two further abstractions connected with the implication elimination steps produce the final result

$\lambda f.\lambda g.\lambda u.(fu)gu \in \forall u(P(u) \rightarrow Q(u)) \rightarrow (\forall u P(u) \rightarrow \forall u Q(u))$

An existential formula such as

$\exists u \in U.P(u)$

may be concluded if the instantiation of a particular type (say a) from the universe of types U gives a proof object p of the formula $P(a)$. As a result, the proof object for an existential formula has two parts: a type a from the universe of types and proof object $p \in P(a)$ formed from that type. The resulting proof object is a pair (a,p) but differs from the proof object of conjunction because the second component depends on the first.

We wish to develop a natural deduction proof of the formula

$(\exists u \in UP(u) \rightarrow Q) \rightarrow \forall u \in U(P(u) \rightarrow Q)$

and to discover the proof object of this formula. As in previous examples, it is convenient to make implicit the requirement that u is chosen from the universe of types, rather than show it explicitly each time it is used. Thus the formula becomes

$(\exists u P(u) \rightarrow Q) \rightarrow \forall u(P(u) \rightarrow Q)$

$$\frac{\lambda f.\lambda u.\lambda p.f(u,p) \in (\exists u P(u) \to Q) \to \forall u(P(u) \to Q)}{\frac{\lambda u.\lambda p.f(u,p) \in \forall u(P(u) \to Q)}{\frac{\lambda p.f(u,p) \in P(u) \to Q}{\frac{f(u,p) \in Q}{f \in \exists u P(u) \to Q \quad (u,p) \in \exists u P(u)}}}} \quad \begin{array}{l} \to \text{intro} \\ \\ \forall \text{ intro} \\ \\ \to \text{intro} \\ \\ \to \text{elim} \\ \\ \exists \text{ intro} \end{array}$$

$$u \in U \quad p \in P(u)$$

Figure 9.23 An existential introduction: proof objects are in medium type, propositions in bold type

and a natural deduction based on this form is shown in Figure 9.23. Clearly the central implication symbol is the principal connective, so an implication introduction rule detaches a hypothesis $(\exists u P(u) \to Q)$ that is then available to be used as a leaf formula. Equally clearly, the next step has to be a $\forall$ introduction generalising the formula $P(u) \to Q$ over all possible values of u. This step is justified if we have derived the unquantified formula from the hypothesis that $u \in U$ is an arbitrary type from the universe of types. Another implication introduction then reduces the formula to be proven to the simple statement Q and adds one more hypothesis. At this point, we have all of the hypotheses that are going to be used in the deduction: $\exists u P(u) \to Q$, $u \in U$, and $p \in P(u)$. The objective now is to derive Q from these hypotheses and the strategy is to derive the fragment $\exists u P(u)$ then use this in an implication elimination to obtain formula Q. An existential introduction produces the required formula from an arbitrary element in the universe of types and a formula with that type as a free variable.

A proof object for the whole formula is again constructed by assigning objects to each of the hypotheses as follows:

$f \in \exists u P(u) \to Q$
$u \in U$
$p \in P(u)$

then working back up through the tree to produce a composite proof object. A proof object for the existential formula is a pair consisting of an arbitrary element u and a proof p showing that it has property P:

$(u,p) \in \exists u P(u)$

An implication elimination corresponds to the application of function f and an implication introduction corresponds to abstraction over element p (the proof object of the antecedent). A universal introduction corresponds to an abstraction over all types from the universe of types, then comes a final abstraction over the proof objects of $P(U)$. The final result is

$\lambda f.\lambda u.\lambda p.f(u,p) \in (\exists u P(u) \to Q) \to \forall u(P(u) \to Q)$

In the same way, any type might be instantiated into the slightly more complex structure

$$\exists u \in U.A(u) \times A(u)$$

but whatever the type instantiated here, this structure always represents a Cartesian product. In its simplest case it might represent values of $(5,7)$ or of $(true, false)$, but the components may be complex.

A particularly interesting situation arises when an existentially quantified formula contains both the existential type to be instantiated together with some fixed type, e.g.

$$\exists u \in U.A(u) \times (A(u) \to nat)$$

This again represents a pair, but we are able to reason about the proof objects of this statement without knowing what types might be instantiated. Suppose that xs is the proof object of some type a instantiated into this formula:

$$xs \in A(a) \times (A(a) \to nat)$$

It follows that $(snd\ xs)\ (fst\ xs)$ yields an object of type nat and this must be so for any instantiated type. The type $A(a)$ defines a set of objects whereas the second component defines a function from this set to the set nat. This striking resemblance to an abstract type signature like those described in Chapter 6 is not a coincidence: existential types are equivalent to the earlier abstract types and the form of proof object xs is that of a simple signature. Existential types have an "information hiding" effect that allows reasoning to take place without a specific commitment to a given representation. Since universal quantifiers equate to parametrised types and existential quantifiers to abstract types, we should not be surprised that a combination of the two quantifiers equates to the parametrised abstract types described in Section 6.4.

CHAPTER TEN

Languages and databases

10.1 RELATIONAL AND FUNCTIONAL LANGUAGES

A logic language such as Prolog obtains its results by backward chaining through a series of relations in a database of clauses until a unification is achieved. Bindings occur through the unification of the goal with database clauses, but each binding may be undone through backtracking to allow subsequent attempts at unification. Prolog keeps track of all the substitutions made in reaching a certain point, so at unification it can report the full set. At this point, the goal is said to be satisfied. The Prolog search mechanism does not and could not substitute terms in the relations themselves because it is an animated form of logic without equality. Instead it keeps track of the substitutions in a separate list. Functional languages, on the other hand, admit the concept of denotational equality and compute a result by rewriting terms until the simplest possible result is obtained. Clearly there is no backtracking in a functional language.

A logic language might for example include the following facts:

```
colour(door,green)
colour(door,blue)
colour(chair,green)
```

and from this database a user might be informed that doors are available in either green or blue:

```
?colour(door,X)
X = green, X = blue
```

Here a user presents a goal and Prolog attempts to unify the arguments in the goal with those of the same relation in its database. Since the unification procedure is a two-way process, nothing prevents a user from presenting goals in which the first argument is unspecified, for example

```
?colour(X,green)
X = door, X = chair
```

The user could go even further and present the goal ?colour(X, Y) to Prolog, obtaining every possible set of arguments for the relation. Prolog clauses are said to be non-deterministic because they do not predefine any of their terms to be either input or output. The Prolog append relation is often offered as a good example of non-deterministic behaviour: it either appends two lists together to form a single larger list or it can supply all possible pairs of lists that could construct a given list. Nothing in the definition of the relation determines which way it has to be used. This dual usage makes Prolog very expressive and allows clause definitions to be used for more than one purpose, but there are problems. In practice the majority of Prolog clauses do not have this dual behaviour because there is no operational mechanism to support it.

A naive attempt to submit a definition something like that above to a functional interpreter might take the form

```
colour("door") = "green"
colour("door") = "blue"
colour("chair") = "green"
```

but would be immediately rejected by the interpreter. Identical arguments are, by definition, mapped to identical results because the result denotes the value of the function. The same function cannot denote two different objects. Fortunately, a similar effect is achieved with the following functional definition:

```
colour("door") = ["green","blue"]
colour("chair") = ["green"]
```

Thus a one-to-many relation is represented in Prolog as a collection of facts but in a functional language the argument is mapped to a variable-length list of elements. A functional language draws a very clear distinction between the arguments to which the function is applied and the denotation of the applied function. The arguments are pictured as the input and the denotation as the output; there is a clear direction in the computation and the process is deterministic. Unification in Prolog is inherently a two-way process that might produce many satisfying results, whereas the substitution mechanism of functional languages is a one-way process that produces just one result. Functional programs generally have a much clearer operation than logic programs, even when the logic programs do not include procedural features. As a result, the implementation of functional languages on parallel machines is much more straightforward.

Since logic languages are derived from first-order logic, the only form of quantification allowed is over terms in predicates. Furthermore, no substitutions of terms by equivalent values are permitted in a language without equality. As a result, Prolog has to transmit its computations through a series of intermediate variables in a clause such as

```
r(x,z) :- f(x,y),g(y,z)
```

If z is some constant to be computed from x, it might be computed via an intermediate y as in the above clause. Clearly y has no purpose other than to transfer the output from relation f to the input of relation g. There can be no doubt that the proliferation of intermediate variables is a problem in logic languages. Such variables are essential to pass information from one relation to another, but they do create a great deal of inefficiency in the language.

If there is only one value of y for each value of x, the relation is functional and if both f and g are functional relations, then r is also functional. But the relations in a logic language do not have to be functional. In the case that they are both functional, the above composition of relations may be rewritten in a functional language as a composition of functions:

```
r(x) = f(g(x))
```

Functional languages permit higher-order functions that take other functions as their arguments, removing the need for intermediate variables that transfer results. If a relation is functional it can be written much more compactly in a functional language; but as many relations are not functional, the logic program has advantages.

Declarative languages allow a user to describe a relationship between what is known and what is required without explicitly telling the computer how to compute one from the other. Nevertheless, the method of computation is much clearer for a functional language than for a logic language. Different program definitions influence the operational behaviour of the program and might significantly affect the efficiency with which a result is obtained. Logic languages are particularly prone to efficiency problems because they achieve their results through exhaustive database searches. One solution to this problem is to incorporate procedural features such as the cut described in Chapter 4, allowing a user to manipulate the search mechanism. In fact, almost any practical use of Prolog requires the use of such procedural features and this is a major disadvantage of the language. Lazy functional languages require no extra procedural guidance in order to run efficiently or to read from and write to files. As a result, the semantics of functional languages are much clearer than those of logic languages.

One feature that Prolog and Miranda have in common is that both read a file containing a program into the main storage of the computer and work from that stored program. Changes made in program definitions during a particular session are incorporated when the whole program is written to a file, replacing a previous version of the file. File data may also be changed by explicit reading and writing of files, opening up the possibility of unwelcome side-effect style programming.

Many of the examples in this book apply complex programs to relatively small amounts of data, but in the commercial data-processing world the opposite combination is common. Many applications are of simple programs to massive quantities of data and in this case the process of reading and writing whole files is not efficient. Such systems maintain data in secondary storage and allow modifications to be made incrementally, without loading all the data into primary storage. Modifications to data are said to be "persistent" because they are retained in secondary storage without explicit file-writing instructions such as those used in Prolog and Miranda. Languages using persistent storage have to ensure that results obtained from the database are independenet of the order in which information is added. The remaining sections of this chapter describe some languages with these features.

10.2 THE RELATIONAL DATABASE MODEL

The relational database model is "set oriented" and many of its most characteristic features are a direct consequence of set theory. A database table consists of a set of tuples, so the order in which tuples appear in the table is of no consequence. Each tuple in turn consists of a set of attributes whose order is unimportant. In practice the columns of attributes have to be entered in some order, so a consistent but arbitrary order is defined.

A number of restrictions are applied to a table of tuples and their attributes, some of which are a direct consequence of the fact that a database is a set of tuples:

a. No two tuples are the same because the second copy of any one item in a set is redundant.

b. Every tuple in the set of tuples must contain the same set of attributes.

c. Attribute values must be atomic, i.e. they cannot themselves contain substructures such as lists or functions.

d. Each attribute value must be chosen from a fixed domain that is characteristic of the attribute set, e.g. integer or string.

Since relational database tables are sets, they may be manipulated by the usual set theory operations and also by a number of new operations defined especially for the purpose. The set union, intersection and difference operations are familiar and might be written as

```
Table1 ∪ Table2
Table1 ∩ Table2
Table1 - Table2
```

These three arity-two operations are only applied to union-compatible arguments, i.e. to argument tables that contain the same set of attributes. The result of each operation is another table, consisting of those tuples that appear in either table, those that appear in both or those that appear in the first but not the second. Consider as an example the following two tables:

```
BOOKS
BKNO        AUTHOR        TITLE            PRICE
4536        Beethoven     Sonatas          21.45
5274        Jones         Yoga             10.45
5728        Adjei         Africa           15.74

DISCS
RECNO       ARTISTE       TITLE            PRICE
2121        Clarke        Greensleeves     10.55
4536        Beethoven     Sonatas          21.45
4637        Beatles       Midnight         15.26
```

in which two separate tables called BOOKS and DISCS contain details of the books and compact discs in a certain library. A relatively small number of items might occur in both tables because a book and a compact disc may be borrowed as a single package. These two tables are certainly union-compatible because they contain the same set of attributes: two numbers and two character strings. As a result, the following tables might be formed from the set theory operations:

```
BOOKS ∪ DISCS
BKNO        AUTHOR        TITLE            PRICE
4536        Beethoven     Sonatas          21.45
5274        Jones         Yoga             10.45
5728        Adjei         Africa           15.74
2121        Clarke        Greensleeves     10.55
4637        Beatles       Midnight         15.26
```

This set contains five elements representing every tuple that occurred in either of the two argument sets. Observe, however, that the column titles have been taken from the first table. Union-compatible tables do not have to have the same column headings: it is the types of the columns that have to be compatible.

An intersection, on the other hand, contains only those elements that are common to both arguments:

```
BOOKS ∩ DISCS
BKNO        AUTHOR        TITLE        PRICE
4536        Beethoven     Sonatas      21.45
```

Finally a set difference contains those elements of the first set that do not appear in the second:

```
BOOKS - DISCS
BKNO        AUTHOR        TITLE        PRICE
5274        Jones         Yoga         10.45
5728        Adjei         Africa       15.74
```

Union and intersection are symmetric operations but difference is not: if the arguments of set difference are reversed, a different result is obtained.

The set operations above are expressed in relational algebra form: each of the symbols $\cup$ $\cap$ and $-$ represents an arity-two operation applied to two union-compatible tables. These three algebraic operations might also be expressed in the form of comprehensions as follows:

BOOKS $\cup$ DISCS = {t | t $\in$ BOOKS $\lor$ t $\in$ DISCS}

BOOKS $\cap$ DISCS = {t | t $\in$ BOOKS $\land$ t $\in$ DISCS}

BOOKS $-$ DISCS = {t | t $\in$ BOOKS $\land \neg$(t $\in$ DISCS)}

A union of the tables BOOKS and DISCS is the set of all tuples t such that t is an element of the set BOOKS or is an element of the set DISCS. Of course, the same element might be an element of both sets, but a duplicate copy of that element in the resulting set is then redundant. Similarly, the intersection of the two tables is the set of tuples t such that t is an element of both sets, BOOKS and DISCS. Finally, the set difference is the set of tuples that occur in the set BOOKS and not in set DISCS. In the context of relational databases, the expressions within the comprehensions are called relational calculus.

The Sequel (SQL) relational database language contains the infix operations UNION, INTERSECT and MINUS that apply the set theory operations to union-compatible arguments. Thus BOOKS UNION DISCS represents a union of two tables to produce the table shown above; the other operations are similarly applied. Although Sequel generally follows the calculus form, these operations have an algebraic form.

In addition to the three classical set operations above, a further four set operations may be defined:

a. selection

b. projection

c. Cartesian product

d. join

Selection is an arity-one operation, taking one set of tuples as an argument and denoting a new set with perhaps fewer tuples, but each tuple retains the same number of attributes. In terms of tables, the resulting table has the same number of columns but perhaps fewer rows. Tuples appear in the new table if they satisfy a selection criterion added as a subsript to the select operation. The relation algebra expression for the set of books costing less than 20 currency units is expressed as follows:

$\text{select}_{\text{PRICE<20}}$ (BOOKS)

and the equivalent calculus expression has the form

{t | t $\in$ BOOKS $\land$ t[PRICE] < 20}

Thus the set denoted by this operation contains all tuples t such that t is an element in the set BOOKS and the price attribute of the tuple, shown as t[PRICE], is less than 20 currency units. Sequel allows a slightly more user-friendly version of the calculus expression:

```
SELECT * FROM BOOK
      WHERE PRICE < 20;
```

and, like the other expressions above, this represents the table

```
select_PRICE < 20 (BOOKS)
BKNO     AUTHOR     TITLE      PRICE
5274     Jones      Yoga       10.45
5728     Adjei      Africa     15.74
```

Projection is also an arity-one operation. It takes one set argument, this time denoting a table with the same number of rows, but perhaps with fewer columns. Columns to be projected from the argument table are included as subscripts to the project operator applied to a table containing those column headings. For example, relational algebra and relational calculus expressions denoting a table containing just the TITLE and PRICE columns of the BOOKS table are written as follows:

$$\text{project}_{TITLE, PRICE}(BOOKS) =$$
$$\{t \mid \exists u \in BOOKS \wedge t[TITLE, PRICE] = u[TITLE, PRICE]\}$$

This set contains all tuples t such that t has two attributes, TITLE and PRICE, and these attributes exist in a tuple u of the set BOOKS. An existential quantifier is introduced to assert that "there exist" tuples u in the set BOOKS. Sequel again provides a much more user-friendly version of the calculus expression

```
SELECT TITLE, PRICE
      FROM BOOKS;
```

and again this represents the same table as the expressions above:

```
project_TITLE, PRICE (BOOKS)
TITLE       PRICE
Sonatas     21.45
Yoga        10.45
Africa      15.74
```

In practice many queries will be neither pure selections nor projections but combinations of the two. We might wish to project out the BKNO and TITLE attributes from just those tuples in which the PRICE attribute is less than 15 currency units. Since relational algebra is an applicative language, the result of one operation may be the argument for another, and the query described above may be expressed in the form

$$\text{project}_{BKNO, TITLE}(\text{select}_{PRICE<15}(BOOKS))$$

The same set may be expressed in calculus form as follows:

```
{t | ∃u ∈ BOOK ∧ t[TITLE,PRICE] = u[TITLE,PRICE]
u[PRICE] < 15 }
```

Sequel once again provides a compact form of the calculus expression:

```
SELECT TITLE,PRICE
       FROM BOOK
       WHERE PRICE < 15;
```

Relational databases generally contain collections of separate tables and information has to be extracted from combinations of these tables. In the examples being used here, book and disc items in the library may be borrowed by individuals listed in a MEMBERS table, with member number, name and location attributes:

```
MEMBERS
MNO     NAME     LOC
1234    Lewis    Sales
3645    Morse    Finance
```

A third table then connects tuples in the BOOKS and MEMBERS tables through the BKNO and MNO attributes:

```
SERIAL
BKNO    MNO      RETURN
5728    1234     12-APR-98
4536    1234     06-JAN-99
```

A Cartesian product of the SERIAL and MEMBERS tables might be expressed simply as cprod(SERIAL,MEMBERS) and is equivalent to the following relational calculus expression:

```
cprod(SERIAL, MEMBERS) =
        {t | ∃u ∈ SERIAL ∧
        t[BKNO,MNO,RETURN] = u[BKNO,MNO,RETURN] ∧
        ∃v ∈ MEMBERS ∧
        t[MNO,NAME,LOC] = v[MNO,NAME,LOC]}
```

These expressions denote a table with the following structure:

```
cprod(SERIAL, MEMBERS)
MNO     NAME     LOC       BKNO     MNO     RETURN
1234    Lewis    Sales     5728     1234    12-APR-98
1234    Lewis    Sales     4536     1234    06-JAN-99
3645    Morse    Finance   5728     1234    12-APR-98
3645    Morse    Finance   5728     1234    12-APR-98
```

In fact, the product form used in relational databases is better described as a complex product because the order in which columns appear is unimportant: a given tuple is characterised by a set of attributes rather than a list. As a result, every attribute has to be distinguished by name not by its position in the tuple, and one of these columns should be renamed in the complex product. In practice this is not a problem because products are only formed between tuples in which the common attribute has the same value. A product of this kind is called a join, or perhaps more correctly an equijoin, because it depends on an equivalence between two attributes. When applied to the example above, we obtain

```
join(SERIAL, MEMBERS) =
        {t | ∃s ∈ SERIAL ∧
        s[BKNO,MNO,RETURN] = t[BKNO,MNO,RETURN] ∧
        ∃m ∈ MEMBERS ∧
        m[MNO,NAME,LOC] = t[MNO,NAME,LOC] ∧
        s[MNO] = m[MNO]}
```

Once again, Sequel provides a very user-friendly implementation of the calculus expression:

```
SELECT S.MNO, NAME, LOC, BKNO, RETURN
      FROM SERIAL S, MEMBERS M
      WHERE S.MNO = M.MNO;
```

Here the symbols S and M are used as pseudonyms for table names and are then used to avoid the ambiguity that might arise from two similarly named columns. The resulting table contains only one copy of the joined attribute:

```
join(SERIAL, MEMBERS)
```

MNO	NAME	LOC	BKNO	RETURN
1234	Lewis	Sales	5728	12-APR-98
1234	Lewis	Sales	4536	06-JAN-99

This table might be subjected to further operations, perhaps becoming an argument in a further join with the BOOKS table. Alternatively, some combination selections and projections may be applied to the table above. We might write a relational algebra operation extracting the MNO and BKNO attributes for all books due back after a certain date:

$$\text{project}_{\text{MNO, BKNO}}(\text{select}_{\text{RETURN>14-DEC-98}}(\text{join}(\text{SERIAL}, \text{MEMBERS})))$$

Complex products and joins inevitably produce tables with increased numbers of rows and columns. Often a large table formed in this way is then subjected to projection and selection operations, removing columns and rows that need never have been included in the table. For example, it is possible that only a small number of tuples in the SERIAL table satisfy the restriction RETURN > 14-DEC-98, but every SERIAL tuple is involved in the joining operation. This will not be the case when the expression is rewritten in the form

$$\text{project}_{\text{MNO, BKNO}}(\text{join}(\text{select}_{\text{RETURN>14-DEC-98}}(\text{SERIAL}), \text{MEMBERS}))$$

so that the SERIAL table is first reduced in size before the join is carried out. Term rewriting of this kind is the basis of the optimisation techniques used in relational databases.

Current commercial database systems almost invariably use the Sequel query language, largely a sugared form of relational calculus. Adherents of the calculus often claim it is more declarative than the algebra, but a number of large-scale working systems have shown that use of the algebraic form also has advantages. The fact that the algebra is a higher-order language allows compound expressions such as those above to be constructed and used as arguments in other expressions. Intermediate tables built up from base tables in this way are called views, creating virtual tables that allow a great deal of data and software reuse. Views may also be defined through relational calculus expressions, but the procedure is not as elegant and flexible as in the algebra.

Relational database tables obviously have to be created in the first place and their tuples entered. A database structure is created by this Sequel instruction:

```
CREATE TABLE BOOKS
     (BKNO NUMBER(5),
     AUTHOR CHAR(14),
     TITLE CHAR(14),
     PRICE NUMBER(5.2));
```

then the tuples are entered with a series of instructions of the form

```
INSERT INTO BOOKS
     VALUES(4536,'Beethoven','Sonatas',21.45)
```

Further tuples may be added in the same way, either at the same time or in subsequent sessions on the computer. Each time data is inserted into the table, it persists after the user has logged off, without any special file storage instructions.

A comparable database might be constructed in the Miranda language by including the following instructions in a script:

```
books :: [ (num,[char], [char],num)]
books = [(4536,"Beethoven","Sonatas",21.45),...]
```

Here a structure is declared by a type description, then the tuples of the table are enumerated. The books database is stored as a program and might be written to a file using the file instructions described in Chapter 8. A new tuple is added by editing the file. Each column of the table has a name in the Sequel implementation, but not in the Miranda implementation. This means that attributes are accessed by name in Sequel; the order in which they appear is of no importance. In contrast, the Miranda version depends on the positions of attributes in each tuple for its method of access. We could obviously include a conversion routine that would accept names and produce appropriate positions in the tuple, but this is not required here.

If the discs database is specified in a Miranda script in the same way as the books example above, the three classical set operations might be applied in the way described in Chapter 8:

```
union books discs
intersect books discs
difference books discs
```

and the same results are obtained. Selection, projection, Cartesian product and joining are also implemented in the way described in Chapter 8, using the Miranda list comprehension facility. The similarity between list comprehension definitions of the relational database operators and the set comprehension descriptions above is quite obvious.

There are in fact two forms of relational calculus expression, one described as tuple oriented, the other as domain oriented. Languages such as Sequel are tuple oriented, so this form has become well known, but other languages derive advantages from the domain-oriented form. The difference is clear when we write a comprehension for the algebraic expression

$$\text{project}_{\text{BKNO,TITLE}} \, (\text{select}_{\text{PRICE}<15} \, (\text{BOOKS}))$$

in domain-oriented form as

$$\{(\texttt{bkno},\texttt{ti}) \mid (\texttt{bkno},\texttt{au},\texttt{ti},\texttt{pr}) \in \text{BOOKS} \land \texttt{pr} < 15\}$$

This comprehension labels individual domains in the tuple rather than giving a single symbol t for the tuple then expressing attributes in terms of the tuple. More important, it takes very little effort to convert this form of the comprehension to a Miranda list comprehension.

Although both languages store the information as a list of tuples, there is a significant difference in the addition and deletion of tuples from a database. Sequel allows individual tuples to be added to the database incrementally and changes to the database persist in secondary storage without any explicit file storage instructions. A Miranda definition has to be recompiled to incorporate such changes, then the changed script is stored or an explicit instruction moving the data to a storage file is required.

Relational databases allow a primitive form of null element and its exact meaning has been a major point of discussion since Codd first recognised its interpretation as a problem. Sequel permits an instruction

```
INSERT INTO BOOKS(6738,'Patel','Meditation',NULL);
```

but it is not clear whether this means that the price attribute is unknown or inappropriate. Nevertheless, it is very useful in practice and many database queries are defined when some attributes are NULL, providing a form of lazy evaluation.

Relational database theory is attractively simple and relatively easy to implement on computing systems, but this simplicity is itself the source of problems. Soon after Codd first described such systems in the early 1970s, it became clear that special methodologies are required in order to convert real-world situations into relational database models. One major problem with the relational model is that all the tables in a given system are quite separate, even though they might model interconnecting objects in the real world. Tables BOOKS and MEMBERS in the example above are said to be entity tables because they describe distinct entities or objects. The SERIAL table, on the other hand, is called a relationship table because its purpose is to provide a relationship between the two entity tables. Each of the base tables described above is just one component of a single library system, but any connection between these components is contained in the queries, not in the data structures themselves. Tables isolated in this way might suffer from integrity problems, in particular they might lack referential integrity. This arises when an attribute in one relation (a foreign key) is supposed to match a defining key in another relation (a primary key), but does not do so. As a result, we have either a reference to a tuple that does not exist or no reference to one that does exist.

Relationship relations may be divided into three groups; one-to-one (1:1), one-to-many (1:M) and many-to-many (N:M). Often (1:M) and (N:M) relationships are a source of problems in developing relational database systems. Table SERIAL above is clearly a (1:M) relationship because each member might borrow any number of books. More important, the number of books borrowed is variable and the only way of expressing this in a relation is to have separate tuples for each book. The entity–relationship model was the first of many semantic data models intended to capture the behaviour of systems but is still the most widely used approach.

10.2.1 Manipulating one-to-many relations

Consider an example with two base tables called STAFF and PLACES defined as follows:

```
STAFF
NAME       SPEAKS
tim        french
tim        english
tim        german
donna      italian
mark       spanish

PLACES
LANGUAGE   COUNTRY
english    canada
english    australia
french     canada
spanish    bolivia
```

Both of these tables represent one-to-many relations: a person named in the staff relation might speak more than one language and a particular language might be spoken in more than one country. Suppose that we want to know the names of people in the STAFF table who can speak to the natives of each country in the

PLACES table. Clearly a join between the two tables is required and, because we want to make repeated references to the resulting table, we define it as a view called VISITS:

VISITS = join$_{\text{SPEAKS=LANGUAGE}}$(STAFF, PLACES)

The table might equally well have been described in calculus form and in the Sequel language this might appear as follows:

```
CREATE VIEW VISITS AS
      SELECT NAME, SPEAKS, COUNTRY
           FROM STAFF, PLACE
           WHERE SPEAKS = LANGUAGE;
```

An extra instruction CREATE VIEW defines a virtual table in terms of the STAFF and PLACES tables. Once defined in this way, the table VISITS can be used as though it were a base table:

```
VISITS
NAME      SPEAKS       COUNTRY
tim       french       canada
tim       english      canada
tim       english      australia
mark      spanish      bolivia
```

If we are only interested in the staff names and the countries they might visit, we might obtain a further view of the database:

VISITS2 = project$_{\text{NAME, COUNTRY}}$(VISITS)

Or in its Sequel form:

```
CREATE VIEW VISITS2 AS
      SELECT NAME, COUNTRY
            FROM VISITS;
```

producing a view which, according to the base tables above, has the content

```
VISITS2
NAME      COUNTRY
tim       canada
tim       canada
tim       australia
mark      bolivia
```

Notice that the final table above contains a repetition of the tuple (tim, canada) because it can be derived in two ways: once through french and once through english. This repetition is removed from an SQL definition by adding the DIS-TINCT keyword after a SELECT command.

The same database may be defined in Miranda with statements such as

```
staff :: [([char],[char])]
staff = [("tim","french"),("tim","english"), ... ]
```

The `visits` and `visits2` views might then be defined in the domain-oriented form as

```
visits = [(n,s,c) | (n,s) <- staff ; (t,c) <- place; s = t]
```

```
visits2 = [(n,c) | (n,s,c) <- visits]
```

Just as in SQL, the resulting table contains a repetition of the tuple `(tim,canada)` but this is easily removed by an application of the `mkset` operator described in Chapter 8.

10.3   FUNCTIONAL DATABASES

Functional databases are much more expressive than their relational counterparts and are much more easily related to the semantic data models used to model systems. Unfortunately, they are more difficult to implement on current computers, so their development has lagged behind the relational model.

In order to provide a comparison with the relational model, we shall reuse an example from above, this time using Miranda to mimic a functional database system. As a first step, the STAFF and PLACES tables are expressed through functions:

```
speaks :: [char] -> [[char]]
speaks "tim" = ["french","english","german"]
speaks "donna" = ["italian"]
speaks "mark" = ["spanish"]

country :: [char] -> [[char]]
country "english" = ["canada","australia"]
country "french" = ["canada"]
country "spanish" = ["bolivia"]
```

These functions handle a one-to-many relation by containing the many elements in a single list that may be treated as a set. The elements could themselves be complex structures. If we now want to know the languages spoken by a certain person, we simply apply the function, e.g.

```
?speaks "mark"
["spanish"]
```

A query that previously required the joining of two tables now requires a composition of two functions, but a little care is required here. If we want to find the countries in which `tim` can speak to people, we first find which languages `tim` speaks then find the countries where these languages are spoken. A first attempt might simply compose the two functions as follows:

```
countries(speaks(tim))
```

but this does not work, because function `speaks` denotes a list whereas the function `countries` requires a single string argument. A small comprehension provides a general function for all such queries:

```
visits x = concat[ country y | y <- speaks x]
```

using the built-in `concat` function to flatten a list of lists into a single list, as in the following example:

```
?visits "tim"
["canada","canada","australia"]
```

Once again, the `mkset` function could be applied to remove duplicates.

Poulovassilis and King developed a functional database language called FDL that has the features of a strict functional language and a database system. This system has the familiar base types, integer, Boolean and string, together with the ability to define abstract types, called non-lexical types in FDL. Most important of all, instances of the abstract types are labelled by surrogate keys that identify each instance in later references. For example, a person is declared as an abstract type and three instances of the type, labelled $p1, $p2 and $p3 are declared by

```
person :: nonlex
create person $p1,$p1,$p3
```

Information about the abstract type is then added to the database by defining signatures and equations (shown as ⇐ in FDL) as follows:

```
name : person -> string
name $p1 ⇐ "tim"
name $p2 ⇐ "donna"
name $p3 ⇐ "mark"

speaks : person -> (list string)
speaks $p1 ⇐ ["french","english","german"]
speaks $p2 ⇐ ["italian"]
speaks $p3 ⇐ ["spanish"]
```

FDL defines abstract entities by the functions that may be applied to the entity, and new signatures and equations may be added incrementally to the database. This is quite different from a functional language such as Miranda, where functions are only extended by recompiling a script. For example, the constructors of a disjoint union are changed in Miranda by modification of the original definition and recompilation. In FDL the new constructor is simply added to the database. A database system also has to accept modifications to instances of abstract types without loading the whole database, but has the additional advantage that the abstract type itself may be modified in the same way.

Once an abstract type has been declared in this way, a number of functions may be defined to manipulate the stored data in much the same way that functions are defined in Miranda. A polymorphic function to test whether a particular element is contained in a list is written as follows:

```
member : alpha (list alpha) → bool
member x [ ] ⇐ false
member x [y|z] ⇐ (x = y) or (member x z)
```

Apart from differences of notation (alpha in FDL is * in Miranda, and list alpha is equivalent to [*]), this function looks like its Miranda equivalent. Many of the functions described in Chapter 8 could be used in FDL with small syntactic changes, but in other ways the languages are quite different.

As we have noted in connection with Sequel, a database system often contains large quantities of data items that are added as they become available. FDL functions such as those shown above are added to a persistent storage area, changing the number of instances of each abstract type and even dynamically extending the abstract type itself. Secondary storage devices accommodate persistent data, and runtime management systems are supplied to handle its movement.

Incremental addition means that the top-to-bottom method of pattern matching functions with program functions used in Miranda has to be modified. Since FDL defines its equations incrementally, by repeated insertion and deletion of modified definitions, it cannot rely on an order of appearance of functions in the database. Instead it uses a special pattern-matching algorithm that is independent of program functions.

Another major difference is obvious when no pattern match is found between a query and a database function. Miranda assumes that functions are defined for all arguments and therefore considers a unification failure to be an error. However, we should expect a database to draw a blank from time to time and this should not be seen as an error. For this reason, FDL provides an explicit polymorphic null value @ that might be inserted explicitly by a user or is returned when the system fails to find a pattern match.

10.4 DEDUCTIVE DATABASES

Declarative languages have developed separately and quite distinctly, according to the intended applications of each language. Relational database (RDB) languages have evolved in a form suited to enable fairly simple queries applied to large volumes of data. Although the structure of relational databases is fairly simple and queries written in relational query languages are straightforward, they can be efficiently implemented on currently available computers. Thus, implementations of the Sequel language in database systems such as Oracle have been widely adopted in the commercial data-processing industry. Prolog, on the other hand, has been the servant of the artificial intelligence community, responding to a demand for complex reasoning applied to a limited collection of base tables. It is a more expressive language than Sequel in the sense that it permits the formulation of queries that would not be possible in a relational database system, but this expressiveness is obtained at the cost of efficiency. Given the efficiency of relational database systems and the expressiveness of logic programming, there is a great incentive to try to integrate the schools in some way and obtain the best features of each one. One major hindrance in attempts at coupling logic languages and relational databases has been a basic mismatch in the way in which these languages obtain their results. Although both languages deal with relations, Sequel treats a relation as a set of tuples whereas Prolog works on individual tuples. Fortunately, the mismatches between the two different kinds of language can be removed by defining a new logic language called Datalog that has some of the set-oriented properties of relational databases while retaining most of the desirable features of a logic language.

Before any attempt is made to describe this modified logic language, it is perhaps wise to look again at the correspondence between the operations of relational algebra and their Prolog equivalents. First of all, we have to distinguish between the base tables of a relational database system and any derived tables that might be defined through views. Base tables might be considered as "real" tables because the content of these tables is physically contained in some storage device. Views, on the other hand, are "virtual" tables because all that exists in storage is a description of a table that has to be constructed from existing base tables. All databases consist of an extensional database of base tables and an intensional database of views. A Prolog extensional database consists of a collection of facts and an intensional database consists of a collection of rules. It follows that a collection of ground facts for a single relation is equivalent to a base table, and a rule is essentially a view or a derived table. In practice an extensional database changes with time as new items are added and old ones deleted, but intensional databases encapsulate relationships between base tables and are less likely to vary with time. Factual details change, but the relationships between the factual items are less prone to change.

In order to illustrate the relationship between relational algebra operations and Prolog, we rewrite the earlier database tables in the form of Prolog facts:

```
books(4536,beethoven,sonatas,21.45)
books(5274,jones,yoga,10.45)
books(5728,adjei,africa,15.74)

discs(2121,clarke,greensleves,10.55)
discs(4536,beethoven,sonatas,21.45)
discs(4637,beatles,midnight,15.26)
```

These relations again contain details of the books and discs in a certain library. Once again, a few items might occur in both relations because a book and disc might be borrowed as a single item.

The classical set theory operations union, intersection and difference may be applied to these relations because they are union-compatible. Thus a union of the two relations is defined as follows:

```
items(W,X,Y,Z) :- books(W,X,Y,Z) ; discs(W,X,Y,Z).
```

An intersection arises when the same tuple occurs in both the books and discs relations:

```
in_both(W,X,Y,Z) :- books(W,X,Y,Z).discs(W,X,Y,Z).
```

Set difference takes those elements of one set that do not occur in another; it is encapsulated in the Prolog rule

```
no_disc(W,X,Y,Z) :- books(W,X,Y,Z).not(discs(W,X,Y,Z)).
```

This last set operation is especialy interesting because it requires the use of a special Prolog negation operation called not that is applied in the style of a higher-order operation. Some further explanation of the not operation is provided later in this chapter.

Chapter 4 showed how Prolog is able to mimic the behaviour of each of the remaining relational algebra operations. Thus pure projections and selections might be defined as follows:

```
title(Y) :- books(W,X,Y,Z).
```

```
cheap(W,X,Y,Z) :- books(W,X,Y,Z), Z < 10.
```

Cartesian products and joins between Prolog relations are described in Section 4.2 and are in many ways simpler than the database operations themselves. But notice that Prolog rules are inherently domain oriented because the variables represent domain elements.

10.4.1 Differences between Prolog and relational databases

Remember that relational databases deal only in flat tables that contain simple atomic arguments as opposed to structured objects such as functors or lists. Prolog, on the other hand, can accommodate complex terms of any size and lists of arbitrary length.

Relational algebra always produces a result table even if this might sometimes be an empty table. The order in which tuples appear in the table is unimportant, and algebraic operations may be applied in any order consistent with the term-rewriting rules. Prolog does not necessarily produce a result because the search path can get trapped in an infinite branch of the SLD tree, a direct consequence of the depth-first left-to-right search mechanism adopted for the language.

Relational algebra is a purely declarative language and might be seen as a primitive functional language in which arguments are always sets of tuples and operations are limited to set operations. Prolog is not a purely declarative language because the order in which clauses appear in the program sometimes decides whether a given program terminates. Worse still, the language provides operators such as the cut, allowing programmers to manipulate the search path taken by the program.

This form of direct interference makes it difficult to define the meaning of the program, reducing its clarity almost to the level of a machine-oriented program.

Relational databases are "set oriented" in that their operations are always applied to sets of tuples, i.e. to whole tables. Prolog is tuple oriented because each step in the solution of a query involves a unification of individual tuples. This feature alone accounts for the large efficiency difference between Prolog and a relational database language.

In spite of these differences between Prolog and relational databases, some research groups have managed to couple the systems together effectively, in some cases to great advantage. Nevertheless, the majority of workers in the area seem to support the idea of a specialised logic language with characteristics similar to those of a relational database. A language called Datalog has been defined and is essentially a subset of Prolog with a clear declarative semantics. Since it is a subset of Prolog, we can now list the modifications that have to be made in order to overcome the problems enumerated above.

10.4.2 Reducing the mismatch between logic and RDB languages

Complex terms and lists are prohibited in pure Datalog, making a relation in the new language directly comparable with a table in relational algebra.

The non-termination problem in Prolog is a direct consequence of the top-down backward-chaining mechanism adopted for the language. An initial goal is unified with a program clause to generate subgoals that are treated in the same way until satisfaction is achieved. Each time a subgoal has to be matched with a program clause, the search begins again from the top of the Prolog script, generating a depth-first search. Instead of attempting to completely satisfy the subgoals of a successful unification before looking at any lower possibilities, all unifications in a script might be investigated to the same level. This provides the effect of a breadth-first search and would produce a result wherever one was possible. Unfortunately, a breadth-first search mechanism of this kind is still tuple oriented, leaving a considerable mismatch between the logic and relational database approach.

Of course, a logic program does not have to adopt the goal-oriented top-down mechanism used in Prolog. Chapter 3 included a description of a bottom-up forward-chaining mechanism that starts with a logic program and repeatedly applies program rules until no further ground facts are obtained. This is the fixed point of the program. Forward chaining takes a mixture of facts in an extensional database and rules in an intensional database to produce a single extensional database that defines the program. If a goal is found in this derived database it is proven; otherwise it is unproven. Forward chaining has the advantage of being set oriented, because the clauses of a relation are treated as a set to be expanded at the same time. It has the great disadvantage that it generates many more results than are required for a particular query. In any practical application it is very inefficient, but has one very important job: it defines the meaning of a Datalog program. In fact, the naive forward-chaining approach can be considerably improved by removing duplicate tuples as they arise and by a number of other optimisation techniques. However, it is still tuple oriented and does not take advantage of the information contained in a goal to reduce the work that needs to be done. There are relatively efficient implementations of Datalog that may be shown to have the same semantics as the simple forward-chained implementation. For example, an approach called the query–subquery algorithm is a goal directed top-down approach, but it is set oriented and processes whole relations rather than individual tuples. Equally important, it uses a breadth-first search mechanism and always terminates. This means that a Datalog program adopts the same set-oriented processing approach as the relational database and always terminates. The problems caused by procedural features such as the cut are easily resolved by not including them in Datalog.

A Datalog program consists of extensional and intensional parts and looks much the same as the facts and rules of its Prolog equivalent, but there are important differences. A predicate symbol may be used repeatedly in Prolog with different numbers of arguments, so a program might contain the two facts

```
staff(123,tom,5000)
staff(34,bill)
```

Datalog requires that a given predicate symbol always has the same number of arguments in a given program. This is in line with the requirement that every tuple in a relational database table has the same number of attributes. There is another restriction connected with the requirement that forward chaining must produce a finite result, i.e. a fixed point must exist for a program. A Datalog program must satisfy the following safety conditions:

a. Every fact in the extensional database must be a ground fact. A fact such as any(X, Y) that would be acceptable in a Prolog program is prohibited in Datalog.

b. Each variable that occurs in the head of a rule must also occur in the body of that rule.

Taken together with the restrictions above, these conditions ensure that the collection of facts derivable from a given program is finite and that a fixed point always exists. It is important to note that the first condition above rules out the use of "built-in" predicates such as $X < Y$ and $X = Y$. These predicates are equivalent to extensional facts even though they are not part of a user-defined program.

Pure Datalog differs from Prolog in that no negation operation is defined for the language. As a result, the set difference operation does not occur in pure Datalog whereas it is available in relational algebra. Pure datalog is therefore equivalent to a subset of algebra operations called positive relational algebra RA^+ that does not include difference. On the other hand, Datalog is capable of answering some queries that could not be expressed in relational algebra.

To illustrate the sort of query that is possible in a recursive language, but not in relational database theory, we introduce the OFFSPRING table:

```
OFFSPRING
PARENT     CHILD
mary       joe
marie      patsy
stan       zoe
lee        ann
joe        marie
```

Any person entered as a child in this table might also appear as a parent, allowing us to trace all of the descendants of a particular person. It is not difficult to write a Datalog expression that will find all the descendants of one particular person. For example

```
descendant(X,Y) :- offspring(X,Y).
descendant(X,Y) :- offspring(X,Z),descendant(Z,Y).
```

and a query of the form ?descendant(mary,X) produces satisfactions for joe, marie and patsy. This is just a version of the recursive rules explained in Chapter 4.

A pure relational database system is unable to search a table to some arbitrary depth in this way. It would be possible to write a nested query such as

```
SELECT CHILD
     FROM OFFSPRING
     WHERE PARENT IN
          (SELECT CHILD
          FROM OFFSPRING
          WHERE PARENT = 'mary');
```

but this only reveals grandchildren. It would produce neither the first-generation offspring, joe, nor the great grandchild, patsy. There are other ways of expressing this in a relational system, but they are all equivalent to queries set at a fixed depth. Commercial relational database systems are often augmented with a number of ad hoc impure features that allow queries such as the one described above.

10.4.3   Extended Datalog

It should be clear from the description above that pure Datalog allows the query-processing facilities of a logic language to be coupled with and to take advantage of the mass storage facilities of a relational database. At the same time, it sacrifices some of the greater expressiveness that can be achieved in a logic language. Later work has extended Datalog to include the following features:

a. built-in predicates

b. negation

c. complex objects as terms

In fact, the extension to include built-in predicates turns out to be quite straightforward. A built-in predicate may be used safely provided every argument used in the predicate is also used at least once in a user-defined predicate of the same rule body.

Negation presents a much greater problem because its use depends on an assumption beyond the definition of negation provided in Chapter 1. Consider as an example a database of animals of the type

```
dog(fido).
dog(rex).
cat(tiddles).
rat(rufus)
animal(X) :- dog(X);cat(X);rat(X).
```

This database might in fact be much larger, containing many other animal facts, so the animal rule is further extended to include badgers, rabbits and others. If we now wish to extract information about all the animals except rats, we might add a rule to the database

```
cuddly(X) :- animal(X), not(rat(X))
```

then the query ?cuddly(tiddles) might be presented as a query. This would generate a subgoal animal(tiddles) that would be satisfied because tiddles is indeed a cat. A search for rat(tiddles) then fails to unify with a database fact, so the subgoal not(rat(tiddles)) is deemed to be satisfied and the original goal is satisfied. This is the principle of negation by failure, quite different from the concept of negation described in Chapter 1, where it was defined by the equivalences

```
not false = true
not true = false
```

Subgoal rat(tiddles) is not proven false in the above example: it is just not derivable from the program. Thus, any fact that cannot be derived from a program is assumed to be false, and negation by failure assumes the negation of such a fact to be true.

The Microelectronics and Computer Technology Corporation in Texas have implemented a powerful version of Datalog called LDL. Not only does this system extend Datalog in all the ways suggested above, it also compiles the program into a form of relational algebra that runs on a parallel-processing machine. This implementation allows large "data dredging" operations that would not be possible on single-processor machines. The language has also been implemented in a form that runs on most Unix machines.

10.5 LANGUAGES OF THE FUTURE

Several times in the preceding chapters we have contrasted the model theoretic, semantic approaches to logic with the alternative proof theoretic, syntactic approaches to the subject. A model theoretic approach proceeds by evaluating formulas in different interpretations to decide which interpretations are models of the formula. Those interpretations that make the formula true are models whereas those that make it false are not. In contrast, a proof theoretic approach takes a collection of first-order formulas and uses these formulas as premisses from which further formulas may be deduced. Deduction steps proceed in the style of the Hilbert proof systems of Sections 1.7 and 2.7 to produce derived logical statements.

The view of relational databases presented earlier is model theoretic in that the table of information is an interpretation of a particular complex product. At the very simplest level, a query is answered by comparing a formula with each of the tuples of a database relation until a complete match is obtained. More subtle queries place variables in the formula so that the formula may be proven true by zero or more tuples in a particular database interpretation.

Reiter has suggested that relational database theory could be reformulated in proof theoretic form, as opposed to the model theoretic form described earlier. He claims that many of the problems arising in relational databases are associated with the algebraic nature of Codd's original proposals. In particular, the lack of expressive power of the relational model means that various semantic modelling devices such as entity–relationship modelling have to be introduced to convert real-world situations to database models. Another major problem area is the ad hoc and uncertain use of null values in tables. Although a proof theoretic approach to relational database implementation is of little practical interest, it does provide a perspective of the traditional approach that is only possible when an alternative exists.

If the relational tables BOOKS, MEMBERS and SERIAL listed earlier are simplified by removing all of the attributes in BOOKS and MEMBERS except the primary keys, we obtain a modified database:

BOOKS	MEMBERS	SERIAL	
4536	1234	5728	1234
5274	3645	4536	1234
5728			

These three relations may be considered as interpretations of the arity-two predicate Serial and the arity-one predicates Books and Members. Notice that the predicate is written with an initial capital letter followed by lower case letters whereas a relation or interpretation is written entirely in capitals. As always, an interpretation defines a set of values from which the truth of a formula may be decided. Thus, the appearance of certain values in the tables allows us to deduce that Books(4536) and Serial(5728,1234) are true while Members(9876) is false. This last deduction is based on the closed-world assumption, a device that allows the nonappearance of an item to be equated to the value false. A given formula might then be judged on the basis of the table values; for example, the formula

$$\forall x \forall y. \text{Serial}(x,y) \rightarrow \text{Books}(x) \land \text{Members}(y)$$

asserts that, for all x and y, the truth of Serial(x,y) implies the truth of Books(x) and Members(y). This formula is true in the interpretation provided by the tables above, so we conclude that the table is a model for this formula. A query presented to the database is defined by a domain-oriented form of the set comprehension described earlier:

$\{x \mid \exists(x,y) \in \text{SERIAL} \land y = 1234\}$

indicating the set of values x such that there exists a tuple (x,y) in the SERIAL relation with a y attribute 1234.

A proof theoretic approach begins by recasting the table into the form

```
Books(4536), Books(5274),Books(5728), ...
Members(1234),Members(3645), ...
Serial(5728,1234),Serial(4536,1234), ...
```

and in this form the database begins to look like a Prolog knowledge base. These formulas are ground atomic formulas from which further formulas may be derived. For example, the formula

$\exists x.\text{Books}(x) \land \text{Serial}(x,1234)$

is derivable and is satisfied by Books(5728) and Books(4536). In order to allow the same deductions that are possible in the algebraic, interpretational approach, Reiter has to define several other general formulas to accompany the ground atomic formulas above. First of all, he has to include the equality axioms described in Chapter 5, so all proofs are implemented in logic with equality. An explicit axiom stating that different symbols represent different objects is then required, because this assumption is built into the interpretational model. In effect, this is a syntactic version of the initial semantics described in Chapter 5. Finally some closure axioms are required to implement a version of the closed-world assumption in terms of formulas. For example, the Books predicate is defined as follows:

$\forall x.\text{Books}(x) \rightarrow x = 4536 \lor x = 5274 \lor x = 5728$

Reiter claims that a proof-based approach is more easily extended to model incomplete information with devices such as null values. Suppose a book may be loaned to an unknown member; this fact is represented as follows:

$\exists x.\text{Members}(x) \land \text{Serial}(5728,x)$

The existentially quantified variable here may be replaced by a Skolem constant, as described in Chapter 2, to give

Members(a) $\land$ Serial(5728,a)

and the constant instantiated here is used as a null value. Each null value is then distinguishable, allowing a much more general and flexible treatment of incomplete information. A proof theoretic approach provides a framework within which knowledge representation techniques may be formulated and used to specify real-world situations. One of the problems with the model-based relational model is that various semantic modelling techniques have to be used to capture some real-world situation. Specifications written in one of these modelling techniques are then implemented as relational tables and queries. A proof-based approach allows the modelling technique to be seen as an extension of the database itself. Unfortunately, the prospect of animating a proof theoretic procedure such as that described above lies beyond current possibilities. It became clear in Chapter 5 that theorem proving in logic with equality becomes exceedingly difficult because an increased number of axioms leads to many more branches in the search tree. Since Reiter's system is formulated in logic with equality, any attempt to automate the procedure would have to address this issue.

10.5.1 Combined functional and logic languages

Earlier chapters in this book have emphasised a major distinction between two kinds of languages: the early chapters described a system of animating simplified statements in logic without equality and the later chapters described term-rewriting systems in logic with equality. Historically, the animation provided by SLD unification only became possible when equality axioms were discarded from logic programs. Term-rewriting systems, in contrast, are defined by equality axioms but make no direct attempt to handle the relational statements found in logic languages. Given that both kinds of language have been found useful, it seems natural to try to combine them into a single system, and a great deal of effort has been applied to this end. Three approaches to merging functional and logic languages appear possible:

a. Provide a logic language and functional language in one package so that one can invoke the other as required. This approach is not as attractive as it initially sounds because terms are distributed throughout relations in a way that makes the separation difficult.

b. Retain an equational term-rewriting structure and express logic programs in terms of the features available in such systems. For example, the bodies of rules in a logic program have to be true in order to make the head true, and we can mimic this behaviour with a guarded statement. For example, a rule to find the larger of two numbers appears in a logic language as

```
max(x,y,x) :- greater_than(x,y)
```

but might be written in functional form as

```
max(x,y) = x , if greater_than(x,y)
```

An alternative possibility is to recognise that relations are interpretations in which a given tuple may be identified as either true or false. As a result, they may be treated as Boolean functions.

c. Retain the SLD unification mechanism of a logic language and express a functional program in a logic language form. This is of course just the opposite approach to item b and it appears to have some attractive features that we now explore.

Van Emden and Yukawa explored the possibility of implementing an SLD unification system suitably extended to cope with equality. To illustrate their solution, we first examine the problem of implementing terms in the equality axioms of Section 5.2. We take as an example the successor and addition functions described earlier and write the equality axioms (Eq) for these forms:

$$
\begin{array}{ll}
x = x \leftarrow & \text{Eq1} \\
x = y \leftarrow y = x & \text{Eq2} \\
x = z \leftarrow x = y \, , \; y = z & \text{Eq3} \\
\text{suc}(x) = \text{suc}(x) \leftarrow x = y & \text{Eq4} \\
\text{add}(w,x) = \text{add}(y,z) \leftarrow w = y, \; x = z & \text{Eq5}
\end{array}
$$

The first three rules here are the reflexive, symmetric and transitive rules of equality, followed by two instances of the function rule given in Section 5.2: one for suc and one for add. Further equations (E) are required to specify the meaning of the two functions

$$
\begin{array}{ll}
\text{add}(0,x) = x & \text{E1} \\
\text{add}(\text{suc}(x),y) = \text{suc}(\text{add}(x,y)) & \text{E2}
\end{array}
$$

Function add denotes the sum of two natural numbers, 0 represents zero, and x and y are any natural numbers. Before looking at the evaluation of a term in a logic system, we recall the method of evaluating expressions through term rewriting. A term such as add(suc(0),0) is evaluated through the following steps:

$$
\begin{array}{ll}
\text{add}(\text{suc}(0),0) = \text{suc}(\text{add } 0,0) & \text{E2} \\
\phantom{\text{add}(\text{suc}(0),0)} = \text{suc}(0) & \text{E1}
\end{array}
$$

A logic language evaluates the term by presenting it as a goal in which variable x is found through substitution σ:

$$
\text{Eq} + \text{E} \vDash (\text{add}(\text{suc}(0),0) = x) \; \sigma
$$

The problem now is that the SLD mechanism produces a large number of correct but useless answers such as add(suc(0),0) = add(suc(0),0), telling us that the term is equal to itself. A term-rewriting system rewrites expressions into simpler forms until the simplest possible, canonical value is obtained. Unfortunately, this simplest form has no special significance in a logic language; it is just one of a number of satisfactions to be discovered by the search mechanism. Furthermore, the SLD tree for a program with equality produces non-terminating branches that could prevent the program from producing any result at all.

Van Emden and Yukawa's solution to the problems above is quite simple in principle: they mimic term rewriting in a logic program by controlling the order in which an SLD search takes place. In what they call the interpretational approach they recast the equality axioms in the form

$$eq(x,x) \leftarrow canonical(x) \qquad \text{Eq' 1}$$
$$eq(x,z) \leftarrow non\_canonical(x), eq2(x,y), eq(y,z) \qquad \text{Eq' 2}$$
$$eq2(x,y) \leftarrow x = y \qquad \text{Eq' 3}$$
$$eq2(f(x_1,\ldots,x_n), f(y_1,\ldots,y_n)) \leftarrow eq(x_1,y_1),\ldots, eq(x_n,y_n) \qquad \text{Eq' 4}$$

This form of program distinguishes two equality predicates, eq and eq2, from an equality predicate labelled = that is used for the defining equivalences. All three predicates represent the same equality but are distinguished from each other to control the order in which axioms are used. Axioms 1 and 2 are equivalent to the reflexive and transitive rules of equality, but the one is only applied to canonical arguments whereas the other is only applied to non-canonical terms. Axiom 3 applies equations defining an object such as the equivalences given by E1 and E2 above. Axiom 4 is the substitutivity axiom, allowing the arguments of a function to be replaced by terms of equivalent value. In Chapter 5 we saw that the symmetric condition of equality is redundant in the presence of the the other axioms and its absence from the above program does not limit the results that might be obtained. In effect, the rules above implement the strategy when a problem is presented in the form eq(term,z):

```
if the leftmost argument is canonical
        resolve the goal with the reflexivity axiom
else
        resolve the goal with the transitivity axiom
```

When eq2 is invoked, an attempt is first made to resolve the goal with one of the defining equations; failing this an attempt is made to substitute arguments in the non-canonical form. If the order of equations 3 and 4 is changed, the reduction order followed is equivalent to innermost evaluation.

EXERCISES 10.1

1. Trace the evaluation of query add(suc(0),0) to give the result suc(0) through the interpretational approach above. Observe that, although the desired result is obtained, substantially more effort is required than is necessary in a simple term-rewriting system.

Bibliography

Classical logic

GALLIER J. H. (1987) *Logic for Computer Science.* New York: Wiley

GALTON A. (1990) *Logic for Information Technology.* Chichester: Wiley

REEVES S. and CLARKE M. (1990) *Logic for Computer Science.* Reading MA: Addison-Wesley

SMULLYAN R. M. (1968) *First Order Logic.* Berlin: Springer-Verlag

SPERSCHNEIDER V. and ANTONIOU G. (1991) *Logic – A Foundation for Computer Science.* Reading MA: Addison-Wesley

Logic programming and Prolog

BRATKO I. (1990) *Prolog Programming for Artificial Intelligence.* Reading MA: Addison-Wesley

CLOCKSIN W. F. and MELLISH C. S. (1981) *Programming in Prolog.* Berlin: Springer

DEGROOT D. and LINDSTROM G. (1986) *Logic Programming.* Englewood Cliffs NJ: Prentice Hall

HAMILTON A. G. (1989) *Prolog.* London: UCL Press

LUCAS R. (1996) *Mastering Prolog.* London: UCL Press

NILSSON U. and MALUSZYNSKI J. (1995) *Logic, Programming and Prolog.* Chichester: Wiley

Abstract types

BERGSTRA J. A., HEERING J. and KLINT P. (1991) *Algebraic Specification.* Reading MA: Addison-Wesley

EHRIG H. and MAHR B. (1985) *Fundamentals of Algebraic Specification*, Vol 1. Berlin: Springer

FUTATSUGI K., GOGUEN J. A., JOUNANNAUD J. and MESEGUER J. (1985) Principles of OBJ2, in *Conference Record of the 12th Annual ACM Symposium on Principles of Programming Languages*. Association of Computing Machinery, pp. 52–66

GOGUEN J. A., THATCHER J. W. and WAGNER E. G. (1978) An initial algebra approach to the specification, correctness and implementation of abstract data types, in *Current Trends in Programming Methodology*, R. Yeh (ed.). Englewood Cliffs NJ: Prentice Hall, pp. 80–140

Miranda

BIRD R. and WADLER P. (1988) *Introduction to Functional Programming*. Englewood Cliffs NJ: Prentice Hall

CLACK C., MYERS C. and POON E. (1995) *Programming with Miranda*. Englewood Cliffs NJ: Prentice Hall

HOLYER I. (1991) *Functional Programming with Miranda*. London: UCL Press

THOMPSON S. (1995) *Miranda*. Reading MA: Addison-Wesley

Intuitionistic logic

DUMMETT M. (1977) *Intuitionism*. Oxford: Oxford University Press

TURNER R. (1991) *Constructive Foundations for Functional Languages*. New York: McGraw-Hill

Database systems

CERI S., GOTTLOB G. and TANCA L. (1989) What you always wanted to know about Datalog (and never dared to ask). *IEEE Transactions on Knowledge and Data Engineering*, **1**, 146–66

GRAY P. M. D., KULKARNI K. G. and PATON N. W. (1992) *Object Oriented Databases*. Englewood Cliffs NJ: Prentice Hall

HUGHES J. G. (1991) *Object Oriented Databases*. Englewood Cliffs NJ: Prentice Hall

McCABE F. G. (1992) *Logic and Objects*. Englewood Cliffs NJ: Prentice Hall

STANCZYK S. (1990) *Theory and Practice of Relational Databases*. London: UCL Press

ULLMAN D. (1988) *Principles of Databases and Knowledge Based Systems*. New York: Computer Science Press

VAN EMDEN M. H. and YAKAWA K. (1987) Logic programming with equations. *Journal of Logic Programming*, **4**, 265–88

Index

For Product Safety Concerns and Information please contact our EU
representative GPSR@taylorandfrancis.com
Taylor & Francis Verlag GmbH, Kaufingerstraße 24, 80331 München, Germany